Unsettling India

Unsettling India

Affect, Temporality, Transnationality

PURNIMA MANKEKAR

Duke University Press *Durham and London* 2015

© 2015 Duke University Press
All rights reserved
Printed in the United States of
America on acid-free paper ∞
Typeset in Chaparral Pro by
Westchester

Library of Congress Cataloging-in-
Publication Data
Mankekar, Purnima, 1961–
Unsettling India : affect, temporality,
transnationality / Purnima Mankekar.
pages cm
Includes bibliographical references and index.
ISBN 978-0-8223-5822-0 (hardcover : alk. paper)
ISBN 978-0-8223-5836-7 (pbk. : alk. paper)
1. East Indian diaspora.
2. East Indians—United States—Ethnic identity.
3. Mass media and culture. I. Title.
DS432.5.M28 2015
909'.04914—dc23
2014032513

ISBN 978-0-8223-7583-8 (e-book)

Cover art: Meera Sethi, *Anamika
Sengupta (Ann)*, from the Foreign
Returned series. Courtesy of the artist.

For Akhil, with love

....

ACKNOWLEDGMENTS

....

This book has been a long time in the making and has, along the way, gathered a number of debts. I would like, first of all, to thank my informants in New Delhi and the San Francisco Bay Area for their generosity and patience: so many of them met with me repeatedly for over a decade and shared their insights, experiences, anxieties, and aspirations. Expressing one's sense of unsettlement is never an easy or comfortable experience and, in doing so, my informants, some of whom became friends over the years, also shared their sense of vulnerability. I have learned much from them. They provided me with many examples of how the affects that suffuse longings, dreams, anxieties, and fears are generative of agency and of subjectivity. Like others before them, these informants reminded me of the ways in which coping with the temporalities of everyday life, of learning to make do, of yearning and despairing, of struggling to change one's circumstances, of losing and then regaining hope all represent modes of making sense of one's life that are also modes of theorizing one's place in the world. This, then, has become an objective of all my ethnographic work: to bring, with deep humility, my informants' modes of theorizing into conversation with conceptual frameworks that I have developed as a feminist anthropologist, a scholar of media and public cultures, and a student of the transnational and the global.

I must also thank the institutions that provided support for the research and writing of this book. My very first forays into researching this book were enabled by a seed grant from the South Asia Initiative at Stanford University. The conceptualization and initial writing of this book were supported by a fellowship at the Radcliffe Institute of Advanced Study at Harvard University. My colleagues at the Radcliffe, chiefly, Rita Brock, Cynthia Enloe, Dhooleka Raj, Francesca Sawaya and Vicki Schulz patiently read and listened to iterations of papers that were later to become chapters. At Harvard, Michael and Nea Herzfeld, Charles Hirschkind, Engseng Ho,

Saba Mahmood, and Mary Steedly were a wonderful community of friends and interlocutors: without their company I would never have felt at home at Harvard or in Cambridge. While in residence at the Stanford Humanities Center, stimulating feedback from my colleagues, chiefly, Keith Baker, John Bender, Johannes Fabian, Wendy Larson, and Rob Polhemus enabled me to rethink and revise the architecture of this book. An exemplary institution, the Stanford Humanities Center provides those privileged to be fellows with outstanding resources and, most importantly fiercely protects the time of faculty who, in their home institutions, are overextended with teaching and advising. Final revisions to this manuscript were carried out in the summer of 2013 while in residence at the Asia Research Institute at the National University of Singapore (NUS): I am grateful to Prasenjit (Bhaity) Duara and other colleagues at NUS, chiefly, Ann Brooks, Beng Huat Chua, Annu Jalais, Vineeta Sinha, Malini Sur, Shawna Tang, and Sharon Quah for making my stay in Singapore so productive and enjoyable.

I am immensely appreciative of my colleagues at the Center for the Study of Race and Ethnicity at Stanford University for providing me, and many other minority faculty and students, with an oasis and a safe space for sharing work and ideas. Larry Bobo, Gordon Chang, Hazel Markus, David Palumbo-Liu, Claude Steele, and Dorothy Steele provided moral support at a very difficult time and proved, once again, that intellectual work and political solidarity must always go hand-in-hand. Colleagues in my former department at Stanford, chiefly, Sylvia Yanagisako, Akhil Gupta, Lochlann (Sarah) Jain, Barb Voss, and Matthew Kohrman were terrific interlocutors; the staff in the department, chiefly, Ellen Christensen and Shelly Coughlan took care, with great competence and grace, of the "infrastructure" that enabled my research. My students at Stanford quickly became my peers and colleagues: to this day, my writing and research are shaped by their voices and insights. These include (in alphabetical order) Tania Ahmed, Lalaie Ameeriar, Jocelyn Chua, Cari Costanzo, Rozita Dimova, Rachael Joo, Jisha Menon, Karen Morris, Marcia Ochoa, Sima Shakhsari, Mukta Sharangpani, Aradhana Sharma, Celine Parrenas Shimizu, and Miriam Ticktin—all of who continue to inspire me with the integrity and creativity they bring to their work and to their lives. Rozita Dimova and Ulka Anjaria provided diligent research assistance: their insights have shaped chapters 5 and 6. My undergraduate students at Stanford often took my breath away with their dynamism, commitment to combining a life of ideas with political activism, and sheer brilliance. I recall with particular affection and respect Veena Dubal, Amisha Patel, Aly Remtulla, Nisha Varia, all of whom have now become an invaluable part of my life. Mamta Ahluwalia, Ritu Bhatnagar, and

Veena Dubal provided indispensable research assistance: without them I could never have written this book. Special thanks to Rachael Joo and Marcia Ochoa for their comments on these chapters.

At UCLA, I am grateful to my department chairs, Chris Littleton, Beth Marchant, and Jenny Sharpe of the Department of Gender Studies and Cindy Fan, Lane Hirabayashi, and Jinqi Ling of the Department of Asian American Studies for their support. I am particularly thankful to the staff in both my departments, Jenna Miller-von Ah, Samantha Hogan, Richard Medrano, Van Nguyen, Jessie Singh, Natalia Yamashiro-Chogyoji and Anne Bautista for their hard work and patience. My colleagues at UCLA have been a wonderful source of intellectual stimulation and camaraderie: these include (in alphabetical order) Victor Bascara, Lucy Burns, John Caldwell, Keith Camacho, Jessica Cattelino, King-kok Cheung, Michelle Erai, Lieba Faier, Cindy Fan, Aisha Finch, Mishuana Goeman, Sondra Hale, Sarah Haley, Grace Hong, Marjorie Kagawa-Singer, Rachel Lee, Jinqi Ling, Beth Marchant, Saloni Mathur, Valerie Matsumoto, Kathleen McHugh, Aamir Mufti, Don Nakanishi, Thu-huong Nguyen-vo, Kate Norberg, Chon Noriega, Paul Ong, Sherry Ortner, Kyeyoung Park, Sanjay Subrahmanyam, Renee Tajima-Pena, Tim Taylor, Sharon Traweek, David Yoo, and Min Zhou. Members of my writing group, Lieba Faier, Hannah Landecker, Abby Saguy, and Juliet Williams were generous and rigorous readers of drafts of many of the chapters of this book and I am deeply grateful to them. Ali Behdad and Juliet Williams made me and my family welcome when I first moved to Los Angeles. I have been delighted to have students who have provided me with intellectual companionship and stimulation. These include Amanda Apgar, Diya Bose, Sudeep Chowdhury, Chloe Coventry, Brian Hu, Jessica Martinez, Naveen Minai, Esha Momeni, Trung Nguyen, Lai Wa Wu, Stephanie Santos, Preeti Sharma, Mihiri Tillakaratne, Saundarya Thapa, Iris Yellum, and Ger Xiong. I am particularly grateful to Amanda Apgar, Priya Patel, Preeti Sharma, Darci Sprengel, and Saundarya Thapa for their assistance as I revised this book.

Beyond Stanford University and UCLA, Lila Abu-Lughod, Anne Allison, Anjali Arondekar, Steve Caton, Carla Freeman, Faye Ginsburg, Michael Herzfeld, Engseng Ho, Arthur Kleinman, Fred Myers, Arvind Rajagopal, Parama Roy, Louisa Schein, and Mary Steedly have been generous colleagues: I have learned a great deal from their work and their feedback has shaped much of the analysis that has gone into this book. In reading this book, my teachers from graduate school, E. Valentine (Val) Daniel, Lorna Rhodes, and Ann Anagnost will find that their mentorship still shapes my scholarship so many years into my career.

I cannot thank enough my editor at Duke University Press, Ken Wissoker, for his patience with this project. If it weren't for his confidence in me and this project, this book would perhaps never have seen the light of day. Willa Armstrong, Jade Brooks, Amy Buchanan, and Sara Leone at Duke University Press have been a pleasure to work with. I am very grateful to Anitra Grisales for editing earlier drafts of the chapters of this book. I thank the anonymous reviewers of this book for their rigorous feedback.

In addition to the professional and institutional support that I have received, I have been sustained by a close community of friends-turned-kin. In India we have a wonderful term, "family friends," that encapsulates how friends become family when bonds of affection strengthen over the years and, very often, across distances. Veena Dubal has become my older daughter and is one of the most important members of my family: her sparkling intelligence, infinite capacity to love, unflinching commitment to an ethical life, and generosity always fills me with awe. I have been privileged to acquire a wonderful network of family friends in the San Francisco Bay Area which, despite my move to Los Angeles, provides companionship, good humor, and affection. These include Lawrence Cohen, George Collier and Jane Collier, Cari Costanzo, Eleni Kapur, and Kai Kapur, Julia Jaroch and Ethiraj Venkatapathy, Arun and Poornima Kumar, Sylvia Yanagisako and John Sullivan, David Palumbo-Liu and Sylvie Palumbo-Liu. Arun and Poornima, in particular, have always opened up their home to me and I will always love them for that and many other kindnesses. Dan Neuman, Sherry Ortner, and Tim Taylor were the magnets that drew my family and me to UCLA and, thanks to them and to Saloni Mathur, Aamir Mufti, and Jalal Mufti, Kathleen McHugh and Chon Noriega, and Arundhati Neuman, Los Angeles is now my home. Ken Wissoker, Cathy Davidson, Inderpal Grewal, David Nugent, and K. (Shivi) Sivaramakrishnan have been generous with their affection and friendship. Ulf Hannerz and Helena Wulff in Stockholm; Rachel Dwyer and Michael Dwyer in London; Kirin Narayan and Ken George in Canberra; Tara Mohanan and K. P. Mohanan in Singapore and now in Pune; Prasenjit Duara, Juliet Duara, Arpana Vidyarthi and Rajiv Ramanathan in Singapore; Minal Hajratwala, Arjun Kalyanpur and Sunita Maheshwari, Lata Mani, Devesh and Bhavani Nayel, Saritha Rai, Ayaana Bhojwani, and Namas Bhojwani, Sajai Singh and Sapna Taneja in Bangalore; Dhananjay Date in Pune; Vandana Chak, Razia Ismail, and Ritu Walia in New Delhi are my diasporic family friends who make me feel at home every time I am with them.

In October 2008, I met with an automobile accident and incurred a head injury that took away my ability to read for close to a year. I was terrified and, occasionally, filled with despair. Throughout this time, Akhil Gupta took over the challenging task of managing our household and our move to Bangalore. It was his profound compassion, patience, and love that, eventually, enabled my recovery. I owe him more than words can express. Ken Wissoker extended unwavering support, and Lata Mani was a living example of courage and fortitude. Louisa Schein was generous with her sympathy and patience during this challenging time and, at UCLA, Chris Littleton, Lane Hirabayashi, and Alessandro Duranti extended support that went beyond the call of duty.

My family has been a source of tremendous love and support: they have been the "steel frame" of my life and have always stood by me. Silvia Flores, Lucy Mankekar, Aruna and Harsh Bhargava, Anita and Rahul Aggarwal, Gauri and Amit Gangolli, Akash and Elizabeth Bhargava, Aaron Mankekar, Nina Mankekar Pandya and Tushar Pandya, and Shefali Aggarwal Patel have provided me with much companionship and good humor. My life has been enriched by loved ones who are no longer with me: my father, D. R. Mankekar, my father-in-law Jwala Gupta, and my brother Ajit Mankekar. Not a day goes by when I do not miss them. My mother Kamla Mankekar always inspires me with the dignity, integrity, and courage with which she lives her life: quite simply, I would not be the feminist, parent, and scholar I am if it were not for her. My mother-in-law, Meena Gupta, has taught me so much about resilience, grace, and the capacity to forgive: she has been my "guru" in many ways.

This book is shaped by the presence of two of the most important people in my world. My daughter Deeya Shivani Gupta has given me unending joy: her capacity for happiness, her sense of empathy and compassion, her creativity, and her never-say-die attitude have filled my life with magic. My partner in all things, Akhil Gupta, has been unfailingly generous: his ability to find humor in every situation, his strong sense of ethics, and his innate sense of dignity have all been a source of tremendous strength for me. Akhil is my moral compass, my collaborator, my best friend, and the love of my life: I dedicate this book to him as a token of my gratitude for everything that he is to me and does for me.

A portion of chapter 1 first appeared in "Reflections on Diasporic Identities: A Prolegomenon to an Analysis of Political Bifocality," in *Diaspora: A Journal of Transnational Studies* 3, no. 3 (Winter 1994): 349–71. Earlier versions of chapters 2, 3, 4, and 6 in a different form appeared respectively in the following: "Brides Who Travel: Gender, Transnationalism, and Nationalism in Hindi Film," in *Positions* 7, no. 3 (1999b): 731–62; "'India Shopping': Indian Grocery Stores and Transnational Configurations of Belonging," in *Ethnos: Journal of Anthropology* 67, no. 1 (2002): 75-97; "Dangerous Desires: Television and Erotics in Late-Twentieth Century India," in *Journal of Asian Studies* 63, no. 2 (2004): 403–31; and "Becoming Entrepreneurial Subjects: Neoliberalism and Media" in *The State in India after Liberalization: Interdisciplinary Perspectives,* edited by Akhil Gupta and K. Sivaramakrishnan, 213-22. New York: Routledge, 2011.

CHAPTER 1

Unsettlement

One frigid, gray December afternoon, I sat with Omvati on a low stool on her kitchen floor. As she sliced potatoes for the evening meal, I hugged the steaming cup of tea she had just handed me, scalding my tongue as I sipped it gingerly. Omvati lived with her son, grandson, and daughter-in-law Radha in a tiny, one-bedroom flat in a working-class neighborhood in New Delhi. Her son, grandson, and daughter-in-law used the bedroom. The kitchen was where she lived, where she spent most of her days and all her nights; this side of the shut bedroom door was suffused with the smells and sights of food, of lunches packed in small plastic boxes for her son and daughter-in-law and frugal dinners lovingly tended over a kerosene stove. The kitchen was where she chatted with her son and grandson (and, occasionally, her daughter-in-law) and where she spent solitary mornings and nights. One corner of the kitchen was decorated with pictures and small statuettes of family deities, some unfamiliar to my upper-caste eyes, the incense ash on the foreheads of her gods redolent with prayers offered, entreaties made, and dreams fulfilled and dashed. This was the room where she spent her afternoons with her grandson as they watched their favorite serials on a small black-and-white television set perched on a high, rickety shelf; this is where she spent long evenings waiting for her son (and daughter-in-law) to return from work.

I had first met Omvati on an earlier field trip, and continued to meet with her every time I visited New Delhi. It had taken a while for us to get to know each other: she was new in the neighborhood, and took pride in staying aloof from her neighbors. Our conversations were ostensibly about her avid engagement with dramatic serials shown on satellite television channels but often segued into recollections of her experiences as a new migrant from Uttar Pradesh some thirty years ago. A lower-caste widow, she and her two children had moved to her brother's home in New Delhi in order to start a new life. Since arriving in New Delhi she had eked out a living cleaning the homes of people living in the middle-class neighborhoods nearby. It had been tough because she also had to work late into the night sewing clothes for a garment exporting factory. By about the early 1990s, her family had acquired some degree of financial stability. It had all been worth it, she said. "All my hard work paid off when my son got a job in a government office. He got a stable income, we moved into this flat, and I was able to marry off my daughter. We have worked very hard to get to where we are. It is still a struggle, but at least I am no longer afraid of where my next meal will come from."

Suddenly, her eyes blazed with anger, and she added, "I wish my daughter-in-law would understand what it took for us to get to where we are. She always wants more and more." When I looked puzzled, Omvati continued, her voice low but trembling with rage: "Radha constantly wants to buy the new things being advertised on television. She wants them for herself. Whether she needs them or not, and whether we can afford them or not." I was taken aback by her abrupt change of mood and by the intensity of her fury.

She then looked away from me and pursed her lips tight, worry settling heavily across her careworn face: "It is not just things. She also wants more from her husband. She wants him all the time. Always. They shut their bedroom door for hours on end. That is the way she is. He is losing sight of his other responsibilities. He is in her control [uske vash mein hai]." It dawned on me that it was the conjunction of Radha's desire for commodities with erotic desire that had made Omvati furious. This was the first of many ethnographic encounters in which Omvati described to me how her authority as a mother-in-law was being undermined by the intimacy between her son and daughter-in-law. She was very anxious that this would destroy their family and their traditions. Clearly, patriarchal discourses of sexuality, conjugality, and family, together with the conjunction of caste and class, profoundly shaped her sense of feeling marginalized in her own home. Deeply unsettled by the changes under way, she was extremely uncertain about what lay ahead.

About five years later, my research assistant, Ritu Bhatnagar, and I walked into the small Silicon Valley office of Ashutosh Sen, the founder and CEO of an IT company, hoping to interview him about the South Asian community in the San Francisco Bay Area. It was the week following the Fourth of July and his office was festooned with U.S. flags. Ritu and I snaked through cubicles inhabited by earnest-faced young men and women of dif-

ferent nationalities and races, the low hum of the cavernous room punctuated by a large, booming voice emanating from the CEO's glass-enclosed office. Everybody was dressed informally in jeans, sweatshirts, and sneakers,
but there was nothing casual about the focused expressions on their faces
as they sat in front of monitors, their bodies tight with concentration. The
room was crackling with the intense productivity of a high-energy Silicon
Valley startup during the boom years. The sense of excitement in the air
was palpable.

Peeping into Sen's office through a large glass wall, we saw that he had
on a headset and was talking to someone in a loud voice, his fingers tapping rapidly on the keyboard of the laptop in front of him. A trim man in
his forties, he wore an elegant Ralph Lauren polo shirt with his blue jeans
and his hair was slicked back. We were on time for our appointment but
it seemed that Sen was not yet ready to meet us. Just as Ritu and I were
starting to steel ourselves against his infamous arrogance, he looked up
at us hovering outside his door and waved us in, but continued to talk on
the phone for the next ten minutes. I glanced at my watch several times,
discreetly at first, then more openly to indicate my growing impatience at
being kept waiting. "I have fifteen minutes to give to you," he said, when
my impatience finally got under his skin. "I have to get back to my work as
soon as possible." As I described my project to him, his eyes began to flit
restlessly around the room. Then, just as I was starting to despair of ever
getting his attention, I mentioned that among the media I was researching
were Bollywood films. He was silent for a moment, then remarked that
watching Bollywood films was one of the few ways in which he was able to
relax. In a voice turned soft with longing, he explained that in the small
town where he had gone to engineering college there had been few opportunities to "chill" apart from movie theaters, and that was when his love
affair with Bollywood films had started. Ritu and I were taken aback by the
change in his demeanor: from being arrogant and loud, he had suddenly
become mellow, even a bit shy, as he spoke of his passion for Bollywood
films. Leaning forward across his desk, he said that when he first came to
the San Francisco Bay Area to go to graduate school, it had been difficult
to keep up with Bollywood films. But, he added, his voice quickening with
excitement, now these films were easily available on video and DVD and
he could also watch them on satellite television and in local theaters: they
were now a part of his life.

He became animated, and we spoke of some of his favorite films. "Did
you see *Dilwale Dulhaniya Le Jayenge*?" he eagerly asked. I responded that I
had and, in fact, had written an article on it. He interrupted me and began

to describe how moved he was by this film's portrayal of the estrangement between a man and his young daughter over her desire to marry a man of her choice. To our utter astonishment, his eyes filled with tears. "This is a dilemma a lot of us confront," he mumbled, visibly moved but also embarrassed by the emotions stirred by his recollections of this film. He added, "How do we hold on to our daughters, our culture, our identity? How do we explain to them what it means to be Indian?" He was clearly anxious about his daughters, how he could "hold on" to them, and how he could teach them what it meant to be Indian. Like Omvati, he was uncertain about what lay ahead.

Omvati and Ashutosh were separated not only by geography (one lived in New Delhi, the other in Saratoga, California), but also by class, gender, and social location. Yet much seemed to connect the two. They were extremely anxious about the changes that seemed immanent in their respective families; in their distinct ways, they were articulating that something was shifting and they were uncertain as to how to navigate these changes. Their engagement with transnational media, television in one case and Bollywood cinema in the other, was voracious, intimate, and affectively charged: the slow boil of anger fueled by Omvati's fears that the commodities being shown on transnational satellite television were unleashing turmoil in her family, and the passions and anxieties engendered by Ashutosh's engagement with Bollywood films will always stay with me. Both were deeply afraid that the desires of young women in their families might unstitch the social relationships and cultural patterns that they held dear.[1] For each of them, the position of women symbolized cultural continuity and authenticity; for both, gender, culture, and Indianness were irrevocably entangled. In their own ways, Omvati and Ashutosh pointed to how transnational public cultures were unsettling notions of gender, culture, and belonging.[2]

My book is about how transnational public cultures participated in the creation of India as an archive of affect and temporality for my informants in New Delhi and the San Francisco Bay Area. I begin with the foregoing ethnographic vignettes not to set forth an empiricist record of what happened, who said what to whom, or the contexts in which my informants lived. Instead, I craft ethnographic scenarios that are intended to be evocative rather than (merely) descriptive: my intention is to stage particular landscapes of affect and temporality that shaped the lives and imaginations of women and men with whom I worked. In the rest of this book, I juxtapose the ethnographic with the textual to demonstrate how they might articulate—or disarticulate—to produce fields of force, agency, and affect: contrary to presumptions that the ethnographic is more "real" (or more empirical) than the textual, the mediated texts with which I engaged became mediated worlds, sites of intimate habitation for my informants and me. Moreover, far from providing me with a stable ground for theorization, my fieldwork for this project has reminded me of the irrefutable volatility of ethnographic research: as the following chapters demonstrate, ethnography has become a means for me to enact the contingency of cultural analysis.

In this book, I draw on the acute sense of unsettlement experienced by informants as an ethnographic lens to trace the role of public cultures in the (re)constitution of notions of India and Indianness. Simultaneously, I deploy unsettlement as an analytic toward a feminist project of denatural-izing and unpacking the totalizing claims of nationhood. Conducting eth-nographic research was, for me, a deeply embodied and affective process. In what follows, I attend to everyday practices, corporeal intensities, and shifts in tone that recall affects of longing and resignation, aspiration as much as despair, rage as well as fear. I reflect on conversations that I had with my informants and on much that was left unsaid between us. I write of sense memories that generated particular conjunctions of sociality and affect. Some of these ethnographic scenarios enable me to evoke for my readers the different ways in which bodies might register the slow passage of time, or enact how the temporalities of everyday lives are punctuated by moments that collapse past, present, and future. These are volatile sce-narios that do not stand still but quiver with the potentiality of struggle, or with the quickening of intensities that can change a life irrevocably. Through my ethnography I scramble the banal and the everyday with the momentous.

I remix the ethnographic and the textual in order to examine how affect and temporality enable the constitution of notions of "India" and "Indian culture" that circulate through transnational public cultures.[3] By focusing on the circulation of television programs, films, commodities, images, and texts between India and the United States, I reverse persisting conceptions of the transnational in which commodities, texts, and images flow from the West to the rest of the world (see also Mankekar and Schein 2012). Rather than engage in a comparison of two discrete sites, New Delhi and the San Francisco Bay Area (as, for instance, in Shukla 2003) or analyze community and identity formation at two ends of a migration chain (Raj 2003), I draw out how transnational public cultures mediate conceptions of India and In-dianness for my informants at two nodes in a global circuit of images, texts, and commodities, New Delhi and the San Francisco Bay Area.[4] I examine media that traverse national and territorial borders (popular film, televi-sion, and advertisements) as well as the social spaces created through the circulation of commodities, such as grocery stores in the San Francisco Bay Area.

Rather than focus on a single medium (as in Mankekar 1999a), I attend to the intertextual and extratextual modalities of transnational public cultures as they circulate between New Delhi and the San Francisco Bay Area. I conceive of public cultures in terms of the affective and sensorial ecologies produced by the circulation of media and commodities: in so doing, I wish to eschew stubborn dichotomies of production versus consumption, text versus context. This shift in my focus was necessitated, in part, by the saturation of Indian public cultures by transnational media following the introduction of CNN during the Gulf War in 1992. In the years that immediately followed I witnessed the intense intertextuality of the media that proliferated: television programming borrowed freely from cinematic techniques of narration; print media poached off the narrative logics of television; advertising and music television genres entered into promiscuous partnerships; and commodity images became ubiquitous in the visual landscapes of cities, small towns, and many villages. As I observed how these media fed each other, it became clear to me that analyzing a single medium—either television or cinema or advertising—was no longer viable from an ethnographic or theoretical perspective.[5] I had only to wander through a busy market in New Delhi to experience the multiplicity of public cultures engendered by the heterogeneity of media and the accelerated circulation of commodities: Punjabi and Urdu magazines sat cheek by jowl with issues of *Cosmopolitan* and *Vogue*, Hindi movies ran alongside the latest Hollywood film, and several movie theaters screened matinees of films made in other Indian languages. I learned that public cultures are more than the sum of their parts; instead, they are generated precisely through the frisson produced by the uneven circulation of media, commodities, and peoples.

Several studies have focused on the role of public cultures in creating zones of debate (for instance, Appadurai 1996; Breckenridge 1995; Gupta 1995; Rofel 2007). My book builds on these works and extends them by examining how public cultures engender a range of affective regimes with profound implications for social relationships (see especially Berlant [2008] and Stewart [2007] on the affective dimensions of public cultures). My conception of public cultures suggests their intimate entanglement with the cultural politics of states (see, in particular, chapters 2 and 5). Public cultures exist in nonequivalent and hierarchical relationships with each other; for instance, those supported by the state or a hegemonic bloc might exist in relations of superordination to those produced and consumed by minority communities or working-class communities (see also Rajagopal [2001] on split publics). Yet public cultures are not hermetically sealed: they often feed off each other, even when they might exist in opposition. Transnational public cultures have been shaped by the global consolidation of media industries (Mankekar and Schein 2012): the proliferation of indigenously produced media notwithstanding, many are owned by the same conglomerates (for instance, the India Today Group, Essel [Zee] industries, or Yash Raj Films are major, if not dominant, players in the print media, television, and film industry respectively).[6] However, rather than conceive of these media as monopolistic, I prefer to see them as rhizomatic and nodal, as formed through contingent relationships with historically specific institutions like the state and the media industry (see, especially, Caldwell 2013). As I demonstrate in the following chapters, the circulation of media articulates with the circulation of capital and labor; at the same time, rather than conceive of the circulation of media in terms of flows, it makes sense to also trace the disjunctures that emerge in their wake (compare Appadurai 1996; Tsing 2004).

In interweaving policy analysis, cultural analysis, and ethnography I engage the complex relationships between regimes of affect, temporality, and discourse as they implicate the production of India.[7] A new sensorium came into being in India after the proliferation of transnational media and the flooding of Indian markets (and landscapes) with commodities. Following Amit Rai, I emphasize not how older representations, affects, and sensations were replaced by new ones but how the "old" and the "new" remediate each other (2009: 71). Put another way, I am interested in how these representations, affects, and sensations crisscross different media platforms and how they articulate with the circulation of capital, marketing strategies, and policies of the Indian nation-state to create what Rai describes as "feedback loops of capital, affect, pleasure, and time" (2009: 71).

Constituting India

The central argument of this book is that transnational public cultures constitute India as an archive of affect and temporality. For instance, a number of television serials and Hindi films now depict Indians living overseas and are aimed at them. What are the affective regimes suffusing these portrayals and engendered by them, and how do they mediate the constitution of Indianness and national belonging within India and beyond? And what do these dynamic and unstable representations of Indianness and national belonging tell us about temporalizing processes in a transnational world?

To be sure, the traps inherent in invoking India are legion. At the very least, invoking India risks attributing an unshakeable solidity to what was a shifting signifier of affiliation and identity for most of my informants. The affective salience of India varied sharply for all of them, ranging from indifference and irrelevance, to fervent nationalist engagement, to passionate antagonism. In New Delhi, India meant something entirely different to those informants who subscribed to Hindu nationalist discourses of national purity, as opposed to those who adhered to secularist conceptions of nationhood or those from minority communities positioned at the margins of the Hindu/Indian nation-state. Similarly, in the Bay Area, India held a vastly different affective salience for informants who had migrated recently from India, as compared with those who claimed descent from India but hailed from other parts of the world such as Africa, the Caribbean, or Southeast Asia. As can be expected, religious affiliation, class, gender, and sexual preference mediated my informants' conception of India in significant ways in both New Delhi and the Bay Area.

As the chapters that follow demonstrate, I conceive of India as an extraterritorial category that neither elides nor dismisses the political-economic and geopolitical materiality of the Indian nation-state. I am concerned with tracing how modes of belonging, affiliation, and, indeed, disaffiliation and alienation might exceed and, on occasion, subvert the interpellatory claims of the contemporary Indian nation-state both within India and beyond its territorial borders. Most importantly, rather than assume a substantialist notion of Indian culture as something that is affixed onto India, I explore how it is constantly re-produced, reinvented, and unsettled within India and in diasporic communities with varying relationships to India. Here, I build on scholarship within South Asian studies that seeks to remap and open up the category of India and, indeed, South Asia.[8] Scholars have long recognized that India has always been produced at the intersection of the local and the translocal through, for instance, pilgrimages (van der Veer 1994), as a result of centuries of trade in and around the Indian Ocean (Bose 2002; Bose 2009; Choudhuri 1985; Ghosh 1992; Subrahmanyam 1998, 2013), migration (van der Veer 1995), and travel (Grewal 1996; Markovits et al. 2003).

I problematize conceptions of India as a locus or source of Indian culture or tradition (compare Gupta and Ferguson 1997b). The lives and subjectivities of my informants in the San Francisco Bay Area were shaped not only by their heterogeneous (and often contradictory) positionings vis-à-vis India but, equally, by their locations within class hierarchies and racial landscapes in the United States. Here, I build on and intervene in analyses of identity and community formation produced by scholars in Asian American studies, particularly those who incorporate dimensions of diaspora and transnationality into their conceptions of racialized identities.[9] My ethnographic research suggests that while the production of hegemonic discourses on gender and sexuality across these two nodes is filled with contradictions and disjunctures, there are also some striking parallels. For instance, many of my informants in New Delhi were deeply concerned that the sexual purity of women might have been endangered after the perceived opening up of India following the liberalization of the Indian economy and the expansion of transnational media (chapters 2, 4, and 5); for my informants in the San Francisco Bay Area, these anxieties were most visible with regard to the preservation of women's sexual purity, which, in turn, became emblematic of the cultural purity of the (heterosexual) family and community (chapters 2, 3, and 5).

As the chapters that follow demonstrate, I am concerned with the citationality of India at particular nodes of transnational public culture: my ethnographic goal is to trace the temporality and historicity of these very processes of the invocation, evocation, and unsettlement of India and Indianness across transnational space. Hence, far from conceiving of India and Indian culture as stable objects and hence reinscribing the nationalist assumptions on which they are sometimes predicated, I invoke the category of India as an optic precisely to foreground the processes of citation and elision that these invocations produce.

Sites of Inquiry

My book draws on ethnographic fieldwork conducted in two overlapping parts. One part of my research for this project occurred between 1993 and 2005 in New Delhi, and consisted of ethnographic research on transnational television and advertisements, changing notions of the erotic, representations of overseas Indians in Hindi film, Hindu nationalist discourses of national and cultural purity, and the cultural implications of the expansion of the business process outsourcing (BPO) industry in India. The second, overlapping part of my fieldwork was conducted in the San Francisco Bay Area between 1997 and 2001, and included ethnographic research on Indian grocery stores, the reception of Hindi films by heterogeneous audiences, and public events convened by Indian community organizations. Then, just when I believed that my research had been completed, the series of events now memorialized as September 11 occurred. Affect and temporality emerged as critical factors in how my informants experienced and responded to racially motivated harassment and violence. I draw briefly on some of this research in the coda to this book to sketch the contours of a theoretical framework that enables me to unsettle the U.S. nation.[10]

My choice of New Delhi and the San Francisco Bay Area as locations for fieldwork and as sites of inquiry is shaped by the work of feminist cultural geographers who have sought to rethink historical processes of place making. For instance, Massey argues that, rather than conceive of places in terms of "introverted, inward-looking history, based on delving into a past for internalized origins," it is essential that we seek a "sense of place which is extroverted" (1991: 27, 29; see also Moss 2002; Moss and Al-Hindi 2007; Rose 1993). Building on this and similar frameworks, I conceive of New Delhi and the San Francisco Bay Area as nodal spaces produced through the traffic in peoples, commodities, and media. For centuries, New Delhi (and Delhi) has been a city of newcomers and migrants who brought with them their own distinct cultural practices. After Indian independence in 1947, New Delhi became home to refugees from Partition, middle-class youth in search of education and employment opportunities, and migrants from all over the country seeking ways of making a living. New Delhi is thus a palimpsest of an ongoing traffic in people and commodities. As Paolo Favero points out in his brilliant ethnography of this city, "Contemporary Delhi is the result of this long history of dialogue between local and foreign influences. It is a modern metropolis, while it keeps history alive amidst its chaos" (2005: 197).

Although New Delhi is not a center of film or television production, its physical landscape and the social practices of its inhabitants have been radically transformed by the proliferation of transnational public cultures. Until the early 1990s, New Delhi was deemed primarily a city of government where bureaucrats and politicians held sway but, after the liberalization of the economy, it rapidly acquired a reputation as a commercial and business center as well. As in other Indian metropolitan centers (for instance, Mumbai, Bangalore, Hyderabad, or Chennai), New Delhi's middle-class, lower-middle-class, and upwardly mobile working-class residents are energetic, if anxious, participants in the cultural transformation of their city. In recent years, New Delhi has also become host to a burgeoning business process outsourcing industry, accelerating the migration of youth from different parts of India (see chapter 6). As these youth began to build careers and lives in New Delhi, they left their mark on the city with their labor practices and globalized lifestyles. Throughout my fieldwork in New Delhi, I was struck by a perpetual sense of flux. New Delhi, with its refugees, migrants, and transients, felt like a space of unsettlement as much as settlement.

A dwelling place for some of the earliest South Asian communities at the turn of the century in rural California, the San Francisco Bay Area was my second research site.[11] Over the course of my fieldwork, the Bay Area became home to a diverse South Asian community, with residents hailing from all over the subcontinent and ranging from Silicon Valley entrepreneurs to assembly-line and convenience store workers. The dizzying traffic in transnational public cultures played a crucial role in making the San Francisco Bay Area a distinctive place of habitation for its Asian and Asian American residents.[12] These transnational public cultures mediated how the area's Asian and Asian American inhabitants negotiated their positions in a social and political-economic landscape produced at the intersection of class, national origin, gender, sexuality, and race.[13]

Indeed, South Asian immigration to California exemplifies the ways in which immigration policy has been shaped by the U.S. economy's changing needs for labor and capital and, simultaneously, refracted by race and national origin. The turn of the twentieth century witnessed the migration of laborers from Punjab to California and other parts of the West Coast, and constituted the first wave of immigrants from the South Asian subcontinent (Leonard 1992). The Alien Land Laws of 1913, 1920, and 1923 cast all Asians as ineligible for citizenship, and the 1917 Immigration Act explicitly excluded Indians from naturalization. In 1946, the Luce-Cellar Bill repealed the "barred zone" clause of the 1917 Immigration Act. Thereafter, between 1946 and 1965, there was an increase in South Asian immigration into the United States. The second wave of South Asian immigration started after the 1965 Immigration and Nationality Act: the entry of Indians into the United States rose from 12,296 in 1960 to 51,000 by the end of 1965 (Hing 1993: 70, 72). By the 1980s, about 20,000 to 30,000 South Asians were emigrating every year (Khandelwal 1995), and in 1985 Indian immigrants ranked third (at 28,498) behind Filipinos and Koreans. According to the 2010 U.S. Census, over 3.4 million South Asians live in the United States, of which the largest segment (80 percent) consisted of self-identified Indians or Indian Americans.[14] The San Francisco Bay Area was among the top five metropolitan areas in terms of South Asian population, with San Jose in the South Bay and Fremont in the East Bay representing the highest concentration of self-identified Indians or Indian Americans (43,827 and 38,711 respectively; Springer 2012).

My fieldwork in the San Francisco Bay Area spanned periods when the local economy boomed (in the mid- and late 1990s, during the heyday of information technology [IT] and its ancillary industries), when the so-called tech bubble burst (during the early years of the new millennium), and in the immediate aftermath of September 11, 2001. Each of these sharply contrasting periods shaped how my informants positioned themselves in the ever-shifting racial landscapes in which they lived; they also refracted the range of relationships that they constructed with India.[15] As Favero (2005: 199) argues, "Places are 'processes,' not 'essences.' Their meanings accumulate through what Massey [1993] calls a 'progressive sense of place,' i.e., through the activities that centre upon them and the routes that bring people and objects to meet there." New Delhi and the San Francisco Bay Area are, for me, not just points on a map. They are places with deep histories of movement, migration, and cultural traffic. Through the generation and circulation of regimes of affect and temporalization, transnational public cultures have articulated with the longer histories outlined above to reconfigure these sites as places of habitation and emplacement (Ahmed et al. 2003; Kaplan 1996; Massey 1993).

Media, Affect, Temporality
THE CIRCULATION OF AFFECT

My theorization of affect extends Raymond Williams's theorization of structures of feeling. Williams provides a succinct definition of structures of feeling in *Marxism and Literature*: "Structures of feeling can be defined as social experiences in solution, as distinct from other social semantic formations which have been precipitated and are more evidently and more immediately available. The effective formations of most actual art relate to already manifest social formations, dominant or residual, and *it is primarily to emergent formations (though often in the form of modification or disturbance in older forms) that the structure of feeling, as solution, relates*" (1977: 134, emphasis added).

Williams was primarily concerned with the relationship between literature and social change. He insisted that a structure of feeling is most easily tracked during moments of struggle or transition. Dissatisfied with some Marxist models of false consciousness and determination dominant at the time and preoccupied by the gap between experience and articulation, he argued that analyzing the aesthetic conventions and formal properties of a work of art or literature enables us to trace the structure of feeling of a particular social group (Williams 1954). There is a curious doubling in Williams's notion of structures of feeling: at the same time that aesthetic conventions enable us to trace it, a structure of feeling is always "in solution" rather than something that has "precipitated" (1977: 134). A structure of feeling, he believes, becomes "evident" in moments of struggle and transition through shifts in artistic practice and, hence, in conditions of emergence (1954: 122). Thus, even though it is often inchoate, a structure of feeling may be traced through shifts in semantics or aesthetic convention. In sum, Williams is interested in tracking the relationship between experience (in particular, how feeling is experienced), consciousness, and social formation.

Building on but also diverging from Williams's notion of structures of feeling, my conception of affect draws on the formulations of Deleuze (1997) and Massumi (2002), who insist that affect is distinct from feeling (the domain of individual subjectivity) and emotion (the domain of the linguistic; see also Spinoza 1985). Thus, my conception of affect extends scholarship on the anthropology of emotions and sentiments by Michelle Rosaldo (1984), Catherine Lutz and Lila Abu-Lughod (1990), Sylvia Yanagisako (2002), and my own earlier explorations of the role of television in the construction of the affective bases of nationalism (Mankekar 1999b); it also draws on theorizations of affect by Sara Ahmed (2004), Teresa Brennan (2004), Patricia Clough (2007), Ann Cvetkovich (2003), and Kathleen Stewart (2007). Lutz and Abu-Lughod (1990) have argued that emotions cannot be tied to tropes of interiority and are, therefore, not exclusively located within the domains of the psychic, the cognitive, or the subjective. As I conceptualize it, affect is also not tied to tropes of interiority. The relationship between affect, individual agency, and social action is complex and multilayered. Affect cannot be located solely in an individual subject, nor can it be relegated to the psyche or to subjective feelings. Subjects are not where affect originates; rather, affect produces subjects through the traces it leaves upon them.

Drawing on the work of Charles Sanders Peirce, affect can be described in terms of abduction—a sense of intensity that exists prior to its capture by language. A complex relationship exists, therefore, between affect and narration; as stated by Clough, "affect constitutes a nonlinear complexity out of which the narration of conscious states such as emotion are subtracted" (2007: 2). Further, as I argue in my analysis of objects displayed and consumed in Indian grocery stores in the San Francisco Bay Area (chapter 3), affect affixes itself to particular bodies and objects. This is not to say that affect inheres in objects or resides within subjects; instead, affect is engendered through the encounter of bodies with each other and with particular objects (Ahmed 2004: 4). Subjects and objects function as nodes in the circulation of affect (Wissinger 2007: 247). Affect is often experienced in the body yet cannot be biologized.[16] It does not seem to me worthwhile to try to locate affect in terms of precognitive versus cognitive intensities, or in terms of a dichotomy between the cognitive and the corporeal (which, after all, presupposes and is predicated on artificial binaries of thought versus emotion, mind versus body). Instead, affect entails both forms of apprehension and bodily forms of feeling.

Additionally, affect transects and therefore blurs the binary between private feelings and public sentiments (Berlant 2008; Stewart 2007). As I elaborate in chapter 3, affect circulates between and across objects and subjects—and, here, public cultures play a critical role. Above all, affect is socially consequential: affect is what makes us invest in, or rage against, particular social formations. Certainly, affective investments in ideologies of public and private have particular consequences for gender, sexuality, and, indeed, feminism (Berlant 2008). In hegemonic discourses of gender, affect is often associated with femininity; yet, as I demonstrate in several chapters of this book, discourses of masculinity are affectively charged in potent ways. Nor is affect confined to realms of domesticity; as my discussion of affective labor in chapter 6 suggests, affect is constitutive of forms of labor central to the global capitalist economy.

Although affect is irreducible to the social, it is profoundly refracted by sociality. As Ahmed argues, "Affective economies are social and material, as well as psychic" (2004: 46). Like a structure of feeling, affect is not reducible to ideology. Yet ideologies gain considerable political force through the ways in which they acquire affective freight. Consider the affective potency of ideologies of nationalism. Benedict Anderson's (1991) groundbreaking and classic work on nationalism foregrounds the role of the imagination in the formation of national communities. Yet affect remains strikingly undertheorized in Anderson's analysis: he neglects to consider what it is that affectively binds subjects into a national community.

My deployment of terms like affective investment, affective regimes, affective value, and affective circulation is intended to foreground the material and institutional aspects of affect: affects are neither free floating nor unmoored from the sociohistorical conjunctures of which they are a part.[17] Transnational public cultures are both constituted by and enable a range of affective regimes, and this circularity is both fundamental and inevitable. Affects are generated and mobilized by media to produce webs of relationality between subjects.[18] For instance, a popular singing competition telecast on the South Asian transnational television network Zee TV called *Sa Re Ga Ma Pa* illustrates how affect is generated and circulated through Hindi film music in communities across the world with a range of affiliations with India: these communities may be constituted by immigrants, those whose ancestors migrated abroad several centuries ago, or those with no direct migratory connection with India. These competitions are usually staged in front of live audiences who display intense affective responses to the music. The camera frequently lingers on members of these audiences to show us how they are moved by the music to weep, tap their feet, and sway their bodies to its rhythm, or shake and nod their heads in response to the melodies being sung: these affective responses are visceral and corporeal. Thus, the affects generated within and across public cultures are often ambient and, at the same time, experienced in intimate, embodied, and often visceral ways.

Affect entails the circulation of intensities across spatially and temporally located subjects. Hence, although affect is not reducible to mediation, mediation is crucial to its generation and evocation: affect is what sometimes results when signs rub up against one another (Ahmed 2004; Mazzarella 2009). Signs may be regnant as well as generative of affect. Even as individual feelings vary, certain signs become suffused with affective potency at particular historical moments: once again, one has only to compare the range of affects that might be evoked by a national flag during times of relative peace as opposed to those it might generate in conditions of war.

In part, my effort in this book is to draw out the relationship between transnational public cultures and the affective regimes that undergird processes of in/habitation, being moved, feeling attached, and feeling in or out of place. Ahmed, Castaneda, Fortier, and Sheller point out that "the affectivity of home is bound up with the temporality of home, with the past, the present, and the future" (2003: 9). Media like Bollywood cinema, satellite television, and, as I argue in chapter 3, the circulation of commodities enable the reterritorialization of space through the construction of a phantasmic India that cannot, ultimately, be located in a specific place. Thus, for instance, transnational public cultures participate in the production of phantasmic notions of India in both the homeland and diaspora by generating a range of affects spanning nostalgia and longing, as well as disaffection, alienation, and, at times, antagonism—as in the case of some members of minority communities placed at the margins of the Indian nation-state. In contexts where memories of India were painful, as for an informant who left India to flee the homophobia of her family and community, satellite television generated for her an entirely different kind of affective connection—this time, of antagonism shot through with relief—with the India she had "left behind."

Moreover, while not minimizing the significance of physical movement, I am wary of reifying it as the defining feature of subject formation across heterogeneous contexts of mobility. For one, privileging the mobility of bodies as singularly constitutive of subject formation is conceptually and politically problematic because it implies a static notion of culture based on a metaphysics of sedentarism (Malkki 1997). In such formulations, whereby bodies migrate and culture stands still, the purported homeland becomes a space marked by stasis hence eliding, for instance, the imaginative travel engendered by transnational public cultures as a form of migration.[19] Despite the fact that they had never set foot outside India, several of my middle-class informants in New Delhi could imaginatively navigate the streets of London (and, increasingly, New York City) through their engagement with films about Indians abroad: to the extent that these films enabled them to inhabit other worlds and experience other forms of being, imaginative travel was neither marginal nor epiphenomenal but was central to the constitution of subjectivity. For some informants, media such as television shows produced in India and abroad, films, advertisements, and the Internet generated a range of fantasies about "life in the West." These media played a crucial role in inciting their aspirations to travel and, in so doing, refracted their conceptions of futurity. Other lower-middle-class and middle-class informants aspired to move overseas to make what they saw as a better life for themselves in the future—in large part because they were driven by an overwhelming desire to acquire the commodities they saw flashing on their television screens, on billboards all over the newly configured landscapes of New Delhi, and in films. For, even though commodities had begun to flood the Indian market after the liberalization of the Indian economy, most of my informants believed that the commodities they so fervently desired would be more readily accessible in "the West": in their fantasies of upward mobility through migration, commodities became iconic of (an easier, more affluent, more successful and, at times, more glamorous) life in the West.

As will be clear from my argument in this book, affect and temporality are enfolded into each other to simultaneously constitute and unsettle conceptions of India and Indianness. Affect and affectivity (that is, how we affect others and are affected by them) are intrinsically temporal processes on several registers. The temporality of affect is shaped by the fact that it is transitive and cannot be located in any one place or location; it is generated when signs, texts, bodies, and objects rub off one another to create feedback loops. As Ahmed (2004) points out, affect is economic: it acquires social force through circulation. I have noted elsewhere (Mankekar 2012, 2014) and earlier in this chapter that this circulation can occur in seconds or over years; it happens over time. Second, emotion is affect retroactively signified and re-cognized, hence underscoring the temporality of affect. For instance, my analysis of grocery stores (chapter 3) suggests some of the ways in which affects and temporalities get scrambled: the sensuous knowledges produced by these stores underscore the temporalities of memory, antagonism, and ambivalence that shift across terrains of class, gender, and race. Furthermore, the conjunction of affect and temporality enables us to trace the circulation of discourses to foreground the place of movement in social processes. Thus, in chapter 5 I trace the circulation of discourses of morality across nonsynchronous and disparate nodes ranging from the Indian state's policies to evoke affiliative ties with wealthy Indians, Hindu nationalist protests against Valentine's Day, the consonances of a popular Bollywood film with notions of a resurgent Global India, and the struggles of a young woman situated at the margins of discourses of nation, community, and race to create her own version of Global Indianness: my objective here is to trace the feedback loops between nodes previously conceived in terms of the static grid of production versus consumption.

Foregrounding the temporality of affect and the affectivity of temporality is particularly useful in understanding the dynamism of subject formation. While I disagree with theorists who assert that ideological interpellation leads inevitably to "gridlock" or "freeze frame" (for example, Massumi 2002), I have come to realize that ideological interpellation does not tell the whole story about how media move us. In addition, I join forces with scholars like Mazzarella (2009) who insist on bringing mediation back into our understanding of how media produce us as subjects in ways that problematize schisms between body and mind, mind versus heart, cognition versus corporeality, and passion versus reason.

Similarly, affect, conceptualized as the capacity to affect and be affected, enables us to arrive at a conception of agency that takes us beyond dichotomies of resistance versus compliance. I am interested in the ethical dimensions of affect, in how (mediated) affects enable us to situate ourselves in the world and, equally, in how we are imbricated in processes of change. Thus, my conception of affect underscores how our understandings of subject formation and social process may take into account movement, passage, and potentiality rather than stasis and arrival. To put this differently, affect is about the capacity to navigate the world, about world making (Das 2006) and about worlding (Stewart 2007). Yet it is important to note that these processes are contingent on temporalizing regimes. At the same time, as the rest of this book demonstrates, I want to insist on conceiving of affect and temporality as particular kinds of regimes, which is to say, as imbricated in institutions of power such as family and kinship, class formation, caste, state policies, and, last but not least, media. Thus, for example, in chapter 5 I examine how discourses of Resurgent India generated by a Hindu nationalist state, which were predicated on affectively charged conceptions of a nation that has to be woken up after "centuries of sleep," worked across class and gender to constitute some of my informants as particular kinds of subjects.

Yet, for the sake of analytical clarity, it has made sense for me to pry affect and temporality apart in order to trace how India is constituted at specific nodes of transnational public cultures. Below I discuss the "work" of time to foreground that time has affectivity: as I argue, this entails an understanding not simply of how time was phenomenologically experienced by my informants but, more pertinently for my argument in this book, in terms of how time shapes subject formation and social process; stated another way, I am concerned with the affective potency of temporality.

Finally, as I note above, this book is about unsettlement as an ethnographic lens as well as an analytic. Unsettlement occurs on two registers here: at the level of subject formation, as when subjects are formed through unsettlement; and as a framework for thinking about the relationship between media, public culture, and culture/cultural change. In foregrounding the temporality of subject formation and of social processes, I am indebted to Peirce's insistence on the dynamism of semiotic processes (see also Mankekar [1999a] for a theorization of subject formation as always already in medias res). Deploying unsettlement as an analytic enables me to skirt the conceptual trap of thinking of cultural change in terms of transitions between prescripted (and predetermined) stages (of growth, capitalism, modernity, postmodernity, and so on) by insisting on movement as intrinsic to culture. Thus unsettlement allows me to think of culture and cultural change neither in terms of unchanging continuity (a representation of India that continues to have tremendous salience in popular and scholarly representations) nor in terms of radical transformation, rupture, or a sea change.

For my informants, unsettlement was an affect that was temporally charged; it shaped their abilities to situate themselves in a rapidly changing world. Unsettlement was thus not simply something that they experienced but was affective in that it was profoundly consequential for the formation of their subjectivities.[20] Tracing the conjunction of affect and temporality provides us a mode of apprehending the fullness of time and the disjunctions it sometimes brings in its wake; the onward march of nations sprinting to the future and the women, men, and communities that are left behind; and the yoking and rupturing of individual and collective destinies.

THE WORK OF TIME

Ahmed's (2004) notion of affective economies is particularly helpful to understanding the temporality of affect. She insists that the circulation of signs is fundamental to the generation of affect and to the accumulation of affective value (2004: 45) and is, hence, implicated in processes of temporalization in fundamental ways. In arguing that transnational public cultures participated in the constitution of India as an archive of affect and temporality, I draw attention to multiple dimensions of time, from the passage of time as engaged by some of my informants and the work of time in their lives and the relationship of temporalizing processes to the formation of nations.[21]

Building on a long-standing interest within anthropology in how time shapes sociality and, indeed, the ethnographic project itself (including Evans-Pritchard 1969; Fabian 1983; Geertz 1966; Munn 1992; Pandian 2012; Rabinow 2007), I conceive of temporalization as an affective process that is constantly produced through everyday life.[22] Rather than restricting myself to an analysis of my informants' subjective or phenomenological experiences of time, I am concerned with how time, or what Henri Bergson (1910) has termed *durée* or duration, crisscrosses, transects, articulates, and, equally importantly, disarticulates the lives of my informants with the temporalizing processes through which nations are made and unmade.[23]

As Bergson (1910) reminds us, duration or durée is substantial and resistant; it contracts, expands, and intensifies; it is dynamic and continuous. My informants' engagements with the passage of time were deeply refracted by the circulation and consumption of transnational media and were affective rather than subjective or located in individual consciousness. For instance, many of my informants in New Delhi structured their household routines around their favorite television shows, so that viewing television literally punctuated the durée of family life: they would plan their mealtimes, rush home from work or social events, and organize their daily lives around the broadcast of their favorite television programs— and this continued to be the case even after cable and satellite television introduced a plethora of channels into people's homes and lives. Thus conceived, time was not measured in abstraction or in discrete units: the durée of family life, indeed of domesticity, intermingled with rhythms of viewing and consumption in patterned, yet constantly shifting, ways.[24]

As Munn puts it, "We may think of temporalization as going on in multiple forms, 'all the time'" (1992: 104). Transnational media play a crucial role in processes of iteration and temporalization: for example, we need to look no further than the televised spectacle of the destruction of the twin towers of the World Trade Center on September 11, 2001, to see how electronically mediated images acquire (in this case, an excess of) affective value through their reiteration over time. Yet as my ethnographic work with Sikhs and Muslims taught me, September 11 did not inaugurate a new period of hate violence for many communities of color but represented one of many events in a longer durée. My informants reminded me that processes of temporalization are hence unpredictable and nonteleological; they may consist of moments of rupture and interruption, or a prolongation and protraction. More importantly, my informants provoked me to see that, as much as affective regimes were refracted by diverse temporalities, the converse was equally true: temporalities were fundamentally affective in how they shaped the production of subjects, and how subjects negotiated and positioned themselves in the world: in this crucial sense, then, affect and temporality were mutually imbricated.

My analysis of transnational public cultures foregrounds how temporalization entails moments of unsettlement, as when patterns of thought and practice are unstitched or are rearticulated with new ones. Rather than engage the work of transnational public cultures in the production of epochal time, I examine how they both are embedded in particular sociohistorical conjunctures and are constitutive of them.[25] For instance, during the late 1980s and early 1990s, state-run Indian television played a central role in the shaping of an entire historical conjuncture in terms of the consolidation of Hindu nationalism as a political formation, the constitution of middle-class subjectivity, and the formulation of discourses of Indian Womanhood (Mankekar 1999a). Media and temporalizing processes are also closely implicated in how we remember (and, equally significantly, forget) aspects of the past, interpret and live in the present, and imagine the future. In fact, rather than conceptualize the past, present, or future as a priori or autonomous realms of experience, it makes sense for us to think of the ways in which transnational public cultures constitute the past, present, and future through, for instance, their mediation of memories of the past, experiences of contemporaneity, and discourses of futurity (Mankekar 2008). Some of my informants in the San Francisco Bay Area experienced India as a homeland that belonged in the past: these affect-laden memories were, as noted earlier, far from uniform and ranged from nostalgia to ambivalence, disaffection, and antagonism. Their constructions of homeland in terms of the past were refracted through their engagement with transnational media like satellite television and Bollywood films, including films that represented a phantasmic Indian culture that was "vanishing" in the face of an allegedly invasive modernity (compare Ivy 1995).

Yet it is crucial to note that transnational public cultures also participated in the production of a phantasmic past for my informants living in New Delhi. Despite (or perhaps because of) the proliferation of imported programs like *Oprah* or *Baywatch*, spectacular renditions of Hindu religious serials like *Ramayan, Shri Ganesh, Draupadi, Om Namah Shivay,* and *Raavan* on television formed an archive of collective memory for many of my Hindu informants in New Delhi: these serials portrayed "the national past" in terms of the "golden age" of Hinduism. As I demonstrate in chapter 5, these representations shaped not only the construction of the national past but also of contemporaneity and futurity. These examples illustrate the ways in which temporalizing processes are heterogeneous and multiple rather than homogeneous or unitary (Bergson 1910: 100).

Veena Das asks: "What is the work that time does in the creation of the subject?" (2007: 95). Many of my informants in both New Delhi and the San Francisco Bay Area would remind me that time has agency or, at the very least, a force of its own: time works upon us, our relationships, and our lives. They would speak of how time engendered their conceptions of the arc of a life. As I've suggested above, time was neither shaped by nor a product of their individual experiences. Instead, time constituted their lives and produced them as particular kinds of subjects. Some of my Hindu informants would recall the generative power of time in Hindu mythology through their invocation of time as *kaalchakra* (the wheel of time).[26] Contrary to stereotypes about so-called Indian fatalism, these informants were alluding to the temporality of their actions in how they dealt with crises or triumphs: put another way, time was generative of agency. Thus, for instance, Ramesh Jog described how, during a long period of illness in the family, time taught him how to live with the unsettlement "it" brought in its wake (samay hi hamein sikhata hai). Another informant emphasized the culpability of perpetrators of anti-Muslim pogroms in Gujarat by quoting a Sanskrit phrase: *vinaash kaale vipreet buddhi* (when the time of destruction is near, you lose all judgment). Some of my Muslim and Sikh informants were equally insistent in their belief that time has agency; time makes things happen; sometimes we wrestle with or against time, often to no avail (compare Das 2007: 86, 87, 95–96). As one informant, Fehmida Khan, who had moved to San Jose after the anti-Muslim pogroms in Mumbai in 1993, insisted, "There is no saying what time will bring" (kuch keh nahin sakte ki waqt apne saath kya layega). Thus, as I note above, temporality was affective in that it was productive of subjectivity, sociality, and the capacity to act and be acted upon.

On a different register, as the voluminous scholarship on nationalism attests, nationalist ideologies are enmeshed in temporalizing processes. In order to come into being nations have to acquire a past and look to a future: notions of the past, contemporaneity, and futurity are thus central to the formation of nationhood. Against the empty, homogeneous time of the nation (compare with Anderson's [1991] interpretation of Benjamin [1973]), I foreground the fullness of time and heterogeneous temporalities of the lives of my informants in New Delhi and the San Francisco Bay Area. When individual and national aspirations were coconstructed, as in the case of call center workers I worked with in Gurgaon, individual and national destinies acquired the temporality of emergence and potentiality: the aspirations of these informants were fraught with a hopeful waiting in which anticipation was weighted by an acute sense of uncertainty. In contrast, my informants who were positioned at the margins of the nation-state felt that they were out of step with the dominant temporality of nationalist self-representation, whether conceptualized as a particular kind of (Hindu) past or in terms of the nation's purported progress toward global dominance. As I describe below, at such times, my informants experienced the brutality of excision when they felt left out or shut out of the (un)steady march of the nation toward its prescribed future. Throughout my fieldwork in New Delhi and the San Francisco Bay Area, I was made aware of the intertwining of these multiple, sometimes disjunctive, temporalities. And, similarly, I was constantly reminded of the myriad ways in which homeland and diaspora were connected through displaced temporalities rather than a linear temporality of movement from the homeland to the diaspora.

Transnational Connectivities: Resituating Diaspora and Homeland

My intention, in this section, is to focus on how regimes of affect and temporality denaturalize conceptions of diaspora and homeland as territorially based. To clarify: this is not to minimize the importance of place or location (see, for instance, chapter 3 for an argument about the continuing significance of place and location to the formation of subjects in diaspora) but, rather, to underscore the constitution of India as an archive of affect and temporality through the circulation of transnational public cultures. Contrary to conceptualizations of the relationship between home and diaspora in binaristic terms, my objective is to draw out the transnational connectivities between the two. At the same time, there is a theoretical and political value to rethinking and also retaining the concept of diaspora. For one, the presence and vitality of diasporic cultures problematize essentialist conceptions of culture by breaking apart the isomorphism of place and culture (see Gupta and Ferguson [1997b] for an early discussion of these issues): as chapters 3 and 5 demonstrate, diasporic communities create India(s) as an archive of affect and temporality even as they unsettle them. Second, in some historical contexts, the resilience of diasporic communities enables a resistance to the assimilationist claims of nation-states—and here perspectives from critical ethnic studies scholarship are indispensable. At the same time, as I demonstrate in chapters 2 and 5, diasporic aspirations and affects might also lead to a resurgence of hypernationalist discourses, some of which are predicated on the elimination of minority communities in the homeland (compare Appadurai 1996 and 2006). As this book demonstrates, diasporic identities are neither singular nor homogeneous: they are contingent on specific histories of migration, geographic location, relations with "host" nation-states, and shifts in local, national, and global political economies. More importantly, as I insist in chapters 3 and 5, diasporic identities are frequently multiplex and are shaped as much by how communities and individuals navigate local landscapes of race, gender, and class as they are by (heterogeneous and contingent) relations with the purported homeland.

Once again, I draw on the work of feminist geographers who, in their pioneering work, insist that we rethink our sense of place in the context of the transformations wrought by the traffic in global capital, labor, and media (see, for instance, Massey 1991, 1993, 1994; Moss 2002; Rose 1993). For one, territoriality, configured at least in part by states and capital, remains a crucial modality through which identity and subject formation occur (for an excellent discussion of the territorial fantasies of Indian diasporas, see Shukla [2003: 5, 27]). Territoriality never ceased to be salient for my informants in either New Delhi or the San Francisco Bay Area, and was sometimes articulated in terms of intense affective attachments to land.[27]

In both New Delhi and the San Francisco Bay Area, some of my informants invoked territory in terms of erotic longing. A young man in New Delhi poignantly articulated an erotically charged love for the home/land (the word he used was *dharti*, which literally means land or earth) by describing soldiers who had died in the 1999 Kargil War with Pakistan as men who had consummated their love for the nation and, in the consummation, lost their lives. It is noteworthy that this young man used the erotically charged word for love, *mohabbat*, rather than the more neutral *pyaar*.[28] Another powerful articulation of this conjoining of erotic longing with longing for the homeland is expressed in a song in the film *Dilwale Dulhaniya Le Jayenge* titled "Ghar aaja pardesi tera desh pukare re" in which the homeland (*desh*), troped as female, is described as longing for the return of the man who has abandoned her by going abroad. Indeed, in films like *Dilwale Dulhaniya Le Jayenge* and *Pardes*, India is represented as the locus of affectively charged erotic desire.[29]

At the same time, a transnational analytics compels a rethinking of territorial notions of homeland versus diaspora as dichotomous categories of analysis and identity. These formulations are predicated on binaries of diaspora versus homeland to foreground spatiotemporal rupture, such that the homeland belongs to the past (as opposed to the diasporic present) and is located elsewhere. The temporality that adheres to the homeland is thus deemed one of anteriority: it is the locus of an originary identity and the place left behind. Yet the discourses of some of my informants in both New Delhi and the San Francisco Bay Area suggest that even when the homeland represents roots and therefore the past, the diaspora does not represent an unmoored present.

My informants' discourses displayed significant variations shaped, at least in part, by their class positions. The idea of a spatiotemporal rupture was affectively charged in potent ways for some of my working-class informants in the San Francisco Bay Area, who frequently spoke of "back home" as a place rooted in a distant place and time. Most of my middle- and upper-class informants insisted that recent technological developments like the Internet (in particular, Skype) enabled them to stay in such close touch with people and events in India that, as one of them remarked, "It feels like we are living in the same time zone." Furthermore, my upper-class informants tended to speak of an "emergent India" in terms of discourses of futurity. For my middle-class and upper-class informants, then, communication technology and transnational media had profoundly redefined their experiences of both space and time. Many of them remained in close touch with family members, friends, colleagues, and political and social developments in India and used a range of media to establish regular and dense lines of contact. For almost all my informants in the San Francisco Bay Area, satellite television services such as Dish Network and the simultaneous release of films in India and in the United States enabled them to keep up with popular cultural developments in India. The relationships these particular informants forged with India were shaped by a temporality of simultaneity rather than by spatiotemporal rupture.

Nevertheless, the idea of going back to India remained affectively charged for some other informants in the San Francisco Bay Area, indicating not simply the resilience of a fantasy of return but, more significantly, the shifting place of India in an unfolding trajectory of subject formation. In these particular instances, India became part of discourses of potentiality and futurity and, hence, was closely imbricated with complex processes of temporality. In some cases, India represented the telos, the end point of a journey constituted by sojourning in the West. In other instances, India was one node in a series of travels. For instance, Salim Choonawala's life suggested the trajectory of multiple migration (Bhachu 1986), and thus problematized normative constructions of diaspora as unlinear (see also chapter 5). The son of middle-class migrants whose ancestors left India close to a hundred years ago, he grew up in Kenya but moved to Gujarat in his early twenties to set up a business. When the business failed, he returned to Kenya for a few years before moving to Canada. Then, when he was in his forties, he found his way to the Bay Area where he started life anew as a gas station attendant. He described his life in the United States with great zest but always insisted that he would move to Gujarat. This, he claimed, was his dream for his future because he always believed that once the Indian economy "got developed," he would be able to reestablish his business and "settle down" there. How did he perceive himself? I asked. He replied that he felt he had the ability to "take on the culture" of wherever he lived. He had always thought of himself as Kenyan when he was growing up, and moving to Gujarat and Canada had done nothing to change that. But when he moved to the Bay Area and found himself in the midst of large and diverse communities of people from India, he felt he was slowly becoming "more Indian." He believed that moving to India "eventually" would enable him to become more "fully" Indian because he would then be surrounded by other Indians.

His discourses of futurity foreground the shifting registers of his identity (for instance, his ability to take on "the culture" of where he lived).[30] On the one hand, India emerges as a locus of his dreams for the future— and, on the face of it, this did not appear to be very different from the fantasies harbored by some of my other informants who also dreamed of "returning" to India. Yet Salim was not implying that an essential Indian identity somehow underlay his other identities. Instead, he insisted that his identity was something that changed according to his surroundings.

His dreams of "settling down" in India were not based on a conception of India as a land of an originary past to which he would return. On the contrary, Kenya, Canada, and the United States were where he located his past, while India was a land of future habitation or settlement.

My insistence on displaced temporalities builds on Massumi's (2002) argument that we move away from conceptualizing identity in terms of a spatial grid of axes and look instead at movement as a process of becoming. Much like Salim's itinerancy, relationships between diasporas and homelands may be conceptualized through modalities of potentiality, as always emergent, and as constituted by processes of both habitation and unsettlement. I thus problematize the binary between formulations of homeland predicated on assumptions of origin and authenticity versus those of diaspora, as tied exclusively to tropes of loss, exile, or inauthenticity. Instead of conceiving of diasporic subjectivity "in terms of" India (Axel 2005: 42), I am concerned with the heterogeneous, yet often politically charged, relationships some of my informants in the San Francisco Bay Area had with India; more importantly, their subjectivities were shaped by allegiances and ties to multiple locations rather than circumscribed by the binary of homeland versus diaspora. These (re)positionings underscore how the identities of migrants, immigrants, and diasporic subjects are formed not just—or even primarily—through relationships with purported homelands but through multiple relationalities (Espiritu 2003; Siu 2007).

An increasing number of professional and upper-class Indians that I worked with in the San Francisco Bay Area were, in fact, able to relocate to India. In the course of my research with lower-middle-class informants in New Delhi, I also met some upper-class former nonresident Indians (NRIs), or RNRIs (returned NRIs) as they liked to call themselves.[31] Narinder Singh Dhaliwal was one such RNRI. He was a software professional who had moved from Austin to New Delhi, where he opened a company that did software outsourcing. During the peak years of the IT boom in the United States he moved back to New Delhi, where he had grown up and gone to engineering school, because he firmly believed that India was the land of the future. I first met him in 1999, when the IT industry was booming, and we continued to meet over the years that I conducted my fieldwork. One evening in 2003 we sat in his tastefully appointed living room in New Delhi, surrounded by European crystal and original art by celebrated Indian artists; beneath our feet were plush silk carpets. Over dinner, I asked him why he chose to move to India when he did. He sat back, stroked his beard, and smiled reflectively; then, seeing that I was awaiting his reply, he leaned forward earnestly. His voice quiet with a self-

assurance gifted by professional success, he replied that while the IT industry in the United States was always going to be subject to ups and downs,
it would grow steadily in India. He said that, despite the liberalization of
the economy, it was still very difficult to start a business in India and that
he had had to deal with many obstacles. Yet, he asserted, "In the long run,
this [India] is the place to be. This is the place of the future." He ran an
office in Austin and would travel "back" on a regular basis, but he insisted
that he felt equally at home in both places: certainly, his cosmopolitan lifestyle indicated that. Narinder added that another, perhaps equally important, reason for moving to India was to engage in social activism, because
he believed that it was now time for him to "give back to Indian society."
So, despite the fact that they were Sikhs, he and his wife had joined the
Bharatiya Janata Party, the Hindu nationalist party then in power, and
had committed much of their free time and resources to working for the
party.

In subsequent years I met several other upper-class entrepreneurs and
professionals who worked in the IT industry or with corporations interested in setting up shop in India. These men and women were often selected by their companies to open branches or diversify their corporations'
undertakings in India precisely because of their Indian background: perceived as mediators, they were identified as bringing together the "cultural
knowledge" and "technical knowledge" necessary to set up operations in
India. India, for these upper-class men and women, was not just a place of
the past but of the future and, indeed, of futurity.

Because the chronotope of rupture implies the splitting of an a priori
authentic subject, of severance from "context," another trope conjoined
with diaspora is that of loss—loss of the homeland, of "tradition," of roots,
of authenticity—such that diasporic affect is frequently represented in
terms of mourning this loss.[32] Yet growing up in India during the 1970s
and 1980s and throughout my fieldwork, I was frequently confronted by
similar articulations of mourning for a lost culture or tradition. As I elaborate in chapter 5, the reconstitution of Hindu nationalism over the past
several decades has, in many ways, been predicated on mourning a "glorious Hindu past." Hence, far from being unique to diasporic subjectivity,
notions of temporal rupture and loss haunted the discourses of several
of my informants living in New Delhi, who spoke of the "real India" as
something that belonged in a past left behind. This was particularly true
of those who subscribed to discourses of Hindu nationalism and believed
that the vanishing past could be resurrected through religious revivalism
and, in particular, through Hindutva.

In the case of many of my informants in the San Francisco Bay Area, the density and the modalities of their transnational connections with India were contingent on particular histories of immigration, class positions, and on heterogeneous formations of family and kinship. Discourses of gender and sexuality centrally mediated the relationships that many of my informants constructed with India. For instance, Tehmina Ali, a young, upper-class woman who lived in the Mission District in San Francisco, had not been back to India since she came out as a lesbian.[33] We used to meet regularly at a café in her neighborhood and our conversations would be frequently interrupted by friends who would stop by our table. One crisp October afternoon we decided to go for a walk, and we traversed the hills of Diamond Heights and Noe Valley, our faces covered with the sweat of our exertion, our hearts racing with exhilaration. As we paused to look over Dolores Park, Tehmina said she wanted to stop for a bit. I thought at first that she wanted to stop because she was tired. But then she started to speak of how her memories of India were intimately linked with her acceptance of her sexuality. She became pensive and remarked that coming out had entailed loosening her ties with biological family and kin who lived in India and painstakingly building new kin networks within the United States. Yet Tehmina insisted that she was committed to "staying in touch with India," and her primary modes of doing so were the friendships and political alliances she constructed with South Asian LGBTQ networks within the United States and through her consumption of popular Bollywood film.[34] She said that every few months she would host a Bollywood night at her home and she would invite all her friends ("South Asian or not") to watch the latest Bollywood release over biryani and beer: "We call it my Bollywood, Biryani, and Beer nights," she laughed wryly, clearly wanting to change the mood of sadness that seemed to have fallen like a blanket upon us. Then, becoming serious once again, she added that when she decided to come out as a lesbian, she recognized that it meant that she would have to "move once and for all from India." Nevertheless, despite (and perhaps because of) her sense of displacement, India continued to play a central role in the construction of her subjectivity as a lesbian and a woman of color in the United States. Active in the "mainstream" LGBTQ community as well as in South Asian networks, she asserted that there was "no question" in her mind that India was "at the foundation" of her sense of self. As she said to me, "I can never forget where I came from, and that does something to me and my sense of who I am. It will always be a part of who I am."

Yet it is crucial to note that the India Tehmina asserts as foundational to her sense of self is an extraterritorial India created through affect and temporality rather than one based on territory or one circumscribed by the Indian state's claims to citizenship. In her persuasive theorization of the Sinophone, Shu-mei Shih (2007: 184–85) critiques discourses of "Chinese diaspora" that privilege an ideology of origin. Shih insists that "identity is a temporal category" and argues that it is important to ask "not so much what is Taiwanese American, but also *when* is Taiwanese American" (2007: 186, emphasis added). In like fashion, I wish to foreground the temporality of identity for subjects like Tehmina for whom India constitutes an ambiguous and disjunctive point of reference. Representing herself at different moments as Indian, South Asian, "Gujarati babe," and dyke activist, Tehmina's identity shifts along heterogeneous, sometimes discontinuous, temporal registers, all of which are affectively charged in distinctive ways.

Narratives of Unsettlement: Homeland and Diaspora

Another ubiquitous mode of defining diaspora is in terms of displacement and dislocation. This conflation of diaspora and displacement has implications that are political as well as epistemological. First, conflating diaspora and displacement has political implications in that it suggests that all diasporic communities are intrinsically out of place because they belong elsewhere: that "elsewhere" is where they are authentically located; *that* is their place of origin and, therefore, their proper place. This conceptualization has concrete consequences for the ability of migrants and, in particular, immigrants of color to construct a sense of belonging within the United States: the implication is that they do not belong in America and that the only way to earn a place here is to break ties with there. Thus, assimilationist assumptions underpinning this paradigm—the notion that migrants and immigrants alike have to "leave behind" lives, political affiliations, histories—undergird nationalist discourses on migration and immigration (Chuh 2003; Espiritu 2003). Second, displacement and dislocation are often posited as uniquely or singularly diasporic experiences, thus (over)privileging the physical movement of individuals and communities from one nation to another.

In the following ethnographic example, I problematize assumptions that, in contrast to diaspora where one presumably feels unsettled, the homeland is where one is supposed to feel settled. When I first met her, Harbhajan Kaur lived in a working-class neighborhood in New Delhi. She was a widow who supported herself and her three small children by work-ing as a housemaid in the homes of middle-class residents of a neighbor-ing cluster of apartments. Dominant discourses of gender, sexuality, and family on the one hand, and her position as a poor woman belonging to a religious minority community on the other, intersected to profoundly shape her sense of unsettlement.

Harbhajan's late husband's uncle and his family lived in a tenement across from her, while her two sisters-in-law lived in an adjoining lane. Yet she always spoke tearfully of how alone she felt: it was clear that she grieved deeply for her husband but, as our friendship grew, I realized that her sense of being alone had been exacerbated by her tense relations with her husband's relatives. Far from extending any material or emotional support, her in-laws would always gossip about her when she found a job as a housemaid and would allege that she was a "bad mother" and a "dis-loyal" wife to her late husband because she would go out to work. Harb-hajan's loneliness in New Delhi was compounded by her memories of her childhood: she remembered her life in her natal home in Ferozepur with considerable sadness and longing, and missed her parents' love and, in particular, how her brothers would "protect" her. "I felt their hands were always there, protecting me, covering my head with protection and with their blessings" (unka haath mere sir pe hamesha rehta tha), she said. She had not wanted to get married but her parents had forced her to do so because, they claimed, a daughter's place is not with her parents but with her husband and his family. The following is extracted from one of many conversations in which she compared her life in New Delhi with her past in Ferozepur:

> Delhi seems strange after Ferozepur. It seemed even more strange when I first came here after my marriage. . . . I felt alone [in New Delhi] for a long time. I still do. I didn't want to marry. I wanted to keep living in my parents' house. That [her parents' home] is not my home any more. My parents made that clear. I didn't want to marry and move here. But I am afraid in this neighborhood. After what happened in 1984 I can never feel safe here. I never felt afraid in Ferozepur. But now I can never sleep well at night here. I really don't belong here. But then I now have no home left anywhere.

On the one hand, Harbhajan's sense of the strangeness of New Delhi seemed to stem from her "aloneness" after her marriage and reveal the shifting temporalities of identity. Her narrative of displacement is any-thing but linear: she moves back and forth between her childhood, her life as a married woman, and her fears living as a widow in a city that had been hostile to her as a Sikh woman. It was evident that she had been married against her will: her parents made it clear that she had no other option, thus revealing the discourses of sexuality surrounding unmarried women and the politics of gender that circumscribe the place of daughters in patrilocal and patriarchal families (see also Mankekar 1999a). Harbhajan's childhood, while not idyllic, had been marked by some sense of security: her brothers' protection of her was a theme she reverted to in several of her conversations with me. At the same time, her memories of their protection was also marked by an undertone of an acute sense of betrayal (after all, she was forced to marry by the very brothers who protected her) and anguish (she felt so acutely displaced as to feel homeless). Her affect was that of an unsettled subject who has lost one home and has not found another.[35]

But her sense of unsettledness was made all the more profound by the betrayal of her Hindu neighbors who were either passively or overtly complicit when violent mobs rampaged through her neighborhood in November, looking for Sikhs to target, ostensibly to avenge the assassination of then prime minister Indira Gandhi by her Sikh bodyguards. This sense of betrayal remained powerful many years after 1984 and surfaced in several of our conversations. She would tell me of how her body had retained memories of the terror and rage she had felt during those long nights and days: there were still times when she would awake with a start because she would hear the roar of mobs in her sleep. She said that sometimes when she accidently burned something while cooking, the smoke and the smell of burning would burn her eyes and nose—it would remind her of the acrid smells that filled the days and nights when Sikh homes and taxis were burned by Hindu mobs. She spoke of how there were times when her body would stiffen when she heard Sikh devotional music from the neighboring Sikh temple. It reminded her of how all the men in her community, including her husband, had gathered at the temple to defend it against Hindu mobs, and she had been so frightened that he would never return that she crouched "like a crumpled *dupatta*" in a corner of her room all day and night. She told me that it felt as if time had stood still: she thought the nightmare would never end, except that it wasn't really a nightmare—it was what was happening. She claimed that her life in New Delhi had been transformed by what had happened: she now thought of her life as divided between what had happened before and after 1984.

When I last met Harbhajan, her financial condition seemed to have improved a bit, as evident from the furniture and DVD player that graced her one-room apartment. One afternoon, we watched a popular Hindi film, *Hum Aapke Hain Kaun*, that had been released more than a decade earlier. Harbhajan commented on the ostentatious home in which the film's characters lived and said that as India had progressed (desh aage badha hai), while rich people had moved forward, poor people, like herself, had stayed exactly where they had always been (ameer log aage badhe hain aur hum gareeb log waheen ke waheen rah gaye hain). She added, "I worry about how my children will keep up. I hope they don't get left behind" (kaheen yeh peeche na rah jayein). This worry about being "left behind" was reiterated by many of my working-class informants in New Delhi and foregrounded their sense of precariousness. Harbhajan's words, in particular, foregrounded the sense of unsettlement exacerbated by her feeling that time was slipping away, and of feeling shut out and left out by the time of the nation.

As I was leaving her house that afternoon, Harbhajan added, "My bad time isn't over yet" (mera bura vaqt abhi khatm nahi hua). Once again, I was reminded of how time had its own agency: it held a power over her life and that of her children. Women and men like Harbhajan Kaur felt chronically unsettled because of their location at not just the spatial margins of the nation but its temporal margins as well. Although Harbhajan was not part of what might be conventionally defined as a diasporic community, her narratives of displacement underscore how exclusionary discourses of national(ist) belonging, backed by state-sanctioned violence, produce affects of unsettlement for marginalized subjects within, as much as across, nations.

Archiving India

Nothing starts in the Archive, nothing, ever at all, though things certainly end up there. You find nothing in the Archive but stories caught half way through: the middle of things; discontinuities.
—Carolyn Steedman, *Dust*, 2002

I want to close by reverting to the claim with which I began this chapter: that transnational public cultures constructed India as an archive of affect and temporality for my informants in New Delhi and the San Francisco Bay Area. My use of the term "archive" is motivated by the methodological, political, and epistemological interventions I wish to make. For one, by insisting that India is constituted as an archive of affect and temporality, I draw on the interrogation of the notion of the archive in critical historiography and cultural theory. For instance, Steedman insists that fragments "become archives only when they've been ordered, classified, and indexed in particular ways. They're thus remade each time they are used according to the purpose of the individual researcher" (2002: 68). I therefore use the term "archive" to unsettle assumptions that India might be an originary locus of identity and culture for subjects in both the so-called homeland and the diaspora. My broader interventions are political: to radically destabilize conceptions of nation predicated on the sublation of disparate forms of belonging; they are also conceptual in that I wish to demonstrate how using unsettlement as an analytic enables us to rethink the complex relationships between media and transnational public cultures on the one hand, and nationhood, gender, and subject formation on the other.

Drawing on a voluminous critical literature that has problematized the archive as an artifact, epistemological object, and site of theorization (for instance, Arondekar 2009; Cvetkovich 2003; Derrida 1996; Guha 1999; Steedman 2002; Stoler 2009), I examine the production of India as an extraterritorial site constituted through distinct affective regimes and through displaced temporalities that contravene the anteriority of homeland to diaspora. Diverging from substantialist conceptions of nationhood, I wish to point to ways in which we might destabilize the continuing hegemony of the nation-state in our imaginings of subjectivity and community: I wish to examine the modes of inquiry and forms of politics enabled and foreclosed when we conceive of India and Indianness as objects of knowledge production and of mediation.

I use the term "mediation" in its most capacious sense to include not just the work of transnational media such as film and television but, equally, the strategies of mediation I deploy in constructing my ethnographic archive. Like many archives, my ethnographic archive is fragmentary, incomplete, and impermanent (Arondekar 2009; Cvetkovich 2003; Steedman 2002). It is constituted by particular motivations: to disclose and withhold; to conceal and make publicly available; to order, render coherent; and, then, to unsettle.

The formation of archives is sometimes carefully planned, at other times fortuitous; as Steedman has argued, "The archive is made from selected and consciously chosen documentation from the past and also from the mad fragmentations that no one intended to preserve and that just ended up there" (2002: 68). Yet the building of archives is fundamentally imbricated with the manifold agendas of states (Arondekar 2009; Guha 1999; Stoler 2009) and hence with the workings of power.[36] To reiterate: when I posit the construction of India as an archive of affect and temporality, I am by no means minimizing the role of the state and of other political, economic, and social institutions. On the contrary, I trace some of the ways in which the contemporary Indian nation-state participates in the constitution of India and Indianness through the generation and circulation of specific affective and temporal regimes (for example, in financial policies designed to attract capital investments by NRIs; see chapter 5).

Steedman (2002) eloquently and poignantly describes the "dust" constituting and surrounding historical archives in terms of its materiality, obduracy, and corporeal implications for all who engage it. Extending her metaphor, I wish to insist on the obduracy and materiality of the affective and temporal regimes surrounding the construction of India as archive. Further, I wish to clarify that by focusing on the unsettlement of India and Indianness in the present moment, I do not by any means wish to imply that that which was stable has suddenly become unsettled.[37] Indeed, in focusing on a particular sociohistorical conjuncture, I have sought to claim that unsettlement is *intrinsic* to the production of India, such that Indian culture is conceptualized as chronically in flux, as always emergent. Contemporary battles over Indian identity and Indianness in political and popular culture seem to be circumscribed either by assumptions of cultural stasis (as in conceptions of tradition that have existed since "time immemorial"), in terms of cultural contamination, and/or of cultural transformations of such magnitude as to be unrecognizable. Ultimately, I am concerned with what happens when India—as epistemological object and locus of identity—is itself unsettled, destabilized, imagined anew. For my assumptions about temporality are, in the end, imbricated with how I conceive of India as an epistemological formation. On the one hand, the project of unsettling India implicates how I conceive of subjects on the move. But then again I wish to steer clear of an empiricist preoccupation with individual experiences and think instead of the kinds of subject effects produced by an unsettlement of India. Such a conception of India is predicated on the impossibility of India: not only do I believe that it is impossible to talk about India in monolithic or homogeneous terms, but I insist that India is produced through mediation, emplaced by mediation and, in fundamental ways, unsettled by it.

In sum, mediation operates at several different levels in my attempts to unsettle India. In staging fragments culled from my ethnographic research, I implicitly critique positivist assumptions about the archive as that which consists of original sources and yields primary data that are more directly reflective of "reality" (as opposed to secondary data, which are deemed secondhand and, therefore, less authentic)—in other words, as yielding "data" that are unmediated by processes of ethnographic inquiry and writing.[38] Here, I build on critiques of the archive as framed by the hermeneutics of recuperation (Arondekar 2009) or a locus of originary narratives (Derrida 1996). My ethnographic archive is formed through my modes of production and collation, my motivated reading and writing practices and, last but not least, my affective engagements with the objects and subjects of my inquiry: far from seeking to "find" or "discover" the truth of India that is waiting to be recuperated, I have attempted to trace the construction of India as fundamentally emergent.

Further, rather than crafting my archive on the basis of an unproblematic assumption of authorial agency, I have tried to be vigilant to how I, as authorial subject, am constituted by some of the very affective regimes I strive to trace. Far from presuming a unitary subjectivity, I found myself positioned in complex and fraught ways in an ethnographic mise-en-scène that was inherently unstable, not least because of my often visceral and embodied engagements with the objects and subjects of my inquiry. These engagements involved processes of recognition and misrecognition; identification, misidentification, and disavowal; affinity and alienation; pleasure, empathy, fear, and disgust—and affection, as in being affected by and affecting the objects and subjects of my inquiry.

Derrida (1996) writes about the traces that constitute the practice of writing, and the gathering of signs (consignation) that constitute the formation of archives. Taking its place as one of many processes by which India is entextualized, my ethnography is constituted through reading and writing practices that are contingent and temporal—and hence are unsettling—precisely because it is vulnerable to the irruptions of surprises, emergences, and potentialities, and to the ineffable, the inarticulable, and the inscrutable. Yet for all the volatility of the ethnographic scenarios I construct, like the dust of Steedman's archives, there is an obduracy to my ethnographic archive; its materiality is shaped by a generative tension between ethnographic longing—my desire to narrate, order, emplot—and the opacity of much that I have grappled with; it cannot be swept away.

....

The remaining chapters of this book are organized to delineate the multiple modalities through which, at specific nodes in a transnational circuit of images, texts, and commodities, India was constituted as an archive of affect and temporality for my informants in New Delhi and the San Francisco Bay Area. Instead of following the chronological arc of my ethnographic research, the sequence of these chapters demonstrates the nonlinear and discontinuous movement of regimes of affect and temporality across specific locations. Accordingly, rather than group the following chapters on the basis of particular media, the organization of this book enacts the busy traffic across media platforms. I hence intersperse my analysis of film and television with the movement of commodities, the proliferation of erotics, the potency of discourses of morality, and the unsettling valences of aspiration: my objective is to examine how specific nodes of public cultures generate flows, interruptions, feedback loops, and disjunctures in the circulation of regimes of affect and temporality. The thread that links these disparate nodes is the simultaneous (re)constitution and unsettlement of India and Indianness.

Chapter 2 examines a popular Hindi film, *Dilwale Dulhaniya Le Jayenge* (*DDLJ*), to trace how India and Indianness were at once unsettled and reconfigured at a specific historical moment shortly after the liberalization of the Indian economy. Drawing on ethnography, textual analysis, and policy analysis, I argue that this film demonstrated a shift in the relationship between belonging and territoriality such that India emerged as an extraterritorial formation that existed in the "hearts of Indians." Even as the film's representation of NRIs reinforced hegemonic discourses of gender and sexuality, it unsettled the binary of home versus abroad.

If the ideal NRIs of *Dilwale Dulhaniya Le Jayenge* carried India in their hearts wherever they went, they were also represented as unlocatable and as unshaped by their emplacements in the social and racial landscapes in which they lived: these representations of NRIs indexed the primacy of Indianness to their subjectivities. I contrast the idealized, placeless NRIs of the film with the subject positions of my informants in the San Francisco Bay Area whose identities were considerably more multiplex, emplaced as they were in sedimented landscapes of race, gender, class, and national origin. Hence, my chapter on *DDLJ* is followed in chapter 3 by my analysis of how Indian grocery stores in the Bay Area were crucial nodes in the production of sensuous knowledges about India. These stores also enable us to examine the interpellation of my informants by discourses of race, class, and national origin specific to where they were located. I describe these stores as complex social spaces in which objects and people on the move collide. Complicating assumptions about diasporic affect in terms of nostalgia or loss, the affective charge of the objects displayed and sold in these stores enabled the production of spaces of solidarity as well as ambivalence or hostility, and suggest how the intertwined discourses of affect and temporality unsettle conceptions of India even as they sometimes generate them

In chapter 4, I examine other modalities of the affectivity of objects in the simultaneous reification and unsettlement of notions of Indianness in my delineation of commodity affect. This chapter takes us back to New Delhi to examine how the proliferation of transnational television enabled the intertwining of distinct affective regimes and temporalizing processes pertaining to commodities and erotics so as to unsettle my informants' conceptions of desire, family, and Indianness. Concerns about the renegotiation of Indianness also refracted the production of Global India as an affective-temporal formation sustained by the interpellation of subjects by transnational discourses of morality. Thus, in chapter 5, I strategically juxtapose four apparently discrepant nodes of the circulation of discourses of morality: the moral and affective claims made by the Indian state's Resurgent India campaign for wealthy NRIs; the violent moral policing of Hindu nationalist groups against the celebration of Valentine's Day in different parts of India; the affectively and temporally charged discourses of family, gender, and nation in a popular Hindi film, *Kabhi Khushi Kabhie Gham*; and the struggles of a young Sikh American woman in the San Francisco Bay Area who constructed a discourse of Global India that diverged from statist and Hindu nationalist conceptions. Each of these nodes points to how transnational discourses of morality shape the production of Global India and Indianness in multifarious ways.

If conceptions of Global India were undergirded by morality for certain subjects in the San Francisco Bay Area, aspiration was a crucial modality for the production—and unsettlement—of India for call center agents in a suburb of New Delhi, Gurgaon. These informants' aspirations for the future enabled a different form of unsettlement: an excitement about what the future held in store that was, inevitably and irrevocably, marked by the temporality of uncertainty. In chapter 6, I examine aspiration as an affective-temporal formation that shaped the lives of the call center agents in Gurgaon as well as the trajectories of the protagonists of a popular Hindi film, *Bunty aur Babli*. Individual aspiration is sutured to national aspirations for growth and success in a context marked by neoliberal discourses of individual responsibility and entrepreneurship. At the same time, Aspirational India necessarily coexists in uneasy tension with an Other India: while Aspirational India engages a temporality of self-advancement and futurity, the Other India gestures toward a temporality of lag. These multiple, ostensibly contradictory temporalities remind us that, even as India is constituted as an archive of affect and temporality, it is also a formation that is profoundly and intrinsically unsettled.

In the coda to this book, I briefly trace the modalities of unsettlement experienced by my informants in the San Francisco Bay Area as they struggled against racial violence that followed September 11, 2001. In U.S. nationalist discourses, September 11, 2001, is often represented as a watershed event or a rupture; however, for many of my informants, particularly Sikhs and Muslims, the hate violence they faced in its aftermath was an exacerbation of what many of them had already experienced at different points in their lives. Nevertheless, it deeply unsettled their sense of where they were located in the larger racial and political landscape of the San Francisco Bay Area. Reverting to my claims here about deploying unsettlement as both an ethnographic lens and an analytic toward the political task of unsettling the nation, I draw the contours of a conceptual framework that enables me to extend my project of unsettling India to the U.S. nation-state and, more broadly, to the totalizing and repressive claims of nationalisms.

CHAPTER 2

Moving Images

Reconceptualizing Indianness in *Dilwale Dulhaniya Le Jayenge*

Roughly two-thirds of the way through the film *Dilwale Dulhaniya Le Jay-enge*, Dharamveer Malhotra and Baldev Singh, overseas Indians who live in London, meet for the first time in Punjab. Baldev exclaims that, despite the fact that Dharamveer wears Western clothes, he seems very close to India (aap Hindustan ke bahut kareeb hain). Leaning forward earnestly, Dharamveer responds: "Don't be deceived by my appearance, Choudhry Sahib. I carry India in my heart wherever I go." This exchange between two expatriate Indian men foregrounds a reconceptualization of Indianness that lies at the core of *Dilwale Dulhaniya Le Jayenge*. In unyoking belonging from territoriality, *Dilwale Dulhaniya Le Jayenge* contrasts sharply with earlier films that depicted overseas Indians using tropes of betrayal that equated leaving the nation with losing one's Indianness. Dharamveer's insistence that he carries India in his heart wherever he goes and, by extension, on the portability of Indianness, epitomizes a reconfiguration of nationalist affect at a critical juncture in postcolonial India.[1]

Released in 1995, *Dilwale Dulhaniya Le Jayenge* (which roughly translates to *The Lover Carries Away the Bride*, and which many middle-class Indian viewers know as *DDLJ*), narrates a somewhat clichéd story about the struggles of young lovers to win parental approval to marry. *DDLJ* is about Simran and Raj, nonresident Indians (NRIs) living in England, who fall in love while traveling in Europe. When Simran's father, Baldev Singh, learns of their love, he moves the family to his village in Punjab, where he arranges for Simran to marry the son of his childhood friend. Raj follows Simran to Punjab. When he arrives there, he announces that he is interested in buying land in India so that he can open a factory there. Raj is immediately befriended by Simran's fiancé, Kuljeet, and is welcomed with open arms by his and Simran's families. But when Baldev and Kuljeet learn that Raj is really there so he can marry Simran, they are enraged. Raj and his father, Dharamveer Malhotra, who had arrived in Punjab to help his son win Simran's hand in marriage, are forced to leave the village. But just as they are about to depart, Simran appears at the railway station where Raj and his father are waiting for the next train out. At the last minute, Baldev relents and approves of their marriage, and she leaves with Raj and his father. The lovers are finally reunited and, presumably, live happily ever after.

   DDLJ was neither unprecedented nor unique in its focus on overseas Indians. Nevertheless, the film signaled the realignment of the axes of location and identity occurring in postliberalization India. When I first watched the film, I felt that it was suffused with a longing for places and landscapes (ostensibly) located in India. It seemed to suggest that love of the land, nostalgia for place, and location within the territorial boundaries of the nation are fundamental bases for national identity and belonging. However, watching it repeatedly with my informants in New Delhi and the San Francisco Bay Area over the course of several years of fieldwork compelled me to revise my initial interpretations of this film.[2] I now believe that, at the same time that it aligns with state-endorsed discourses of nationalism, *DDLJ* signals the affective production of India as an extraterritorial entity, a "place" that (some) diasporic Indians might carry in their hearts wherever they go. The gendered figure of the NRI is of central significance to this renegotiation of nationalist affect: even as the film reifies gendered notions of Indianness, its portrayal of NRIs unsettles the binary of home versus abroad and, hence, problematizes the relationship between territoriality and belonging.

   DDLJ has been deemed a critical milestone in the history of Indian cinema for several reasons. For one, several years after its release, it was one of the longest-running films in the history of the Bombay film industry: as of 2012, it had broken all continuous-exhibition records in India for playing nonstop in a central Mumbai theater since its release in 1995. According to Anupama Chopra (2002), it raked in an estimated Rs. 600 million in revenues, and its music broke all records. In the San Francisco Bay Area's Indian cinemas, it achieved phenomenal success when it was first released. According to Shiraz Jiwani, the owner of Naz 8 Cinemas in Fremont, *DDLJ* was screened from dawn until well past midnight. For the first several months every one of its screenings attracted standing-room-only crowds, with long lines of hopeful viewers snaking around the building.[3] Although my interview with Jiwani occurred six years after the release of the film, his eyes still lit up with excitement when he described its runaway success. He claimed that DDLJ put Naz 8 Cinemas and, indeed, Hindi cinema "on the map" in the Bay Area.[4] The film's unprecedented popularity in India and overseas consolidated the careers of its leading actors, Shah Rukh Khan and Kajol, who play Raj and Simran respectively, and transformed them into international stars. DDLJ evinced a crucial shift in how filmmakers in the Hindi film industry would henceforth conceptualize, and hence target, its overseas audiences.[5] The film grossed unprecedented sums in box-office revenues alone, thereby reminding the Hindi film industry of the importance of overseas markets to its films.

More significantly, the film represented a turning point in how expatriate and diasporic Indians were represented in the popular imagination in India. In the aftermath of the liberalization of its economy and the introduction of transnational media, the very notion of Indianness had been thrown into crisis, necessitating the repositioning of the nation vis-à-vis the discursive and imaginative entity of "the global."[6] In this particular context, the global was a shifting and slippery signifier invoking, at different moments, fantasies of progress and modernity on the one hand and, on the other, the spectral presence of "the West" (against which the cultural, political, and economic sovereignty of the nation had to be protected) and/or "the foreign" (which represented a threat to the cultural purity of the nation). Through the gendered figure of the NRI, DDLJ provided one of several modalities through which India was constituted as an archive of affect and temporality for many of my informants in New Delhi and the San Francisco Bay Area.

It is difficult for me to delineate precisely when I conducted my ethnography of DDLJ. Conversations about the film surfaced throughout my fieldwork for this project irrespective of the topic under discussion. The citationality of this film never ceased to astound me: DDLJ was ubiquitous as a referent and a subtext in my conversations with informants across a range of topics, particularly those relating to family, gender, sexuality, and class. Although my focus in this chapter is on informants in the San Francisco Bay Area, DDLJ cropped up in my conversations with men and women from diverse national and cultural backgrounds, including Sri Lankans, Pakistanis, Fijians, Trinidadians, and Kenyans; not all of them could speak Hindi and many barely understood it. Yet most were able to talk about the film with tremendous passion and eloquence. My Hindu, Muslim, Sikh, and Christian informants in New Delhi as well as the San Francisco Bay Area claimed to have enjoyed it in equal measure. In the San Francisco

Bay Area, IT professionals from Silicon Valley waxed eloquent about the film. Taxi drivers in San Jose and Emeryville would pop in its CD the moment I stepped into their cabs and would launch into lengthy discussions of scenes from the film. Senior citizens and their grandchildren watched the film together. Men and women of different sexual orientations appeared to be profoundly moved by it. I would hear the film's songs in malls and at weddings, in upper-middle-class homes and in convenience stores.

Here, as elsewhere in my scholarship (for example, Mankekar 1999b, 2012, 2014) I join with other scholars committed to taking seriously the pleasures afforded by popular cultural formations as a point of entry into cultural and political critique (see, especially, the work of scholars working within the so-called British cultural studies paradigm, for instance, Hall 1981, 1990; Gray 1992; McRobbie 1994, 2000; Morley 1992, 2000, as well as scholarship in Asian American studies, most notably Kondo 1997, but see also Gopinath 2005; Manalansan 2003, 2007; Nguyen and Tu 2007). I am interested in what it was about the film that was so appealing to my informants, what made it meaningful to them, and what its pleasures and meanings suggest about the affective regimes it generated. Certainly, my informants' reasons for enjoying *DDLJ* varied sharply by class, gender, sexual orientation, and their affiliation with the contemporary Indian nation-state. My interest in the reception of this film, however, lies less in the variations in viewers' responses to it than in how it generated affective economies that spanned the heterogeneities of its viewers. Curious about why this film was so moving and pleasurable for such disparate viewers, I conducted a multitude of ethnographic interviews over the course of my fieldwork; I organized focus groups of students at an elite university and at a less-prestigious community college in the San Francisco Bay Area; I entered into informal conversations and structured interviews with informants in their homes and, occasionally, in public spaces like cafés and restaurants; I discussed *DDLJ* with informants in cabs, stores, offices, and classrooms.[7] Some of my informants would smile as they recounted how Raj and Simran fell in love, and then appear sad when they spoke of the obstacles they faced. Stern-faced men would express their anxieties about their children "going astray" as they described the dilemmas that Simran's father faced. Young women giggled when they recalled Raj's flirtatious ways. Young men would speak earnestly of how Simran embodied the kind of woman they wished to marry. Discussions about *DDLJ* often seeped surreptitiously into conversations about workplace politics, romance, and, in the Bay Area, immigration narratives. Many of these discussions would be woven into stories about family members and aspirations for the future.

My informants were extremely voluble about how much and why they loved the film and would provide me with a plethora of explanations. Some young women would talk about how they "identified" with Simran because they faced similar dilemmas in deciding between an arranged marriage and a "love" marriage. A significant number of the college-age women I worked with in the Bay Area asserted that they liked Simran because she was beautiful "despite" being dark skinned; as one young woman put it, "Simran is so pretty—she has an Indian beauty. Unlike women here, she is neither fair nor thin." Young men frequently confided that Simran represented all that they wanted in a partner and a spouse. Some women, in particular, were deeply touched by the portrayal of Simran's close relationship with her mother. Almost everybody that I interviewed spoke at great length about how much they loved the music. Many of my informants, including those who couldn't speak Hindi, could recite some of Raj/Shah Rukh Khan's dialogue. Every time I convened focus group meetings consisting of a screening followed by a group discussion of the film, I would be struck by how deeply moved my informants seemed to be. What was I to make of the pin-drop silence that enveloped them when Simran's mother explains to her that, while she could dream of love, she should never expect those dreams to turn into reality? What explained their tears when Raj and Simran finally reunite? The potency of my informants' highly charged engagement with this film cannot be captured in words.[8]

For despite the fact that my informants were so vocal about how much they loved the film, the pleasures they derived from its music, and the intimate relationships they forged with its characters, I was perpetually haunted by an acute sense that the power of this film could not be represented by what my informants said to me: it was as if their words simply could not articulate what they felt when they watched this film. I felt that our conversations about the film barely skimmed the surface of the affective intensity of their engagements. What accounted for DDLJ's power, its hold on their imaginations and feelings? After all, there are so many films that deal with dilemmas regarding love versus arranged marriages, and there is no shortage of films with catchy songs. It became evident to me that, despite my informants' effusiveness, there was much about their engagement that was indeed impossible to put into words. I faced an interesting ethnographic conundrum marked by the simultaneous volubility and inarticulacy of my informants.

I became curious about what was left unsaid by my informants. My project, however, was neither a hermeneutic one to "uncover" the silences or inarticulacy of my informants with the goal of parsing out their individual ("real") feelings, nor was it an empiricist one that aimed at transposing or mapping out the variable responses of viewers onto their diverse socioeconomic or cultural backgrounds. I could sense that the film produced affects that transected the responses of individual viewers and, hence, went beyond individual emotions. Furthermore, I gradually realized that I would have to rethink my earlier focus on state-endorsed ideologies of nationalism in *DDLJ* (Mankekar 1999b) and consider, instead, how it generated and circulated affective economies that exceeded ideological interpellation.

Patricia Clough describes affect as an intensity that is in "excess of consciousness"; she argues that affect is not presocial but can be traced from the "reflux back from conscious experience to affect" (2007: 2; see also Massumi 1997). In my earlier research on the role of television in the production of nationalist affect, I had been struck by the profound political potency of nationalist affect but did not, at the time, have a theoretical vocabulary that enabled me to articulate how it implicated the interface of texts and lives (Mankekar 1999a). It had been clear to me, even then, that the power of nationalism extended beyond ideological interpellation. At the same time, my earlier research also foregrounded the ruptures and slippages within nationalist affect; while it could not be conflated with or reduced to subjective feelings, neither could it be subsumed under totalizing conceptions of "mass" passion.

Gregg and Seigworth locate affect in immanence, "in the complex assemblages that come to compose bodies and worlds simultaneously" (2010: 6). There was much that was inchoate in my informants' engagement with *DDLJ*, suggesting that the range and scale of affects that the film aroused in them could not be described as particular kinds of emotions. My informants' responses to the film were extracognitive and exceeded what they could put into words; these responses enacted an intensity that was deeply affective. It was clear to me that *DDLJ* formed a vital node in the generation and circulation of the inchoate, inarticulable affective economies pertaining to shifts in nationalist affect.

My conception of affective economies draws on Sara Ahmed's delineation of affect as a form of capital. Drawing on Marx and Freud, Ahmed argues that "affect does not reside positively in the sign or the commodity, but is produced as an effect of its circulation" (2004: 45). Analogous to the production of surplus value in capitalism, affects assume value cumulatively through circulation: "The movement between signs or objects converts into affect. . . . Signs increase in affective value as an effect of the movement between signs" (45). Ahmed also provides us with a crucial qualification to the analogy she wishes to draw between surplus value (as formulated by Marx) and affective value. As she rightly points out, her analogy does not account for the Marxian distinction between use value and exchange value. Therefore, she also draws on Freudian conceptions of displacement. Yet, and critically, she refuses to locate affect in the psyche. She posits: "Where my approach involves a departure from psychoanalysis is in my refusal to identify this economy as a psychic one (although neither is it not a psychic one), that is, to return these relationships of difference and displacement to the signifier of 'the subject'" (Ahmed 2004: 45). Affect is presubjective in that it does not emerge from a subject; rather, affect is productive of subjectivity (52–53). Subjects, texts, and objects (and cinematic texts) are nodal points in the economy of affects.

As I argue throughout this book, media play a pivotal role in the generation and circulation of affective economies. Against the argument that affect is, in some ways, "beyond" semiosis (see, for instance, Massumi's [1997] insistence on the "autonomy" of affect), I wish to underscore the relationship between affect and mediation by foregrounding the political potency of affective economies that congeal around particular images and representations (Mazzarella 2009; see especially Ochs and Schiefflin 1989 on the linguistic expression of affect). Drawing on the semeiotic theory of Charles Sanders Peirce, I argue that while affect might be in excess of symbolization, it inheres in iconicity (a sign relation by virtue of resemblance; icons exist as pure potentiality) and indexicality (as when a particular signifier might point to and constitute the signified; indexical signs are formed through an existential relationship with the object being represented). Icons and indexical signs anticipate the cognitive and the discursive and therefore evoke a different temporality than the symbolic. A more nuanced and capacious understanding of semeiosis and mediation thus enables us to trace how affects are communicated and how they circulate between bodies and across bodies and objects (such as cinematic images and, equally importantly, nonvisual and synesthetic signs, including haptic signs). Moreover, while affect is irreducible to narrative, as the materialization of inchoate longings narrative can give form to affective economies (Ngai 2004). Rather than engage the diegesis of this film, I am concerned with how, even as it made these affects available for narrativization, DDLJ's affective economies resonated with and affirmed the inchoate longings, dilemmas, and anxieties of many of my informants.

As I have argued elsewhere, processes of semeiosis are historically specific (Mankekar 1993, 1999a, 1999b; compare Daniel 1996). I begin by describing the articulation of affective and political economies in 1990s India as an important context for the production, circulation, and reception of

DDLJ. I next examine how affective regimes surrounding *DDLJ* reconfigured the binary between India and "the foreign," home and diaspora, through landscapes that iconicize diasporic affect. This is followed by my analysis of representations of NRIs (exemplified by Raj and Simran) as indexical of shifts in nationalist affect that occurred in the 1990s. Finally, I turn to how *DDLJ* participates in the production of the imagination of a New India that is not tethered to territorial location but is, instead, constituted through affect and temporality—an India that expatriate Indians and Indians in India may carry in their hearts wherever they go.

Political and Affective Economies

The liberalization of the Indian economy in 1991 followed on the heels of political-economic changes that had already occurred in the 1980s, such as a shift from heavy industry to a consumer economy, the introduction of advertisements on state-controlled Indian television (Doordarshan), and the launch of transnational satellite television in 1991 (Mankekar 1999a).[9] This sociohistorical conjuncture witnessed a proliferation of Hindi films that were not only set abroad but, more importantly, depicted the lives and dilemmas of diasporic Indians. For the most part, the NRIs featured in these films were upper or middle class; further, and more significantly, their portrayals articulated with the aspirations of expanding "middle classes" in India.[10]

From the mid-1980s onward, the Indian state inaugurated policies aimed at opening up the economy to privatization and multinational investment.[11] In accordance with these policies, the state streamlined procedures to make it easier for private companies to get clearance for projects. For instance, in early 1987 the number of approvals required from the Reserve Bank of India (the Indian equivalent of the U.S. Federal Reserve) was reduced from fourteen to four. Liberalization policies launched by the state of India in the mid-1980s had immediate effects. For example, after the entry of foreign banks and the deregulation of banking in 1985, in a single year profits for foreign banks doubled to Rs. 61.7 crore or $51.3 million ("Foreign Banks" 1988). Foreign investments accelerated at an unprecedented rate. In the first nine months of 1988, overseas investment peaked at Rs. 170 crore or $124 million ("Foreign Investment" 1988). An increasing number of multinationals began to recognize the importance of gaining a foothold in India, both for its potentially huge domestic market and as a springboard to markets in the rest of the region. The state introduced other policy changes, such as changing Reserve Bank regulations to make it easier for multinationals to employ foreign nationals in India and permitting overseas organizations to establish joint ventures without Indian partners.

To a large extent, the state acted with the approval (if not in response to the prodding) of upper- and middle-class elites. For instance, an editorial in the metropolitan newsmagazine *India Today* hailed then-prime minister Rajiv Gandhi, who had been credited with introducing economic reforms, as "the original glasnostian." The editorial proceeded to explicitly conflate "modernism" with privatization and liberalization: "In the context of India's development modernism must mean . . . decreasing the role of the state and getting the state off the backs of the people. Modernism must mean freeing the productive and creative energies of the people—a genius they have demonstrated whenever hampering state controls are lifted" ("The Challenge of Modernism" 1988).[12] By 1990 more changes had been introduced. Despite the trepidations of multinationals, the left-leaning National Front regime then in power continued to "reform" the Indian economy.

By 1991 India's external debt amounted to $70 billion and was the third largest in the world after Brazil's ($122 billion) and Mexico's ($101 billion; Nayak 1991). The Indian state had to seek a substantial structural-adjustment loan of $5–7 billion from the International Monetary Fund to withstand this grave fiscal crisis. Conditionalities for the loan included devaluing the currency, liberalizing the foreign trade sector, cutting subsidies, and initiating the privatization of industry.

In 1991 the Indian state introduced economic reforms in response to conditionalities attached to the International Monetary Fund's structural adjustment loans. The state did away with licensing for all but eighteen industries (Lakdawala 1991). It also reduced the number of procedures required for multinational investment. For example, multinationals were now permitted to invest up to 40 percent equity in Indian companies (provided that imported capital goods did not exceed 30 percent of the total value of outlay).[13] By 1995 the private sector was permitted to pursue oil and gas exploration, the lending rates of banks were deregulated, airlines were privatized and, in some sectors, industrial licensing was almost completely deregulated. In 1996 some economists were advocating the emulation of China's economic reforms. They claimed that in China the nonstate sector was virtually free of "most regulatory impediments—it pays few taxes and is free to hire and fire labor, and has no restrictions on foreign investment" ("Economic Liberalisation" 1996).

Many commentators were concerned that liberalization would plunge India into neocolonial dependency. For instance, one analyst remarked, "the nexus between direct foreign investment and promotion of consumerism among upper and middle classes is . . . palpable from the behaviour of multinational corporations already operating in India" (M. 1991).[14]

Nevertheless, despite these changes in the state's economic policies, many supporters of liberalization within the state and in industry were dissatisfied with the pace of the reforms. Skeptical of the state's commitment to completely liberalize the Indian economy, they turned to a different kind of foreign investor, the NRI. This targeted group was made up not of multimillionaires such as the U.K.-based tycoon Swaraj Paul but upper- and upper-middle-class Indians all over the diaspora. Some supporters of liberalization in policy circles believed that the remittances and deposits of NRIs would enable India to survive the serious foreign exchange crisis. Indeed, in his budget speech the finance minister tried to court NRIs by announcing the appointment of a chief commissioner whose primary responsibility would be to attract NRI investment ("NRI Remittances" 1991). Comparisons were made between Israel's drive for funds from Jewish communities overseas and India's appeals for inward remittances. The state offered a range of incentives, such as a higher rate of interest on the Foreign Currency Nonresident Deposit Scheme (FCNR). In fact, the interest rate for this scheme was often much higher than the London Inter-Bank Offered Rate (LIBOR) at which international banks lent to one another.

Obviously, only wealthy NRIs with the capital to invest in India were wooed. Political and economic refugees, migrant laborers, and exiles were completely erased from these discourses. The newly discovered wealthy NRI became the new messiah of liberalization. By 1991 the state had launched an increasing number of schemes as incentives to draw NRI investment. Ranging from the sale of gold to raise foreign exchange to the devaluation of the rupee, these policies were designed to encourage NRIs to remit money to India through regular banking channels and, in fact, they led to an increase in the total number of NRI deposits. Under the 1991–1992 budget, the following special incentives were offered to NRIs to invest in India: a tax exemption on interest earned on nonresidential external (NRE) accounts held by persons characterized as residents under the Foreign Exchange Regulation Act (FERA), remittances in foreign exchange to persons in India, India Development Bonds, Double Taxation Agreements, and NRI Bonds ("Exchange Reserves" 1992). Relaxations under FERA and income tax laws would enable NRIs to stay up to 150 days in a financial year and still retain their NRI status under income tax rules; further, under FERA, NRIs with foreign citizenship could work in India for up to three years without having to repatriate their foreign assets to India.

India was packaged as an attractive investment opportunity, and NRIs emerged as an important source of foreign investment. A special advertising supplement aimed at NRIs in North America claimed, "Over the last few months, were it not for the . . . NRI deposits that continued with banks in India, India would have defaulted on its foreign repayments. . . . Most NRIs showed their confidence in India by retaining their hard-earned foreign exchange in banks in India" ("NRIs" 1991). In 1992 the net inflow of funds into NRI deposits was estimated at $4.35 billion ("Exchange Reserves" 1992).

As noted above, the NRIs being valorized were those who had the wealth to invest in India. In addition to being classed in this manner, the NRIs being courted for their capital were gendered as male. The following description is emblematic of the masculine subjectivity imparted to NRIs.[15] It is equally significant for how it expresses the love-hate tone of popular representations of them, thus underscoring the intersection of affective and political economies congealing around the figure of the NRI:

> He is the Indian everyone loves to hate: flashily dressed, he drinks bottled water, books airline seats en bloc during the holiday season, complains bitterly about "Indian efficiency," and walks away with prime allotments of land, blue chip stocks and Maruti 1000s. He is the Non-Resident Indian (NRI). But many Indians prefer to call him Not Required Indian. Yet, it seems it is he who might turn out to be the *knight in shining armour* to rescue the *damsel in distress* that is the Indian economy with its many woes: 12 per cent inflation, foreign exchange reserves of Rs. 3, 050 crore (three weeks' imports); Gulf crisis bill of Rs. 71,000 crore; budget deficit of Rs. 13,000 crore, and industrial growth target downgraded from 10 percent to 7.5 per cent. ("Non-resident Indians Asking for More" 1990, emphasis added)[16]

Since complete liberalization was deemed out of reach by most elites, the wealthy, male NRI, the foreign-based son of the soil, emerged as the harbinger of privatization and increased foreign investment.[17] Although DDLJ portrays two different classes of NRIs (emblematized by the middle-class Baldev Singh and multimillionaire Dharamveer Malhotra), in general, depictions of NRIs in popular media—as male, affluent, and peripatetic—represent some of the ways in which affective economies of nationalism were altered in the aftermath of the liberalization of the Indian economy.

Certainly, the political and economic changes described above seem to resonate with DDLJ's representation of shifting notions of belonging and Indianness and enact discontinuous moments in the trajectory of postcolonial nationalism. In the remaining sections of this chapter I demonstrate how *DDLJ*'s constructions of NRIs, with its attendant discourses of nation and identity, point to some of the new dispositions of power emerging in postliberalization India.

There is no question that the preoccupation with NRIs in Hindi films such as *DDLJ* was the result of the fact that Indian diasporas represent a crucial segment of their market. But films like *DDLJ* also perform the affective work of representing the diaspora to itself and to "those back home." For, if the Indian state defined the category of the NRI largely in financial terms, the claims it made on NRIs were fundamentally affective. *DDLJ* paved the way for countless films that focused on the longing, anxieties, and trials of diasporic Indians (such as *Pardes* [Foreign land, 1997], *Aa Ab Laut Chalein* [Come, let us return, 1999], *Kabhi Khushi Kabhie Gham* [Sometimes happiness, sometimes sadness, 2001], *Kal Ho Na Ho* [Tomorrow may never come, 2003], *Salaam Namaste* [2005], *New York* [2009], and *Kabhi Alvida Na Kehna* [Never say goodbye forever, 2009]). Some of these films (in particular, *Pardes* and *Kabhi Khushi Kabhie Gham*) articulate the longings and dilemmas of many Indians who may have made it abroad but are concerned about losing their "culture." In keeping with the reconceptualization of notions of culture, belonging, and Indianness occurring in India in the mid- and early 1990s, these films were about NRIs who might or might not return to India but are "reassured and reassuring about traditional [Indian] values" (filmmaker Govind Nihalani, quoted in Jain and Chowdhury 1997).

Moving Images: Home and Abroad

The term "diaspora" foregrounds a field of relationships with a purported homeland, with the homeland signifying an imaginative, and occasionally imagined, site of longing, struggle, and ambivalence. *DDLJ* is ostensibly about members of the Indian diaspora. The film begins by constructing a particular form of diasporic affect, a sense of loss most powerfully expressed through landscapes that iconicize longing, displacement, and, eventually, emplacement.

In *DDLJ*, affect is generated and accrues through other processes of semeiosis, specifically, through iconicity and indexicality; therefore, it seems worthwhile to clarify what I mean by iconicity (firstness) and indexicality (secondness) in terms of their place in processes of semeiosis.[18] According to theories of semeiosis formulated by Peirce, iconicity (firstness), indexicality (secondness), and symbolization (thirdness) are indivisible. Hence, at different moments, a sign can be iconic, indexical, or symbolic. Semeiosis is thus an intrinsically temporal process: it can be infinite, stretch over a duration of time, or be episodic, singular, or irruptive. As a sign redolent of firstness, an icon bears a constitutive resemblance to its objects (or what it represents); for instance, an icon of a divine being embodies divinity. As Peirce puts it: "An icon is a representamen [sign] of what it represents and for the mind that interprets it as such by virtue of its being an immediate image. . . . We extend the term icon to the outward objects which excite in consciousness the image itself" (1958: 4.447). A sign is iconic when it evokes particular qualities: an icon is religious insofar as it "excites" a sense of its divinity. Yet the qualities evoked by an icon are inchoate, preindexical, and presymbolic. An icon's qualities of firstness are evanescent; an icon can be redolent or regnant with affect. As J. Jay Zeman points out: "Firstness is immediacy, firstness is prereflexive. When reflection does occur, however, we enter the realm of secondness" (1977: 24). Zeman adds, "The difficult thing about talking about firsts is that when we recognize that something is grasped as a first its firstness effectively evanesces" (1977: 23). An indexical sign, on the other hand, might not bear any resemblance to its object (for instance, a weathercock is an index of the wind or smoke indexes the presence of fire) but, instead, bears a direct existential relationship to the object of representation; it exists by virtue of its coexistence, causal relationship, or contiguity with the object. Finally, symbols are products of conventions and rules; symbols are arbitrary signs that require cognition and learning to be interpreted. Symbols are generated through some degree of consensus or agreement as to the relation between a sign and its object; for instance, there is a general agreement that a given national flag represents a nation. To reiterate, these different dimensions of signs are indivisible, which is to say, signs are seldom purely or solely iconic, indexical, or symbolic. Therein lies the dynamism and temporality of the process of semeiosis.

Affects may be rendered or communicated through iconic forms of semeiosis because they might embody firstness, a quality that is immanent and precognitive: these affects exist prior to their capture by language and other forms of symbolization. Thus, for instance, Kathleen Stewart analyzes how affects, as "moving forces," are "immanent in scenes, subjects, and encounters" (2007: 128). In what follows, I trace the immanence and circulation of affects through the deployment of landscapes as particular cinematic "scenes." Through their enactment of qualities of firstness, certain images and scenes in DDLJ iconically generate and circulate affects that are in excess of (rather than preclude) and anticipate symbolization. Put another way, while the semeiotic form predominant in these scenes is that of iconicity and firstness, these scenes are not devoid of indexical signs or symbols: tracing the iconicity of signs hence allows us to understand not

2.1. Baldev and the pigeons in London.

only why affect is ineffable and inchoate, but also how affect may be recognized and categorized retroactively through its symbolic forms.[19]

In sum, the ineffable presentness of affects may be analyzed retroactively through the iconicity of specific images. These images are moving in multiple senses of the word: they generate affects and are nodes in the circulation of affective economies. It bears repeating that, even as the responses they evoke are frequently visceral, embodied, and corporeal (as, for instance, when the eyes of many of my informants filled with tears as they watched Raj and Simran suffer pangs of separation, or when they cringed when they saw Raj being brutally thrashed by Kuljeet and his henchmen), the affects produced and circulated by these scenes are irreducible to individual passions or feelings.

DDLJ opens with a frame (a scene) of a cold, soggy morning in central London. Into this frame walks an Indian man, Baldev Singh, in "traditional" Indian clothing (figure 2.1). Baldev begins to feed pigeons that have gathered around him. His sense of displacement is presented to us in his voice-over: he remarks that just as the pigeons are homeless and must fly to where they can find food, so must he. But, unlike the pigeons, his wings have been cut by his financial needs and constraints. He remarks that, despite the fact that he has lived in London for twenty-two years, the land still feels alien to him. He walks these streets every day, and every day these streets ask: "Who is Chaudhry Baldev Singh? Where has he come from? Why has he come here?" Nobody knows him here, except the pigeons. He dreams that one day he will return home to his nation, to his Punjab. In these scenes the gray and dank landscape is iconic of Baldev's affects of diasporic loss; it produces a sense of his estrangement from the city in which he lives; here, iconicity or firstness evokes "an instance of that kind of consciousness which involves no analysis" (1.306, in Zeman 1977: 243). Baldev's words represent only some of the affects pervading this scene. Much of the affect of loss and displacement suffusing this scene

2.2. Baldev remembers his home in Punjab.

is produced through the iconicity of the landscape itself: the wet, lonely streets that are silent and appear bereft of all life except for the presence of Baldev and the pigeons.

Cut to images of fields blooming with iridescent mustard flowers, which contrast with the grayness and loneliness of the spaces Baldev inhabits in London: the sensorium produced here contrasts sharply with the previous scenes. The iconicity of this landscape works synesthetically. Lively Punjabi music fills the air and, in the background, we see women in colorful *dupattas* dancing and singing: "Come home, O traveler, your land beckons." In the very next frame, we see Baldev in the foreground once again feeding pigeons; but, this time, he stands in the sunshine, surrounded by the lush fields (figure 2.2). He has been transported to another time and another place, and the landscape is regnant with other affects. The colors and the vibrant music that suffuse the next few frames iconicize (his) nostalgia for the homeland; their liveliness and vitality contrast sharply with the empty stillness of the bare, dank streets of London.[20] These scenes foreground the ways in which DDLJ represents the temporalities of diasporic affects. Baldev's love for his home/land evokes his memories of the past and his sense of alienation in the present, even as it gestures toward his longing to return to Punjab in the future.

Suddenly, the pealing of church bells fills the air. Abruptly, Baldev is pulled back into the present, to his sense of alienation in London. He collects himself with a start. He picks up his umbrella and starts striding through the streets that do not know his name, passing what are for him alien landmarks (Trafalgar Square, Parliament, Tower Bridge) that potently iconicize his estrangement from his life in the present. This apparently conventional rendition of diasporic longing encapsulates aspects of mediation that are presymbolic. The contrasting landscapes Baldev inhabits also iconicize the displaced temporalities of diasporic loss by enacting his simultaneous inhabitation of landscapes of the past (the land that he

2.3. Raj and Simran reunite.

has, ostensibly, left behind) and the present (the land in which he currently lives).

We see another rendition of the affective iconicity of landscape when, much later in the film, Raj and Simran reunite in Punjab. Restless with longing for Raj and unable to sleep, Simran hears the strains of the mandolin that Raj used to play in Europe. Her hair disheveled and eyes heavy with longing, she dashes into the mustard fields that surround her; they are lush and sensuous as the mustard sways in the predawn breeze. She is wearing white, which symbolizes virginal purity. Looking into the distant horizon she suddenly sees Raj standing with a mandolin in his hand, backpack on his back, looking exactly as he did in Europe. The two run toward each other to the crescendo of music that is rousing as well as arousing. They hold each other in a fervent embrace, surrounded by swaying mustard blossoms: the tactility and haptic quality of these scenes foreground the erotic longing of the lovers (figure 2.3). They sing of the madness of their passionate love for each other and pledge to die in each other's arms. Here the landscape of Punjab iconicizes sensuality, erotic longing, and fertility.

This landscape acquires a different kind of affective iconicity in yet another scene when, close to the climax of the film, Raj and Baldev sit in the mustard fields feeding pigeons (figure 2.4). Raj has been joining Baldev there on a regular basis as part of his campaign to win him over. Baldev reminiscences that he was very young when his father would bring him to these fields on his shoulders; he has been friends with these pigeons since that time, and finds solace in their company. Raj asks Baldev if he thinks there is a difference between these pigeons and those in London. Baldev replies with a knowing smile that there is a difference: "The pigeons here know me, recognize me. They belong to the same soil as I. There, even the pigeons are alien to me." Then, Raj, with a quizzical expression on his face, responds by asking if it could be possible that the "difference" might lie in his perception (*nazar*) since one of the pigeons in London could well have

2.4. Baldev and Raj bond briefly in the fields of Punjab.

flown there from Punjab, might "belong to the same soil," and might know and recognize him. Could it be that it is Baldev who doesn't recognize that pigeon? Baldev whirls around to face Raj as if seeing him for the first time. But, before he can speak, a shot rings through the air. A wounded pigeon falls to the ground, shot by Kuljeet, Simran's fiancé, who is out hunting. Raj runs over to pick up the pigeon from the ground and lovingly smears mud on him. When Baldev asks him what he is doing, he replies, "My mother used to say that the soil of our country is magical. This pigeon will recover." As nonarbitary signs, icons embody a constitutive resemblance to their objects: in this case, the soil is iconic of the healing properties of the home/land itself. Baldev turns to Raj and says, his face creased in a rare smile, "You are right. It is I who failed to recognize [the pigeon that flew to London from here]." The scene of the two men feeding pigeons is transformed into a landscape that iconicizes recognition and reconciliation in the face of diasporic estrangement and loss.

These scenes, these representations of the landscape of Punjab, are central to the film's generation of affects of loss and longing. At the same time, these representations of Punjab also suggest how the love of the land may be subsumed within state-endorsed nationalism. The diasporic affect iconicized in this landscape is, in fact, fundamentally (Hindu) nationalist; what we get is the resolutely Hindu Punjab of state-sponsored Indian nationalism. Significantly, all traces of Sikhism and Islam are erased from this mythic representation. DDLJ's depiction of Punjab-as-India illustrates how some affective recuperations of the homeland can erase all signs of Others within the nation and all traces of violence against them. Not surprisingly, what we see is not the war-torn landscape of Punjab but a nostalgic rendering of the Hindu-Indian homeland through affectively charged representations of verdant fields, the love of extended kin groups, and bonds of community. In this slippage between Punjab and India, the homeland is depicted as a site for the consolidation of family and the forging of marriage alliances.

Despite the anxiety underlying Simran's marriage preparations (what if Raj is unable to rescue her?), music, dancing, feasting, and, most importantly, affective ties and traditional customs predominate in the film's production of nationalist affect through its rendition of the homeland. Diasporic loss is thus sublated to nationalist affect.

Additionally, at the same time that it is troped as the motherland, India is also eroticized. The title scenes described earlier enact a diasporic longing that is overtly erotic and affective. We see young women dancing in the fields, singing a song in which the homeland (literally embodied as female) beckons the traveler (*pardesi*) back. The lush fertility of Punjab forms a constant backdrop for the last two-thirds of the film. This is where Raj and Simran's romance is tested; this is where their love blossoms; India is the place to which NRIs must return to consummate their desires within the confines of marriage.

At first glance India appears to be part of a semeiotic chain linking territoriality with Indianness, an Indianness rooted, as it were, in the soil of Punjab. The homeland is represented by Baldev's village in Punjab, a place that represents the continuity of family and community. On the face of it, the landscapes described above suggest an affective investment in territoriality. Yet, for all the emphasis on place and landscape, as the homeland, India becomes an unstable signifier of Indianness because the film's affective economies revolve around a problematization of the assumed isomorphism between identity and place, location and belonging. For instance, as in its first few frames, much of the film's affective power stems precisely from Baldev's longing for the landscape of a mythic Punjab, its lushness contrasting sharply with the dreary wetness of England; the opposition between these two depictions of landscape frames the narrative that follows.

But there is a twist to this rendition of the presumed relationship between attachment to place and the affective economies of belonging, and herein lies the power of the film. It is crucial to note that, in DDLJ, Indianness is not constructed as static or unchanging but instead is portable and flexible. As illustrated in the itineraries of Raj and his father, Indianness can (and must) adapt to the transnational movements of migrants and capital. When Raj's father sets foot in Punjab, he pauses for a few moments as if to imbibe the very air of his homeland and exclaims, "My country! My land! My Punjab!" Yet, significantly, in the exchange with Baldev cited at the beginning of this chapter, he defines his Indianness by insisting that, despite his Westernized appearance and the fact that he has lived abroad for so many years, he carries India in his heart wherever he goes.

Indianness is hence constructed as an affective formation rather than contingent on territoriality. This reconceptualization of Indianness lies at the core of the film, and this is where it contrasts most sharply with earlier films, for instance, *Purab Aur Paschim* (1970), which constructs a decidedly more rigid and territorially based definition of Indianness such that overseas Indians automatically endanger their cultural purity by living in the West. In contrast, in DDLJ Indianness is constructed as responsive to the demands of migration and late capitalism.[21]

Perhaps it is this deterritorialized conception of Indianness that enabled some of my informants in the San Francisco Bay Area to engage so viscerally with DDLJ.[22] For all the ways in which the film generates diasporic loss as subsumed by state-endorsed nationalism, it also produces India as a place that some diasporic subjects might carry in their hearts wherever they go. For many of my informants in the San Francisco Bay Area who had never been to India and were unlikely ever to go there, this film enabled them to inhabit India as an extraterritorial space. And for many of my informants in New Delhi (as much as in the San Francisco Bay Area), the notion that Indianness could be preserved—both abroad and in the face of rapid globalization—was deeply comforting. As indexed by the relationships that Raj and Dharamveer forge with India, (select) NRIs could stay authentically Indian even when they no longer lived in India: resonating with the love-hate feelings prevalent in India toward NRIs, this film was reassuring in its suggestion that those who lived abroad had not forsaken India financially, culturally, or affectively.

At the same time, the very term "NRI" unsettles assumptions of territorially bound notions of India and Indianness in that it pushes the boundaries of location by signifying a nonresident who can, nonetheless, be Indian. Extending this aporia, DDLJ articulates a constitutive tension between territoriality and belonging: instead of confining Indianness to territorially based notions of identity, the film locates Indianness affectively in the hearts and bodies of (authentic) NRIs. Ultimately, this tension between territoriality and belonging is displaced onto the gendered and eroticized bodies of NRIs.

Moving Bodies: Indianness, Sexuality, and Nationalist Affect

Ochs argues that "part of the meaning of any utterance (spoken or written) is its social history, its social presence, and its social future" (1992: 338). Extending to cinematic signs her formulation of utterance as linguistic signs, I wish to, once again, foreground the temporality of processes of semeiosis. What do *DDLJ*'s constructions of NRIs teach us about the reconstitution of nationalist affect during a historical context in which the Indian economy was undergoing major transformations? This was also a time when, for my informants in New Delhi, the cultural landscape was being reconfigured so as to unsettle their understanding of what it meant to be Indian.

As figures that mediate past and present, India and "the global" NRIs are indexical of an Indianness that straddles multiple temporalities. In their ability to remain authentically Indian they embody a past ostensibly left behind; at the same time, they also embody futurity conceptualized in terms of the ways in which India, via the bodies and capital of NRIs, can reposition itself vis-à-vis "the global." NRI bodies combine different moments in the process of semeiosis and enfold iconicity (firstness), indexicality (secondness), and symbolization (thirdness). My concern, however, is with how these NRIs are indexical of shifting notions of Indianness: as indexical signs these representations of NRIs both point to these shifts and are constitutive of them.[23] These NRI bodies demonstrate how nationalist affect shapes and circumscribes the body's capacity to affect and be affected, to act and be acted upon. I am, therefore, concerned not with the embodiment of specific NRIs in phenomenological terms but with the NRI body as a recursive sign and as a nodal point for the circulation of affect between objects/images on screen and the implied bodies of spectators. As I elaborate below, I am interested in what the NRI body can do, how this body is affected by other bodies, and how it might engage in feedback loops in spaces occupied by spectating bodies.

In its focus on bodies on the move, *DDLJ*'s affective power is deepened by the kinesthetic pleasures it offers to spectators in diasporic communities and, perhaps even more potently, to members of the middle classes in India whose worlds have expanded since the liberalization of the economy and the influx of transnational media (Mankekar 2012b). NRI bodies, by definition, are formed through mobility and through practices of dwelling in travel.[24] Certainly, *DDLJ*'s world is produced through movement. Its frames are filled with the movement of NRIs striding the busy streets of London, wandering through the rolling hills of Switzerland or the fields of Punjab; of NRIs traveling from one place to another by trains, cars, buses, and airplanes.

In addition to these bodies in motion, the film is filled with objects on the move: the movement of suitcases that spill open and of backpacks bursting with memories from days and nights spent roaming the world. Yet it is important to note that the mobility of wealthy NRIs is neither generalizable to other transnational subjects nor can it be conceived in voluntary terms. As evident in Simran's struggles to travel to Europe and her father's ability to force the family to move back to Punjab, the movement of NRIs is frequently circumscribed by class, gender, and sexuality.

As an indexical sign, Simran both points to the relationship between sexual and cultural purity and, through her bodily hexis, constitutes it. Until the release of *DDLJ*, most films about overseas Indians portrayed the West as a site of rampant sexuality and promiscuity (as in *Purab Aur Paschim*). Although *DDLJ*'s portrayal of the West is much more complex, as in many previous films, the relationship of NRIs to India is mediated through anxieties about female (hetero)sexual purity in contexts of diaspora. In *DDLJ*, and in many other films about overseas Indians, the sexual purity of unmarried daughters is indexical of the preservation of Indian tradition: while it is always at risk in the West, sexual purity can be protected and family and national honor can be preserved through the constant surveillance and assiduous discipline exercised by NRI males.[25]

Simran indexes Baldev's success in preserving Indian culture in London. For instance, in an important scene set in London we see Simran praying: Indian culture is conflated with Hindu culture, and Simran's docile, pious body indexes the responsibility of daughters to preserve the Indianness of the family, the community, and the nation. Her agency lies precisely in her ability to embody docility and obedience, and in her ability to (re)produce Indianness in the diaspora. Yet despite the fact that her father has promised her hand in marriage to the son of his childhood friend back home in Punjab, Simran meets and falls in love with Raj while traveling in Europe. When she returns to London, she confides her love for Raj to her mother. Her father overhears the conversation between mother and daughter and is enraged. He decides that the family must move to India the very next morning. His draconian decision and the family's precipitous departure for India are driven by his fear of losing control over his daughter's sexuality. Evidently, he believes that he can recuperate the family honor only by returning to India and getting Simran married, thereby transferring control of her sexuality to her husband and in-laws "back home." Thus, at the same time that female sexuality is affectively linked with the fertility of the motherland, it is also embodied in the virginal purity of the heroine, a purity that is inherently precarious and always at risk in the West. The film stresses that even though Simran is an NRI, she neither drinks nor smokes, she respects and obeys her father (in fact, she is in awe of him), and she seems to submit to him at every step. She is the embodiment of filial loyalty and duty, and of virginal sexuality.[26]

At one point Simran's mother begs her to elope with Raj because, she claims, she does not want her daughter to follow in her footsteps and sacrifice her happiness. Significantly, Raj is steadfast in his loyalty to the law of the father. Despite Simran's mother's repeated pleas that he elope with Simran, Raj insists that he will wait until he can marry her "the proper way." Evidently, the fact that Simran's mother has consented to their marriage is irrelevant to Raj; only when Baldev consents can the marriage acquire legitimacy and be deemed honorable.

Thus, Simran is not the only NRI who indexes the preservation of cultural authenticity. Raj, our hero, is even more exemplary in how he embodies a reconstituted, yet hyperauthentic, Indianness. Raj's purported authenticity is reinforced through his contrast with Kuljeet, Simran's fiancé. Significantly, Kuljeet, as the native son of the soil, is clearly undeserving of her; he is the one who drinks and smokes excessively. At the end of the film the man who gets the girl is not the son of the soil but, instead, the NRI male, Raj. Evidently, in DDLJ the West is a place where cultural purity and authenticity can be maintained. The guardians of the heroine's sexual purity and, therefore, her cultural purity are NRI males. The authentic Indianness of DDLJ's NRI hero is manifest in his respect for Indian codes of modesty and in his reverence for the sexual purity of Indian women. NRI women are seemingly unable to manage their sexuality or protect their own honor.

In the first part of DDLJ when Simran and Raj are traveling through Switzerland, one night Simran gets tipsy. She awakes the next morning to find that she might have shared a room, and possibly a bed, with Raj. Fearing the worst, that is, that she and Raj may have had sex the previous night, she bursts into tears. She is pacified only when Raj assures her that, even though he lives in England, he is, after all, an Indian man. He knows the value of an Indian woman's honor, or *izzat*, and would never take advantage of her. Despite the fact that he is an NRI, he knows all too well the importance of the sexual purity of Indian women. In this manner his respect for Indian women's sexual purity illustrates his authenticity, his fundamental Indianness. Hence, in DDLJ it falls to the nonresident but still quintessentially Indian Raj and, eventually, to Simran's father, Baldev, to protect and thereby control the sexuality of "their" women.

DDLJ enacts a desire for a particular type of masculinity that is affluent, cosmopolitan, and modern. If, in the film, diasporic women are especially burdened with the transmittal of Indian culture, NRI men iconicize the mobility of both capital and culture. As noted above, when he first arrives in Punjab, Raj claims that he has returned to the homeland to launch a factory. Even though his real motive is to stake his claim on Simran and marry her, it is this assertion that provides him with a legitimate entry into Simran's family. Raj's mobility is indexical of the mobility of transnational capital; with his backpack on his back, he is always ready to travel. Yet, as I have argued above, he is depicted as essentially Indian in his respect for the sexual purity of Indian women, his deference to his elders, and his reverence for bonds of marriage, family, and community. Even as the female NRI's sexual purity confirms her cultural purity, the male NRI's respect for Indian women and Indian families underscores his authentic Indianness, which exists not despite but because of his mobility.

In an age of economic liberalization, modernity is mediated through the gendered bodies of NRIs. Raj indexes contemporary valorizations of the NRI; he is an Indian at heart who is youthful, virile, and masculine, a knight in shining armor who will rescue the damsel in distress. The NRI is the prodigal come home to participate (if not enable) the liberalization of India; he is authentically Indian. DDLJ represents the paradigmatic NRI as not just male but, more importantly, wealthy, thus belying the struggles of countless working-class men and women of Indian origin who live and work in immiserized conditions all over the world.[27]

As I have suggested above, Simran indexes the ambivalent relationship between nationalist affect and erotics. This ambivalence toward female sexuality is shaped by dominant discourses of heteronormativity so that anxieties about female sexuality are resolved by regulating it within the confines of (parent-approved) marriage; indeed, the moral economy of the film does not permit the expression of nonheterosexual erotics. The metonymy of family and nation in DDLJ foregrounds the salience of heteronormative constructions of nation and family. As Gayatri Gopinath (2005) points out, heteronormative sexuality is foundational to the formation of hegemonic diasporic subjectivity. Gopinath argues that women's bodies are "crucial to nationalist discourse in that they serve not only as the site of biological reproduction of national collectivities, but as the very embodiment of this nostalgically evoked communal past and Indianness" (2005: 9). Same-sex desire, according to Gopinath, is "impossible" within such a framing.[28]

In DDLJ, the indexical figure of the NRI occupies a political and affective space produced through its marriage with notions of the homeland and, in the modern conjuncture, the nation. I use the word "marriage" deliberately, to foreground the role of gender and heterosexual privilege folded into the very construction of the term "diaspora." Stefan Helmreich returns us to the etymology of diaspora by pointing out that it is derived from the Greek terms for dispersion and "to sow or scatter" (1992: 245). Hence, Helmreich points out, "the original meaning of diaspora summons up the image of scattered seeds and, therefore, to male substance, that is, to sperm" (245). He argues that "diaspora, in its traditional sense, refers us to a system of kinship reckoned through men and suggests the questions of legitimacy in paternity that patriarchy generates" (245).

DDLJ raises provocative questions about the agency of NRI women. At first glance the women in the film appear mere pawns in masculinist battles over culture and Indianness. Simran is terrified of her father and seems to obey him unquestioningly; her mother seems unable to stand up to the tyranny of her husband. Unlike some (now-canonical) narratives about women in diaspora, where women's travel to the West signifies eventual self-realization and emancipation (for instance, *Jasmine* [Mukherjee 1989] and *The Joy Luck Club* [Tan 1989]), the women in DDLJ seem equally imprisoned at home and abroad.

On further analysis, however, the women in DDLJ appear to have a more complex subjectivity that might, in fact, unsettle some dominant assumptions about gender, erotics, and nationalist affect. For instance, when she encourages her daughter to elope with Raj, Simran's mother reveals her love for her daughter, her courage, and her insights into gender inequities within the family. She tells Simran that, after sacrificing her own happiness all her life, she had promised herself that she would not permit the same thing to happen to her daughter. But, she laments, she was mistaken. She had forgotten that "a woman does not even have a right to make promises: she will always be sacrificed for the happiness of a man." She begs Simran to forget Raj. Yet, later, when she meets Raj and sees how much Simran and Raj love each other, she changes her mind. She takes her jewelry to them and begs them to run away. In so doing she is willing to defy her husband and his code of family honor, and is prepared to assume responsibility and face the consequences of encouraging Simran and Raj to elope. Finally, in the last scene when Raj is being beaten up by Simran's fiancé and his friends at the railway station, it is her mother who holds her hand and takes her to him (though her father, who is also at the station, prevents Simran from going to Raj). Similarly, Simran's younger sister, who is portrayed as precocious and intelligent, has a mind of her own and has no qualms about expressing her opinions. She is particularly candid about pointing out Kuljeet's flaws and, through her disapproval of him, sets him up as a foil to the NRI hero, Raj.

Significantly, despite restrictions on her mobility, Simran is able to travel to Switzerland where she meets Raj. At first Simran's father does not allow her to go, precisely because he seems all too aware of the sub-versions represented by women (especially single women) who travel for pleasure. Simran uses her wits and works hard to obtain his permission to travel. As noted above, she convinces him by waking up early and singing a Hindu hymn within earshot of her father and is so persuasive that he turns to his wife and says, "I know now that I haven't failed. I have man-aged to keep India alive in the heart of London." In another scene, Simran and her younger sister are dancing to Western music but, as soon as Sim-ran hears their father approaching the house, she changes the music to an old Hindi song: she knows that the song will evoke for him nostalgic mem-ories of India and, hence, will put him in a good mood. Even though, in the ultimate analysis, the law of the father prevails, Simran's (limited) ability to manipulate tokens of duty and tradition so she can travel to Europe suggests how diasporic women might negotiate dominant discourses of tradition and family. Thus, despite all Baldev's efforts to control her behav-ior, Simran's body is a body that travels, a body that is disciplined but not overwritten by patriarchy.

Furthermore, drawing on Deleuze (1997), and Clough (2007), I wish to underscore the potentialities of Simran's eroticized body, recalling lines of flight that threaten to exceed inscription by hegemonic ideologies (De-leuze 1997). While I am by no means claiming that Simran embodies a sub-jectivity that is outside the workings of hegemony, as I argue below, her apparently docile body is also a body whose erotic energies can potentially subvert the rules laid down by her father. Put another way, even as we see her enacting different modalities of docility and piety, we are also con-stantly reminded of the potentiality of her eroticized body to exceed the proscriptions of patriarchy.

Simran indexes the fraught and ambivalent relationship between na-tionalist affect on the one hand and erotics as affective potentiality on the other. Although for much of the second half of the film her bodily hexis is that of docility, throughout, her sensuality and the potency of her erotic desires threaten to defy her father's efforts to impose his will on her, thus foregrounding the eruptive potentiality of the erotic. Indeed, although it is never fully developed through its diegesis, the subversive potentialities of Simran's sexuality are introduced early in the film. When we first meet Simran, we see her standing at a window, the breeze sensuously ruffling her hair; she embodies an innocent sensuality, that of a young girl on the cusp of womanhood.[29]

Shortly thereafter we see her dancing in the rain (figures 2.5 and 2.6). In the semeiotic codes of Hindi film and many other Indian aesthetic

2.5 and 2.6. Simran dancing in the rain.

traditions, rain symbolizes eroticism and (occasionally, transgressive) sensuality, but the force (indexicality) of Simran's wet body dancing in the rain exceeds this aesthetic history. In one frame we see her swaying rhythmically, her legs apart, her eyes closed, as the rain pours down on her. She is wearing a short dress; the camera caresses her wet body.

Indexical signs are forceful; they compel us to pay attention through their immediacy; so too is our attention drawn to the eruptive potentiality of Simran's sensuality. Simran's voluptuous figure is made the object of our gaze throughout the first half of the film. In the second half of the film, set in India, although we see Simran wearing "traditional" (and, therefore, seemingly demure) clothes, we are constantly reminded of her exuberant sexuality (see also Sharpe 2005: 67–68). In a crucial scene portraying the festivities the night before Simran's wedding to Kuljeet, the man chosen by her father, we see her dancing joyfully. Raj, who is still pretending to be a friend of Kuljeet, and Simran lead groups of young women and men, respectively. They sing a song that expresses their longing for each other and anticipates the consummation of their desire. Simran is to wed Kuljeet the next day, but she is confident that Raj will prevent the marriage from taking place and that the two of them will be united at last. The scene is redolent with erotic yearning and the anticipation of their union. Simran's body is indexical, a pointing arrow that reminds us of the fragility of patriarchal control of NRI women's erotic energies. Throughout the film

Simran's youthful sexuality is immanent; it exists as a subversive intensity that threatens to break free from her father's surveillance and tear asunder the India that he so carefully preserves in his home.

The Nation and Its Futurities: The New India(ns)

In conclusion, DDLJ provides a view of how Indianness may be produced through affective economies surrounding practices of mobility, dwelling, and diasporic longing. Although DDLJ creates a discourse of a timeless Indian culture, indeed, a culture rooted in the Punjabi-Indian soil, in contrast to earlier films about diasporic Indians such as *Purab Aur Paschim*, DDLJ suggests that Indian culture can travel in the hearts of diasporic subjects. As suggested by the policing of Simran's sexuality, Indian culture can be kept alive through specifically gendered practices of dwelling-in-displacement (Clifford 1997). Indian women abroad mark their essential difference from Western women by being dutiful daughters and faithful wives. Similarly, as Raj claims when he reassures Simran that he did not seduce her and, later, when he refuses to elope with her, Indian men are essentially different from Western men because of their allegiance to Indian codes of sexuality, gender, and family. In these representations Western men and, in particular, Western women are portrayed as the Others from whom Indian culture must be protected and against whom Indian manhood and womanhood must be defined.

At the time the film was released, DDLJ constituted a vital node for the reconstitution of nationalist affect because its portrayal of NRIs unpacked assumptions about the relationship between territoriality and national belonging. It seems particularly irresponsible, however, to conflate the privilege of the NRIs portrayed in this film with the lifeworlds of other diasporic peoples, such as working-class and undocumented migrants, political and economic refugees, and exiles. Furthermore, as with earlier cohorts of migrant laborers in Britain, the Caribbean, or California, to go abroad was to stay abroad. In prior representations of overseas Indians, as in *Purab Aur Paschim*, the only way to be abroad was to be necessarily inauthentic. Diasporic Indians had to surrender their culture; they had to choose between East and West, between *purab* and *paschim*. Leaving home meant being cut off from home; as a consequence, identity and location were closely tied.

DDLJ suggests that the relationship between cultures and spaces has changed. While earlier, decisions to live abroad were deemed irreversible, the present context of late capitalism has seen an increase in the movements of NRIs between diaspora and homeland. Moreover, DDLJ asserts that it is possible to get the best of both the East and the West; diasporic Indians can live abroad and still be authentically Indian. In earlier films about expatriate and diasporic Indians, to leave the country was to disown the nation, and the West (*paschim*) represented a space where the sexual purity of women could not be preserved; only in India could the law of the father be maintained. However, DDLJ insists that one's cultural identity does not depend on where one lives. In this manner, the film represents fundamental changes in the experience and imagination of foreign places, and the renegotiation of the relationship between mobility, location, and authenticity.

What are the implications of this rearticulation of space, place, and culture for how we may understand nationhood and belonging? A major theme of this book is that diasporas and nationalisms re-create each other and, in so doing, unsettle nation-bound constructions of subjectivity. At the beginning of the film we see Baldev longing for his *vatan* (homeland), his Punjab. As the film progresses, we see that, far from being a postnational longing for the land of his past, Baldev's nostalgia for Punjab and Punjabi culture is conflated with the nation and national culture. His longing for Punjab is enfolded into his identity as an Indian, a Hindustani, and his love of the homeland is subsumed by nationalism. The film is about nonresident Indians, not nonresident Punjabis, reclaimed as prodigal sons by the contemporary Indian nation-state. Thus, even though the film lovingly portrays Punjabi customs, it is not about Punjabi culture but, ostensibly, about Indian culture.

In the final analysis, DDLJ is about Indian manhood and Indian womanhood and about carrying India in our hearts wherever we go. It goes without saying that what it means to be an Indian abroad varies according to one's immigration history, position vis-à-vis host states, relationship with other communities, gender, class position, and so on. Not all forms of travel are privileged; some are the result of coercion and violence, and many occur within highly determined circuits. Diasporic subjects, however, do not just travel. They also forge identities and communities shaped by particular affective economies of dwelling. If travel and contact are "crucial sites for an unfinished modernity," then diasporas are "part of an ongoing transnational network that includes the homeland not as something simply left behind but as a place of attachment in a contrapuntal modernity" (Clifford 1997: 154).

What identities, attachments, notions of belonging, and conceptions of culture travel with diasporic peoples? What gets left behind in processes of dwelling in new lands? And what gets unsettled? As I have argued in the introduction to this book, an analytic that centers on traditional dichotomies of home versus abroad leaves intact the opposition between the two, thereby reinforcing locational and territorial conceptions of identity and belonging. My argument is that, in contrast to formulations in which the homeland is conceived as a place of origin and anteriority, we need to focus on the transnational connectivities that underscore the coproduction of home and diaspora.

The temporal and geographical specificities of diaspora experiences are crucial to understanding the relationship between travel, dwelling, and culture. However, *DDLJ* does not attend to the specificity of diasporic community formation. Instead, it features a generalized diasporic family that, purportedly, could be living anywhere. In stark contrast to *Bhaji on the Beach*, Gurinder Chadha's 1993 film about South Asian women in Southall, England, or Mira Nair's *Mississippi Masala* (1991), about twice-displaced immigrants to the southern United States, *DDLJ* teaches us nothing about the history of Indians in Britain, their social relations with other communities, or their location vis-à-vis formations of race and class in their host country.

Yet when it was first released the film represented a turning point in how expatriate and overseas Indians—and, indeed, Indianness—were represented in the popular imagination. *DDLJ* underscores some of the ways in which transnational media such as Bollywood cinema have participated in the simultaneous reconfiguration of national(ist) belonging and transnational allegiances (compare Rouse 1995: 353–54). If *DDLJ* seemed reassuring to my informants in the San Francisco Bay Area, particularly from those communities whose connections with the contemporary Indian nation were, at best, tenuous, it appeared even more affectively potent for viewers in New Delhi. For the Indian middle classes, conceptions of Indianness were up for grabs in the face of the influx of transnational media and the liberalization of the economy. The very notion of Indianness was thrown into crisis, necessitating the repositioning of the nation vis-à-vis "the global." By representing India as an affective rather than territorial formation, *DDLJ* seemed to offer some of my informants in New Delhi one way in which Indianness could be reconstituted in the face of the global. It appealed to my lower-middle-class and upwardly mobile working-class informants in New Delhi because it resonated with their desire to be cosmopolitan; in many cases, it appealed to their (for the most part, unfulfilled) longings to travel. Circulating at a historical moment when becoming middle class was as much an aspirational identity as a socioeconomic position, this film enabled something for them: it enabled them to feel global and cosmopolitan, yet remain Indian. In this sense, then, DDLJ domesticates the global by making it more accessible, indeed, by Indianizing it.

Some of my informants in the Bay Area were drawn to DDLJ because it portrays NRIs as more authentically Indian than those "left behind." At the same time, the film's NRIs offer the promise, in material as well as affective terms, of potentially mediating between India and the global. In complex ways and with varying degrees of success (note, for instance, the dexterous agility of Dharamveer versus the stasis represented by Baldev), these NRIs embody different temporalities. On the one hand, the retention or reproduction of "traditional" values and portrayals of an authentic Indianness, apparently unsullied by the very forces threatening the cultural purity of the homeland, harkens back to the temporality of the past. At the same time, the careful selection of "modern" values provides a blueprint for the futurity of India. DDLJ's Raj, Dharamveer, and, eventually, Simran index the futurity of the Indian nation which can become a global player even as it retains its cultural authenticity.

In DDLJ the figure of the NRI, the Indian abroad, interrogates and unsettles binaries of national versus foreign, Self versus Other. By straddling the borders of Self and Other, the gendered NRI represents a space of ambivalence in nationalist discourses of alterity. Tölölyan points out in an early theorization of diaspora that "diasporas are emblems of transnationalism because they embody the question of borders, which is at the heart of any adequate definition of the Others of the nation-state" (1991: 6). However, the Others of the nation-state exist not just beyond but also within its borders: the integrity of the nation-state is predicated on its management of alterity, both within and outside it (Mankekar 1999a; see also chapter 5).

Let us not forget that the very category of the NRI was purposefully created by the Indian state in order to make financial and affective claims on select members of upper-class diasporic elites. At a critical moment in India's postcolonial history, the state aimed to woo NRIs primarily to encourage them to invest in an economy that was teetering on the brink of bankruptcy. My effort in this chapter has been to argue that the production of NRIs is not simply an outcome of the ideological interpellations by the Indian state but of the convergence of political and affective economies. Furthermore, rather than being a transhistorical or politically neutral entity, the category of the NRI is contingent on exclusions based on class, gender, and sexuality. Fears of the loss of culture in the diaspora are embodied in the figure of Baldev, who struggles to "keep India alive in the heart of London" through his surveillance of the women in his family. Baldev's fear is that *angrezipan* (Britishness) will contaminate his children and leave them in a liminal space of nonbelonging, neither here nor there (dhobi ka kutta, na ghar ka na ghaat ka). Yet, in the end, he too is forced to rethink his conceptions of authenticity, belonging, and, indeed, Indianness.

For many of my informants in both New Delhi and the San Francisco Bay Area, this film enabled the formation of India as an archive of affect and temporality, an India that was not lost either to those who had left the shores of the nation or to those who had been "left behind" in India. And yet those left behind did not feel forsaken: the NRIs idealized in this film are respectful toward Indian tradition (for instance, Raj's refusal to elope and his respect for all the elders in Simran's family, particularly her father, is noteworthy, as is his deference toward religious rituals).[30] More significantly, these NRIs embody a reconfigured Indianness that is selective and portable yet authentic. Raj and Simran, in different ways, invoke a new temporality, the temporality of the future and of potentiality and, hence, index the New India. This New India is not tethered to territorial location but is predicated on an affective allegiance to the purported core values of Indianness: respect for elders, the containment of (women's) sexuality, and an intense love for the land (recall Raj and Simran's reunion among the swaying mustard fields and Raj's insistence that the soil of Punjab is magical). This is an India that New Indians carry in their hearts regardless of where they are located; this is the India of the future.

As noted above, in *DDLJ* the homeland is no longer a site of anteriority or a site where NRIs were "originally from" before they lost their authenticity; certainly, India is no longer an exclusive locus of cultural purity. *DDLJ* provokes us to rethink the relationship between diaspora and homeland in terms of multiple temporalities rather than a linear temporality of going from the homeland (a site of origins positioned in the temporality of the past) to the diaspora (where subjects are purportedly caught between the temporalities of the past, present, and future). Such a formulation foregrounds the mutual imbrication of diaspora and homeland in that interrogating one necessitates rethinking the other. Hence, by unsettling conceptions of diaspora that assume dispersal from a point of origin, I have also reconceptualized the homeland.

In tracing how India is multiply invoked and produced through affect and temporality, my intervention has been to destabilize the contemporary Indian nation-state as being the primary (or even a significant) constituent of South Asian diasporic identities. In chapter 3 I analyze how Indian grocery stores in the San Francisco Bay Area create sensoria where objects and people on the move collide; these are also social spaces that enable diasporic subjects to negotiate their positionalities in landscapes of class, race, and religion. Critical perspectives in transnational studies, area studies, and ethnic studies that call into question nationalist conceptions of identity and politics offer fecund sites for the formulation of conceptions of multiplex communities. It is this conjunction of transnational studies, ethnic studies, and area studies that I draw upon next.

CHAPTER 3

Affective Objects

India Shopping in the San Francisco Bay Area

Whenever I drove down Highway 101 in Silicon Valley, two features of the landscape would stand out to me: the flat, uniform appearance of the low-rise, glass-paned buildings housing dot-com and other IT companies, and the billboards lining the highways that displayed wares and text (likely to be) incomprehensible to all but those working in the computer industry. But as soon as I extricated myself from the maze of highways intersecting Highway 101 and drove along secondary streets, a different landscape would come into view: streets dense with strip malls and small shopping arcades offering a mix of products, sights, and smells. As it cut a wide swath through Sunnyvale and its neighboring communities, the long stretch of El Camino Real vividly brought to life a jostling of cultures, cuisines, and languages. Large Korean supermarkets sat cheek by jowl with Persian kebab houses and "mainstream" stores like Safeway and Staples; Indian fabric stores bumped up against car repair garages and Vietnamese nail salons; the aroma from Chinese buffet restaurants mingled with the smells emanating from Kentucky Fried Chicken and Indian grocery stores. This is where people from diverse communities came to shop, socialize, browse, and eat. This is where the "familiar" and the "unfamiliar" intersected in unexpected ways.[1]

Of course, the cultural and social complexity of the San Francisco Bay Area is encapsulated neither by the apparent blandness of Silicon Valley nor by the cultural remixing occurring along El Camino Real in Sunnyvale. Nevertheless, in the San Francisco Bay Area, Indian grocery stores were places where people and objects on the move collided.[2] In this chapter,

I argue that these stores are fecund sites for the proliferation and negotiation of affective regimes pertaining to India and Indianness, as well as discourses of community, race, gender, and family; they are, therefore, exemplary sites to observe some of the everyday practices, customs, and rules of social interaction that existed among my informants in the San Francisco Bay Area. As fraught social spaces, these stores and the affects they evoked enabled for some of my informants, in particular those claiming Indian origin, a complex negotiation of temporality, of past and present, through the production of specific kinds of sense memories and sensuous knowledges about India.[3]

In a groundbreaking study, Grewal examines how "America" functions to produce South Asian subjects in contexts of migration, immigration, and neoliberalism (2005). In dialogue with this work, I turn the analytic lens around to how India functions to shape the formation of the subjectivities of my informants in the San Francisco Bay Area and, in so doing, trace the ways in which India is constructed as an archive of affect and temporality. In what follows, I analyze the myriad ways in which, for many of my informants, these grocery stores constituted a vital node for the production—and unsettlement—of India for my informants. Unlike the idealized and placeless NRIs of DDLJ, my informants were emplaced in the complex sociopolitical landscapes of the San Francisco Bay Area: Indian grocery stores provide us with a critical lens to trace these processes of emplacement. My analysis of these stores elaborates on some of the themes explicated in the introduction: first, that diasporas and homelands are co-implicated. Second, and perhaps more pertinently, while these stores participated in the production and circulation of India, they also foreground how India was one of many modalities of the subject formation of my informants who had to negotiate their place in landscapes of gender, race, and class in the San Francisco Bay Area.[4] Their identities, therefore, were multiplex and heterogeneous in that they conceived of themselves as Indians, immigrants, Indian Americans, or South Asians with a range of ties to India.

As in the rest of this book, by foregrounding the constructed and contested nature of India, my objective in this chapter is to denaturalize and, hence, unsettle India. For many of my informants living in the San Francisco Bay Area, the social spaces of these stores, and the objects they displayed and sold, formed sensoria that evoked a range of affective connections with a phantasmic India. Phantasms refer to the shifting meanings of the uncanny that irrupt into our conscious ways of thinking about the world. Agamben (1993) argues that the phantasm mediates between the imaginary and the real; phantasms render experientially accessible and bring into the realm of the everyday such abstractions as desire, absence, or loss.

The genealogy of the concept of the phantasm as an analytic goes far back in Western social theory. In the work of Plato, for instance, the phantasm is opposed to the icon. As Favero points out, "While an icon expresses a sense of likeness to reality, the phantasm is a simulacrum deprived of any ground in it," in contrast to the work of Aristotle, who "sees the phantasm *as the sensorial instrument* used by human beings to grasp abstract concepts" (2005: 15, emphasis added). Favero adds that for Lacan, "the phantasm domesticates our perception. It helps us to make sense of, understand and accept the world that surrounds us" (2005: 15). In foregrounding both its imaginary constitution and its constructed nature, I want to trace the production of India as phantasmic precisely through its displacement, iteration, and circulation for my informants in the San Francisco Bay Area. Drawing on Agamben (1993), Favero (2005), and Ivy (1995), I conceive of phantasms as epistemological objects "whose presence or absence cannot be definitively located" (Ivy 1995: 22) but which, nevertheless, have material and tangible implications for lives and subjectivities.

In focusing on the objects displayed and sold in these stores, I am interested in the ways in which they generate a range of affect, spanning longing and desire, as well as ambivalence, alienation, and antagonism. As Ahmed argues, "Affect does not reside positively in the sign or commodity, but is produced as an effect of its circulation" (2004: 45). It goes without saying that this circulation is mediated by history and memory, and by sociality and politics. The affects generated in these stores were ambient and, at the same time, experienced by many of my informants in intimate, embodied, and often visceral ways. Thus, while I want to insist on the obduracy of objects, their social consequentiality, and the fact that their materiality is not collapsible to semiotics, I argue that affects congeal around particular bodies and objects (cf. Ahmed 2004: 4). Rather than posit that affects inhere in objects or reside within subjects, I trace how they are engendered through the encounter of subjects with particular objects. What transpires when the patrons of Indian grocery stores encounter (through physical contact or through their memory or imagination) objects that constitute nodes in the circulation of affect? The stores that I describe here are important sites for the staging of such encounters, where the affective charge of particular objects is intimately entangled with their sensuous apprehension. Although not reducible to bodily sensation, the evocation of affect in these stores brings into play senses of touch, smell, sound, sight, and taste. Laura Marks points out that "commodities, though they are subject to the deracinating flow of the transnational economy and the censoring process of official history, retain the power to tell the stories of where they have been" (2000: 78). What sorts of stories are told by the objects displayed in Indian grocery stores in the Bay Area?

I am interested in the affectivity of objects displayed and sold in these grocery stores, their contribution to the creation of grocery stores as sensoria, and their role in shaping regimes of temporality through the production of knowledges of the past and present. Indian grocery stores are spaces where the affective and the political, the social and the sensuous converge. At the same time that I engage the affective charge generated by the collision of objects and subjects on the move, I am also concerned with the centrality of these stores to processes of place making and emplacement: simply put, my analysis of Indian grocery stores in the San Francisco Bay Area underscores the different ways that, in contexts of the dizzying traffic in capital, objects, and texts, place matters.

As we will see, Indian grocery stores are implicated in processes of place making and emplacement along several different registers. Marks (2000: 2) argues that migrants and diasporic subjects produce culturally defined sensuous geographies. The stores in which I conducted my research transformed the spaces in which they were located into particular kinds of places. Conversely, these stores were themselves deeply marked by where they were located within the San Francisco Bay Area: characteristics of location and locale shaped what got displayed and sold, the demographics and expectations of customers, the affects the stores evoked, and the spaces of sociality they constructed. Last but not least, these stores played a crucial role in the emplacement of their customers, particularly those affiliated with the Indian subcontinent, along axes of nationality, race, class, and gender in the San Francisco Bay Area.

India Shopping: Retailing "the Familiar"

During the time when I conducted my ethnographic research, Indian grocery stores in the Bay Area performed a number of cultural functions. On the one hand, they marked the urban landscape with specific signifiers of ethnicity and Indianness. For many of my informants, these stores were a means of self-representation both to themselves and to the so-called dominant community (it is not surprising that, in some U.S. cities, the neighborhoods in which Indian grocery stores are located are known as Little India; compare Shukla [2003] and Sen [2012] for excellent analyses of these so-called ethnic enclaves). These stores also provided spaces where community members gathered and exchanged news about community events, and where new arrivals could learn about neighborhoods, schools, and employment opportunities. This is where some women could exchange recipes, obtain information about religious rituals, and, in the stores that also sold clothes, keep up with Indian fashions. For other women, these stores represented spaces that extended community surveillance of their sexuality and agency. By transforming their neighborhoods into particular kinds of places, and by shaping through their very presence the physical and cultural landscapes in which they were located, these stores problematize conceptions of diasporic identity in terms of simple binaries of assimilation versus resistance.

Grewal argues that consumer culture produces "transnational identifications for subjects whose desires and fantasies crossed national borders but also remained tied to national imaginaries" (2005: 11). I take my title, "India Shopping," from one of the store owners I interviewed for this project. He said to me, "Oh, people don't just come here to buy groceries! They come for the whole package. They come for India shopping." I found that, to some extent, this description held true not only for customers who had traveled from India but also those from other parts of the world. Although many stores were called grocery stores, this label might be a bit misleading. For while the stores I describe primarily sold groceries, they also sold other goods imported from India—namely, cosmetics, music, religious icons, and, in some cases, clothes and jewelry. Moreover, these stores also displayed and sold products produced outside India (for instance, spices, pickles, or clothes manufactured in the United States and in other locations) many of which were, nevertheless, generative of powerful discourses of Indianness. In addition, most of the stores where I conducted my ethnographic research offered for rent videos and DVDs of films and television programs from all over the South Asian subcontinent. For many of my informants, these stores invoked a phantasmic—and highly contested—India. As I demonstrate below, this phantasmic India was constituted through sense memories, affect, and temporalizing processes. Furthermore, the social landscapes in which the production and consumption of these phantasmic constructions of India occurred were marked by, among other factors, gender hierarchies, regional differences, and class differences.

Most of these stores catered primarily to people from all over the South Asian diaspora. Thus, despite the fact that an overwhelming majority called themselves "Indian" grocery stores, it is important to note that all the store owners I interviewed were extremely savvy about the diverse

3.1 and 3.2. Indian stores in the Bay Area. Photograph courtesy of Veena Dubal.

ethnic and national identities of their customers. Store owners astutely employed different marketing strategies to reach customers from all nations in the South Asian subcontinent, including Pakistan, Bangladesh, Sri Lanka, and Nepal, as well as the Caribbean, Africa, and other parts of the world where people of South Asian origin live. Indeed, even though a majority of the stores in which I conducted my research were owned by migrants or immigrants from India, depending on their locations they were

3.3. Indian stores in the multicultural streets of Berkeley. Photograph courtesy of Veena Dubal.

traversed by shoppers and browsers of diverse national, racial, and cultural affiliations, including European Americans. Not surprisingly, these stores performed different functions for the latter (from satisfying their curiosity about their new and not-so-new neighbors to enabling them to purchase exotic "ethnic Indian" products).

In short, the stores in which I conducted my research varied sharply in their ambience, the objects they displayed and sold, and the customers they attracted. For instance, in Berkeley, most of the stores in which I conducted ethnographic fieldwork catered not only to people from all over South Asia and its diasporas, but also to members of what one store owner termed the "larger [European American] community." One store comes particularly to mind. Called Taste of India, this store displayed an India that appealed to different senses and, indeed, to different tastes. It was far cleaner than most other Indian stores in the area, with objects tidily displayed in the shop windows and shelves. Shoppers would browse to the accompaniment of piped sitar music. The subtle fragrance of sandalwood incense contrasted sharply with the pungent aroma of spices that pervaded the other stores. I would often see European Americans as well as middle- and upper-class Indians in this store; certainly, the expensive clothes and objets d'art suggested that only certain kinds of customers could afford to shop there. Commenting on the representational significance of this store, its owner claimed, "We represent India to people living here. People come from all over the East Bay to get a taste of India."

Stores like Taste of India contrasted even more sharply with those located in the Peninsula and in the South Bay which catered primarily to members of South Asian communities. In fact, many of the stores in the Peninsula and the South Bay did not bother to translate the names of products into English: they simply transliterated the original names of the products into the English alphabet (for instance, *khandvi, bissi bele bhaath, sarson da saag*, and so on). As the owner of a store in Sunnyvale remarked to me somewhat wryly, "If we see a white person in our store, we wonder what they are doing here. We go up to them and do our best to help them but they really look out of place here." It goes without saying, then, that Indian grocery stores in the Bay Area were complex social spaces, and the commodities and texts they displayed and sold were multivocal and evoked a range of affects for the men and women who patronized them. I train my focus, however, on the memories, longings, and often ambivalent, if not contradictory, range of affective connections these stores produced for those among my informants who had traveled from India: immigrants and their children, H-1B visa holders who lived in the area as "guest workers" in the 1990s, and working-class and undocumented men, women, and their families.

Since objects are inextricable from social life, I find it helpful to trace the trajectories of objects in motion as they travel across contexts and track the regimes of value they produce and incite. For my analysis of the objects displayed and sold in these stores I draw, in part, on an early discussion by Arjun Appadurai (1986) of regimes of value in processes of commodity exchange. According to Appadurai, the notion of regimes of value emphasizes that acts of commodity exchange and consumption do not presuppose "a complete cultural sharing of assumptions, but rather that the degree of value coherence may be highly variable from situation to situation, and from commodity to commodity" (1986: 15). The consumption of commodities and other objects is always already embedded in other social and semiotic practices; hence, regimes of value are inseparable from other domains of politics. What sorts of regimes of value were created by the objects displayed and sold in Indian grocery stores? And how did these regimes of value participate in the creation of a phantasmic India?

Extending the work of Bergson ([1911] 1988) on the sensuous embodiment of memory, Marks reminds us that we "hold knowledge in our bodies and memory in our senses" (2000: xiii). What kinds of knowledges and memories did Indian grocery stores produce for those who frequented them, browsed through them, gazed through their windows, smelled them down the street, or drove past them? In tracing the affective connections generated by the sensoria of these stores, I am interested in exploring the relationship between the senses, affects, and knowledges. I am also concerned with how, at the same time that these stores are sensoria redolent with affect and sensuous memory, they are also dense with sociality. I draw on Marks's insistence that sense memories, and sensuous knowledges, are "cultivated, that is, *learned* at the level of the body" (2000: 145, emphasis added). How did these stores participate in "educating" the senses of their customers in particular ways (Marks 2000)? My analysis of the sensoria of Indian grocery stores is predicated, therefore, on the assumption that these sensuous knowledges, as much as the affective connections they generated, were culturally contingent; they were learned, cultivated, and mediated by practices of sociality.[5]

The Grocery Store as Sensorium

Eight years had passed since I had last been in Spice Bazaar, an Indian grocery store in Sunnyvale. I noticed many changes: from a dingy one-room shop, catering to Indian students and professionals in the area, it was now a dingy three-room store. But, as in times past, I was struck by a familiar smell as soon as I walked in: the musty aroma of spices combined with dust. There were tables on the sidewalk displaying vegetables, and, as I walked past them, I could smell the tomatoes ripening all too rapidly in the blazing July heat. Despite it being a weekday afternoon, the sidewalk was full of people, mostly women of different ages, buying produce. From the way they were dressed, some women looked like they were making a stop there on a lunch break from their offices.

But not everyone there was on break from work. One elderly woman in a white polyester sari, her white hair pulled back in a severe bun, was going through a big bin of okra with meticulous care. She would pick up each pod, and put it to what I want to call the snap test: if it snapped under the pressure of her fingers, she would grimace and throw it back into the pile; those that survived the snap test were placed in a plastic bag. For this woman, as much as for many others in this store, shopping for vegetables was a sensuous experience involving the senses of touch, smell, sight, and, quite often, of taste. For many customers, shopping was also a social activity. As I stood taking in the sights and smells, I noticed a middle-aged couple greeting a *salwar-kameez*-clad younger woman with great enthusiasm; it was obvious that they were friends and had not seen each other for a long time. When she saw the older couple, the younger woman immediately draped her *dupatta* over her head and bent to touch their feet in a customary Hindu gesture of showing respect to one's elders; the older woman embraced her and they started to exchange news.

I randomly picked the middle of the three doors leading into the store; it turned out to be the main entrance. One wall was pasted with flyers of all kinds: for nanny and housekeeping services, posters of upcoming film screenings, advertisements for roommates, and real estate notices. Lining a second wall were shelves of videotapes and DVDs. The young woman behind a counter covered with stacks of ledgers stared blankly back at me in response to my somewhat timid smile. Intimidated and a bit self-conscious, I walked on: unlike my usual trips to Indian grocery stores, when I rushed in with a list of things to pick up, this time I was there as an ethnographer and, accordingly, planned to browse. Inside, the store was even more crowded than the sidewalk outside. All the spices were on a row of shelves in one of the rooms, lying in what seemed to me to be utter disarray. Daals, icons of Hindu deities, and posters of Sikh gurus were placed together on another shelf. One middle-aged woman, who seemed to be the owner, glared balefully at her customers as she rang in their purchases; with a start I was reminded of the kind of "customer service" I received in stores in New Delhi. But it was not just the customer service (such as it was) and the visual clutter that reminded me and several of the people I interviewed of shopping experiences we had had "back" in India. Marks insists that "the senses often remember when nobody else does. The memory of the senses may call forth histories of transnational objects, histories that have been lost en route" (2000: 110). Through the objects they offered for sensory consumption—their sights, sounds, and smells—Indian grocery stores were sensoria regnant with a range of affect for many of us.

The dominant impression most of my interviewees had of Indian stores was their distinctive smell. If, to other communities, these stores represented sites of (olfactory) alterity, to many of my informants who went to these stores, they represented spaces of familiarity. To several men and women I spoke with, Indian grocery stores felt familiar in a foreign land where Indians are marked as alien by the smells we embody.[6] Smell, according to Marks, is an "indexical witness" (2000: 113). Smell also encodes affect: we react affectively, often viscerally, to a smell before we can even name it or identify it.

Varsha, a second-generation Indian American woman, described her changing feelings toward the smells of Indian stores thus: "When I was a kid, one of the things I hated was [that] you came out smelling of spices, smelling of India. I used to say, Mom, we can't go anywhere afterwards because we smell like India. But later I started liking the smell. I liked that pungent smell." Varsha's responses to the smell of these stores had, evidently, shifted over the course of her life: from feeling ambivalent about how she smelled ("like India") after being in a store, she had started to like the smell. Yet, for others I spoke with, the smells of these stores brought forth a different sort of response. For example, another woman spoke of how "disgusting" she found the stores. "They are so disorganized. It's a stressful experience. And the smell!" she exclaimed, her eyebrows arched, her lips turned down in an expression of disdain. She added, "It's not just the smell of the spices and the daals, it is the smell of the press of people, of Indian bodies." Clearly, the smell of the stores reminded this woman of India and, in her case, it generated an affect that was anything but nostalgic.

While smell, sight, and taste were ubiquitous in the sensoria created by these stores, my informants also described other sensory cues. One woman I spoke with mentioned that she made it a point to go to Spice Bazaar on weekends: "It is just like bazaars in India. There is always music blaring in the background; everybody talks loudly. If the owner wants to check on the price of a particular product, she shouts across the store to someone in the back to look it up. I always have a headache by the time I leave. But it's always fun. It is not like Safeway or Walmart." Echoed by several of my informants, this woman's comparison of Indian stores with stores like Walmart reminds us that most migrants and diasporic subjects simultaneously inhabit multiple sensoria.

These stores provided other auditory cues through the music they played and sold. Most stores had Indian music (usually film music but, occasionally, classical or religious music) playing in the background. Other stores would have a film playing on a big-screen television mounted on a wall in the corner; it was not unusual, therefore, to do one's shopping to the backdrop of a passionately erotic Bollywood song or the loud sounds of an action scene in which the hero was single-handedly thrashing a dozen thugs. Some stores sold music from India and from South Asian diasporic communities all over the world. For instance, India Palace was a chain of stores that opened in Sunnyvale and Milpitas in the late 1990s, famous for its large selection of music from India. When I first visited it, I was struck by the range of Indian music it carried. I saw three long shelves with CDs and audiotapes, of which two were lined with South Indian film and classical (Carnatic) music. On top of the shelves were signs declaring "South Indian Music." Tapes and CDs in different southern Indian languages—Tamil,

Malayalam, and Telugu—all lay mixed together in stacks. I commented to the saleswoman at the counter that this was a huge collection of music and asked if they got a lot of customers. Yes, she replied, "these South Indians" love their music no matter where they are. The store obviously catered to a large number of people from the southern regions of India, their musics all lumped together under the homogenized category "South Indian Music." The display reinforced a system of categorization whereby the music and, by extension, the diverse cultures of southern India were lumped together. This homogenization underscored the dominance of North Indian assumptions about a normative "Indian culture" and reflected some of the regional tensions seething in India.

It is important to note that the affects generated and circulated through the modality of the familiar were not always pleasurable or nurturing for all my customers, and gender seemed to be a crucial variable in this regard. For some women, the soundscapes of Indian grocery stores represented an extension of the surveillance exercised within the community (compare Maira 2002; Shankar 2008). Younger, second-generation women frequently confided to me about how, when they accompanied their parents to these stores, they were repeatedly admonished for "loud" behavior. They were expected to exercise restraint and speak softly and politely so as not to acquire a reputation for "unrestrained" or "immodest" behavior. As the nerve centers or, rather, gossip centers of the community, these stores were spaces where some women were subjected to particularly gendered forms of surveillance. As Seema, a colleague in a domestic violence organization based in Berkeley, pointed out to me, in instances where women's mobility was restricted by their abusive spouses, they were "allowed" to go by themselves to Indian stores even when they were prohibited from going to "regular" stores because Indian stores were deemed safe by their husbands; they knew that they would hear about their wives' behavior from community members present there. Thus, while the stores provided opportunities for women whose mobility was otherwise curtailed, the very fact that abusive men felt that their wives were unlikely to do anything "inappropriate" while in them suggests that they also represented an extension of community surveillance and patriarchal control.

Again, the soundscape of surveillance in these stores was constituted by talk, the whispers of gossip to which women were subjected; evidently, the affect of familiarity staged by these stores had a dark side as well. One informant, Bindu Singh, spoke of how, after her divorce from her abusive husband ten years ago, she had been stigmatized by the Indian community in Berkeley, where she then lived. She recounted that she had felt like an outcast and this sense of stigma was most vivid when she went grocery shopping at the Indian stores lining University Avenue. She spoke of how much she used to dread the whispers that would start up as soon as she entered these stores: "I felt everybody's eyes were on me. Maybe I was being paranoid, but I'd walk into a store and I knew everybody was talking about me. The community in Berkeley was very small in those days, and everybody knew what was going on in each others' homes." But, she said, their attitude had changed recently. After her divorce she had seen some very hard years as a single parent to her two children, but she had managed to train herself as a real estate agent and had achieved tremendous success in her profession. Furthermore, her children were now grown up: her son was at Stanford and her daughter at UCLA. Having become wealthy and having provided a "good upbringing" to her children, she had earned the acceptance of her community members. "[Then] I ignored their stares and, now, when I go to their stores or meet them somewhere else, they are so nice to me. Now they want to ask me for advice," she added sarcastically. From being soundscapes of hostility and suspicion, these stores had become spaces in which Bindu, with her independence and, more importantly, her upward mobility (indexed by both her successful career and the fact that her children went to elite colleges), was greeted with grudging respect by her community members.

THE TASTE OF MEMORY

Spices and "exotic cuisine" have acquired an iconic, and stereotypical, significance in popular cultural representations of India (and "the Orient" more generally). As Marks points out, "Food, oral signifier of exoticism, is the locus of displaced Western notions of Asian sensuality; and by extension, of the threat of the foreign . . . [of] exoticism and paranoia that surround imported cuisines and, implicitly, the less-manageable immigrants they represent" (2000: 236; see also Roy 2002). Further, as Martin Manalansan (2007: 179, 180) reminds us, Asian Americans have had a deeply complicated historical and symbolic relationship with food production, distribution, and preparation, ranging from Asians who came to the United States to provide cheap labor in plantations to meat packers and restaurant workers in contemporary times. Within the United States, the complex and deeply sedimented relationship between cuisine and orientalist tropes about Asian and Asian American communities lends a particularly fraught valence to the discursive contexts in which Indian food and, by extension, spices and other Indian food products are situated.[7]

Spices and "Indian" food are thus double-edged in their signification: at the same time that they evoke the affect of familiarity and "home" for some and offer touristic ventures into the exotic for others, they symbolize irrevocable alterity to yet others. Nevertheless, food is of particular significance to communities that travel across transnational space; Parama Roy (2002), for instance, analyzes the power of nostalgic gastronomy for diasporic subjects. The affective power of food underscores the ways in which memories and knowledges are embodied in powerful ways. As I argue below, food acquires a distinctive, and distinctively gendered, valence in transnational and migrant communities.

Marks argues that "sense memories are most fragile to transport, yet most evocative when they can be recovered" (2000: 110). Extending my interest in the relationship between affect, the senses, and notions of the familiar, I would now like to focus on the sense of taste, or the palate, as a site of individual as well as collective memories. Roy reminds us, "Food, in the migrant/diasporic subject's cosmos, becomes—whatever it might have been at its place of putative origin—tenaciously tethered to economics simultaneously and irreducibly national and moral" (2002: 472). As markers of cultural continuity as well as difference, hybridity, and/or assimilation, the gastronomic habits of transnational subjects become especially fraught areas for contestations and negotiations of gender, community, and kinship. One woman, Farah Merchant, described to me the importance of being able to buy "suitable" ingredients so that she could cook "proper" Indian food for her husband and children. As a busy, professional woman, she gave priority to cooking Indian food because, she said, this was one way of keeping her culture alive. "Language and food are two ways to retain our culture," she explained. "Now that the kids are in school, they're forgetting their Gujarati. But the least I can do is to give them one Indian meal a day."

I came across many instances of how the politics of gender mediated the play of (gustatory) memory. One woman, Rukhsana Sheikh, spoke to me about how, when she first arrived in the United States fifteen years ago after marrying a man she didn't know very well, cooking her husband's favorite Indian dishes helped "develop" her marriage. She continued, "It helped me get to know him, his needs. And on weekends we would together to buy groceries in Jackson Heights [in New York, where the couple lived at the time], and we both looked forward to that." For both these women, and for many others I interviewed, cooking Indian food was integral to their roles in the family and to their constitution as national and gendered subjects—indeed to their identities as Indian women. As dutiful wives and mothers, they believed they could keep their respective cultures "alive" through the food they cooked, a task made infinitely easier and, in some cases, pleasurable by being able to buy the necessary groceries at Indian stores.[8]

The relationship between food preparation and ideas of "suitable" or dutiful womanhood becomes still clearer when we hear what some women store owners told me about their efforts to teach younger and second-generation Indian American women how to cook Indian food. One woman store owner in Berkeley recounted:

> Very often, young women who've grown up here come to my store because they are missing something their mom used to cook. They describe it to me, and I tell them how they can make it in their own apartments. They don't know anything about Indian cooking. But if you're Indian of course you'll want Indian food. Sooner or later you'll miss it. After all, how long can you eat hamburgers? It is not in our culture. And then they come to me. I tell them what to buy, how to cook. What basic ingredients to always keep in their kitchen. I tell them how to use shortcuts so it is not necessarily what their mothers cook, because they don't have the time to cook authentic recipes. But it is Indian food that can be made in America. I tell them what to do. It is obvious they've never cooked before.

These words bring together discourses of food, gender, and culture in suggestive ways. According to this store owner, second-generation women, marked as such by their appearance and their accents, would "of course" want to eat Indian food because, despite how they might look or sound, they are after all Indian (note how the longing for Indian food is naturalized—or rather nationalized—here). Drawing on a discourse that collapses the immense diversity of the culinary traditions of the subcontinent, this woman implied how cooking or learning to cook "Indian food" enabled the reproduction of Indianness for young, second-generation Indian American women.[9] While the recipes these store owners gave to young Indian American women might not be "authentic" (to the extent that they entailed improvisation, shortcuts, and the hybrid use of ingredients) they were, nevertheless, deemed Indian or, at the very least, were Indian recipes that could be made in the United States.

The store owner quoted above obviously homogenized "Indian culture" and "Indian food." Most store owners, however, were extremely knowledgeable about the diverse culinary habits of their customers. They were all too aware that they had to cater to a regionally and culturally heterogeneous community. For instance, while in the past most stores sold only ingredients used in North India, they now made it a point to offer products used in different regional Indian cuisines. Store owners were proud of their niche marketing practices shaped, in turn, by their knowledge of local demographics and patterns of settlement. As the owner of a chain that has branches in Berkeley and Sunnyvale said to me, "I always keep *gongura* [an ingredient used in Andhra food] in my store in Sunnyvale because there are lots of Telugu-speaking people there. In Berkeley, there aren't that many Telugus [*sic*], so I don't bother." Another store owner who called his business Indian Bazaar spoke proudly of selling "food from all over India." On the one hand, this is the story of U.S. multiculturalism meeting savvy marketing; at the same time, it also expresses the nationalist "unity in diversity" narrative promoted by the postcolonial Indian state.

Each of these memories produces sensuous knowledges about Indian food, Indian culture, and, indeed, India. These sensuous knowledges, in turn, are deeply inflected by heterogeneous affective regimes pertaining to generational politics and the gendered politics of marriage and family. For instance, the consumption of a favorite food might lead an individual to selectively remember the warmth and laughter surrounding family gatherings and celebrations of the past (rather than the conflicts and politics of family and kinship surrounding them). I came across several instances of this selective remembering and forgetting evoked by a favorite food, but one stands out particularly vividly in my mind. I was interviewing a middle-aged couple, Ramesh and Savi, in their living room about the place of Indian grocery stores in their lives in the Bay Area when Ramesh started to speak of how the fragrance and taste of saffron brought back fond memories of family celebrations of the Hindu festival Diwali. As he waxed lyrical about the mountains of food prepared for the occasion, Savi slyly remarked to me that Diwali in her in-laws' home meant that the women of the family would be "stuck" in the kitchen all day preparing the grand meal. "No way am I going to do that here," she added. The gendered division of labor surrounding food preparation in her in-laws' home meant that Savi could not share in her husband's (selective) memories of Diwali celebrations of the past.

Obviously, the memories evoked by favorite foods were neither reflective nor constitutive of homogeneous collective memories for these customers. There are two additional caveats I would like to insert here. As I noted earlier, the affective regimes congealing around objects were clearly shaped by the contexts in which their consumption occurred. Commodities and other objects consumed in the United States acquired a different affective valence than when consumed in India. Thus, a favorite shampoo was simply a favorite shampoo when used in India; in the diaspora, however, this shampoo acquired particular affective value because it evoked specific memories of home and childhood. Second, I do not intend to paint a fuzzy, soft-focused picture of memories of home or family that were uniformly pleasurable. For some women that I worked with, these memories evoked sorrow or fear; Indian grocery stores were thus not just familiar but for these women deeply familial, with all the complicated emotions the familial evoked. For those for whom the home was not a safe place, the familiar and the familial evoked neither longing, pleasure, nor security but instead brought forth emotions of ambivalence, claustrophobia, resentment, and, in some cases, terror.

BRANDED TEMPORALITIES

For several years now, some spices and other groceries have been processed within the United States. Interestingly, print and television advertisements highlight the fact that these products are made "here." For instance, the television advertisement for one company emphasizes that its products are unadulterated and of higher quality because they are processed in the United States ("made here, made pure," goes the voice-over for the ad). This marketing strategy underscores how, in recent years, Indian culture is now considered portable. Indeed, just as India can now be found abroad, Indian culture can also be produced and experienced outside of India in an even purer, more authentic form than in India itself (as we saw in chapter 2). For the most part, however, the shelves of Indian grocery stores in the Bay Area, and perhaps those in other parts of the United States as well, were stacked high with brands that are hugely popular in India, for example, Maggi Noodles, Amul Butter, or Glucose Biscuits. Thus, it was not at all unusual to find customers from India reaching for the very brands that they consumed "back home." In his explanation of this phenomenon, Rajiv Chopra, the owner of a store in Berkeley, exclaimed to me, "There are three reasons why my customers reach for the same brands they used in India: nostalgia, nostalgia, nostalgia!"

In unpacking what Chopra is describing, I find it necessary to flesh out how I conceptualize nostalgia. For one, I would like to caution against reducing diasporic affect to nostalgia or conceptualizing nostalgia in terms of a simple longing for the past.[10] Second, it goes without saying that these branded commodities did not evoke nostalgia for all customers; moreover, even among those who nostalgically reached for the same brand names that they consumed in India, the range of affects these commodities generated were quite varied. Finally, as Marks points out, nostalgia cannot be reduced to "an immobilizing longing for a lost past: it can also mean the ability of past experiences to transform the present" (2000: 201).

I am interested in unraveling the intimate relationship between temporality and nostalgia as affect. I noted earlier in this book that if affect is rendered as a result of the circulation of signs, this circulation occurs over time: in this sense, affect is fundamentally tied up with processes of temporality. Moreover, as we will see shortly, memory is central to the accumulation of affective value evoked by particular brands of commodities in grocery stores (compare Ahmed 2004). If, as Daniel Miller observes in another context, commodities are "brought to life in the consumption practices of the household" and "enact moral, cosmological and ideological objectifications," the branded objects of Indian grocery stores "create the images by which we understand who we have been, who we are, and who we might or should be in the future" (1995b: 35). Through the products they displayed and sold, Indian stores enable the cathexis of different fragments of the past and future onto brand-name objects, enabling the consumption and (re)production of Indian culture across transnational space.

I do not, by any means, imply that all memories were nostalgic for my informants. Nostalgia, in fact, was only one of many affective modalities for negotiating temporality. Indeed, as I have argued earlier, my informants experienced and engaged multiple temporalities entailing the copresence of the past within the present rather than as a radical break or rupture vis-à-vis a past that had been "left behind." Furthermore, the relationship between nostalgia and memory was rendered particularly complex since, for some of my informants, the object of their memory, India, was itself phantasmic.

Nostalgia and memory got cathected onto some of the branded objects sold in Indian grocery stores (here I refer particularly to commodities produced in India) to produce multiple temporalities. Marks terms material objects that encode collective memory as "recollection-objects" that "condense time within themselves, and . . . in excavating them we expand outward in time" (2000: 77). Recollection-objects can embody different, sometimes conflicting, pasts. Many of the store owners I interviewed echoed the words of Rajiv Chopra quoted above: they all claimed that most Indians came to their stores to buy the same brands that they had used in India. As one of my informants, Sunita Gupta, who had been frequenting Indian stores in Sunnyvale for the past eight years, informed me, some of these brands "brought back memories of home," a home that had moreover been "left behind" in the past. Sunita was a thirty-something professional who worked in a Silicon Valley company. She spoke of how she always reached for the same products. For instance, she always bought Glucose Biscuits to eat with her morning tea because they reminded her of early mornings in her parents' house:

> Every morning, I would waken to the sounds of tea being served in our living room. My parents used to wake up very early, go for a walk, and then drink their tea when they returned. My father would sit with a pile of newspapers, and my mother would sit beside him, serving tea. I would walk in bleary-eyed, dip my Glucose Biscuit into my tea, and sip it slowly. As soon as I was done, I would rush off to get ready for school. My mother would scold me every morning for dawdling over my tea; I would always have to eat my toast on my way to the bus stop. It was a set routine: every morning I would drink tea with them; my mom would yell at me; I would ignore her and sip my tea, my father and I smiling slyly at each other. No matter what else happened, this happened every single morning, every morning. . . . Here, so far away, I still dip my Glucose Biscuits into my tea. And I skip breakfast because I never have time to eat before I leave.

Other informants also described how particular product brands evoked very specific memories of their pasts in India. Indira, who taught in a primary school in Fremont, spoke of how she always bought Brahmi Hair Oil because, every Sunday, her mother would massage her hair with this oil. Similarly, every year she bought Mysore Sandalwood Soap because that is what they used in her family on Diwali. As she said, "You're so far away and you want links with those days. And the smell of the soap, and how soft it makes my skin feel, brings back those days." The smell of the soap and its feel on Indira's body suggest how temporality is experienced affectively, through the senses, and through the embodiment of memory.

In *Cinema 2: The Time Image*, Deleuze remarks, "The present itself exists only as an infinitely contracted past which is constituted at the extreme point of the already-there" (1989: 98). For most of the men and women that I interviewed, the experience and negotiation of multiple temporalities were mediated by the fact that, for them, nostalgia was not just a simple, romantic longing for the past: it consisted of a range of affects, many of which were shot through with ambivalence. Indeed, in some cases nostalgia entailed contradictory affects, sometimes in the same individual, who would at once feel a sense of loss regarding certain elements of the past, and a sense of relief at having left that past behind. For others nostalgia entailed an acute sense, sometimes experienced viscerally, of the haunting of the present by the past. As Daphne Berdahl (1999: 202) points out, nostalgia is about the production of a present rather than the (simple) reproduction of a past. Furthermore, nostalgia often draws on a selective remembering and forgetting of the past (see also Berdahl 1999: 198). In fact, as in the case of Berdahl's informants, nostalgia can "evoke feelings of longing, mourning, resentment, anger, relief, redemption, and satisfaction—often within the same individuals" (203).

Conceptualized thus, nostalgia also complicates our understanding of the relationship between temporality, memory, and territoriality. Some scholars of diaspora have defined nostalgia as stemming from a desire to return to the homeland (for example, Naficy 1993). This definition did not hold true for many of the men and women that I interviewed in the course of my research. Many of those that I interviewed did not want to actually return to India, but felt nostalgic all the same. In their case, nostalgia was not driven by a desire to return to the homeland, whether it was their hometown, their state, or, more generally, the Indian nation. One informant claimed that going into Indian stores was like "going into a time warp. It is messy, it is loud. It is fun while you're there. But you can then return home to your clean and quiet house. You don't have to stay there [in the store]." For her and for several other customers, the disjunction of the spatial with the temporal (the "time warp") entailed in the chronotope of grocery stores engendered a nostalgia that kept alive an ambivalence toward a phantasmic "homeland."

As branded commodities, some objects function as cultural mnemonics (compare Naficy 1993: 152), enabling the production and consumption of particular narratives of the past—a past rooted, as it were, in the shifting signifier that is the homeland. Indian grocery stores exemplify the sensuous geographies, affective connections, and dense socialities that ensue when people and objects on the move came together. Next I analyze how, as nodes within a transnational circulation of people, objects, and discourses, Indian grocery stores are also crucial to the emplacement of subjects in landscapes shaped by race, culture, and class.

Emplacements: Race, Culture, and Class

The racial order is equilibrated by the state—encoded in law, organized through policy-making, and enforced by a repressive apparatus. But the equilibrium thus achieved is unstable, for the great variety of conflicting

interests encapsulated in racial meanings and identities can be no more than pacified—at best—by the state.
—Omi and Winant, *Racial Formation in the United States: From the 1960s to the 1990s*, 1994

Beauty products and cosmetics represent how objects in motion produce specific regimes of value that travel and get re-created across transnational space. The relationship between chromatics or skin color (manifest in the obsession with fairness in many communities in India as well as across Indian diasporas), beauty, and femininity is one example of how certain objects articulated distinct regimes of value in terms of discourses of racialization circulating in the United States and India. This articulation was particularly striking in the case of cosmetics produced in India, some of which evoked discourses of femininity and beauty that were racialized in specific ways. Let me demonstrate what I mean with an ethnographic example. Lata Kapoor, an MBA from an elite East Coast university, told me that she only used Margo Neem soap because, she felt, it was better for her complexion than the soaps she bought in the United States. She added that, after coming to the United States, her mother had always bought Margo Neem soap and had told her that it would enable her to get a "clear" complexion. A clear complexion, she explained, was skin that was not only free from pimples and acne but, perhaps more importantly, was a "glowing, wheatish" complexion. Now, "wheatish complexion" is often used to describe relatively fair (rather than white) skin in India. Lata, a single woman who defined herself as a second-generation South Asian American, said that her mother placed a great deal of importance on looking beautiful. She said that she was grateful for this "upbringing" because now, she said, "no matter how busy I am, I always make sure I wash my face with Margo Neem soap before I sleep at night."

These desires for fair or wheatish skin suggest the intersection of racialized discourses of beauty in India with those hegemonic in the United States. Among the many cosmetics and beauty products displayed and sold in Indian grocery stores, some of the most popular among young women, especially second-generation women, were skin-whitening creams. For instance, when I asked Lata if she bought other cosmetics from Indian stores, she replied that she always bought Vicco Turmeric Cream because it also "cleared" her complexion. I knew from mutual friends that Lata was under considerable pressure to marry. The fact that she was a successful career woman was not enough; her parents were anxious that she would not really be settled until she was married. In her late twenties, her single status was a source of considerable anxiety to her parents and, I was beginning to sense, to her as well. I then remembered that many young women in northern India used Vicco Turmeric Cream to lighten their skins. I recalled ads for the cream that promised young women that they would become "fair and beautiful brides" if only they used it. I also knew that in many Indian communities, a fair complexion was as highly valued in the United States as in India. As in the case of many young women in India who were on the verge of entering the marriage market, Margo Neem soap and Vicco Turmeric Cream represented the promise of beauty (indexed by a fair complexion) and femininity.

This ethnographic example suggests how the North Indian fetishization of fair skin, with its embeddedness in discourses of race and caste, overlaps with conflations between fairness, race, and beauty in the United States. Indeed, the issue of skin color or chromatics is one of many complex ways in which Indians in America are racialized. As Rosemary George argues, "Skin color becomes the surface on which racial identity is read, and sometimes, evaded" (1997: 32).[11] George points out that "much of the everyday experience of being migrant/immigrant is grounded precisely in 'chromatic issues'—skin color is neither simple nor uncomplicated. Nor are skin color dynamics only to be understood in relation to whiteness and passing for white" (1997: 33). The relationship between chromatics and race constitutes a shifting terrain within the United States. As I argue later, brown skin assumed a particularly fraught salience in the context of the racial violence against South Asians and those perceived to be of Muslim or Middle Eastern descent after September 11, 2001. Within the framework of the ultranationalist and racist discourses that flourished, brown skin connoted racial and cultural alterity, so much so that many South Asian and Middle Eastern men, women, and children with brown skin were singled out as enemies of the (white) nation.

In addition to chromatics, the discourses of culture and cultural difference produced and circulated through Indian grocery stores were central to how my informants were emplaced within the racial order of the United States.[12] On the one hand, Indian grocery stores enabled alternative cultural practices vis-à-vis assimilationist constructions of national culture. At the same time, they also produced discourses of culture and cultural difference that, in fact, enabled either the skirting of issues of race or, on other occasions, the production of discourses of race that drew upon white supremacist discourses hegemonic in U.S. nationalism.

In his pioneering work on Filipino grocery stores, Rick Bonus argues that Filipino store owners use the term "oriental" as a contestatory business strategy. Bonus describes these stores' representation of Filipino culture as the "strategic marketing of difference" (1994: 664). This seems equally applicable to Indian grocery stores that sought to represent and market Indian culture to Indians as well as to non-Indians. While the consumption practices enabled by these stores unsettled dominant narratives of cultural assimilation, these stores also trafficked in difference in ways that reified culture and enabled the displacement of racial conflicts and hierarchies onto the terrain of cultural difference.

Depending on their location, the migration histories of their clientele, and the racial composition of surrounding communities, Indian grocery stores in the Bay Area enabled performances of identity in terms of ethnic and cultural difference (compare Marks 2000: 124). Throughout the time that I was conducting my field research, I would see crowds of second-generation Indian American youth hanging out in Indian stores in Berkeley. Frequented by customers with longer histories of settlement in the area (as compared with most stores in the South Bay, which were newer and catered to customers who were relatively recent arrivals), these stores provided second-generation youth with public cultural sites for the performance of ethnic identity often expressed in terms of cultural difference. One young second-generation man explained why he and his friends liked to hang out at the stores in Berkeley thus: "It is cool to be Indian now."[13] There were some stores where, during the weekends, while parents bought groceries and socialized with their friends, their teenaged children hung out on their own, sometimes on the sidewalk, but also sometimes in the stores themselves (compare Maira 2002). Groups of young men and women had become increasingly visible in (and outside) stores that displayed and sold these hybrid cultural products, especially those with large collections of Bollywood and Indipop music. As one young man who was a regular at such a store in Berkeley commented, "We're different. We're building our own culture. It is not American culture. But it is not pure Indian culture [either]. It is similar to our parents' culture, but it is also different."[14]

But, for the most part, the consumption practices enabled by these stores reified essentialist notions of identity and culture. For instance, when I asked one young woman, Henna Singh, why she always bought cosmetics made in India, she responded that it was because they allowed her to express her identity, an identity that was essentially different from that of her

European American friends. For many youth, this notion of cultural difference stemmed from ideas of a distinctive (and usually ahistoric) Indian culture instilled in them by their parents and, also, from discourses of multiculturalism present in some pockets of the Bay Area in the late 1990s.

Multiculturalism not only is characterized by the aestheticization and commodification of cultural difference, but has more pernicious consequences as well. As Lisa Lowe argues, U.S. multiculturalism is fundamentally nationalist: "If the nation proposes American culture as the key site for the resolution of inequalities and stratifications that cannot be resolved on the political terrain of representative democracy, then that culture performs that reconciliation by naturalizing a universality that exempts the 'non-American' from its history of development or admits the 'non-American' only through a 'multiculturalism' that aestheticizes ethnic differences as if they could be separated from history" (1996: 9).[15]

At the same time that some of the stores enabled alternative cultural practices resistant to an assimilationist model of U.S. national culture, they also participated in the reification, aestheticization, and commodification of cultural difference.[16] Later in this book, I elaborate on how this reification of cultural difference slid into the discourses of irrevocable alterity that proliferated after September 11, 2001. For now, it is sufficient to note that, throughout the time that I conducted my research, for some of my informants in the San Francisco Bay Area "culture" was reified in terms of loss or fears of loss—something that had to be consciously retained, produced, or disavowed. These reifications of culture and of cultural difference on the part of these informants drew sustenance, in large part, from constructions of phantasmic notions of India and Indianness. This phantasmic India emerged as an extraterritorial space that had tangible and concrete effects on how my informants lived their lives, constructed their identities, and, most pertinent to my argument here, were emplaced vis-à-vis other racial and national groups. Such reifications of culture and cultural difference enabled many of my informants to disavow their own racialization by displacing racial difference onto the terrain of ethnic and cultural difference.

Ironically, my informants' assertion of cultural difference and their opinions on race indicate that, even when they disavowed their own racialization, their disavowals were, in fact, symptomatic of their interpellation by dominant discourses of race and racism (Mazumdar 1989; Prashad 2000). For example, one morning, my research assistant, Mamta Ahluwalia, and I went to meet a store owner in Berkeley just as he was setting up shop. As he pulled up the shutters of his store, he started to scold his African American employee for not doing a good job of cleaning his car.

His employee was barely out of earshot when he turned to us and launched into an ugly tirade about "these blacks": about how lazy they were, and how they could never be trusted to do their job properly. He went on, "Look at us Indians. We come here with nothing but the shirts on our backs and our values of hard work. When I first came here, I lived in a poor neighborhood in Oakland. But I was able to work hard and move up in the world. Now I own a store. I have moved out of Oakland and now live in El Cerrito. I never claimed to be a victim of race [sic]. But those black people! They are always complaining. And they are exactly where they were years ago."[17]

The slippage between racial and cultural difference is not uncommon in discourses of racial antagonism between minority communities in the United States. For instance, in her analysis of black-Korean tensions in Los Angeles, Kyeyoung Park (1996) points to how African American as well as Korean community leaders explain tensions between their communities in terms of culture rather than their discrepant structural locations. Park is particularly insightful in her discussion of tensions between Korean store owners and their African American neighbors and customers; she argues that, rather than consider the commercial roles of "minority middlemen," racial conflict is attributed to immutable cultural characteristics (Park 1996: 492, especially 495–97). She insists, however, that it would be reductive to attribute these tensions wholly to economic relations; instead, she argues, it is essential that we see how particular symbolic meanings are ascribed to material practices (492–93). Indeed, my informant's remarks were in keeping with comments made by several other Berkeley store owners who alleged that their (former) African American neighbors "lagged behind" because of their culture (or lack thereof): they allegedly had dysfunctional families, children who didn't go to school and did drugs, and daughters who became pregnant before marriage. Their culturalist—and irrefutably racist— explanations for the alleged failures of (some) African Americans and for their own successes elided the fact that many of them could buy a store because they had affluent relatives and friends that they could turn to for loans even if they were not, at the time, wealthy themselves.[18] They thus had access to capital via networks in their communities (compare Park 1996: 493; see also Mazumdar 1989; Prashad 2000; Visweswaran 1997; George 1997).

Park (1996: 497) points to the emergence of a racial discourse of "race as culture" in which larger structural and historical factors such as positioning of Korean store owners as middlemen and their imbrication with the reproduction of specific regimes of capital and labor are elided. Like the store owners described by Park, many of the store owners I interviewed insisted that they had succeeded because of their "culture." Thus,

Indian American success was attributed to "Indian culture" (purportedly, the unity and durability of family structures, respect for parents and for tradition and, most importantly, the respect for hard work); conversely, African American failure was attributed to their alleged "lack of culture."[19] It goes without saying that these discourses reveal the dangers of cultural-ist explanations for understanding the varying positions of communities unequally situated vis-à-vis the dominant racial formation. Disparities in class and in racial position are elided; instead, we get a discourse of culture in which it is "values" that enable Indians to "move up in the world" rather than the privileges of education and class.[20]

Furthermore, as George argues, "What is refused by nearly all upper- and middle-class South Asians is not so much a specific racial identity but the very idea of being raced" (1997: 31).[21] George also points out that this denial was reinforced by immigrant bashing in California in the wake of Propositions 187 and 209.[22] Because of their centrality to the produc-tion of reified discourses of culture and cultural difference, Indian grocery stores enable us to trace the complex processes of the racialization of In-dians in the Bay Area. I would add that this denial is enabled, at least in part, by a displacement of issues of racial inclusion and exclusion onto the terrain of cultural difference. Indeed, this denial has a deep history and, indeed, may partially be traced back to the displacement of racial dif-ference onto cultural difference in the discourses of indigenous elites in colonial contexts (compare Ghosh and Chakrabarty 2002). Thus, while it is important to note that the denial of race in colonial and postcolonial contexts cannot be transposed to the racialization of my informants in the San Francisco Bay Area, relationships between colonial discourses of civilizational and racial inferiority were extremely complex and suf-fused with contradictions. For instance, as Ghosh points out, the silence around racial humiliation among middle- and upper-middle-class Indians in the immediate aftermath of independence was rendered all the more fraught because these experiences were "so much at odds with their vision of themselves as high-caste, *bhadra* patriarchs" (Ghosh and Chakrabarty 2002: 153). Ghosh follows with a question that is both poignant and per-tinent to my discussion of my informants in the San Francisco Bay Area: "The ideology of race is an ugly subject; is it possible that we Indians flinch from it partly in self-preservation, and partly because it so hopelessly con-taminates that aspect of liberal western thought in which our own hopes of social betterment . . . are often founded? But then don't we have to ask also, at what point does our aversion to this subject become either com-plicity or denial?" (154).

For the most part, race struggles were frequently sublated as cultural struggles on the part of many of my Indian American informants, whose unassimilability into the fabric of dominant U.S. national culture was metonymic of their racial unassimilability. The racial unassimilability of Indians must, however, be situated in a larger ideological context of constructions of Asia and Asian culture in the dominant U.S. national imaginary. As several Asian American scholars have argued, Asia and Asians in America have long represented the space of alterity against which dominant notions of citizenship and belonging are constructed in the United States. As Lowe posits, "'Asia' has always been a complex site on which the manifold anxieties of the U.S. nation-state have been figured: such anxieties have figured Asian countries as exotic, barbaric, and alien. . . . On the other hand, Asian immigrants are still a necessary racialized labor force within the domestic national economy" (1996: 4–5; see also Palumbo-Liu 1999). This depiction of Asians seems particularly pertinent to the ambiguous and ambivalent racialization of (some) Indians in the Bay Area, who have been portrayed as embodying the quintessentially "American" values of capitalist entrepreneurship, ingenuity, and hard work, and simultaneously, as always already foreign because of their unassimilability into U.S. national culture and their recalcitrance to blending into the so-called melting pot. These discourses of cultural and racial unassimilability had tragic consequences after September 11, 2001, when South Asians—in particular, Sikhs and Muslim South Asians—were marked as radically Other and, therefore, a threat to the U.S. (white) nation.

Finally, it is crucial that we remember that my informants' discourses on race and cultural difference were overdetermined by the larger political and historical contexts in which they are located—and here, again, the racial locations of South Asian store owners have much in common with those of some other Asian store owners in California. For instance, as analyzed by Park, the "African American-Korean American discourse is a triadic relation, not a dyad. It begins with their respective relationships to whites, and it puts Asians, in particular Koreans, in a paradoxical position in U.S. race relations" (1996: 494). Further, Park argues, the very experience of running a store is itself part of the process of becoming racialized: the experience of running small business enterprises also helps to structure Koreans' "emergent ideologies of race and ethnicity" (494). More significantly, I have noted above that many of my lower-middle-class informants worked in stores, either as employees or as partner-owners, precisely because they were unable to penetrate what they believed was a job market shaped by exclusionary discourses of cultural capital and networks based on race and class; similarly, some of my upper-class informants in-vested in stores because they had hit a glass ceiling in their white-collar professions.

Here we have much to learn from Asian American scholarship on how structural location and historically specific processes of racialization and class formation undergird antagonisms between racial minorities in the United States. It goes without saying that the racialization of Indians in the San Francisco Bay Area is mediated by class. While the number of Indi-ans working in blue-collar occupations, the service industry, and in small businesses increased substantially in the past few decades, the story of this community continues to be told in terms of the dominant (upper-class) narrative of "Indian success" in the Bay Area, most notably in Sili-con Valley. The narrative of Indian success in Silicon Valley—a story that is told largely in cultural-nationalist terms—reinserts Indians in the Bay Area into the dominant racial order in particular ways and, ironically al-though not surprisingly, this narrative has contributed to race blindness on the part of a majority within this community. In particular, the race blindness of upper-class Indians in Silicon Valley is shaped by specifically local political-economic and historical factors that are distinct from other communities with large populations of Indians, such as New Jersey, or Queens, New York, or, for that matter, other parts of California.

This race blindness perhaps explains the astounding response of some of my upper-class Silicon Valley informants to racial violence against South Asians after September 11, 2001. At first these informants reacted with outrage that they had been singled out for "random" security checks at airports or subjected to hostile stares in restaurants and other public spaces. But, as one of them related to me, they soon realized that it was "counterproductive" to stay outraged or angry. He reported that he and his friends told each other, "Let's keep our heads down until this blows over." Meanwhile, without their class position to function as a buffer against the onslaught of racial prejudice, working-class South Asians—for instance, those who manned gas stations, worked in small convenience stores, or drove taxis—continued to face the brunt of the racial violence that ensued in the months and years following September 11, 2001.

The uncritical celebration of the successes of upper-class Indians in Silicon Valley (particularly during the years when the economy was boom-ing and the self-confidence of the Indian community in Silicon Valley was at its zenith) is blind to the racial foundations of the U.S. economy and the U.S. national imaginary.[23] Bonnie Honig cautions us that the myth of immigrant success reveals the intimate relationship between xenophilia and xenophobia: "The foreigners whose immigration to the United States daily reinstall the regime's most beloved self-images are also looked on as threats to the regime. And this is no accident. . . . 'Their' admirable hard work and boundless acquisition put 'us' out of jobs. 'Their' voluntaristic embrace of America reaffirms but also endangers 'our' way of life. The foreigner who shores up and reinvigorates the regimes also unsettles it at the same time. Nationalist xenophilia tends to feed and (re)produce nationalist xenophobia as its partner" (1998: 3). Insightful as Honig's argument is about the relationship between xenophilia and xenophobia, it ignores the prevalence of hegemonic constructions of cultural difference. Also, her argument is itself based on an assimilationist narrative because, contrary to what it presumes, not all immigrants can or wish to embrace America: for many, being positioned as racial and cultural Others forestalls such an embrace. Nevertheless, Honig's broader point about the dangers of the myth of the successful immigrant might give us pause in the context of the dominant narrative of the success of some Indians in the Bay Area and especially in Silicon Valley because, within xenophobic and ultranationalist discourses, there might indeed be something unsettling about the always already foreigner whose upward mobility might leave "us" behind (the "us" in Honig's argument obviously refers to the normative European American Self against whom the foreign Other is constructed).

More importantly, rather than foreground or even acknowledge the intersection of race and class in the regulation of immigrant labor, these narratives of immigrant success have crucial consequences for Indian Americans' representations of their communities to themselves as predominantly middle class or upper middle class by rendering poor and working-class Indians in Silicon Valley, and the Bay Area more broadly, voiceless if not invisible. I found that, in some cases, the class positions of my poor and working-class informants had become invisible even to themselves. One of the most poignant moments of my field research occurred during my interactions with Manjeet Kaur, a Sikh woman who worked nights in a computer parts factory in San Jose and in her brother-in-law's grocery store during the afternoons. I knew that she worked long hours in the factory and at the store; this, combined with the clothes she wore and the lines of fatigue and anxiety furrowing her forehead, suggested to me that Manjeet was facing considerable financial hardship. In one of my initial conversations with her, I asked what her husband did. Without batting an eyelid, she replied, "He owns his own business." At first I was a bit taken aback because what she said didn't fit with my perception of her financial struggles, but I told myself that it was possible that his business had fallen on tough times. It was only several weeks later that I learned that her husband was a taxi driver who leased his taxi from a wealthy relative. Several others of my working-class informants confirmed my sense that, for many of them, the path to upward class mobility had been narrowed to two, largely unviable, options: either owning a (successful) business, or working in a white-collar job in the computer industry. For those who had neither the financial nor the educational capital to avail themselves of these two options, there appeared to be no other means of acquiring upward class mobility or indeed financial security.

It should come as no surprise then that, even though store owners insisted that they treated all their customers equally, they and their employees developed ways of identifying the class positions of their customers from their clothes, demeanor, and, supposedly, how they conducted themselves in the stores. For instance, one store owner told me, "Educated people, the professionals, behave differently from taxi drivers." Certainly, my participant observation in several stores confirmed that most store owners treated their working-class customers very differently. Some store owners complained to me that working-class customers tended to haggle more; they also alleged that, in some cases, they had to watch these customers and, in particular, their children carefully because they were afraid they might shoplift. The owner of Indian Bazaar in Sunnyvale claimed, "We don't have to do this with educated people."

Thus, the social contexts in which the production and circulation of phantasmic notions of India occurred in these stores were profoundly marked by class differences. These differences highlight how class fissures Indian communities in the Bay Area and suggest how my informants were emplaced in a larger landscape shaped by class. Class distinctions also existed among stores, so that some stores considered themselves more upper class than others. The owners of these stores went to great pains to distinguish themselves from other, smaller stores. Not only did they try to reach out to wealthier customers, their self-representation was shaped by an acute sense of their store's superior position vis-à-vis other stores. For instance, the owners of one well-known store in Fremont made a special effort to display extremely expensive designer outfits in the store's windows. These exorbitantly priced clothes were often displayed, somewhat incongruously, next to sitars and other classical musical instruments. It was clear that the store was attempting to appeal to customers with a certain amount of financial and cultural capital.

Finally, class distinctions existed within stores as well, not just between owners and employees but also, in the case of family-owned stores, between owners and the rest of the family, especially poorer relatives whose labor was exploited. Many store owners spoke to me of how they preferred to hire relatives or people from their own communities to work in their stores because they felt they could depend on their loyalty and honesty. Yet it was clear to me that intricate relations of power, obligation, and dependency tied these relatives and kinfolk to their wealthier relatives. Thus, even though they addressed each other using intimate or even deferential forms of address (consisting, for example, of kinship terms like *mamaji* [uncle or, more specifically, mother's brother], or *bhabhiji* [sister-in-law or brother's wife], or *anna* [elder brother]), there was no question in anybody's mind as to who was boss. For instance, one employee told me that she was allowed very short lunch breaks by her boss, who was also her niece. Another elderly woman spoke with quiet resignation of how exhausted she would get from standing at the cash register at her daughter-in-law's store all day. When I suggested that she bring a stool to sit on so that she wouldn't have to stand all day, she gazed back at me with an expression that combined incredulity with pity at my naïveté. "I don't want my daughter-in-law to think I am complaining," she explained, as she proceeded to ring up the purchases of a long line of customers. Very often, I would have to arrange to meet some of these employees at a different store or coffee shop because it was clear to me that they felt deeply uncomfortable discussing their working conditions in the stores in which they worked under the close supervision of their relatives.[24] Although I was careful never to inquire about any of my informants' legal status, I have no doubt that undocumented employees were particularly dependent on their store-owner relatives for their security and their ability to live in the United States.

The stores themselves changed in accordance with shifts in the demographic composition and political economy of the region and, in fact, provide us with a useful lens to trace some of these broader processes. The stores in which I conducted my ethnographic research varied. Some had been established in the 1960s and 1970s, and their owners were among the cohort that migrated to the United States after the passage of the 1965 Immigration Bill. Many of these store owners had been trained as professionals who then changed tracks and decided to take up this business. Their reasons for doing this ranged from having to confront a glass ceiling at work to their need or desire to provide a second income for their families and, since most of them were male, a job for their wives. It was not unusual, therefore, for engineers and other professionals to invest in a small store that would be managed by their wives and, once their business picked up, to resign from their jobs to devote themselves full time to their stores. Many of the stores that were established in the 1980s and afterward were owned by immigrants who came to the United States under family reunification quotas and would co-invest in these stores with capital borrowed from wealthy relatives who had been in the United States much longer.[25]

Indian grocery stores in the San Francisco Bay Area were impacted by other shifts in immigration and political economy. During the late 1990s, the IT industry was booming and the region was witnessing the influx of several hundred thousand IT workers from India (and from other parts of the world) on H-1B visas. The presence of Indian H-1B visa workers in the area, most of whom were under temporary contracts with computer firms, lent a huge boost to local business, particularly Indian grocery stores and restaurants located in and around Silicon Valley.

H-1B visas are given to men and women that Immigration and Customs Enforcement (ICE) classifies as highly trained workers with skills that satisfy the prevailing needs of the U.S. economy. During the 1990s, a majority of H-1B visas were given to computer programmers and software engineers from India, Taiwan, Ireland, Israel, and so on. According to Immigration and Naturalization Service (as ICE was known at the time) statistics, in 1999, 52 percent of all H-1B visas were given to computer-related professionals. These visa holders played a pivotal role in the transformation of the economic and cultural landscape of Silicon Valley. According to the INS, during the first half of 1999, 46 percent of all computer-related H-1B workers came from India. A majority of the H-1B visa holders were recruited directly by employment agencies that hired them out to computer companies. In Silicon Valley, these agencies were known as body shoppers.[26]

The H-1B visa holders were a new breed of migrant worker. While companies usually sponsored the visas of employees, H-1B visa holders were often contracted to the body shoppers who recruited them. In the 1990s, most H-1B workers from India were well paid by Indian standards but earned considerably less than U.S. citizens and permanent residents (according to some estimates, many of them were paid about a third of what U.S. citizens and permanent residents would make for the same tasks). These H-1B visa holders thus complicate our understanding of the relationship between class, labor, and immigration. Because their visas were the property of either computer companies or body shoppers, their legal status was always precarious, making it difficult for them to change jobs. Of course, there was no question of their unionizing, organizing, or overtly participating in politics. Most H-1B visa holders sought to eventually gain permanent residency in the United States, and quite a few were successful in doing so. However, in times of economic crisis or downturns, H-1B visa holders became extremely vulnerable and were among the first to be fired.

The liminal status of H-1B visa holders reminds us of the fraught relationship between migration and immigration. For, even though many H-1B workers might have aspired to become immigrants, they remained migrant workers as long as they had H-1B visas; thus, they represented the gray area, the interstitial space, between migration and immigration. In addition, the case of the H-1B visa holders reminds us that immigration policies enact and produce a tiered hierarchy sedimented by race, class, and age. Contrast, for instance, the urgency surrounding calls to raise the annual quotas for H-1B visa holders in the 1990s, when there was an urgent need for their labor in the computer industry, with the stagnancy and backlog in all other quotas, especially those pertaining to family reunification, so that parents, less wealthy relatives, and the (generally female) spouses of residents had to wait for years before gaining entry as legal residents.

Immigration policies articulate both the needs of the U.S. economy for an "appropriate" labor force and an imperative to restrict its inflow to prevent a so-called excess of labor supply. In an economic context marked by mixed production and flexible accumulation, race emerges yet again not as a fixed singular essence but, as Lowe argues, "as the locus in which economic, gender, sex and race contradictions converge" (1996: 26). Not surprisingly, after the dot-com crash in the late 1990s, a majority of the H-1B workers from India were sent back, leading to the bankruptcy of many small businesses in the Bay Area. Scores of Indian grocery stores and small restaurants, most of which had been set up explicitly to cater to this population of H-1B workers, went out of business.

Predictably, the tragic events of September 11, 2001, and the racial violence that followed in their wake also left their mark on Indian businesses in the San Francisco Bay Area. The atmosphere of hostility, fear, and suspicion that proliferated after September 11 was devastating for many stores, particularly in locations where the population of immigrants and people of color was relatively small. Even in areas like Sunnyvale, Mountain View, Cupertino, and San Jose, where Indians and other South Asians had been visible for at least the past two decades, this visibility itself became a source of vulnerability: as icons of radical alterity in a landscape that had suddenly turned hostile, many South Asians and their businesses became marked as targets of violence. Small convenience stores like 7-Elevens and South Asian–owned gas stations were particularly vulnerable to racial attacks.

In the days and months following September 11, most South Asian businesses in the San Francisco Bay Area began to display the U.S. flag prominently. While I cannot do justice here to the complex reasons why these business owners chose to display the U.S. flag, several admitted that displaying the flag made them feel somewhat safer.[27] The owner of a store in Sunnyvale where I had spent a considerable amount of time conducting my research for this chapter admitted to me that, as soon as she heard about what had happened in New York City and at the Pentagon, for the first time in the thirty-plus years that she had lived in this country she had felt afraid for her life and that of her family. The first thing she did, she said, was to go and buy two U.S. flags and a large poster that said, "America open for business." She reported that she wanted to express her solidarity with those who had died, but it was clear to me that she had also felt that she might obtain some degree of safety by displaying these signs of patriotism. When I visited her store about five days after the attacks in New York City and Washington, I was struck by the hushed tones in which customers were speaking, their eyes glued to a CNN telecast of search crews sifting through the wreckage of the World Trade Center in New York City. CNN had replaced the Bollywood film that was always playing in the background. In a matter of just a few days, the noise and bustle of the stores in which I had conducted my fieldwork had been temporarily transformed by an overwhelming sense of sorrow, uncertainty, and, most significantly, fear.

Affective Objects and Transnational Space(s)

In chapter 2 I discussed how the category of the NRI emerged as a financial and cultural entity at a critical moment in postcolonial Indian history. As represented in the film *Dilwale Dulhaniya Le Jayenge*, the ideal NRI was affluent, masculine, and peripatetic with a mobility that was responsive to the circuits of capital. Although *DDLJ*'s NRIs were portrayed as living in the United Kingdom, the film's disengagement with the politics of their location implied that they were both ideal and generalizable: they were unlocatable because they could have been living anywhere. Most importantly, ideal NRIs carried India in their heart wherever they went, thus indexing the primacy of Indianness to the identities of diasporic subjects. In this chapter I have analyzed how Indian grocery stores were crucial nodes in the production and circulation of India as a phantasm for my informants in the San Francisco Bay Area. However, even when my informants claimed strong ties to India, their identities were multiplex: unlike the unlocatable NRIs of DDLJ, these subjects were formed through processes of displacement as well as emplacement as they negotiated their positions along landscapes marked by gender, class, notions of cultural difference, and race.

Yet, as Grewal points out, nationalism's ability to "move, change, spread across different kinds of boundaries suggests that it remained a powerful imaginary which developed in tandem with changing modes of citizenship and consumer culture" (2005: 13). By foregrounding the place of Indian grocery stores in the construction of India as an archive of affect and temporality, I have intended to unsettle the givenness of India and its anteriority to the formation of the subjectivities of my informants. As I argue throughout this book, far from residing exclusively in either the socius or in the "individual psyches" of subjects, affects are generated through the circulation of signs across and between objects and subjects. Hence, affects transgress binaries of private and public. In this chapter I have underscored how affectivity is intimately tied up with how spaces are experienced and materialized (Thrift 2007). For many of my informants, the affective charge of objects enabled the production of grocery stores as spaces of surveillance, solidarity, ambivalence, and/or hostility. The range of affects evoked by objects displayed and sold in Indian grocery stores was also refracted by temporal processes, such as my informants' past encounters with them— whether these encounters occurred in a real or imagined past or in a phantasmic place (in these particular instances, India): the range of affects generated and circulated thus precludes any simple conceptualization of diasporic affect in terms of nostalgia. Furthermore, at the same time that they enabled some of my informants to emplace themselves within landscapes of race, class, and culture, these stores also enabled a disavowal of processes of racialization and class formation, and facilitated the displacement of race and class struggles onto the terrain of essentialist discourses of culture and cultural difference. Indeed, these reifications of notions of culture and cultural difference were sustained, to a large extent, by the construction of phantasmic notions of India and Indianness.

As I noted at the beginning of this chapter, the stores I have analyzed here catered to customers from all over South Asia and, in some locations, from all over the world; they also carried products made in the United States and in other parts of the world inhabited by South Asians such as Pakistan, Sri Lanka, Fiji, Britain, and Canada. Yet many, if not most, of these stores represented themselves as Indian stores. On the one hand, the purported Indianness of these stores was a product of the canny marketing strategies of store owners who hoped, on the one hand, to retail the familiar to their Indian customers. On the other hand, foregrounding their Indianness also enabled some store owners to appeal to Western customers by trafficking in exotic difference and drawing on the discourses of multiculturalism circulating in some pockets of the San Francisco Bay Area. My intention in referring to these stores as Indian, however, stems not simply from a desire to stay faithful to my informants' (both store owners' and their customers') characterization of them but, equally importantly, from my insistence on foregrounding the modalities through which their Indianness was crafted and staged. Certainly, the centrality of Indian grocery stores to productions of India and Indianness compel us to reexamine the relationship between culture and territory—particularly territory as policed by nations and states—in an increasingly interconnected world.

Second, these stores foreground the phantasmagoric construction of place occurring in the contemporary conjuncture: as Anthony Giddens has pointed out, "In conditions of modernity, place becomes increasingly phantasmogoric: that is to say, locales are thoroughly penetrated by and shaped in terms of social influences quite distant from them" (1990: 18–19). It is critical that we recall that these phantasmic constructions of India enabled the (sometimes uneasy) coexistence of Indianness with other modalities of subject formation that drew upon regional and religious affiliation and discourses of multicultural belonging within the United States. My emphasis on the phantasm is as much an epistemological framework as it is a political intervention in how it enables me to avoid the trap of trying to locate a "real" India and, therefore, of seeking originary truths or definitive meanings; at the same time, I wish to underscore that these phantasmic constructions of India and Indian culture are central to symbolic and other contests over cultural purity, authenticity, and community (see chapter 5).

In chapter 4 I examine another aspect of the consumption of commodities in terms of what they meant or, rather, what they did (their affectivity) by tracing the co-implication of commodity affect and erotics for my informants in New Delhi. But for my informants in the San Francisco Bay Area, the reiteration and circulation of these phantasms of India and Indianness occurred precisely at the moment of its (ostensibly) impending erasure in contexts of diaspora and travel. Indian grocery stores in the San Francisco Bay Area represented an in-between space in which binaries of production and consumption, alterity and familiarity, and the national and the transnational were held in productive tension, blurred, and reinvented. For many of my informants, Indian grocery stores, and the objects they displayed and sold, engendered a complex range of affects (spanning nostalgia, ambivalence, and overt antagonism) refracted by the haunting presence of a phantasmic India—its loss, its absent presence, and, in many instances, its attempted retrieval—such that India was simultaneously unsettled and reconstituted through regimes of affect and temporality generated and circulated in these spaces.

CHAPTER 4

Transnational Hindi Television and
the Unsettlement of Indianness

Raju was an upper-caste man who lived with his three children and widowed sister in a working-class neighborhood in New Delhi; his wife had died at the birth of their youngest child, a daughter. I first met him in the mid-1990s. Over the following decade, I witnessed how he worked his way up through a variety of jobs. After starting as a domestic servant in an upper-class neighborhood, he worked as a driver for a diplomat, taught himself how to read and write, and, by the time I met him again in 2003, had found a job as a security guard in the local chain of a multinational retail outlet in a posh neighborhood in South Delhi. One December afternoon I sat with him in his kitchen as his sister ironed his children's school uniforms. I looked around and noted how his house had changed over the years, and how he had changed. When I first met him he was skinny, with furrows between his brows that belied his thirty-something years; he wore clothes that looked grungy and tattered. Ten years later, he looked different, carried himself differently. He was still thin, and the furrows between his brows had deepened, his hair now streaked with gray and receding. But his lanky frame was covered in clothes that always seemed, if not ironed, at least freshly washed; his shoes, although worn, were always polished; his hair carefully combed and slicked back. His house had been quite bare when I first started visiting him and his family. At that time, I had to sit on a low stool or on a metal chair in his living room; the family's only possessions were a nine-inch color television, a string bed, a kerosene stove, and some very basic kitchen utensils. Now they owned a large television set, a two-in-one transistor radio-cum-cassette player, a gas stove, a mixer-blender and, the pride of the family, a small refrigerator, from which he distributed cold water to all his less-fortunate neighbors during the long summer months. His tiny flat was regnant with the triumphs and frustrations, longings and struggles that he had experienced over the past decade.

Raju frequently spoke to me of how not just his life but "society" had changed, *poora samaj badal gaya hai, ji* (all of society has changed, *ji*). So, that December afternoon, I asked him to elaborate. He observed that, while earlier the stores in the South Delhi neighborhood in which he now worked had been frequented by upper-class customers, over the years "different types of people" (*alag kisam ke log*) had started to come, and it was his job to ensure that they did not do anything "untoward" (in English), which meant that they did not shoplift or transgress any unspoken norms of appropriate behavior. I asked him to clarify what he meant by "different types of people." He explained that, more recently, working-class and lower-middle-class people had started going to stores and markets that had previously been "exclusive" (in English) to "gentry" (an English word he used to refer to upper-class people).

Raju attributed most of these changes to the expansion of television from a state-controlled medium with two channels to a plethora of private networks, some of which were based overseas. When I asked him what he meant, he replied:

Earlier, the programs were about social uplift. How to help women. How to bring up good children. Now the programs are about how to move up in the world, what to buy, how to dress. Then they were teaching us how to make the country stronger by helping others. Now they teach us how to make the country stronger by helping ourselves. They show us all these things that can make our lives better. Where to buy them. How to use them. They plant the desire [*kaamna*] for these things in us, love [*chaahat*] for all these things. They give us feelings [*bhavnaaen*] for these things. Even for the things that we cannot own. These programs show us all these things. Earlier programs taught us how to be certain types of Indians. Now we learn how to be other types of Indians. But, the question is, how do we still remain Indian?

The point of Raju's story is not that he exemplifies the upward mobility of the majority of the men and women I worked with; in fact, his (limited) upward mobility was quite exceptional. Rather, Raju's situation evokes the struggles and aspirations of many of my informants. Furthermore, and perhaps more pertinently, Raju's words underscore that if Doordarshan's programs in the 1980s and early 1990s were underwritten by one pedagogical impulse (that of national development and national integration; see Mankekar 1999a), the new transnational television networks were equally pedagogical, even if less overtly so. Television played a central role in the integration of India into the global capitalist economy; at stake was the construction of not just new types of workers and consumers but, perhaps equally importantly, new kinds of subjects and, in Raju's words, new types of Indians. What types of Indians were these? As he and countless others asked themselves and me: How could one adopt new lifestyles, new ways of dressing, behaving, desiring, and dreaming, and still remain Indian?

By facilitating the generation, circulation, and convergence of affective regimes surrounding commodities and erotics, transnational Hindi television programs played a central role in the unsettlement of notions of Indianness and Indian culture. The words Raju used to describe the emotions generated by the commodities displayed on television—*kaamna* (desire, particularly erotic), *chaahat* (love, usually romantic love), and *bhavnaaen* (feelings)—foreground the affectively charged relationship between erotics, commodities, and subjects like him. Yet Raju's articulation of emotional states does not exhaust the affective regimes that surround commodities, but only gives discursive form to them retroactively.[1] The affective regimes I trace here are irreducible to the personal, subjective, or individual.

In chapter 3 I analyzed how the commodities displayed and sold in Indian grocery stores enabled the production of India as a phantasm for my informants in the San Francisco Bay Area and, in so doing, simultaneously reconstituted and unsettled notions of India and Indian culture. Here I turn to how distinct affective regimes and temporalizing processes relating to commodities and erotics intertwined to suffuse the desires and anxieties of my working-class informants in New Delhi. I begin this chapter by situating the role of transnational television in the proliferation of affects surrounding commodities; next, I trace the intertwining of affective regimes surrounding commodities and erotics; finally, I point to how these affective regimes and temporalizing processes enable us to trace not only the cultural and social changes occurring in India at the close of the twentieth century but, more pertinently to my project in this book, the unsettlement and renegotiation of India and Indian culture.

Transnational Hindi Television and Commodity Affect

Modern commodity production, as it increasingly incorporates the aesthetic dimension (in, for example, advertising or contemporary design), develops a discourse that connects with and transforms the sensual awareness of modern subjects; in so doing, it plays, with increasing complexity, across the ambiguities of the real and the fantastic (Haug 1986: 4). As I have argued earlier in this book, the 1990s represented a critical juncture in the history of public cultures in India. The policies of economic liberalization that I describe in chapter 2 occurred in conjunction with the expansion of transnational public cultures. This period was marked by the flooding of Indian markets by consumer goods, many of which had previously been unavailable except to a very small elite; a dramatic shift in the aspirations of many lower-middle-class and middle-class Indians, particularly those living in urban areas; and, last but not least, the erotic recharging of urban public cultures. In many ways, this was a time that was profoundly unsettling—for my informants who experienced these phenomena in visceral ways and, on a different register, in terms of the ways in which the boundaries of India and Indianness were being redefined in the face of global capital flows and transnational media.

By the early 1990s, transnational television was available via satellite to all the men and women that I worked with in New Delhi. Yet it is erroneous to assume that satellite television appeared in India only in the 1990s or that transnational media corporations were the ones to launch it. The Indian state first introduced satellite television in the 1960s as part of a larger strategy for national (specifically, rural) development.[2] Through a program known as the SITE (Satellite Instructional Television Education) project, the Indian state combined communication satellites with terrestrial microwave relay transmitters to telecast instructional programs on farming and new agricultural technologies to villages in select regions of India. While there is no doubt that the number of television channels dramatically increased with transnational satellite networks, it was in the 1980s that the foundation of a mass or, rather, national audience was laid (Mankekar 1999a). Then, too, it was satellite technology that enabled this development. The satellite INSAT-1A, first launched in 1982 in collaboration with Ford Aerospace and followed by INSAT-1B in 1983, became instrumental in enabling the expansion of state-run television, or Doordarshan, across the Indian subcontinent. By setting up low-power relay stations fed by satellite, Doordarshan was launched as a national network. Finally, even though television did not work in isolation from other media (such as cinema or print advertisements), it was state-controlled Doordarshan that inaugurated and solidified the relationship between television and commodity consumption. The very first dramatic serials telecast on Door-darshan were birthed through the marriage of capital and the state; thus, for instance, *Hum Log*, the first Indian teleserial, was sponsored by Maggi Noodles and Nirma Washing Powder (Mankekar 1999a).

However, despite the fact that Doordarshan laid the foundation for the expansion of television as a mass medium and the acceleration of a culture of commodity consumption, it was transnational television networks that intensified these developments in tandem with the expansion of commodity cultures via other media (ranging from cinema and print media to billboards; see chapter 1 for a discussion of the intertextuality of media, and chapter 5 for an analysis of the crucial role of Hindi cinema in representations of commodity culture).[3] Television played a significant role in the proliferation of commodity affect through multiple modalities: by engendering fantasies of upward mobility through the desire for (and, occasionally, the acquisition of) commodities; through the realignment of caste and class; by (re)mobilizing gendered discourses of national culture; and, as I demonstrate in this chapter, the conjoining of commodity affect with erotics. As I have argued elsewhere, the significance of television to the reconstitution of discourses of nation and gender became evident in the late 1980s and early 1990s; after the liberalization of the Indian econ-omy and its attendant shift from the production of capital goods to con-sumer goods, television became all the more salient to the consolidation of cultures of consumption (Mankekar 1999a; see also Rajagopal 1999a, 1999b, 2001). The ubiquity of television in the everyday spaces inhabited by my informants, and the affective regimes and embodied knowledges it generated, only heightened its centrality to the production of spectatorial and viewing subjects as subjects of consumption (Mankekar 2012b).

Transnational television brought about profound qualitative shifts in the mediascapes of late twentieth-century India. In alignment with the liberalization of the Indian economy and in conjunction with exhortations to consume in other media that proliferated at that time, transnational television networks played a crucial role in highlighting India's place as an important emerging market for commodities and, to a large extent, accel-erated its integration into global circuits of capital and consumption (com-pare Mankekar 2004; Mazzarella 2003a, 2003b; Page and Crawley 2001; Rajagopal 1999a, 1999b). While some transnational networks were based overseas (the most notable being CNN and STAR Television), as with media industries the world over, the line between indigenous and foreign capital became increasingly difficult to draw.

Founded in 1992 by Indian entrepreneur Subhash Chandra, Zee TV emerged as a leader in the production of highly popular Hindi soap operas or serials, most of which catered to audiences within India as well as to segments of the Indian diaspora. As I elaborate later, shortly after the introduction of imported programs it became evident that Indian audiences preferred "Indianized" programming; hence, transnational satellite networks like STAR TV, the Sony Entertainment Network, and MTV began to produce programs explicitly oriented to the viewing preferences of audiences in India and across Indian diasporic communities. Furthermore, notwithstanding my focus in this chapter on Hindi-language programs, the proliferation of private television channels spurred media entrepreneurs to set up regional networks targeting specific linguistic communities across India. Thus, for instance, channels like Sun TV, Gemini TV, Asianet, and Udaya TV (in Tamil, Telugu, Malalayam, and Kannada respectively) established their dominance in southern India and across southern Indian communities overseas to draw diasporic television audiences, which represented enormous markets.[4]

Furthermore, as Page and Crawley have argued, "Advertising agencies have the most demonstrable claim to be the midwives of satellite television" (2001: 24). In this manner, the intimate relationship between television and commodity consumption that Doordarshan first established in the 1980s was further consolidated with the expansion of transnational satellite television, with profound consequences for how many of my informants in New Delhi imagined their worlds and their futures. Mary E. John has argued that in the India of the 1990s, transnational media played "a disproportionate role in organising our visual field" (1998: 372). Transnational images of commodities were modified in response to "local" aesthetics and needs; in turn, local representations were reconstituted by transnational images, aesthetics, and narratives. For instance, when Pepsi was launched in India, its first few advertisements cleverly incorporated hegemonic, nationalist representations of tradition (symbolized by Hindi film celebrity Juhi Chawla doing a classical Kathak dance) as well as modernity (in the figure of Goan pop star Remo Fernandes). In contrast to the earlier Gandhian ethos of austerity that had been valorized among some sections of the urban middle classes from the 1950s through (about) the 1970s, consumer goods from the 1980s onward fast became indexical of upward mobility for middle-class and lower-middle-class consumers.[5]

Commodity aesthetics played a crucial role in orienting spectators to engage with consumer goods in particular ways. For, as Haug (1986: 8) has pointed out, commodity aesthetics shape not only our sense of visuality but also our sensual understanding of the material world.[6] Commodity aesthetics influence our ideas of what might be pleasurable to our senses in terms of the exchange value of the commodity. However, more pertinent to my argument about the intertwining of affective regimes surrounding commodities and erotics, commodities are themselves generative of libidinal desire such that "a whole range of commodities can be seen casting flirtatious glances at the buyers, in an exact imitation of or even surpassing the buyer's own glances, which they use in courting their human objects of affection" (Haug 1986: 19).

I use the term commodity affect to indicate how commodities become vital nodes in the production and circulation of intensities that generate and refract desire, agency, relationalities, and potentialities. Commodity affect refers to the ineffable yet potent intensities surrounding commodities that challenge the boundaries between cognition and viscerality, individual passion and collective emotion. Commodity affect does not originate solely from commodities or their representations, or from the subjectivities of those who engage with them. In fact, commodity affect refers to the relay of intensities between subjects and commodities. The line between persons and commodities blurs to produce "affective allegiances"; hence, commodities are not inert objects brought alive by our thoughts, but have a materiality all their own (Thrift 2010: 292). Furthermore, commodity affect does not refer to what commodities symbolize. Rather, it gestures toward the consequentiality of commodities—their affectivity—for subjects' actions, desires, and anxieties. Like other affects, commodity affect refers to "bodily capacities to affect and be affected, or the augmentation or diminution of a body's capacity to act, to engage, and to connect" (Clough 2007: 2).

Early in my fieldwork for this project, I became interested in the feedback loops between representations of commodities on television, the commodities themselves, and the embodied desires of my informants. The shift in Indian television from development discourse to consumption that began in the 1980s and accelerated through the 1990s produced new kinds of spectators and indeed new kinds of subjectivities. Through the generation and circulation of commodity affect, television played a crucial role in the proliferation of affective regimes and sensoria that introduced spectators to the embodied pleasures of a new world of commodities.[7] The power of commodity affect became increasingly clear to me when, in the course of doing fieldwork, I saw how my informants inhabited the texts that they engaged in profound and intimate ways: viewing television served as a point of entry into intense affective engagements with what they watched.[8]

Most of the men and women I worked with could not afford to purchase the commodities they saw on television.[9] I thus learned that desire in commodity affect pertains not just to the pleasure of acquiring a commodity but also to the pleasures of gazing upon it and longing for it. In some instances, these pleasures were corporeal and synesthetic, as in the haptic, multisensorial pleasures that result when, for instance, one's eyes caress a silk sari displayed on television, or when one starts to salivate while looking at an advertisement for ice cream or a dish of *gulab jamuns*. In many cases, these pleasures were deeply embedded in aspirations and fantasies of, in the poignant words of one of my informants, "what life could be like." As several informants suggested to me, gazing at commodities in advertisements and in stores provided them with "a window on the world." It introduced them to the lives and worlds of people removed from them in terms of class, region, and nation. For some of my informants, commodity affect enabled forms of imaginative travel, so that a young woman in a small town in northern India was able to imagine the life of her friend in Bombay. Similarly, a young man who had never traveled outside India but was an avid viewer of television ads could speak at length about youth culture in the United States.

The proliferation of commodity affect via television was part of larger intertextual and sensory contexts. In India during the 1990s, commodities were everywhere. Markets, shop windows, and billboards—literally, the physical landscapes of large cities, small towns, and even some rural areas—were transformed so that the sensory field became thick with representations of commodities in a manner that was unmatched in scale, depth, or magnitude. Alluring photographs of commodities were splashed across the pages of newspapers and magazines. The enormous range of print media that thrived in the 1980s was enhanced in the late 1990s by the emergence of a spate of lifestyle-oriented magazines specifically devoted to the consumption of commodities newly available to Indians with discretionary incomes (e.g., *India Today Plus* and numerous bridal magazines). Popular cinema had always staged commodities in the spectacles that it produced, but films produced at that time revealed an excess of spectacle dominated by commodity aesthetics: these films explicitly focused on the consumerist lifestyles of affluent Indians, newly visible yuppies, and NRIs (e.g., *Hum Apke Hain Kaun* [Who are we to you, 1994], *Kuch Kuch Hota Hai* [Something is happening, 1999], and *Pardes* [Distant land, 1997], respectively).

But perhaps most significant of all was the role of television in the recharging of sensoria in the homes of the men and women I worked with in New Delhi, such that so-called spaces of domesticity became affectively charged spaces of consumption. Indeed, all my working-class and lower-middle-class informants, down to the last man and woman, commented at great length on the changes brought about by the expansion of transnational networks.[10] They spoke in terms of how their apprehension of the material world, their understanding of social relationships, and their conceptions of the possible had been transformed. Most of them were excited by these changes, the options now available for their entertainment, and the unprecedented range of commodities that were advertised on television. Many remarked that they had been unaware of the existence of some of these commodities until they saw them on their television screens. The new television programs, and the advertisements that enabled and surrounded them, participated in the creation of different "types" of Indians through the production and incitement of specific kinds of desires and affects.[11]

Televisual Erotics

Quickly but inexorably, for the lower-middle-class and working-class men and women that I worked with in New Delhi, commodity affect became intimately entangled with erotics, or what I will term erotic affects. For many of my working-class informants, yearning for commodities, even for those they could not afford to purchase, was itself a source of pleasure, a pleasure not dissimilar to erotic yearning.

Anjali Arondekar has critiqued anthropological scholarship for narrating sexuality "through the prism of a short-lived history, often relegating the materialities of colonialism and empire to the nominal status of recurring referents" (2007: 338). Although my focus is on erotics rather than sexual practices or discourses surrounding sexuality, Arondekar's point is well taken. Thus, while engaging premodern and colonial legacies of the erotic in any depth is beyond the scope of this chapter, to avoid "parochialisms of time and space" (Arondekar 2007: 338), I next situate late twentieth-century erotics vis-à-vis genealogies of the erotic in South Asia.

GENEALOGIES OF THE EROTIC

In outlining some genealogies of the erotic in South Asia, I wish to challenge both Eurocentric or universalist notions of erotics (compare Manderson and Jolly 1997: 12, 22) and, equally importantly, the notion that transnational media swept into India to introduce images and discourses of the erotic.[12] Diverse genealogies of the erotic have always coexisted in Indian popular cultures, and I can do no more than list them here.[13] In so doing, however, I want to insert the following caveats. One, I base my delineation of previously existing genealogies entirely on textual sources and do not take into account vernacular or oral traditions. Two, these texts are largely masculinist and, in the case of Sanskrit sources, upper caste. Three, in the case of sources that are affiliated with Hindu traditions, we also run the risk of being complicit with orientalist and/or Hindu nationalist attempts to hark back to a classical Sanskritic past in an effort to outline the genealogies of contemporary cultural phenomena. It goes without saying that multiple traditions have always existed, including Indo-Islamic traditions of representations of erotics. I wish to underscore that late twentieth-century representations of erotics did not emerge in a cultural or historical vacuum and, in all probability, resonated with older, perhaps residual (Williams 1977), conventions of erotics. My goal, therefore, is to trace a very partial genealogy.

Nevertheless, late twentieth-century representations need to be located vis-à-vis heterogeneous traditions of erotics in the premodern past. One example of this is the Kamasutra (said to have been written between the second and fourth centuries CE), a didactic text that conceived of erotics as part of a range of pleasures, including those offered by art, dance, and poetry.[14] Erotics also appeared as an aesthetic category in Bharata's *Natyashastra* (whose origin Dimock et al. [1974] date to before the sixth century CE); in the work of Abhinavagupta (in the eleventh century); in Sanskrit poetry such as Kalidasa's *Kumarsambhava* and Jayadeva's twelfth-century poem *Gitagovinda* (see Siegel 1978, esp. 42–57);[15] in Tamil akam poetry (see Dimock et al. 1974, 172; Ramanujan 1973, 170–81); and in medieval bhakti poetry dedicated to Krishna (see Lele 1981). Many of the bhakti poems were in local languages and continue to be influential in contemporary Hindu popular culture. Some Sufi traditions incorporated the erotic into aesthetic conventions expressing the mystical union of the devout with the Divine Beloved (see Schimmel 1975, esp. 287–89). Among Indo-Islamic and Urdu performative traditions pertaining to the erotic, the most influential in contemporary popular culture is the *ghazal* (see Dwyer 2000; Manuel 1993).

In the modern conjuncture, the most ubiquitous and influential form of popular culture in India and in diasporic communities affiliated with India is popular film. Over the years, film and television have developed a symbiotic relationship, and many representations of erotics on transnational Hindi television—whether in MTV-style music programs or television serials—draw on the representational strategies and narrative conventions of popular Hindi or Bollywood film. The 1990s also witnessed the flowering of heterogeneous print media, ranging from novels, magazines, and pamphlets in English and regional languages to Indianized versions of U.S.-based magazines such as *Cosmopolitan*. A large number of these media focus centrally on intimate relationships and entail the generation and circulation of erotics. These media use a range of aesthetic codes to represent erotics; for instance, a copy of the Indianized *Cosmopolitan* might include excerpts from the Kamasutra alongside articles on safe sex and dating.

In general, in the modern era, representations of erotics in hegemonic popular culture have been predominantly heteronormative, thus (re)inscribing heterosexual erotic desire as normative, if not normal. This does not, of course, preclude readings or interpretations of these representations in terms of homoerotic desire, which might sometimes lie just beneath their surfaces (Gopinath 2005).[16] Furthermore, as my analysis of a music video later in this chapter demonstrates, the advent of transnational television also enabled overt (albeit exceptional) representations of same-sex desires.[17] Despite these rare occurrences of same-sex or homoerotic desire, however, most of the affective regimes generated and circulated by transnational television remained oriented to heterosexual and heteronormative erotics.

Clearly there is no unitary or singular Indian discourse on erotics. Discourses of the erotic proliferating in the Indian public sphere at the close of the twentieth century drew on some preexisting genealogies or existed in uneasy tension with them. It goes without saying that these genealogies of the erotic have not survived unchanged through the ages. As part of larger discursive formations, they are as contingent and contested as other discourses and have been appropriated and reconstituted at different historical moments; for instance, contemporary conflations of middle-class respectability with the sexual modesty of women have been influenced by colonial and Victorian conceptions of gender and domesticity (see Bannerjee 1989; Chatterjee 1993; Tharu 1989). Hence, instead of either harking back to a static tradition of Indian erotics or assuming that transnational media caused the Westernization or homogenization of local discourses of the erotic, we might consider how local cultural forms are produced in articulation with the translocal and, conversely, how the transnational is itself reconfigured as it intersects with the local or indeed the national (Gupta and Ferguson 1997b).[18]

Given that there are such rich and heterogeneous genealogies of the erotic in India, what was so notable about erotics in transnational Hindi television of the late 1990s? First, as I posit in this chapter, late twentieth-century renditions of the erotic were deeply imbricated with the feverish commodity consumption precipitated by the expansion of transnational television, the liberalization of the Indian economy, and the introduction of globalized capital. Additionally, representations of the erotic in postcolonial India provoked discourses of the defense of Indian or national culture (and continue to do so). Notwithstanding older representational conventions, late twentieth-century renditions of the erotic were frequently associated with Westernization and were, therefore, deemed transgressive if not threatening to conceptions of Indian culture. Nowhere was this association stronger than with reference to women's erotic desire.

EROTIC AFFECTS

Shortly after commencing my fieldwork on this project, I realized that a study of erotics presented unique challenges to my ethnographic practice, in part because of the difficulty of talking about these topics with lower-middle-class and working-class women in urban India. For, although interviews and participant observation taught me a great deal about how transnational media shaped my informants' social relationships and everyday practices, the realm of the erotic remained elusive and, at many times, opaque; I felt that I was barely scratching the surface. I learned that I would need to go beyond the verbal, the discursive, and the visible if I were to learn anything at all about the relationship between commodity affect and erotics.

Initially, I assumed that the challenges I was facing were methodological in nature (Mankekar 2004). On later reflection I realized that they were conceptual because I had failed to understand that erotic affects are opaque to conventional ethnographic strategies of participant observation and interviewing. As Clough points out, affects are a "substrate of potential bodily responses, often autonomic responses, in excess of consciousness" (2007: 2). On the one hand, erotic affects are often experienced corporeally and, hence, blur the boundaries between the biological, the social, and the personal. On the other hand, erotic affects are also precognitive and preindividual; they foreground the dynamism and temporality of bodies. Yet if these bodies of entanglement (Clough 2007: 7) are dynamic, so too are their interfaces with commodities, which, I have noted above, also have their own affectivity. It bears repeating that affects, including erotics, are not presocial but entail the "reflux" back from conscious experience (Massumi 2002), as evidenced in the body's capacities to learn and remember.

I became acutely sensitive to the importance of respecting the silences, hesitations, and discursive detours that saturated my conversations with my informants. Rajeshwari Sunder Rajan has observed that the erotic is frequently "clandestine and covert" (1999: 7). I would add that erotic affects are not always decipherable through hermeneutic interpretations of discourse, language, or the everyday practices of individuals (see Zavella 1997). Yet erotic affects might inflect discourses, languages, and practices and enable them to affect us in particular ways by investing them with potency. My informants tended to refer to erotics in the idiom of power rather than pleasure and, more importantly, would do so through the use of metaphors, tropes, and gestures.[19] We thus had to learn to glean each other's thoughts and feelings indirectly rather than solicit or express them directly.[20] Many women I spoke with expressed their erotic longing via their yearnings for certain commodities. Thus, for instance, talking about a particular sari or lipstick would enable a young woman to express her dreams and anxieties regarding her forthcoming marriage; these were instances where the intersection of affective regimes of commodities and erotics were most visible.[21] On other occasions my informants expressed their attitudes and feelings about romance, desire, and conjugality while discussing television programs. But hardly ever did they explicitly talk about their experiences of erotics. In most instances, our discussions were veiled and took the surreptitious form of commentaries on what they saw on television. On my part, I was never inclined to examine how erotics had impacted the sexual behavior of my informants. I deemed it neither ethical nor culturally appropriate to interrogate my lower-middle-class and working-class informants about their attitudes toward sex or, worse, their sexual practices.

Many of the advertisements shown on television explicitly conjoined commodity affect with erotic affect. For instance, a popular television ad for Samsung air conditioners portrayed a group of women literally falling all over a male stripper. The ad starts by showing us a manicured finger turning on a CD player. As the music begins, the camera pans to show us a group of young, elegantly dressed women having a party. A handsome young man, wearing a black suit and with a large red bow tied around his chest, walks into the room and is greeted with raucous cheers from the women. They surround him in a circle and snap their fingers at him, as if to command him. He momentarily covers his face in a mock-feminine gesture of bashfulness. The camera then zooms in to provide us with close-

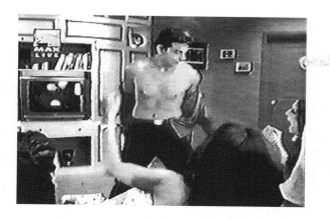

4.1 and 4.2. Ad for Samsung air conditioner.

ups of the expressions of some of the women who smile seductively, all the time continuing to snap their fingers at him. The next frame consists of the young man gyrating to the music, a red rose between his teeth, as he slowly starts taking off his jacket. We see more close-ups of the women, arousal written all over their faces as they watch him remove his tie and then his shirt (figure 4.1).

Although the mood is playful, there is no denying that the women are assertive, if not downright aggressive, in expressing their erotic interest in him. Some of the women start to fan themselves; the heat in the room has obviously gone up. The camera lingers longingly on the male stripper's upper body as he starts to unzip his trousers, all the time dancing to the music (figure 4.2). Our focus is then abruptly shifted to a thermometer, and we see the mercury rising rapidly to 52 degrees Celsius. The music screeches to a halt; the women faint because of the heat. The dancer reaches for a remote and turns on the air conditioner—a Samsung air conditioner.

Cut to a frame that shows us the mercury in the thermometer dropping as quickly as it had risen. The women wake up, and we are provided with a close-up of one of them languorously pushing back her long black hair. A male voice-over informs us in English: "Samsung Instachill. With a unique rotary compressor. The only AC to be effective at 52 degrees Celsius." The music resumes as the women rise to their feet, start converging on the dancer, and once again surround him in a circle. They push him to the floor in their excitement. Cut to a frame in which one of them has flung his trousers into the air. The ad ends with images of air conditioners in different sizes, as the voice-over proclaims: "Samsung Instachill. Especially conditioned for the Indian summer." Although this ad uses humor to mediate (and perhaps, to this extent, neutralize) its representation of women's erotic desires, its focus on women as agential subjects of erotic desire is unmistakable.

The co-implication of affective regimes surrounding commodities and erotics was also reinforced to me by some of my informants. Let us now revisit Omvati, whom we met in the introduction. As I noted earlier, Omvati had been deeply unsettled by her daughter-in-law Radha's desires for commodities which, in her mind, were unmistakably entangled with erotics. Omvati's concerns about her daughter-in-law were mediated by their respective positions in the politics of family. They were also mediated by these women's caste and class positions, and thus need to be situated in a broader sociohistorical context. The struggles, individual as well as collective, to realign caste and class hegemony became extremely volatile after conflicts erupted around the ill-fated Mandal Commission Bill of 1990 (Mankekar 1999a). Introduced by the political regime then in power to create quotas for "other backward castes" in government institutions, the bill stalled after upper and middle castes all over India violently resisted it. The consumption of commodities acquired a particularly potent affectivity in this explosive context. The possibility of acquiring consumer goods presented some lower-caste individuals and families with potential access to a middle-class lifestyle. Although acquiring the commodities advertised on television did not, by any means, enable my lower-caste informants to transcend their caste position, to a limited extent it enabled an apparent realignment of caste and class.

When I first met Omvati, her family was one of the few lower-caste ones in their working-class neighborhood. Her son Satish worked as a clerk in a government office, and Radha was employed as a salesperson in a government-run fabric store. Omvati was extremely proud that Satish was the first in their extended family to receive a college degree and, more significantly, to hold a government job. Radha also had a college degree, but Omvati's feelings about her were mediated by her ambivalence toward the fact that Radha was city-bred and "modern." For Omvati, as much as for Radha, modernity was indexed not only by Radha's college education but, equally, by her fashionable clothes. While Radha embraced what she perceived as the accoutrements of modernity, as noted earlier, Omvati was deeply unsettled by some of the slow but inexorable changes that she was witnessing, especially as they affected her position in the family. The entire family was acutely conscious of two harsh social facts: one, that their struggles to achieve middle-class status were only just beginning and, two, that their (largely) upper- and middle-caste neighbors viewed the family's aspirations to middle-class status and modernity with considerable resentment (compare with Geetha 1998: 323–24). Relations within the family, and the ways in which they navigated the complex and rapidly changing social landscape in which they were situated, were shaped as much by the intersection of caste and class as by patriarchal discourses of sexuality, conjugality, family, and kinship.

When I first met this family, Radha was in an advanced stage of pregnancy and Omvati was very happy at the prospect of having another grandchild. Yet Omvati often commented sarcastically on Radha's "obsession" with beautifying herself and on the couple going out together in the evenings to the movies or to the nearby bazaar.[22] She commented that Radha was "greedy" but, most of the time, I was not sure whether she was referring to Radha's greed for commodities or for her husband. Omvati frequently complained that "city girls" were different from girls in her village: city girls like Radha were independent, ambitious, and always hankered after "more." "They want too much," she said, "and that is dangerous."

As I described in the introduction, for Omvati, the dangers of erotic desire were conflated with women's desires for commodities. This theme was reiterated in my subsequent interactions with her: when Omvati complained to me about Radha's greed, she was talking about not merely Radha's desire to buy things but how she "always wanted more and more" from Satish. It was clear to me that Omvati resented Radha's closeness to Satish. This was confirmed when, on another occasion, Omvati repeated, "Girls these days, especially city girls, want everything." When I pushed her to clarify what she meant, she replied, "They want more things. They always want to have, have, have. But they also want a lot from their husbands." For Omvati, Radha was emblematic of the urban, modern Indian woman whose dangerous desires articulate the co-implication of erotic desire and the yearning for commodities.

One evening, Omvati and I returned from the nearby vegetable market, our arms laden with vegetables for that night's meal. When we walked into her home, we saw Radha sitting in front of the television, a cup of tea in her hand, enrapt in an ad for chiffon saris made by Vimal. The ad showed a beautiful, well-groomed young woman draping a chiffon sari on her body and then holding one edge of it against the side of her face, caressing her cheek with its soft folds. As we watched from the door, Radha put down her cup of tea and held her hand to her cheek, as if to mirror the sensuous gesture made by the visibly upper-class woman on the screen. Omvati turned to me instantly, pointing toward Radha with her chin as if to say, see, this is what I mean: she always wants more and more; her desires are insatiable. Acutely embarrassed by the voyeuristic position in which I found myself, I pretended that I had not noticed anything— neither Radha's sensuous gesture nor Omvati's accusatory gesture to me. Yet so regnant was that scene of the convergence of commodity affect and erotics that it has stayed with me all these years.

Radha reinforced to me how desire is affective in terms of how it animates sociality (compare Stewart 2007). As Deleuze (1997: 189) argues, desire does not imply a lack; instead, desire is the *agencement* of heterogeneous elements that function; it is process as opposed to structure or genesis; it is affect as opposed to sentiment. Omvati was not the only person among my informants to point to the mutual imbrication of desire, erotic affects, and commodity affect. Sunita, a young, lower-middle-class woman, compared her "feelings" for commodities with love. Sunita, who was unmarried, rarely went shopping but enjoyed watching ads on television and going to the nearby market to window shop. One day I asked how she felt about looking at ads and shop windows even when she knew she could not afford to buy the commodities being advertised. She responded that her longing for these goods was like unrequited love. Using words that drew upon the lexicon of romantic Hindi films to impute erotic desire, she said, "It is like when you love someone [jab kissise mohabbat ho jati hai] and they don't love you back. You don't stop loving that person. You get happiness from looking at them and from knowing they are there. It is like that. It is nice to look at these new things that have come into the market. We can't afford them. We may never be able to afford them. But who knows? And in any case, what is wrong in wondering?"

According to Slavoj Žižek, fantasy provides the coordinates or frame for desire: "Through fantasy we learn to desire" (1989: 118). Through wondering or (in my terms) fantasizing, Sunita learned to desire. The fantasies of women like Sunita were engendered not just by their desires to acquire commodities but, perhaps more sharply, by their experiences of longing and deprivation. At the same time, women like Radha and Sunita seemed to get a bittersweet pleasure from their desire for commodities, from the desire to desire (Schein 1999: 366, 369; see Žižek 1989 on the reflexivity of desire). There seemed to be a pleasure in imagining, in fantasizing about the kinds of lives that might be possible if one owned these commodities. This pleasure was like the bittersweet pleasure of falling in love, even when one knew that the love was unrequited.

In the 1990s, state-endorsed discourses of consumerism and mass-mediated incitements to desire commodities resulted in the emergence of a new "brand" of woman (Sunder Rajan 1999). John argues that a new form of subjectivity was produced by "the need to recruit the new middle class woman as a 'consuming subject' of local/global products in a vastly expanded market, . . . a recruitment that cannot take place without her sexualization as an actively desiring subject" (1998: 382). As much as class and caste, discourses of gender and sexuality were central to the constitution of my working-class and lower-middle-class informants as consuming subjects, underscoring the inextricable entanglement of class, caste, gender, and erotics. Most of the men and women I worked with frequently expressed aspirations to upward mobility into the middle class in terms of a greater preoccupation with female modesty and respectability and, in many cases, with an increased surveillance of women's sexuality (see also Mankekar 1999a). These anxieties were heightened in the case of many of my lower-caste informants who, surrounded as they were by upper-caste neighbors, felt particularly subject to their neighbors' surveillance. They frequently expressed their concerns about the purity of "their" women's sexuality in terms of anxieties about the desires and behavior of their young daughters and daughters-in-law. In some cases, they also expressed this concern in terms of worries about young sons.

Let me turn to the example of Prabhakar, a lower-caste man who lived in a lower-middle-class neighborhood in West Delhi with his wife, who was a schoolteacher, and their son. Prabhakar migrated from Tamil Nadu after finishing high school and attended two years of college. One of his biggest regrets was that he had been unable to study further because of financial problems; this, he believed, had hampered his ability to "improve the conditions" of his and his family's life. He and his wife were extremely anxious about how, at the same time that his family was gradually achieving upward mobility, they had less and less control over the behavior of their college student son. Their son, on the other hand, was supremely self-confident and told me on several occasions that he was only going to college to allay his parents' anxieties. He insisted that "social knowledge and not book knowledge" would help him succeed in life. He wished to start his own business and believed that "knowing the right people, being in the right set [original in English], knowing how to talk and how to dress" was what was important. An attractive young man, dressed in the latest fashion of an MTV VJ, he had a reputation in the neighborhood for being quite the ladies' man. Predictably, this reputation filled him with pride. Equally predictably, it caused a great deal of concern to his parents. One day his father confided to me, "My son roams around in the market with his buddies all evening. . . . He often comes home late at night. God knows what he does there; it's not as if he is always buying things there. But it is bad for his character to hang around there all the time. You should see the clothes that he wears and how he reeks of cologne. He is always hanging around in the market. It puts ideas into his head. One of our neighbors saw him with a girl. I hope he never does anything that will bring shame to our family."

Prabhakar and his son had very different opinions as to what would enable him to ascend the ladder of caste and class. While Prabhakar believed that education was the key to upward mobility, his son depended on what he called "social knowledge," which, for him, consisted of not only having the right contacts but also being able to display the outward markers of being "in the right set" by making certain consumerist lifestyle choices such as wearing the right clothes. While this might be indicative of a generational shift occurring in the aftermath of economic liberalization, we also need to attend to Prabhakar's implicit fears about how commodities brought about a change not only in people's appearance but also in their very bodies and desires, and their abilities to affect and be affected. Prabhakar's son literally embodied the conjunction of affective regimes surrounding commodities and erotics as he swaggered through the erotically charged spaces of the market, his perfumed, newly masculinized body raising the anxieties of his parents and upper-caste neighbors about what he might do next. As in Omvati's worries about Radha's "wanting more," the pleasure of being in the market, and presumably of gazing upon the commodities prominently displayed there, is explicitly linked with erotic pleasure: Who knows what ideas come into a young man's head as he roams the (deceptively) anonymous and seductively sensuous spaces of the market? And worse, what if he acts on these ideas and does something that will shame his lower-caste and precariously lower-middle-class family?

Thus, although most of the other examples in this chapter are about women, the most casual observations of households and markets in urban India attest to the fact that men shared equally, if not more, in these longings for commodities. Almost all the men I met in the course of my fieldwork aspired to own at least some of the commodities advertised on television, such as DVD players, refrigerators, automobiles, and, particularly in the case of younger men, fashionable clothes. Several spoke of how, although in the past they had been uninterested (or less interested) in shopping, in recent years, they had become curious about the objects advertised on television. They all insisted that, before the advent of television commercials, they had had little idea of what was available in the markets. Significantly, apart from some concerns about how consumerism was preventing families from saving money, there did not seem to be a moralistic discourse about how men's consumer habits might be undermining so-called Indian culture or tradition. In contrast, women's desires for commodities were more likely to be perceived as a threat to the moral (and not just financial) welfare of the family and, therefore, as symptomatic of an attrition of traditional Indian values under the onslaught of transnational media. Even those men who coveted high-end commodities like automobiles or scooters would complain to me, without the least bit of irony or self-consciousness, of how the extravagant habits of their wives and daughters were not only driving them to bankruptcy but, more pertinent to my argument here, also encouraging them to adopt "Western" or "foreign" lifestyles and aspirations and therefore threatening to erode Indian tradition.[23]

Thus, commodities and the yearnings they evoked were not simply reflective or expressive of individual and collective fantasies but, as distinct affective regimes, were productive of gendered subjectivities. These affective regimes were also generated by changes in programming inaugurated by transnational Hindi television networks, many of which focused on the domain of the intimate.

The Intimacy of Unsettlement

Even as desire constitutes the social field, it simultaneously unsettles it to produce what Deleuze describes as "a whirl, a buckle, a recoding" (1997: 186, 189). In what follows, I point to instances where the articulation of commodity affect and erotics were profoundly disconcerting to my informants and, more broadly, threatened to unsettle dominant discourses of gender, intimacy, and Indianness. Transnational Hindi television's role in yoking the affective regimes surrounding erotics and commodities extended beyond advertisements to include a range of other programs, such as talk shows, soap operas, and MTV-inspired music programs.

Several factors shaped the production of erotics on transnational Hindi television in the late 1990s. I noted above that, initially, transnational networks beamed programs produced in the United States, the United Kingdom, and Australia (these programs included soaps like *Santa Barbara* and *Neighbors*, news programs, and talk shows like *Oprah*). Before long the owners of these networks realized that, once the novelty of watching imported programs wore off, Indian audiences would demand programs that were more familiar to them in their content and, equally importantly, their modes of address, narrative strategies, and aesthetic codes. As the ratings of some of these imported shows began to plummet, the chief executives of transnational networks such as STAR and Sony Entertainment Television realized that, in order to retain the attention of viewers in the South Asian subcontinent and its diasporas, they would need to "Indianize" their programming; slowly but surely they put local talent in charge of producing programs targeting, and creating, Indian audiences.

Furthermore, for many of my informants imported programs raised the specter of cultural contamination through the alleged corrosion of Indian culture. I return to this theme later in this chapter, but for now let me note that the lower-middle-class men and women with whom I worked, as much as nationalist elites, responded to transnational television with a mixture of excitement and anxiety, deeming it a threat to the purity of national culture and to national sovereignty. Most of my informants were very concerned that imported programs and channels such as *The Young and the Restless* and MTV would erode or contaminate Indian culture. Imported programs such as the *Oprah Winfrey Show* or *The Bold and the Beautiful* inspired the production of "indigenous" programs of the same genre, which somewhat allayed fears about Westernization or Americanization. Many of the new programs adopted some of the generic characteristics of the imports, so that there were "Indianized" versions of talk shows, game shows, soap operas, made-for-television movies and miniseries, and music videos. These programs, however, were by no means simple imitations of their Western counterparts; instead, they were hybrid productions that incorporated "Indian" themes and discourses into their narrative frameworks and deployed a diverse range of representational codes and aesthetic conventions.

As Raju and many of my other informants observed, there was a marked shift in television programming from an earlier emphasis on nationalist themes and "social messages" (the mainstay of state-owned television from the mid-1980s to the early 1990s; see Mankekar 1999b). Television was now preoccupied with the intimate.[24] For several of my informants, these representations threatened to undo, or at least unsettle, the delicate balance (what some of my Hindi-speaking informants termed *maryada* or appropriate rules of conduct) so essential to maintaining the stability of the family and, ultimately, the authenticity and purity of Indian culture. The affective charge of these representations of intimacy threatened to undo and reconstitute assumptions about gender, marriage, family, and relationships that they had either taken for granted or had felt were precarious to begin with. For instance, many of the serials that focused on relations of intimacy rendered problematic the delicate balance between conjugality and duty toward the extended family. While these serials had my informants riveted, they were also extremely disconcerting for many of them.

The new preoccupation with the intimate stemmed in part from representations of the erotic that were unprecedented on Indian television (see John 1998: 368). In contrast to earlier Hindi television shows, these programs displayed a fascination with intimate relationships—particularly marital, premarital, and extramarital relationships—and contained new and varied representations of erotics (explicit as well as implicit). These programs included soap operas (e.g., *Tara* [1993–1997], *Shanti* [1994], and *Hasratein* [1995]), sitcoms, talk shows (e.g., *Purush Kshetra* [Men's World, 1994] and *The Priya Tendulkar Show* [1994]), made-for-television films and miniseries, music programs (many of which were based on songs from Indian films), "Indianized" versions of MTV, and television advertisements telecast on transnational networks but produced specifically for audiences in South Asia and its diasporas. Beginning in the mid-1990s and accelerating during the closing years of the decade, the emphasis on the intimate and the erotic was strongest in talk shows (which proliferated after the advent of transnational television), soap operas, MTV-influenced music videos, and television advertisements.

Anjali Monteiro of the Tata Institute of Social Sciences in Mumbai linked this new focus on intimacy in television programming with emerging notions of selfhood: "Traditionally, the distinction between individual identity and group identity was not so sharp. Today there is an emphasis on molding and presenting oneself. The self is something you must work on and talk shows provide an opportunity to look at yourself through others' experiences" (from Chandra 1995: 103). Other theorists have also linked a preoccupation with intimacy to the emergence of bourgeois forms of selfhood (for example, Michel Foucault's [1980] analysis of the history of sexuality and the constitution of the modern subject). Although I hesitate to generalize that the preoccupation with intimacy and erotics in Hindi television programs of the late 1990s heralds the birth of new subjectivities, representations of sexuality and in particular erotics indeed seem to have served as "a prime connecting point between body, self-identity and social norms" (Giddens 1992: 14).

For many of my informants, the affective charge of these representations of intimacy seemed to destabilize prevalent assumptions about intimacy and thus intensified the temporality of uncertainty and unpredictability in their lives and family relations. Unsettlement, quite literally, came home to them. The eroticization of intimacy on transnational Hindi networks was particularly disconcerting for these informants because, despite the sometimes explicit display of erotics in song sequences, they tended to be subordinated to and subsumed under romance in Hindi films of the 1990s (see Dwyer 2000).[25] For although Hindi films have always provided sites for public representations of erotics, the content and modalities on transnational Hindi television programs of the late 1990s were qualitatively different. In Hindi films of that time, erotic desire outside romance was explicitly condemned and was restricted largely to villains and vamps. In contrast, television programs in the late 1990s represented erotic desire in a relatively open-ended manner. Furthermore, the erotic was a central and explicit focus of many television programs.

This was particularly true of talk shows. For instance, hosts, panelists, and live audiences of talk shows like *Purush Kshetra* would analyze, in considerable detail and with unabashed candor, different aspects of male sexuality (ranging from impotence to men's perspectives on polygyny) and male and female sexual desires. For instance, one controversial episode examined the following question: Why do men visit prostitutes? The episode presented a panel of two sex worker, a man who visited a sex worker and eventually married her, a psychologist, and a social worker. The episode's host, celebrated Hindi stage and film actor Kiron Kher, moderated the discussion and asked questions about the sexual and psychological needs that men fulfilled by going to sex worker, while audience members debated whether men's needs could ever be completely fulfilled within the confines of marriage. For example, one of the sex worker on the panel spoke of how some of her clients came to her because their wives would not do "certain things" with them, thus making it "necessary" for them to seek sexual satisfaction elsewhere, at which point Kher brought up the question of women's unfulfilled sexual desires and the avenues available to them to seek sexual fulfillment. Although, in its final few moments, the episode acquired a somewhat moralistic tone with the social worker and the host speaking about the "dirty needs" of men who exploit women, this episode was remarkable in that its participants discussed questions of sexuality, erotic desire, and marriage with unprecedented candor.

Similarly, Indipop music videos frequently focused on women's erotic desires. One popular Indipop music video, *Deewane To Deewane Hain* (Shweta Shetty, Magnasound), has the singer complaining about the number of men who want to have sex with her. In a husky voice pulsating with erotic desire, she humorously describes how, despite her turning them away, these "madmen" persist in their desire for her (deewane deewane hi rahenge). She sings of how her beauty has made it impossible for her to leave her house for fear of causing a sensation. This is no passive, self-effacing beauty; she alternately titillates and rejects her suitors' advances. There is nothing coy or virginal about her; her clothing, demeanor, and voice are all strident with erotic desire. She turns down her lovers' amorous advances not to protect her virtue but because she is weary of their pursuit. Her body language, as she gyrates sensuously to the music, and her expressions, as she alternately arches her eyebrows in mock scorn, waves her hands as if to brush off their attentions, or shrugs her shoulders as if to dismiss their ardor, emphasize that she wants to be in control of when (not if) she will have sex with them. One frame features her tickling one of the men seductively, sensuously, with a feather. Another places her in the foreground complaining about madmen who will not leave her alone; in the background, we see another man lying exhausted on a bed. Throughout, she pokes fun at her suitors and at one point goes so far as to claim that their desire for her has robbed them of their identities. They are so pathetic, she claims, that they have stayed unmarried because they are mad with desire for her.

As in other music videos (and, for that matter, Hindi film songs), the heroine changes her clothes frequently during the song, switching back and forth between leather boots and tights and attire featured in the erotic sculptures of Hindu temples. The video contains several close-ups of the men pursuing her, with the camera lingering voyeuristically (but also parodically) on their bare, buffed upper bodies. A series of frames focuses on one of the men vainly flexing his muscles. These scenes target not just women in the audience but, through the evocation of homoerotic desire, men as well.

The closing frames of this video are particularly significant: tired of turning away the madmen who are trying desperately to woo her, our heroine stands outside her boudoir inviting each of them in. As soon as the last man has entered the room, she locks the door from outside. The camera immediately takes us inside. We see the men bump into each other and

4.3. *Deewane To Deewane Hain* music video.

discover that they have been conned into believing that they would be able to make love to her (figure 4.3). They do not stay disappointed for too long, however, when they discover an erotic interest in each other. We next see them enter into a collective, unmistakably sexual embrace. The video ends with our heroine standing outside the room, smiling smugly, knowingly. She has been able to shake them off and deflect their erotic interest in her onto each other.

Like many Bollywood heroines, the protagonist of *Deewane To Deewane Hain* is represented as an eroticized subject. But unlike the heroines of the time, many of whom were coy about their erotic desires, this woman derives obvious pleasure from her sexual attractiveness and her sexuality. In this music video and in countless others like it, women are no longer simply objects of male fantasy but are represented as active and assertive erotic subjects who choose if, when, and with whom to pursue their desires. Furthermore, while most representations of erotics in transnational Hindi television programs reinscribe it in heteronormative terms, some productions like *Deewane To Deewane Hain* also contain an explicitly homoerotic content, and a few others portray men and women cross-dressing and/or displaying homoerotic desire.

As several of my informants pointed out to me, the struggles and dilemmas of women in the Hindi soap operas of the late 1990s contrasted sharply with those of the 1980s. While in earlier Hindi television serials women struggled to negotiate their commitments to the family and nation (as in *Rajani* [Doordarshan]), the heroines of the late 1990s confronted entirely different dilemmas and conflicts. Even though most Hindi soap operas of the late 1990s continued to depict women in conservative terms (that is, as sexually modest, dutiful toward their families, and so on), there were several that, because of their foregrounding of women's erotic desires, attracted tremendous attention. Even as they were riveted by these new television serials, most of my informants were also extremely disturbed by how they represented women and their erotic desires. Serials like *Tara* or *Shanti*, which drew huge ratings and sparked a new trend, showed women actively, sometimes aggressively, pursuing erotic pleasure and facing the social and emotional consequences of doing so. Indeed, when I began fieldwork on this project, I would sometimes attempt to set the ball rolling by asking viewers what they thought were some of the major differences between the programs that they used to watch in the 1980s and those telecast after the introduction of transnational satellite networks. An overwhelming majority would respond that the most striking change was in the portrayal of women.

One middle-class informant succinctly summarized this contrast between the soap operas of the 1980s and 1990s as "the change from *Rajani* to *Tara*." This woman was pointing to the contrasts in the preoccupations, personalities, and trajectories of the television heroines who had become household names in the 1980s and 1990s, respectively. Rajani was the protagonist of a Hindi serial telecast in the late 1980s on Doordarshan before the advent of transnational satellite television. Rajani was a housewife who committed her energies to correcting "social ills" (e.g., the corruption of bureaucrats, domestic violence, and so on) while remaining a dutiful wife and mother (see Mankekar [1999a] for an extensive analysis of *Rajani*). Tara was the heroine of a serial telecast in the early 1990s, shortly after Zee TV was introduced in India. This serial pioneered a new genre of narratives that dwelled on the intimate lives of modern, urban (frequently upper-middle-class and upper-class) Indian women. Its heroine and some others who followed in her wake were independent, led unconventional lives, were assertive in their pursuit of erotic desire, and had premarital or extramarital affairs. For instance, Svetlana, of the immensely popular *Swabhimaan* (1995–1997), was the mistress of a wealthy industrialist and struggled to maintain her dignity and power. Serials such as *Dard* (Zee TV, 1993–1994) and *Kora Kagaz* (STAR TV, 1998–1999) portrayed strong women who were emotionally and sexually frustrated in their marriages and turned to younger men for satisfaction and comfort. As I learned from my ethnographic observations, the portrayals of Tara and Svetlana were ambivalent, yet they were generally perceived sympathetically, as heroines who struggled courageously to seek fulfillment.

Yet these serials seemed to be particularly disconcerting to my informants because mainstream Hindi cinema at the time was, by and large, much more conventional in its portrayal of relations of intimacy in general and women's erotic desire in particular. Rachel Dwyer has pointed out that the family remains central in Bollywood films: "In many romances, the problem facing the family is the incorporation of erotic love into the family's other relationships" (2000: 139). Thus, for instance, most mainstream Bollywood films of the 1990s (e.g., *Hum Aapke Hain Kaun*, 1994; *Dilwale Dulhaniya Le Jayenge* [The lover carries away the bride, 1995; see chapter 2 for a detailed analysis of this film]; and *Kabhi Khushi Kabhie Gham*, 2001) portray a consistent preoccupation with the articulation of erotic desire with familial obligations and duties.[26] In contrast, some of the Hindi television programs of the mid- and late 1990s constructed a more complex discursive terrain in which erotic desire was at once foregrounded and held in tension with familial obligation. Erotic desire was variably positioned vis-à-vis conjugality, and these representations in turn had consequences for the portrayal of the family.[27]

Indeed, the visibility of conjugality increased in transnational Hindi television programs of the late 1990s. This heightened visibility articulated with the tension that many of my informants experienced between conjugal desire and obligations to the extended family (compare John 1998) and was, for this reason, experienced as profoundly unsettling.[28] Several of my informants spoke explicitly of how the ostensibly new emphasis on the married couple threatened to tear the extended family asunder. About two-thirds of the families I worked with consisted of at least two generations of people living together. All of these multigenerational families were patrilocal, with sons and daughters-in-law (and grandchildren, if any) living with the husbands' families. Many older women spoke at great length about how young women had to realize that they "marry a family, not just a man" and hence had to keep their conjugal life "in perspective." One older woman said forcefully, "Young women have to attend to an appropriate code of conduct [*maryada*] in balancing their attachment to their husbands with their duties to the larger family," thus emphasizing that the marital relationship could not be allowed to weaken the larger family unit.[29] Another woman said to me, "When balance is lost everything becomes messed up, unpredictable, uncertain. *Maryada* is about maintaining a delicate balance which is now getting messed up." Many of my informants frequently articulated this sense of everything getting "messed up" and becoming out of balance when they spoke of the new focus on intimacy on television. Recall Omvati's resentment of the close bond between her son and daughter-in-law, which was ostensibly based on the vitality of their marital relationship. The younger women I spoke with varied in their opinions: while some claimed that the extended family was sacrosanct because it was an integral part of their "culture," others felt that their primary relationship was with their husbands and hence chafed under the restrictions of living with their in-laws.

Erotic desire on television, however, did not relate only to the conjugal relationship. In a hegemonic context in which erotic desire is presumably contained within the confines of heterosexual marriage, representations of erotic desire outside or before marriage were particularly unsettling for my informants. In many Hindi serials and talk shows, women engaged in premarital and extramarital affairs, had illegitimate children, seduced younger men, and defied parental restrictions by pursuing erotic desire. Unlike representations of erotically assertive women in mainstream Bollywood films of the time, these characters were not hyper-Westernized vamps but modern Indian women.[30] For instance, Savitri, the heroine of a popular television serial, *Hasratein*, was depicted as a modern woman who is a partner in a public relations company. Like soap operas all over the world, *Hasratein*'s plot is convoluted and virtually impossible to summarize, but the central story line focuses on the heroine's fifteen-year relationship with a man who is married and has another family. Savitri, or Savi, as she is known in the serial, and her lover live together and have a child. A successful, upper-middle-class professional, she is supremely self-confident as she manages to rise in her career.

I expected my lower-middle-class and working-class informants to disapprove of Savi, and indeed many did. Yet several of them insisted that she remained quintessentially Indian in her devotion to her children and her loyalty to her lover and his parents.[31] In fact, as many of them argued, she provided the links between him and his parents and his other children, and pointed to a crucial juncture in the serial when Savi reminds her lover's father that she is the reason why her lover has maintained his ties with his other family, insisting that this proves that she is not a "bad woman." Despite the fact that Savi is represented as "the other woman," my informants were sympathetic to her; they insisted that until the end, when the narrative reached its denouement, she maintained a cordial relationship with his parents and treated them with the courtesy and respect a traditional daughter-in-law is supposed to extend to her in-laws.

Yet, as the serial draws to a close, Savi is penalized for pushing the boundaries of conventional Indian womanhood. *Hasratein* ends on a highly ambivalent note. Savi's lover is injured in a car accident and loses his memory. His wife and parents take care of him and convince him that they are his (primary) family. He remembers only fragments of his life with

Savi and cannot recognize their daughter. At the same time, he misses Savi and longs for her. When he fails to regain his health and memory, his wife decides to take him abroad for treatment. In the last episode, his wife permits Savi to bid him goodbye. In the end, Savi and her daughter are left alone. Savi is clearly punished for pursuing erotic desire—and with a married man, at that. Yet she is represented with tremendous sympathy. She is always depicted as elegantly yet modestly dressed (frequently in "traditional" Indian clothes); she is soft-spoken and performs all the conventional duties of a wife and mother; and she is dignified and respectful but does not hesitate to fight for her rights. This is in sharp contrast to her lover, who is depicted as loving but confused and weak-willed; after his accident, he is reduced to utter dependency on his wife and parents. He can no longer attend to the business that he and Savi set up because of his amnesia and, in fact, appears incoherent in most of the closing episode.

Savi's portrayal is significant for several reasons. As noted above, her pursuit of erotic desire in this serial is not represented without ambivalence (after all, she does suffer for her transgressions); nevertheless, she is represented as a mature and dignified woman (rather than as immature or promiscuous). Second, in narratives such as *Hasratein*, the pursuit of erotic desire becomes the hallmark of a particular kind of woman: upper class, usually professional, yet "Indian" in her loyalty to her family and to other "traditional" customs and conventions. Although *Hasratein* was by no means the norm, this serial (along with others such as *Tara*, *Shanti*, and *Swabhimaan*) suggests how the pursuit of erotic desire pushes at the boundaries of, and unsettles, conventional assumptions about Indian Womanhood (Mankekar 1999b).

Women viewers' reactions to these representations of eroticized intimacy spoke volumes—not of their own erotic desires per se, but of the imbrication of erotics with shifting configurations of gender, class, and nation occurring in late twentieth-century India. In many cases, these reconfigurations were refracted by class. Many of the lower-middle-class and working-class women I worked with were quick to point out that most of the characters pursuing erotic pleasure on television were upper-middle class or upper class, with successful careers and financial independence. One lower-middle-class woman spoke of how upper-class women inhabited a "different world" in which the "rules for behavior and for conducting relationships" were fundamentally different from those that regulated her world. Most of the women I interviewed insisted that these upper-class women had the means to change their lives by having relationships with whomever they pleased. For such viewers, these women's pursuit of erotic pleasure was explicitly tied to their class positions, specifically their upward mobility and financial independence. As one lower-middle-class woman pointed out to me, the sexual freedom that women such as Tara and Svetlana enjoyed was enabled by their financial independence: "If they had to wait for their men to support them, they wouldn't be able to live like this," she remarked. For many of my lower-middle-class and middle-class informants, upper-class women were emblematic of the influence of Western promiscuity, and they based their opinions of "rich" women primarily on what they saw on television. One upper-caste, lower-middle-class woman suggested that when upward mobility and financial independence were not "anchored" in a "fundamental understanding of our culture, of what it means to be Indian, and what it means for a woman to obey her elders, be loyal to her family, and put her family first," chaos results.

To sum up, unlike programs on state-run television during the 1980s, programs on transnational Hindi television in the late 1990s revealed an overwhelming preoccupation with erotic desire in intimate relationships. The erotics surrounding these representations of intimacy were deeply unsettling for my informants, and indexed an unsettlement of hegemonic notions of Indianness and Indian culture. Some of these programs portrayed women who were not only themselves eroticized but who also actively pursued erotic pleasure in their lives. The erotic agency of these women was mediated and circumscribed in various ways. In some cases, even though they pursued erotic pleasure, they ostensibly retained their Indianness (defined, by many of my informants, in terms of their devotion to their families). Others were represented as upper-class and Westernized women who seemed to embody a threat to the purported purity of Indian culture; these portrayals articulated with the anxieties of my lower-middle-class and middle-class informants who were concerned about how their own identities and ways of life might be unsettled by the changes they observed around them.[32] Some of my informants responded to these unsettling representations of eroticized intimacy by increasing their surveillance of their family members and neighbors; still others responded by aligning themselves with Hindu nationalist and exclusionary discourses of cultural purity and Indianness.

For these informants in New Delhi, the erotic affects generated and circulated by transnational Hindi television constituted a force field of power, pleasure, and danger through their articulation with desires and anxieties pertaining to upward mobility, class, modernity, and tradition.

At stake in these desires and anxieties was not only the unsettlement and reconfiguration of hierarchies of gender, caste, and class within India but also the very definition of Indian culture.

Renegotiating Indianness

The past several decades have been characterized by an unproductive schism in analyses of cultural changes following the liberalization of the Indian economy and the proliferation of transnational media (frequently glossed as globalization) either lauded as intrinsically emancipatory and empowering, or condemned as unleashing sweeping transformations detrimental to the life chances of millions of Indians and to national culture: as I argue in the coda to this book, specific assumptions about temporality and, indeed, culture undergird these conceptions of cultural change. For now, suffice to say that, instead of assuming that transnational television radically transformed India or Indian culture, I have drawn on my informants' practices, experiences, and discourses to examine how it might have participated in the reshaping of affective regimes and in the renegotiation, and hence the unsettlement, of prevalent conceptions of India and Indianness. As I have stressed throughout this chapter, the cultural shifts surrounding transnational Hindi television in the late 1990s did not emerge in a historical or discursive vacuum: state-controlled television had already begun to reconstitute conceptions of national belonging at least a decade prior, and commodity consumption was well under way with the production of the so-called national audience in the 1980s (Mankekar 1999a). Similarly, against assumptions that transnational television introduced unprecedented or new erotic affects into Indian public culture, I have insisted that the erotic recharging of the Indian public sphere both drew on and diverged from previous (including premodern and early modern) aesthetic and performative genres.

Furthermore, it is inaccurate to extrapolate that all programs telecast on transnational Hindi television foregrounded the erotic. Nor is it true that the trend that began in the mid-1990s and accelerated through the late 1990s of portraying the lives and trials of women as agential subjects of erotic desire has continued unabated. Although transnational Hindi television continues to play a central role in the generation and circulation of erotic affects, the following decades also saw a profusion of dramatic serials that valorize "family values," in particular, the virtues of the so-called traditional extended family—as in the *saas bahu* or "mother-in-law–daughter-in-law" genre of Hindi serials that became so ubiquitous in the early years of the twenty-first century.[33] Yet, far from believing that they have replaced or displaced the emphasis on erotics analyzed here, I interpret these markedly conservative serials and their popularity as a backlash against them and, more significantly, as articulations of ongoing debates about the alleged globalization of Indian culture ushered in by the accelerated traffic of texts, images, and commodities. Indeed, I would insist that portrayals of erotics and the more recent valorizations of family values (which, in turn, ostensibly foreground the uniqueness of Indian culture) might be two sides of the same coin. That is, they are part of the redrawing of the boundaries between India and the West provoked by the continuing unsettlement of conceptions of India and Indianness.

The introduction of commercial television in the late 1980s and transnational networks in the 1990s enabled the convergence of erotics and commodity affects in the spaces of everyday life for my informants in New Delhi. By the late 1990s and early years of the twenty-first century, these affective regimes had become inseparably entangled with struggles around gender, caste, class, and nation. Transnational Hindi television generated and circulated affective fields surrounding erotics and commodities that shaped my working-class and lower-middle-class informants' aspirations to upward mobility, their conceptions of erotics and intimacy and, on a different register, the unsettlement and reconstitution of definitions of India and Indianness.

It is crucial that we remind ourselves of the temporality of affects. In the case of commodity affect, I was witness to the entwining of desire and deprivation for many of the men and women I came to know during my fieldwork. Certainly, this combination of desire and deprivation was built into the very structure of commodity capitalism and the specific forms that it acquired in late twentieth-century India. For my working-class and lower-middle-class informants, the affects surrounding commodities, including the desire to desire, were not yearnings for instant gratification (compare Mazzarella 2003a). Instead, for these informants, many of whom could not afford to possess the commodities they longed for, the temporality of commodity affect was based on the brute reality that, for them, gratification would be deferred—in some cases, indefinitely. Yet there was a pleasure in the desire to desire, even if (or perhaps because) it articulated with a sense of deprivation. At the same time, as noted above, several informants spoke eloquently of how the commodities they now saw in markets, on billboards, and on television screens introduced them to "what life could be like": these informants reinforced to me that commodity affect entails potentiality and modes of becoming.

Indeed, the affects surrounding commodities are always emergent rather than predictable, and it is this very aspect of emergence that makes commodity affects both potent and unsettling. Put another way, the affectivity of commodities is never predetermined, but is contingent on circuits of production, circulation, and consumption. For this reason, commodity affect is best understood in terms of potentiality rather than a teleological fixing of meanings, and it is for this reason that commodity affect exceeds symbolization. Thus, for example, for a lower-caste man the commodity affects surrounding a refrigerator evoke possible (if elusive) access to upward mobility in terms of his class position, a potentiality that is not insignificant in contexts where caste and class have been so closely aligned. For his upper-caste neighbor, these very affects might be deeply unsettling precisely because they potentially subvert dominant assumptions about caste hierarchy, social status, and economic power. In another instance, the haptic visuality of a television advertisement for a chiffon sari, the feel of the sari on the eyes (and, hence, on the skin), might offer a lower-middle-class woman like Radha a sense of what her life could be like if she acquired the luxuries that upper-class women took for granted. Her mother-in-law, on the other hand, might interpret her lust for the chiffon sari as yet another index of the insatiability of her appetites not just for luxury but also for sensuality and erotic pleasure.

There were other instances where the convergence of erotics and commodity affect was more overt. A series of print ads for a condom called KS (named after the Kamasutra) was emblematic of this phenomenon and thus acquired iconic status. Released in the early 1990s, these controversial and popular ads portrayed a young, scantily clad heterosexual couple engaging in foreplay. In almost all the ads, our eyes are drawn to the woman, who is depicted in near-orgasmic ecstasy. The KS ads reinscribed orientalist discourses about the Kamasutra in their attempt to invoke a purportedly Indian attitude toward sex (see Mazzarella [2003a] for a detailed discussion of the production of these advertisements; see also Rajagopal [1999a]). These ads contrasted with earlier ads for condoms in important ways. While previous ads emphasized family planning, KS focused unequivocally, if not solely, on erotic pleasure. The second striking feature of the KS ads was that, while they depicted the sexual pleasure of the couple, they also visually foregrounded the erotic desires and pleasures of the woman. As Mazzarella (2003a: 64) has pointed out, this ad generated a desire for the brand so that KS was constructed both as commodity image and as a commodity that was sexualized; desire for the brand was construed as part of the pleasures of anticipating and performing sexual intercourse.

Hindi talk shows, films, and soap operas beamed via transnational networks played a central role in introducing my informants in New Delhi to consumerist lifestyles. These lifestyles entailed the desire for and potential acquisition of commodities such as fashionable clothes, processed foods, cosmetics, automobiles (or, at the very least, scooters), and home appliances such as mixer-grinders, televisions and DVD players, refrigerators, cooking ranges, and so on. Many of my informants were excited about the potentialities offered by commodities, even when most of these commodities were out of their reach. Yet most were also extremely anxious about how these new desires would unsettle their ways of life, their family relationships, the social spaces they navigated on a daily basis, and their intimate lives. According to several of my informants, acquiring a consumerist lifestyle enabled one to display visible signifiers of modernity but, they argued, retaining "traditional" values was crucially important. As Vishnu, who was lower caste and lower-middle class, argued, buying commodities could "help one become modern, have a modern lifestyle, yet hold on to traditional [Indian] values." When I asked him to clarify what he meant by "traditional values," he promptly replied, "Our family, our personal relationships, our culture . . . all the things that make us Indian."

As I have stressed throughout this chapter, my working-class and lower-middle-class informants interpreted the conjunction of erotics and commodity affect in heterogeneous, sometimes contradictory, ways. Nevertheless, a common thread that wove through most of my informants' discourses was the perception that the proliferation of commodity affect and erotics via transnational Hindi television threatened the purported purity of Indian culture.[34] In these circumstances, many of them believed, Indian culture had to be preserved and protected from the onslaught of the global and "the Western." Railing against the proliferation of commodity affect and erotics on television, one of my lower-middle-class informants insisted that it fell to the middle classes to protect their culture and their values (apni sabhyata, apne sanskar ki raksha madhya varg ke logon ko hi karni hai). Like several other informants, this woman claimed that most "rich people," the upper classes, had been "contaminated" by Westernization, specifically by their access to Western education and, in some cases, their ability to travel abroad. Furthermore, several of the women I worked with insisted that the new serials on transnational Hindi television like *Swabhimaan*, *Hasratein*, and *Tara* revealed how Indian culture was changing. These informants insisted that the heroines of these serials were harbingers of other changes that would follow, such as the breakup of families, teen pregnancies, and so on.

Some of my informants responded to the proliferation of erotics in public culture by attempting to hark back to a "traditional culture," one that was untouched by the allegedly contaminating influences of Westernization.[35] For many of my Hindu informants (of different castes), one way to retain ties with Indian culture was to watch reruns or videos of the televization of Hindu epics (Mankekar 1999a; Rajagopal 2001). Several others who were highly critical of the proliferation of erotic affects on television responded with anger and defensiveness. Frequently, those who identified as Hindu reacted by appropriating Hindu nationalist discourses of national purity in which Indian culture was conflated with a pristine Hindu culture. For instance, one upper-caste, lower-middle-class woman said that she felt that "when the winds of change blow," it is important to "return to our roots." When pushed to explain how one might return to one's roots and what these roots were, she advocated a "return" to a pristine Hindu culture (see also Oza 2001; Rajagopal 2001).

I interrogate the seemingly backward-turning temporality of assertions of the need to return to a pristine Hindu-Indian culture in chapter 5. For now, suffice to say that these discourses about roots and Indian culture were aligned with the attempts of Hindu nationalists over the past several decades to recuperate a "glorious Hindu" culture, and were thus predicated on excluding, sometimes eliminating, Other (Islamic, Christian, and lower-caste) cultures. When Hindu/Indian nationalists perceived representations of erotics as foreign or Western in orientation or origin, they saw this as particularly corrosive to the purported purity of national culture. As I demonstrate in chapter 5, fears about the alleged contamination of the purity of national culture also raged in other realms of public culture such as the celebration of Valentine's Day by urban youth in India. Erotics and transnational discourses of morality provided the terrain on which these reifications and renegotiations of Indianness took place.

The spectral presence of the West shaped many of the conflicts and debates that arose at this time about the definition of Indianness and the boundaries between "East" and "West," and these debates and conflicts became especially volatile after the rapid expansion of transnational television. It should not surprise us that if these anxieties, expressed both publicly in the form of protests and privately by my informants, led to an unsettlement of conceptions of Indianness, they also resulted in the (perhaps inevitable) reification of the boundaries between "Indian" and "Western" cultures.[36]

The affective regimes surrounding commodities and erotics provide us with a lens to study the renegotiation of the boundaries of tradition and modernity and, when tradition is conflated with national culture, of the nation itself. I would like to close by returning to informants like Vishnu, who insisted on drawing a distinction between lifestyle and values, such that one could acquire a modern lifestyle yet hold on to traditional (Indian) values. For Vishnu, and for several other informants, the adoption of the accoutrements of modernity did not necessarily endanger one's national identity. In fact, as another informant claimed, it was possible to be proud of being Indian because "we can now get everything here." These informants were alluding to the fact that, in most urban centers in India, people with discretionary incomes could now purchase consumer goods that were once available only in the West. These informants were by no means exceptional; for most of the men and women I worked with, the availability of such a wide range of consumer goods was a crucial marker of India having finally attained modernity. Vishnu's implication, and that of countless others among my informants, was that India had finally arrived on the global stage. The discourse of temporality being invoked here was both of contemporaneity that India had caught up and was no longer lagging behind other nations. It was also a discourse of futurity in that with the availability of commodities that were previously attainable only in the advanced West, India was well on its way to being an advanced nation.[37] In all these discourses, which were highly affectively charged for many of my informants, India itself was reconstituted through the temporality of emergence, of becoming, and of potentiality.

In chapter 5 I continue to track the gendered modalities through which temporality and affect converged to create discourses of morality that spanned transnational spaces by addressing the reconstitution of Indianness implied in discourses of Global India. This is an India that has taken its supposedly rightful place on the global stage while, at the same time, selectively retaining all that is unique about Indianness. These constructions of Global India, I argue, rest on the transnational circulation of heterogeneous discourses of morality across a discontinuous set of nodes. At stake in these discourses is the production of moral subjects with varying affiliations with Global India; in the case of subjects located at the margins of nationalist discourses of India we will see how, at the same time that India and Indianness are reified, they are also decentered and, hence, unsettled.

CHAPTER 5

Global India and the Production of Moral Subjects

In the previous chapter I examined how erotics and commodity affects generated and circulated by transnational Hindi television enabled the renegotiation of the borders of India and Indianness for my informants in New Delhi. Here I analyze another form of this renegotiation by tracing how regimes of affect and temporality inflected the production of "Global India" at the dawn of the new millennium. As we have seen in chapters 2 and 4, the liberalization of the economy and the proliferation of transnational media intensified nationalist anxieties about cultural contamination throughout the 1990s and early 2000s. These anxieties were negotiated and, in some cases, countered by discourses of a Global India that proudly assumed its place on the global stage because of its economic and technological progress. At the same time, Global India emerged as an affective-temporal formation predicated on the production of subjects interpellated by transnational discourses of morality. In what follows, I stage a selection of ethnographic accounts to demonstrate the transnational circulation of these discourses of morality across discontinuous nodes and examine their role in the construction of moral subjects with varying affiliations with Global India.

It is crucial to note that, even as they participated in the production of Global India and Indianness, these transnational regimes of morality did not coalesce into a monolithic discourse. Instead, they were "scattered" (Grewal and Kaplan 1994) and enacted multiple temporalities. Shu-mei Shih points out that "for signification to be possible, . . . meaning has to be temporally and provisionally fixed at nodal points" (2007: 45; see also Grewal 2005: 24–25).[1] I focus on four apparently discrepant nodes in which Global India is temporally and provisionally fixed in terms of specific discourses of morality: conceptions of Resurgent India as they circulate via a government campaign and in the discourses of some of my informants in the San Francisco Bay Area; moral panics surrounding Valentine's Day in India; representations of Global India in a Hindi film, *Kabhi Khushi Kabhie Gham* (2001);[2] and my interviews with a young, working-class Sikh American woman in the San Francisco Bay Area who is positioned at the margins of both the Indian and the U.S. nation-state. In each of these nodes we see how the production of moral subjects undergirds the formation of disparate notions of Global India; at the same time, each of these nodes suggests how subjects, variably situated along axes of class, religion, and gender, participate in the construction of Global India.

I strategically juxtapose these apparently disparate nodes in order to underscore their overlaps as well as disjunctures in order to problematize nationalist conceptions of India. To this end, I deploy unsettlement as an ethnographic strategy and as an analytic to simultaneously trace the production of Global India and decenter it. For instance, at the same time that I analyze the role of Hindu nationalist conceptions of cultural regeneration and moral detoxification, I demonstrate that these discourses were neither monolithic nor totalizing by attending to the ways in which subjects positioned at the margins of the nation might articulate their relationship with Global India. In thus underscoring heterogeneous and counterhegemonic conceptions of Global India, my intervention is conceptual as well as political: rather than assume the stability of the Indian nation, I foreground its construction as an archive of affect and temporality and, in so doing, unsettle it.

The Affectivity of Resurgent India: Hindu Nationalism and the Production of Moral Subjects

On May 11 and 13, 1998, the Indian state, then ruled by the Hindu nationalist Bharatiya Janata Party (BJP), successfully carried out nuclear tests in the Rajasthan desert. Western nations, and the United States in particular, immediately responded with economic sanctions. In retaliation, the BJP-led government introduced the Resurgent India campaign, which consisted of the issuance of bonds that aimed to persuade nonresident Indians (NRIs) to invest in India to counter the potentially devastating economic effects of the sanctions. In so doing, the Indian state was following the example of many nations, most notably Israel, that have turned to their diasporic communities to buttress their economies.

Anupam Chander notes, "Diaspora bonds arise through the convergence of the globalization of capital and of people" (2001: 1060). In the

Resurgent India campaign, Global India was constituted as an entity that was simultaneously affective and material. Diaspora bonds offer significant economic gains to states that issue them and offer a crucial source of capital to states facing fiscal emergencies. However, the Resurgent India campaign's appeal cannot be explained in terms of financial advantages because it offered diasporic and expatriate investors a relatively low rate of return on capital investments. As Chander has argued, Resurgent India bonds were "marketed explicitly to appeal to nationalist sentiments of Indian expatriates, whether they were Indian citizens or not" (2001: 1066). In many ways, the Resurgent India campaign symbolized a reversal of the phenomenon of brain drain and represented a moral imperative to reverse the drain represented by the emigration of the nation's educated and wealthy elites into financial gain for the homeland. Furthermore, in light of the fact that the Resurgent India campaign was launched to off-set international sanctions following the nuclear tests, the Indian state staked a claim on the affective allegiances of NRIs in a manner that aligned them with militaristic Indian nationalism. This was particularly marked in the case of Indian Americans who, by purchasing the bonds, "deliberately flouted the stated policy of the United States—to sanction India for its nuclear testing—and joined India in celebrating its newfound military prowess" (Chander 1995: 2001). Furthermore, as I argue below, the affective regimes that congealed around discourses of Resurgent India naturalized temporalizing processes regarding the progress of the Indian nation.

Of the many ways in which the Indian state crafted its appeals to NRIs to invest in Resurgent India, moral claims based on affective relationships of filiation and kinship were the most ubiquitous. In the face of financial bankruptcy, "India turned 'to its sons and daughters abroad'" in the Resurgent India campaign (Sengupta, quoted in Chander 2001: 1066). In addition to staging direct appeals through carefully orchestrated visits by ministers, bureaucrats, and politicians to affluent NRI communities, the Indian state deployed transnational media through advertisements placed in Indian newspapers and magazines popular within NRI communities and, in particular, the Internet in order to recruit NRI investment.

It is important to remind ourselves that the term NRI indexes the de-coupling of belonging and territory while simultaneously locating identity in a discourse of origins: as noted in chapter 2, the Indian state created the legal and financial category of the NRI with the singular goal of attracting expatriate investment. The relationship of NRIs to the Indian nation-state was complicated by some of the policies of the Resurgent India campaign: the exclusionary implications of Resurgent India bonds were heightened by the ways in which Indian origin was defined. Only those whose parents or grandparents had been citizens of postindependence India were permitted to purchase these bonds, thus excluding citizens of Pakistan or Bangladesh and descendents of indentured laborers in the Caribbean and elsewhere who had migrated in the mid- and late nineteenth centuries (Chander 2001: 1094). The Indian state hence limited the sale of Resurgent India bonds to select segments of NRIs and turned away all others who attempted to buy them.

Resurgent India bonds were launched to promote India's "self-reliance" and "self-respect" and thus reinforced the BJP's appropriation of the Gandhian discourse of *swadeshi* (self-rule). As several scholars have pointed out (for instance, Lal 1999; Rajagopal 2001), Hindutva or Hindu nationalism has acquired tremendous moral and financial support among diasporic communities and NRIs. The discourse of self-respect was crucial to the success of the Resurgent India campaign because of the affective potency it acquired through a temporalizing discourse of avenging past injuries allegedly at the hands of Muslims. Indeed, the congealing of Hindu nationalist affect around the Resurgent India campaign was congruent with other ideological campaigns launched by the Sangh Parivar (a coalition of Hindu nationalist organizations consisting chiefly of the BJP; its student wing, the ABVP; the Bajrang Dal; and the Rashtriya Swayamsevak Sangh (RSS), including the implicit virulence of the slogan *Garv se kaho hum Hindu hain* (Declare with pride that we are Hindus), which had left a trail of blood and mayhem in its wake during the destruction of the Babri Mosque in December 1993, and the (unsuccessful) India Shining campaign of the BJP and its allies in the 2004 national elections. The very conception of a Resurgent India was deeply embedded in Hindu nationalist affect surrounding the vengeful recovery of lost pride and glory.[3] The word "resurgent" also implies an affectively charged but displaced temporality. The Resurgent India campaign, and the discourse of resurging nationhood that it helped consolidate, reinforced Hindutva notions of what Rajagopal describes as "aggressive national regeneration" (2001: 239).

The call to participate in the struggle to reclaim India's lost glory was affectively charged precisely because it was a moral imperative. For instance, Ashok Singhal, the general secretary of the Vishwa Hindu Parishad or World Hindu Organization, which is an important member of the Sangh Parivar, is reported to have said, "The message has reached far and wide throughout the world that the Hindu *will no longer be subdued*. Eventually the world at large will come to the conclusion that after all now they have to deal with a Hindu India" (in Lal 1999: 157, emphasis added). Yet, as noted above, discourses of Resurgent India were not limited to the campaigns formulated by the state and its representatives, nor were their influence and power restricted to the state's fiscal policy of recruiting NRI investment. I learned through my ethnographic work with some of my Hindu nationalist informants in the San Francisco Bay Area that discourses of Resurgent India were contingent on affectively charged and temporalizing processes that exceeded the state's financial campaign to invite NRI investment in India. Let me illustrate with three examples.[4]

I first met Hitesh Kothary, a Silicon Valley entrepreneur who had just launched a start-up in the South Bay, at a Starbucks in Fremont in October 2001. I had been eager to meet him because he was a key figure in the local chapter of the Overseas Friends of the BJP. It was a Sunday morning and I got there early. There weren't too many people at the café, and the sun filtered in through its large windows. I sat by myself for a while, inhaling the aroma of coffee and taking in the air of easygoing busyness characteristic of a café on a weekend morning. A young South Asian couple sat at the table adjacent to mine, chatting companionably. On the other side of me was an older man, sitting by himself, reading the Sunday *New York Times*. Across the room a large family sat with their bagels and scones, their young children noisily arguing with each other.

Hitesh and I had never set eyes on each other before, but when he came through the door we recognized each other right away. He nodded agreeably at me as he walked toward me, and asked if I wanted something to drink. As he approached the counter to order our lattes, I took the opportunity to observe him. He was in his mid-thirties and was casually, but expensively, dressed in designer jeans and a Polo T-shirt; he carried himself with the easy assurance of someone who was comfortable in his own skin. Before I had a chance to introduce my project, he began to speak. He spoke in a self-confident, low voice, with an accent that marked his small-town origins (it turned out that he was indeed from a small town in Gujarat). When I asked him why he became involved with the Overseas Friends of the BJP, he responded that he believed that the BJP would "take India out of the mess of the past into a bright and shining future." He proceeded to speak of the European colonization of California and of the oppression of Native Americans and "Hispanics" and how the "plight" of Hindus in India was analogous to theirs. As I stared at Hitesh in silent disbelief, he added, "After all, we too are oppressed in our own lands. This has to stop. Right now. It has gone on too long."

He paused for an instant, then continued, "It is the dharma of all of us to give our motherland her rightful place in the world." Hitesh was asserting that the condition of Hindus, who are in the majority in India, occupy a position analogous to that of historically disadvantaged minorities in the United States. He believed that it was the dharma or moral duty of all Hindus, particularly those living in the diaspora, to rectify the supposed oppression of Hindus in their "own" nation. His low, calm voice belied the visible tension in his body as he leaned forward, his fist clenched on the table we were sharing.

Instinctively, I moved back in my chair, my pulse quickening as I felt the visceral force of his words. Suddenly claustrophobic in a space where I had felt so relaxed until that moment, I looked around the café anxiously. Nothing had changed. The South Asian couple continued to chat as before; the young man at the table next to mine continued to read his paper; the family across the room continued to enjoy their Sunday morning together. More people had come into the café, and they too seemed to be going about their usual routine, buying coffee, reading the paper, chatting with each other, or greeting friends that they recognized. Yet something had changed for me. I was taken aback by the virulence of Hitesh's assertion about the dharma of Hindus to participate in the struggle of a Resurgent India. I silently berated myself for being so unprepared for the underlying violence of his discourse and for the rage that seemed to simmer beneath his air of calm self-control: Why should I have been surprised, given his public persona as an important member of the Overseas Friends of the BJP? And, anyway, what sort of ethnographer was I to have been so blindsided?

Without missing a beat, and apparently oblivious to the extreme discomfort I was feeling, he continued, speaking the language of modern citizenship: "It is not enough to be legal citizens. It is important to feel that we belong, that we have a voice in what is happening in the country, that we get the same rights as the others." He went on to ask for my help as an anthropologist to refute the allegations of "secularists" in the academy. "Our" struggle, he insisted, had to be based not on passion but on scholarship, on facts, because "facts, as you know, never lie." "We need to construct a database," he added. "It isn't just about religion. It is about how we have to build a modern nation, an India that is awake after centuries of being asleep." It was clear to me that Hitesh was reminding me of my dharma as a Hindu: I was to use my skills as an anthropologist to compile the "database" that would contribute to the morally charged project of Resurgent India. Hitesh and I continued to meet regularly for the next ten months and, every time, he would present me with variations of the same argument. I would try to get his views on other matters facing the

South Asian community in the Bay Area and, each time, we would some-how circle back to the topic of India having to awaken after centuries of sleep and the dharma or moral duty of NRIs like myself to ensure that this happened: clearly, this was something he felt extremely passionate about.

I encountered different, albeit equally virulent, versions of the affec-tive and temporalizing bases of Hindutva in ethnographic exchanges with several other Hindu nationalist informants in the San Francisco Bay Area. It was a muggy August afternoon in 2002 when I met Ramesh Reddy. This meeting was accidental. I was walking to the Festival of India convened by an organization of Indians in San Jose when I fell into step with a young man, perhaps in his early thirties, wearing a Lacoste T-shirt and Tommy Hilfiger jeans. We exchanged names and spoke about what we did for a living. He told me that he was a software engineer at Cisco Systems; I told him that I taught anthropology at Stanford University. He spoke of how proud he was of Indian successes in Silicon Valley. This festival, he said, pointing to the entrance with his chin, showed that we were "not only suc-cessful in IT" but also showed off our "cultural wealth." "It is important to showcase our culture so we do not forget who we are," he added.

We continued to chat as we walked toward the entrance of the festival, and somehow the conversation turned to the pogroms against Muslims in Gujarat earlier that year. When I referred to what had happened as geno-cide, he turned on me, his eyes flashing with contempt and fury: "This is what you secularists always say about what happened [in Gujarat]. You are out of touch with what is happening to Hindus in India. The truth is, you have no idea what it is to be a majority and live like a minority." I was struck by his vehemence, the way the spit flew out of his mouth as he spoke, the audible quickening of his breath, how his voice rose. Serves me right for speaking so plainly, I thought to myself at first. But as his rage mounted, so did mine. When I angrily demanded to know what he meant when he claimed that Hindus "live like a minority," he replied, "I grew up in Hyderabad. Every day, five times a day, the sound of the *azaan* [call to prayer from the local mosque] filled my house. We couldn't ignore it. It was always there. Always. Reminding us of their presence in our neighbor-hood. They don't want to live by our laws, by our rules. They think they can still dominate us. But it's over now for them." He added, "These Muslims! They have no morals. See how they treat their wives? . . . They can divorce them just like that. They have to learn that they cannot live with us if this is how they behave!" Sensing all too clearly that his feelings were sustained by a rage that was so much larger, so much more intense, than his personal feelings of hate, I stood staring at him, my heart pounding and mouth dry. He walked on; he obviously had no time to argue with "secularists" like me. It became clear to me that, like Hitesh and countless other Hindu nationalists among my informants in the San Francisco Bay Area, Ramesh believed that progress (measured through India's success in IT), cultural regeneration, and the moral superiority of Hindu/India were intrinsically linked. And in the ellipses between the Hindu nation and the Indian nation, Muslims were demonized. The violence of his words was inescapable: it was "over now for them."

Some of the most virulent articulations of Hindu nationalist conceptions of Resurgent India were predicated on the exclusion, if not the elimination, of religious minorities: at issue here was not just an ethnic cleansing but a moral cleansing, a detoxification. These conceptions of moral cleansing and detoxification were temporally and affectively charged in that they formed the basis of discourses of futurity: the India of the future had to be cleansed of its minorities, in particular, its Muslims. Beena Chopra was a working-class woman in her early forties who worked as a nanny in the home of upper-class Indian doctors in Fremont. By no means did she have the capital to contribute to the Resurgent India campaign; yet she participated and contributed to the affectively charged discourses of morality that seemed to congeal around it. I present one of many exchanges I had with her on Resurgent India because it underscores how subjects we might deem subaltern (in this case, a working-class, immigrant woman) may be constituted through affects of hate and violence. I met Beena quite regularly over the course of my fieldwork, and we frequently talked about her favorite television serials and movies. Every now and then she would interject her views on the state of "Indian society." She frequently complained that, because of satellite television and "bold" Bollywood films, India was "losing" its cultural purity and becoming morally corrupt. She insisted that it now fell to "right-thinking" people in the diaspora to remind people "back home" about how to bring India "back on track." Beena was particularly worried about how successive Congress governments had "given in" to Muslims in India: she argued that the "permission" to have "many" wives was indicative of the special privileges granted to them by the Indian state. She was even more enraged about "quotas" for Muslims in government schools and colleges.

One afternoon I met Beena in a park near her employers' home in Fremont. As her charge played on the jungle gym, she and I sat by the sandbox and she held forth on how things had "declined" in India. Her voice took on an increasingly shrill tone, and she turned around to look at me and locked my gaze with hers. She put her face close to mine and, slapping her hands down on her lap to emphasize what she was saying, added, "These Muslims do not deserve to live in India. They *should* have gone to Pakistan. They *should* be sent back. They are holding the country back. They remain backward even when we give them so many privileges and rights. And because of them, India cannot progress forward. Because they are stuck, we are stuck. They *just have to be* sent back."

Sent back? I thought to myself. Sent back where? But before I could say anything, she proceeded to argue that what India needed was an *"amruth manthan."* "It is only then that we can really move forward," she insisted, her voice strident even as she casually motioned to her charge to climb down from the jungle gym. As in my meeting with Hitesh, I felt an acute sense of disjuncture between the placidity of our surroundings—the park with children running around us, playing—and the violence underlying her words. And once again I was confronted with the fact that what she was expressing was not (just) her individual or subjective feelings, but affects that blurred the lines between private and public, subjective and collective sentiments, to create an intensity that animates sociality. I remembered the story of amruth manthan that I had heard in my childhood and, recalling the form it had taken in contemporary India, could not bring myself to encourage her to elaborate: my own feelings of extreme discomfort (perhaps fear) compelled me to let what might have been a productive ethnographic moment slip away.

Amruth manthan refers to a Hindu myth from the Bhagavat Puranas in which Lord Shiva churned the ocean of milk to rid it of its poison. This narrative of detoxification has acquired insidious virulence in Hindu nationalist campaigns centering on the moral imperative to create a Hindu Rashtra or Hindu nation that has been cleansed of Muslims and, hence, detoxified. Beena's invocation of amruth manthan drew upon these discourses and reminded me of how stories from Hindu mythology have taken on a new meaning as they are appropriated in Hindu nationalist campaigns to "cleanse" the Hindu nation. Further, as I elaborate shortly, these discourses also deploy particular processes of temporality: the past is rewritten in terms of a lost glory, and the present has to be cleansed, detoxified, so that "we" who represent the Hindu nation are not "held back" from a shining future.

My purpose in selecting and staging the foregoing ethnographic encounters is not to claim that they are representative of Hindutva ideologies in the Bay Area, but because they concretize heterogeneous modes of articulation that nevertheless converge in a profoundly affective vision of Global (Hindu) India. For these informants and for many others that

I worked with, the affectivity of Resurgent India lay in their conviction that it was a moral project, and that it was their dharma to contribute to it. For each of them, discourses of Hindutva are affective to the point of being visceral: Hitesh's apparently calm appropriation of the language of modern citizenship is belied by the intensity of his passionate espousal of the moral duty of all of "us" Hindus in the diaspora to participate in the project of Resurgent India; Ramesh's rage seems to take over his very body; Beena's discourse is soaked in the shrill violence of moral detoxification. All three suggest different ways in which Indian Muslims are Othered and excised in discourses of Hindutva. Hitesh appropriates—and perverts—the language of minority rights to compare the plight of Hindus in India with those of Native American and "Hispanics" in California; Ramesh's discourse about Muslims who do not live by "our laws" or "our rules" slips from a discourse of legality to the brutal language of street violence; and Beena invokes the story of amruth manthan to call for detoxifying the Hindu Rashtra of its Muslims.

Hindutva's affects cut across the boundaries between the personal and social, the private and public, and the cognitive versus the corporeal (see Massumi 2002: 25, 28, 260n3). Even as it inflects the discourses of these subjects, Hindutva affects are in excess of speech acts. Hindutva affects emerge as intransitive: they are neither easily locatable in a single site nor reducible to particular discourses. Hindutva affects are generative of subjectivity. To rephrase Ahmed in another context, affect is "sticky" (2004: 11); the affects that congeal around discourses of Hindutva imbue them with potency. Heterogeneous and (at times) discrepant forms of Hindutva affects slide through and across a range of discourses, such as those pertaining to religious identity, citizenship, and national progress, so as to adhere to them and to charge them with a moralistic fervor. Hindu nationalist affects—in all their varying and nonsingular forms—circulate among subjects and, more significantly, produce subjects in their wake, marking them and constituting them in particular ways. In some cases, Hindu nationalism emerges as an affect of hate that is visceral, in excess of cognition, and experienced corporeally.

The vignettes presented above point to some of the forms assumed by Hindu nationalist affects as they constitute a Global India contingent on particular renditions of temporality. All three of the informants cited above evoke a specific, affectively charged version of the past, one allegedly marked by Islamic dominance, to insist that times have changed, the tide has turned, India is now in the hands of "us," the Hindus, and "it's over now for them," the Muslims, so that the future belongs to us

Hindus. If Hindu nationalist discourses rewrite the past in terms of a lost age of Hindu/Indian glory, they also shape experiences of contemporaneity in terms of the alleged oppression of Hindus as a "minority," and engender specific forms of futurity in terms of a Hindu/India that will finally awaken after centuries of foreign domination. The discourse of self-respect at the heart of Resurgent India is potent precisely because of how it imbues claims about avenging "past injuries" with moral, affective, and temporal freight. Thus, even though Resurgent India appears to be about financial policy, it manifests the Sangh Parivar's success in gaining control over large parts of civil society in India and some segments of its diasporas with regard to how the past, present, and future of the nation must be imagined and fought for. Above all, Resurgent India was a moral project as much as a political one. In the end, Resurgent India manifested how Hindutva discourses of national regeneration and progress acquired normativity and, in the process, produced moral subjects within and beyond the territorial borders of the Indian nation, thus playing a central role in the construction of Global India.

Moralizing Culture: Valentine's Day Protests

Next I examine another instance of the articulation of Hindu nationalist affects with the construction of Global India: the moral panics surrounding Valentine's Day celebrations in India. The celebration of Valentine's Day is relatively recent: it was not until the mid- to late 1990s that middle-class youth in urban India began to do it with such enthusiasm. Yet Valentine's Day continues to provoke violent conflicts about culturally and morally appropriate expressions of romance and intimacy and about how India might position itself globally.[5] In the protests surrounding the celebration of Valentine's Day, Global India is signified in terms of moral purity, which, in turn, is conflated with cultural purity. These notions of moral purity, however, are predicated on the production and disciplining of heteronormative erotic desire.[6] As I suggest below, in these protests, the policing of erotic desire, in particular the erotic desires of young women, was framed in terms of moral interventions on behalf of the nation, with tangible consequences for how belonging and cultural citizenship were redefined by a Hindu nationalist state. At stake was not only the ideological production of morally appropriate womanhood but also of affectively charged discourses of cultural regeneration central to the production of Global India.

My analysis of the protests surrounding Valentine's Day centers on how heternormative erotics are produced and policed so as to enable the affective and temporal generation of conceptions of Global India. For over a decade, Valentine's Day has drawn the ire of Hindu nationalists. On February 11, 2001, Shiv Sena leader Bal Thackeray made headlines by demanding that Valentine's Day be banned because it is "against Indian culture" (Sharma 2001: 1). Thackeray threatened that his men would disrupt celebrations held in defiance of his diktat, and raged, "This shameless festival has been celebrated by our young people for the last 10 years. . . . But it is totally contrary to Indian culture" ("Tough Love for Indian Valentines" 2001). He demanded, "What's this Valentine's Day and who brought in this alien Western craze here? I think this western influence has been imposed on us by a section of leading multinational companies with the ultimate aim of destroying our culture" (2001: 1). The Sangh Parivar immediately joined forces with Thackeray and his followers. The Sangh Parivar organized protests against Valentine's Day in different Indian cities: Nasik, Pune, and Nagpur, all strongholds of the RSS and BJP; Kanpur, in the heart of the Hindu nationalist "cow belt" in northern India; and Bombay and New Delhi, India's commercial and political capitals respectively. The protests were most strident and violent in Kanpur, which, according to some reports, became a "headquarter of the Parivar's 'conscience keepers'" (2001: 1). Terrorized by the Sangh Parivar's threats, many restaurant owners in Kanpur closed their businesses on Valentine's Day. In Pune, 750 volunteers from the BJP's youth wing and the city's Sena unit planned to patrol colleges on Valentine's Day to "save their sisters" from "any untoward incidents of love" (Sharma and Deshmukh 2002: 1). Ingeniously attempting to reclaim love or, more specifically a Hindu way of loving, from multinational companies, Vaibhav Kulkarni, general secretary of the Bhartiya Janata Party Yuva Morcha, insisted, "We don't need Valentine's Day to teach us the meaning of love. We have so many ancient gods and goddesses to do so!" (Sharma and Deshmukh 2002: 1).[7]

The protesters became increasingly violent. In February 2002, Sandeep Khardekar, a BJP activist, boasted, "We have ensured that there are no Valentine's Day celebrations in clubs and restaurants" (Sharma and Deshmukh 2002: 1). In several cities, shops were ransacked, restaurant owners threatened, and "offenders" heckled and humiliated. The Sangh Parivar moral police did not hesitate to publicly punish couples who defied their orders. For example, it was reported that "at a pastry shop in Kakadeo, some boys and girls were humiliated and freed only after they promised 'to maintain [the] dignity of Indian culture'" ("V-Day Couples Humiliated in Kanpur" 2000). In the northern city of Benares, "activists chopped the hair of several celebrating youths and blackened their faces" ("Tough Love for Indian

Valentines" 2001).[8] The moral policing of Valentine's Day was most violent in Kanpur. According to Sharma and Deshmukh, "To the ABVP and other saffron fringe groups like the Hindu Jagran Manch, Shree Ram Sena and Shiv Sena—which, incidentally, has no political base here—go the credit of putting Kanpur on the terror map every February 14" (2002: 1). This is not to say that cities like Delhi and Bombay were immune from the moral interventions of Hindu nationalists. For instance, in 2001, the Shiv Sena attacked Wimpy's, a multinational fast-food restaurant located in Connaught Place in the heart of New Delhi, destroying property in their attempts to disrupt Valentine's Day celebrations.

On many occasions, the state became a willing accomplice. In Kanpur, terrified owners of card stores sought protection from marauding Hindu nationalist mobs by turning to the police. The police responded either by looking the other way when young couples caught celebrating Valentine's Day were publicly punished by the Sangh Parivar, or by transforming Valentine's Day into another opportunity to extort bribes from young men and women seen together in public. In Delhi, the multinational chain Archies Greetings and Gifts sought an injunction against the Shiv Sena and other Hindu nationalist groups from the Delhi High Court. Their plea was dismissed, and they were forced to replace Valentine's Day cards with more generic expressions of love and romance.

As noted above, Shiv Sena leader Bal Thackeray's initial call to ban Valentine's Day was framed in terms of not only defending Hindu/Indian culture but, more interestingly, fighting against the supposed conspiracy of multinational companies to pollute the minds of young Indians.[9] Thackeray's call to defend Hindu/Indian culture from conspiracies allegedly hatched by multinational corporations to corrupt the younger generation was joined by other Hindu nationalist groups who went a step further and linked their anti–Valentine's Day protests with a broader program to "inculcate the feeling of swadeshi in western culture-oriented minds."[10] At first glance, when viewed against their (albeit selective) endorsement of the liberalization of the Indian economy, this stance seems inconsistent. It is, however, in line with a distinction made by many Hindu nationalist ideologues between the modernization of the Indian economy and the "Westernization" of Indian culture. For instance, referring to his organization's opposition to Valentine's Day celebrations, RSS ideologue M. G. Vaidya insisted, "We make a distinction between modernism and westernism [sic]. Modernism is good, but one should not mindlessly ape western practices" (Bartwal 2002: 1).

The Sangh Parivar moral police claimed that one of their primary objectives in protesting against Valentine's Day was to protect young women, replicating a rhetorical move used by many cultural nationalists in which the sexual purity of women becomes metonymic of the cultural purity of the nation.[11] As Rajendra Prasad, general secretary of the Vishwa Hindu Parishad (VHP) Delhi unit, stated, they were staunchly opposed to Valentine's Day celebrations because "they were not only against the basic Indian culture but also led to misbehaviour with women" (Bartwal 2002: 1). It is likely that, in contexts where women were routinely subjected to sexual harassment in public spaces, Valentine's Day may have provided some men with a license to tease and harass women. But the Sangh Parivar's methods of protecting their "sisters" are noteworthy: women caught celebrating Valentine's Day were punished with public humiliation. For example, in 2000, the self-appointed moral police at Kanpur University resorted to the conventional punishment of shaming by blackening the faces of nearly 230 couples for celebrating Valentine's Day. Worse, on one occasion Hindu nationalist activists in Kanpur blackened the faces of two young women for celebrating Valentine's Day and paraded them in the crowded downtown area of the city ("V-Day Couples Humiliated in Kanpur" 2000).

These incidents were part of a larger pattern of moral policing conducted by the Sangh Parivar throughout the past decade in some parts of India. In 2000, the BJP's student wing, the ABVP, requested that the management of schools in Kanpur, particularly those run by missionaries, impose a strict dress code for women. Women students were told to wear only *salwar-kameezes*; skirts and jeans were forbidden in schools and colleges. Furthermore, school authorities were told that women students should not be seen with male friends (Sharma and Deshmukh 2002: 1). The Kanpur University Students Union went so far as to "warn" parents that, if they failed to prevent their daughters from wearing "provocative" clothes, they too would be "punished" ("V-Day Couples Humiliated in Kanpur" 2000).

The enthusiastic adoption of Valentine's Day among middle-class urban youth had something to do with the fact that, for many of them, romance was something to be clandestinely enjoyed, protected from the surveillance of parents and extended families. Celebrating Valentine's Day by presenting the object of one's desire with a card or gifts was, perhaps, all the more pleasurable for being fraught with the risk of public exposure. The moral police capitalized on this fear of exposure by publicly punishing the young men and, in particular, young women guilty of celebrating Valentine's Day. Chilling as these moral interventions were, they were by no means passively accepted by young people in urban India, many of whom continued to celebrate Valentine's Day. This was particularly true of youth in Bombay and New Delhi. Despite the best efforts of the Hindu nationalist moral police to prevent and disrupt celebrations, card stores, restaurants, and other businesses continued to thrive on Valentine's Day. According to several reports, sales for Valentine's Day cards rose to become second only to those for Diwali, a widely practiced Hindu festival. Furthermore, alongside stories of public harassment and "punishment" by the moral police were reports of young people defiantly celebrating Valentine's Day. For instance, Nidhi Mehra, a Bombay college student, was reported to have said, "This occasion comes just once a year, why shouldn't we celebrate?" Hemant Patodia, a college student in New Delhi, expressed his defiance of the Hindu nationalist moral police by quipping: "Do I look like I care about Shiv Sena?" ("Tough Love for Indian Valentines" 2001). Some Indian youth responded to the policing of romance by launching an organization called the All India Lovers Association ("V-Day Couples Humiliated in Kanpur" 2000).

Why did Hindu nationalists become so agitated about the celebration of Valentine's Day, and what spaces did it occupy in their conceptualization of Global India? As we have seen above, Hindu nationalism acquires hegemonic potency not just through struggles that we might conventionally define as political, but also through the invocation of specific regimes of affect and temporality. The affective investment that undergirded the moral panics surrounding Valentine's Day—the shame and rage that spurred the protests—"stuck" to these discourses and imbued them with such potency that they erupted in violence and brutality (compare Ahmed 2004). Despite its internal inconsistencies (see Sarkar [1995], Banerjee [1995], and Setalavad [1995] for analyses of Hindutva in the RSS and Shiv Sena respectively), Hindutva is based on selected interpretations of Hinduism as a blueprint for the organization of community and nation and is, therefore, invested in futurity. Hindu nationalist discourses of morality are also predicated on the articulation of discourses of gender, sexuality, and community, in which the position of the Hindu Woman (and her abject Other, the Muslim Woman) occupy center stage. As Ratna Kapur and Brenda Cossman have argued, "women are constituted in and through communal identity, and conversely, community is constituted in and through women's gender identity" (1995: 83). Thus, while all youth who celebrated Valentine's Day were attacked by Hindu nationalists, women faced the worst of the violence: they were publicly humiliated, subjected to severe restrictions on their mobility and behavior, and, in some cases, physically assaulted.

But how does the violence perpetrated on the women caught celebrating Valentine's Day relate to other Hindutva beliefs about gender and sexuality? Here we get into more complex terrain. In Hindutva ideologies, women are deemed essentially different from men, and the purportedly innate difference of their natures necessitates specific social roles. Women's roles are largely familial, those of wives and mothers; it is their duty to take care of children, instill discipline in members of the family, and ensure the preservation and continuity of tradition. Women are considered vulnerable to erotic temptation (and therefore must be protected from it) and, more importantly, to sexual exploitation at the hands of others. The sexual vulnerability of Hindu women is taken to a horrific extreme in the myth of the lascivious and predatory Muslim male rapist, so much so that "the raped Hindu woman has become a symbol of the victimisation of the entire Hindu community" (Basu 1995: 165; see also Agarwal 1995). The sexual purity of Hindu women is thus foundational to the purity and strength of the (Hindu) community and nation.

Yet it would be a mistake to assume that Hindutva ideologies of gender reduce women to passive victims. On the contrary, these ideologies are striking in their emphasis on women's strength. Women's agency is encouraged, provided it is channeled to the establishment of the Hindu Rashtra or Hindu nation. As several feminist scholars remind us, this emphasis on women's strength has led to the emergence of the militant "new Hindu woman" who is physically fit, disciplined, and resolute in her protection of her family, community, and nation (see, for example, Sarkar 1995). Women can be made strong through physical fitness regimes and, once trained, can protect themselves and, hence, the honor of their communities. Additionally, women's strength is largely based on the concept of *matri shakti*, which roughly translates to "the strength of motherhood" (Kapur and Cossman 1995: 104). According to notions of matri shakti, a woman's strength derives from the conservation of her erotic desires toward the biological and social reproduction of the Hindu community and the Hindu Rashtra. More pertinently, then, women's physical strength has to be matched by their moral self-discipline, especially with regard to erotic desire. Viewed from this perspective, it is not surprising that women celebrating Valentine's Day were so harshly punished, and that discourses of their protection slid so easily into violence against them. These allegedly pleasure-seeking women had violated Hindutva norms of modesty and respectability; far from disciplining their erotic desires, they were guilty of indulging them by exchanging tokens of romance with their partners.

The celebration of Valentine's Day was deemed a threat to the moral foundations of Hindutva for another important reason. The erotic agency of youth who chose their partners struck at the foundations of a central tenet of Hindutva: the consolidation and preservation of the authoritarian Hindu family. The very term Sangh Parivar (family) underscores the dominance of a familial paradigm that not only shapes its organizational framework but also reflects and reinforces the primacy of the patriarchal family by naturalizing unequal gender relations. For instance, Mridula Sinha, president of the BJP Mahila Morcha (Women's Front), has publicly stated, "We maintain that the family and its unity must be maintained. Too much of freedom to women would break up the nuclear family and we resist this" (quoted in Kapur and Cossman 1995: 98; see also Sarkar 1995).

As argued in chapter 4, diverse genealogies and discursive traditions of the erotic (co)exist in contemporary India, many of which preceded representations of intimacy and romance engendered by transnational media. There is also little doubt that the celebration of Valentine's Day in India was engendered by media representations of consumption practices associated with late capitalist nations like the United States. Yet we need to be extremely wary of dualisms that pose "indigenous" notions of love or erotics in opposition to "global" erotics. It seems most productive, therefore, to situate the production of erotic desire surrounding the celebration of Valentine's Day at the intersection of "local" notions of loving and living with those produced through the global traffic in capital, commodities, images, and texts (see also Gupta and Ferguson 1997b).

Multinational companies like Hallmark and Archies were centrally involved in the adoption of Valentine's Day among lower-middle- and middle-class urban youth. As one commentator pointed out, "A whole new industry is now established to market 'love'" (Srivastava 2000: 1). Gifts ranging from candy, flowers, and cosmetics to mobile phones, candles, ballpoint pens, bottled mineral water, and Teflon frying pans were sold and exchanged on Valentine's Day. Businesses thrived: restaurants (like Nirulas in New Delhi) offered special heart-shaped pizzas and pastries, while McDonald's, Archies Gallery, and Cadbury manufactured products especially for the occasion. Indeed, celebrations of Valentine's Day were embedded in global commerce in more ways than one. For instance, by 2000, Bangalore, in the southern Indian state of Karnataka, emerged as a major source for exporting flowers—as much as 80 tons of red roses were shipped to European cities in time for Valentine's Day (Beary 2000: 1).

Globalized media added to the hype surrounding Valentine's Day; trans-national images and texts played a crucial role in enabling, as it were, ex-pressions of romance among middle-class urban youth. For example, on Valentine's Day in 2000, a TV channel took a giant float consisting of a rep-lica of the ship featured in the Hollywood film *Titanic* to different colleges in Bombay. Young couples went aboard the ship to pose as Kate Winslet and Leonardo DiCaprio, the lead actors playing the star-crossed lovers in the film (Srivastava 2000: 1–2).

On the one hand, celebrations of Valentine's Day symbolized the erotic agency of youth (particularly young women) who dared to choose their own romantic partners and, thereby, undermined the authority of the Hindu patriarchal family. Nevertheless, I intend neither to valorize these acts of defiance by young people in urban India as acts of resistance against Hindu nationalists, nor set up a false—and clichéd—dichotomy between "backward" tradition (as exemplified in the trope of the arranged marriage) and romantic love. It is important to note that hegemonic dis-courses of morality, specifically those pertaining to the erotic and the intimate, operate in diverse sites and in multifarious ways. For on the other side of the moral policing of women's erotic desires in India and the South Asian diaspora is the ubiquitous representation in the West of the arranged marriage as a persistent trope for the alleged cultural back-wardness of racial Others.[12] Thus I caution against constructing a teleo-logical narrative of Indian youth throwing off the shackles of repression and engaging in the free or true expression of erotic desire through their celebration of Valentine's Day.

By pointing to the intimate relationship between erotics and global capitalism, I seek to foreground some of the ways in which erotic desire becomes a crucial site for the production of affectively charged discourses of morality. In addition, rather than interpret Hindu nationalist protests against Valentine's Day as nationalist resistance to transnational dis-courses of romance, I problematize the binary between the national and the transnational in constructions of Global Indianness. Hindu national-ist protests were inextricably entangled with the incitement of erotic de-sire in a political-economic and cultural context profoundly unsettled by the workings of multinational capitalism and transnational commerce. Further, as I have argued above, like many other religious nationalisms and fundamentalisms, Hindu nationalist discourses draw financial back-ing and affective sustenance from supporters in diasporic communities scattered all over the world. Thus, far from being a local response against globalization or transnationalism, Hindu nationalist protests against the celebration of Valentine's Day were an articulation of Hindutva regimes of morality that were fundamentally transnational.

Morality Tales: Romancing the Global

Next, I investigate another node for the production of temporally and affectively charged discourses of morality that lie at the heart of Hindutva conceptions of national regeneration. As argued above, despite the patriarchal and masculinist nature of Hindutva (see also Bacchetta 1999; Lal 1999), women are not relegated to the margins of the imagined Hindu Rashtra. Instead, they are expected to energetically participate in the production of Global India. The moral imperative to preserve Hindu/Indian tradition was particularly powerful in some cinematic representations of diaspora, in which women must work hard to protect Global Indianness from cultural contamination.

The conflict between erotic agency and patriarchal authority is a central theme of the Bollywood film *Kabhi Khushi Kabhie Gham*, known to many English-speaking audiences in India and abroad as *K3G*.[13] While I hasten to add that the epic battle between romance and duty toward the family is a well-worn motif in many Bollywood films (Dwyer 2000; Gopal 2011), this film underscores how the disciplining of erotic agency resonates with moralistic discourses of national regeneration in constructions of Global India. *Kabhi Khushi Kabhie Gham*'s significance to my discussion of Global India lies in its didactic impulse: it teaches its implied spectators how they can (and must) position themselves as Global Indians in ways that enable them to preserve their Indianness.

My analysis of *K3G* is based on my textual reading of the film, my experiences of watching the film in two movie halls in the San Francisco Bay Area, and my interviews with informants in the Bay Area. It is not my intention to claim the singularity of this particular text, or to reify its meanings by following its travels across the world as it interpellates members of preconstituted audiences. This film's salience accrues from the fact that it was produced and circulated during a sociohistorical conjuncture marked by the liberalization of the Indian economy in response to the structural adjustment policies imposed by the World Bank and the International Monetary Fund in 1991, the proliferation of transnational media, and the dominance of Hindu nationalism in the state and civil society.

The ostensible mainstreaming of Hindu nationalism has had numerous consequences. I have already discussed some of the ways in which Hindu nationalist discourses of Resurgent India resulted in the production of moral subjects among my informants in the San Francisco Bay Area. For many of these informants, the exclusion and brutal excision of religious minorities, in particular Muslims, was central to the moral imperative to contribute to the construction of Global India. The mainstreaming of Hindutva-inflected discourses of Global India had another consequence: the apparently paradoxical coexistence, on the one hand, of the supreme self-confidence of the Indian business elite regarding their role in the formation of Global India and, on the other hand, anxieties about the so-called contamination of "traditional" Indian culture by "Western culture." Heightened in the context of the globalization of Indian markets and media, these anxieties engendered nationalist discourses of morality, according to which morally appropriate behavior and practices were deemed indexical of Global Indianness.

In the previous section, I argued that these discourses of morality resulted in an increased scrutiny of the behavior, social relationships, and erotic desires of youth and, in particular, of young women. Another essential component of these newly stringent regimes of morality were the temporalizing discourses on which they rested, for instance, through the valorization of the so-called traditional Hindu/Indian family as a metonym of an indestructible nation (*akhand* Bharat). While Hindu nationalism is not unique in its depiction of the heteronormative family as a metonym for the nation, its emphasis on patriarchal authority, endorsement of a hierarchical politics of gender, generation, and kinship, and essentialization of the roles of men and women within the family were noteworthy in how they saturated popular cultural texts circulating both within India and across its diasporas.[14]

But first, a quick plot summary of the film. *K3G* tells the story of Yashvardhan Raichand, a business magnate who is married to Nandini. They have two sons: Rahul, who is adopted, and Rohan. Yash is represented as a stereotypical patriarch: for the most part benevolent, yet dogmatic; obsessed with the importance of maintaining tradition or *parampara*; and extremely invested in maintaining his high social status. All is well in the Raichand family until Rahul, Yash's elder son and heir to his fortune, falls in love with a lower-middle-class girl, Anjali. The relationship that develops between Rahul and Anjali directly contravenes Yash's wish that Rahul marry a woman he has chosen for him who, he claims, will fit in with their family. At first Rahul defers to his father's wishes and decides to forego his relationship with Anjali. But, owing to a twist in the plot, Rahul marries Anjali and disobeys his father, who angrily throws the newlyweds out of the family mansion, reminding Rahul that his disobedience has only proved that he is, after all, adopted ("Now I know you are not my blood"). Rahul, Anjali, Anjali's younger sister Pooja, and Rahul's former nanny

Sayeeda all move to London. Ten years later, when Rahul's younger brother Rohan learns of the circumstances in which his elder brother left home, he vows to bring him back and reunite the family. The rest of this three-hour, thirty-two-minute film is about Rohan's efforts and eventual success in bringing his elder brother and his family home to India. The closing shots of the film portray the Raichand family celebrating the marriage of Pooja and Rohan: the extended family—the family of origin—has not only reunited but has expanded its ranks and is now stronger than ever.[15]

K3G thus narrates the ups and downs in the lives of members of an upper-class Indian family spread across a reterritorialized Global India. The film is set partly in New Delhi and partly in London. It is by no means the first Bollywood film to portray overseas Indians and is, in fact, part of a longer genealogy of films about NRIs (see chapter 2). Moreover, as I argue below, in keeping with the aesthetic of this genre of NRI films, the lavish sets, designer clothes, and upper-class opulence of the visual grammar of the film illustrate the convergence of the transnationalization of the cinematic imagination and the production of consumerist desire.[16]

I first watched K3G in a movie hall in an upper-class area of Sunnyvale on a chilly January evening. This movie theater showed Indian films on occasional weekends but, despite the fact that Sunnyvale had a dense population of residents from South Asia, it did not seem to attract a lot of their patronage. When my friend and I walked into the shoebox-sized room in which K3G was to be screened, we were astounded: no more than eight or ten people were there. Amit Rai talks of media assemblages that bring together "ecologies of media, matter, and sensation" (2009: 8), entailing a form of engagement that is profoundly synesthetic. It was these synesthetic pleasures that I missed while watching K3G at that theater in Sunnyvale: hence, for my friend and I, the experience was profoundly dissatisfying.[17] We wished we had gone to Naz 8 where we would have been surrounded by others watching the film, the sounds of people humming and singing, and the aromas of samosas, chutney, and hot chai mingling promiscuously with the smell of popcorn.[18]

And so it was that two weeks after watching the film in a near-empty hall in Sunnyvale, I dragged one of my favorite informants along to Naz 8 to watch K3G (she was seeing it for the third time). It was a Friday evening and there were long lines everywhere: to buy tickets, to get into the foyer, and in front of the concession stand. As we expected, many (although by no means all) of the patrons appeared South Asian. (As one of my other informants later put it, the scene at Naz 8 depended on the time and day of the week. She claimed that it was an "aunty scene on weekday afternoons and

a family scene on weekends").[19] The foyer buzzed with throngs of customers, and songs from K3G were blasting out of the speakers. The theater where
K3G was screened was large and completely full. As expected, many people
around us sang along with the songs (as my companion commented, it was
like karaoke without a script!) and talked loudly and incessantly. Children
ran around us, a woman three seats to my left changed her baby's diaper,
and the eating never stopped. By the time the film ended, I walked out
content but in a bit of a daze brought on by the sensory overload. As far as
I was concerned, this was the full experience![20]

The affective experience of engaging (rather than simply watching) a
film often precedes and extends beyond its screening. In most instances,
watching one's favorite actors on screen and memories of previous view-
ings combine to make engaging with it a particularly pleasurable experience. Increasingly, in the San Francisco Bay Area (and in New Delhi), my
upper-class and middle-class informants would preview (or review, as the
case may be) scenes from a film on their computers before (or after) they
watched it on screen; many also downloaded Bollywood ringtones onto
their cellphones. And, as one of my informants in Fremont put it, she and
her friends frequently played the CD of songs from a film on their way
to watch it at Naz; this, she insisted, enabled her and her friends "to get
into the right mood." Certainly, if the music booming out of cars pulling
into the parking lot of Naz 8 was any indication, this strategy to get into
the right mood was not uncommon!

K3G was an enormous hit in India as well as abroad, and, indeed, its box-
office success across its dispersed audiences tells its own story; certainly,
the repeated screenings of the film on satellite television channels underscores its continuing popularity in India and beyond (see also Gopal 2011:
64). The lavish production of K3G was somewhat of a milestone in Bollywood history. As a big-budget film that cost its producers Rs 20–30 crore
(Rs 200–300 million), it brought together a formidable cast of some of the
most legendary Bollywood stars. After a year of flops and mediocre show-
ings at the box office, members of the Bombay film industry had placed all
their hopes on K3G's success. They were not disappointed. When it was released on December 14, 2001, the film opened to 100 percent collections in
Mumbai and 100 percent advance collections in other parts of India (Kabhi
Khushi Kabhie Gham . . ." 2001; "K3G Opens to Record Breaking Collections"
2001). More importantly, the film earned Rs 40 crore (Rs 400 million) even
before it was released through sales of satellite and overseas rights.

By the time this film was released in 2001, Hindu nationalists had already
succeeded in seizing the Indian state. As Bacchetta argues, the ascension of

the BJP to state power had irreversible consequences: Hindu nationalism expanded from its attempts to invoke an imagined Hindu community to "the domain of ordering, regulating, and representing that 'community' through the state's apparatus and institutions" (1999: 141). Yet it is not my intention to reduce the ideological and affective work of K3G to Hindu nationalism. Instead, I am interested in the pleasures and complicities enacted in the diegesis of the film. First, there are the pleasures and complicities entailed in the unfolding of patriarchal romance—in particular, the generation and regulation of heterosexual erotics within the context of a patriarchal family/nation. As in many Bollywood films, K3G's spectatorial pleasure involves the production of fantasy at various levels, from a dream sequence in which Anjali and Rahul are literally transported from a *mela* or street fair in Chandni Chowk to the pyramids in Egypt, to the fantasies of upward mobility expressed by the lower-middle-class Ghasitaram, who dreams of leaving Chandni Chowk to become an NRI. As in many Bollywood films, in K3G the consumption of commodities provides the mise-en-scène for desire—be it erotic desire, the desire for travel, upward mobility, or a return to an imagined origin.

As its promotional materials emphasize, the film's visual grammar (its depiction of the interior spaces of homes, landscapes, and its characters' clothes) was carefully designed and marketed as a source of pleasure for its purported spectators. Although it is impossible to obtain precise empirical data about the viewership of the film, like many Bollywood films, the box-office ratings of K3G worldwide suggest that the film reached viewers of diverse cultural and socioeconomic backgrounds, nationalities, and religious affiliations and, therefore, was malleable to multiple interpretations.[21]

At the same time, these implied spectators suggest how consumer culture produces "transnational identifications and subjects whose desires and fantasies crossed national borders but also remained tied to national imaginaries" (Grewal 2005: 11). During a historical moment when Indian identity seemed to have become a precarious phantasm in the face of the allegedly contaminating effects of globalization (see chapter 3), the regime of morality that the film produced was itself a source of pleasure. The film depicts a moral universe that is, ultimately, located in a diegetic movement toward reunion. The yearning that drives its narrative energy consists of a desire for reuniting with extended family and with the nation of origin, a yearning that is ultimately fulfilled when they all return to India, the extended family is reunited, and Pooja and Rohan get married. K3G narrates several intricately interwoven morality tales: about the importance of obeying and deferring to one's elders, the negotiation of tradition versus modernity, the importance of the unity of the family, patriotism, sexual modesty, and so on. But most of all, *K3G* signals and resonates with the reconfiguration of Hindu/Indian nationalism congruent with the moral and affective bases of an emergent Global India. This particular construction of Global India, and of what it means to be Indian in a transnational world, is embedded in affectively charged discourses of morality, specifically through its representation of ideal femininity and of the (heteronormative) Indian family.

Nandini, played by Jaya Bachchan, whose off-screen life crucially mediates the conceptualization of her on-screen persona, is one of the central female characters in the film and its production of Global Indianness.[22] Nandini iconicizes an ideal femininity of an older generation. Indeed, according to director Karan Johar, Nandini is "the soul of the film" (*The Making of Kabhi Khushi Kabhie Gham*, 2001. Respectful and deferential toward her husband and in-laws, Nandini is conscientious in her adherence to family rituals and customs. Although she talks back to Yash at a critical moment toward the end of the film when she protests his autocratic behavior, she is not a feminist in any sense of the word; her role in the film is not to politicize the patriarchal family or to change it in any substantive way. In fact, the resolution of the film's narrative crisis occurs only when her younger son, Rohan, persuades his father to accept Anjali and ask her for forgiveness.

The transformation of Pooja, Anjali's younger sister who moves with her to London, is crucial to the film's construction of Global India in terms of deeply gendered discourses of morality. When we first see her in London she wears skimpy clothes and treats her suitors in a cavalier fashion. However, her latent Indianness surfaces when we see her yearning for a reunion with Rahul's extended family, keeping the *karva chauth* fast (a fast conducted by some North Indian Hindu women to pray for their husbands' long lives), and performing other Hindu rituals. Indeed, the most dramatic moment of her transformation occurs during a crucial *puja* scene, when we see her singing a *bhajan* (a Hindu devotional song). From this point onward, we often see her wearing salwar kameezes rather than Western clothing. During an emotionally fraught scene when Yash runs into her and Anjali in a London shopping mall, she is so deferential to him as to not even raise her eyes to meet his gaze. Her transformation into a moral subject of Global India is complete.

And then there is Anjali, the lower-middle-class young woman from Chandni Chowk, who holds steadfastly to "Indian" culture even while living abroad. She is consistently represented as outwitting and making fun of the white British woman who is her neighbor (this was a source of some laughter and gleeful hand-clapping among viewers in Naz 8). Anjali worries that her son will grow up British because he does not know "our ways," does not sing "our songs" (i.e., the songs she sang growing up in India). We see her perpetually yearning to move back to India to reunite with Rahul's extended family.[23] Anjali insists that her family will be complete only when they return home to Bharat (significantly, the word she uses is not Hindustan or India but Bharat, the Hinduized name for India favored by Hindu nationalists) and when they live with their elders (parents). Anjali's character underscores the duty of Indian women in the diaspora to maintain and reproduce an attachment to the Indian nation and to Indian culture and, thereby, contribute to the production of Global India in the diaspora.

In its moralistic valorization of the extended family, K3G consistently foregrounds the centrality of parental authority, in particular, the authority of the patriarch. From the perspective of some viewers that I interviewed, the patriarch of the Raichand family was domineering and rigid to the point of being cruel: he thinks nothing of throwing out his elder son and separating him from his mother, younger brother, and ailing grandmother. Interestingly, however, the film's advertisements represent Yash's authority in such a way as to soften his portrayal, reminding us that the reception of a cinematic text can never be abstracted from the marketing practices and publicity that surrounds it. In these promotions, we see Yash and his wife Nandini directly addressing the film's (presumed) viewers: both gaze straight into the camera and speak of the radically different ways in which they express their love for their sons. Yash appears first, grave but unmistakably earnest, and asks, "Why is it that a father can never express his love for his son, no matter how much he loves him?" He is followed by his wife, Nandini, who smiles at the camera, and says softly, "And a mother? How much love does she have for her son? So much that neither she nor her son can ever measure it." In addition to portraying quintessentially gendered ways of expressing parental love for sons (daughters are completely marginalized in this narrative of patrilineage and patrimony), the advertisements depict Yash as a loving father whose domineering behavior and gruff manner hide an intense and passionate love for his sons.

One of the most striking features of the diegesis of K3G is its self-conscious citation of other Hindu narratives of patrilineage and patrimony. The theme of obedience to one's parents, in particular to one's father, and of the loyalty of brothers resonates with a dominant theme in the Ramayana that has been frequently invoked by Hindu nationalists for its valorization of the Hindu extended family. However, while in the Ramayana the father sends his heir and eldest son into exile because of circumstances not entirely within his control, in *K3G* Yash throws Rahul out because he is enraged by his marriage with Anjali. In both the Ramayana and *K3G*, however, the eldest sons display an intense love for their respective fathers and an abiding sense of duty and respect. And in both the Ramayana and *K3G*, loyalty between brothers is paramount: the younger brothers are so heartbroken to learn about their elder brothers' departure from home that they do all they can to bring them back. Not surprisingly, in both texts, women play a conspicuously supporting role; even though the presence of some of the central women characters sets off a series of narrative crises, they exist primarily as enablers rather than agents. The two narratives overwhelmingly stress the importance of the unity of the family; politics and power differentials within the family are elided in the face of the overriding message that the family must stay together at all costs—as *K3G*'s title suggests, "through happiness and through tears." And last but not least, the film also makes intertextual reference to other Bollywood films that have recast patriarchal romance in terms of hegemonic interpretations of the Ramayana, most famously Sooraj Barjatya's *Hum Saath Saath Hain* (1999) and, to a lesser extent, *Hum Aapke Hain Kaun* (1994).[24]

In *K3G*, patriarchal romance, or perhaps I should say the romance of patriarchy, is enacted in more ways than one, but its most powerful expression lies in how love for the extended family, the family of origin, frequently slides into love for the Indian nation. This conflation—or, more likely, metonymy—of family and nation is emphasized at several points in the film but, as noted above, is foregrounded in Anjali's insistence on moving back to Bharat and hence reuniting with the extended family. Bharat, then, is the only plausible site for the reunification of the family, so much so that an earlier attempt to reunite the family in London meets with a sorry end. The film is saturated with what one viewer described to me as "NRI patriotism." Participating in a nationalist discourse of anteriority, in *K3G* the nation becomes the family of origin and Indians settled abroad always yearn to return to its embrace.[25]

At the same time, *K3G*'s depictions of the public spaces of London are critical to its production of Global India: London's cityscape is dominated by Indians and by all things Indian, not because whites are invisible or relegated to the margins (as in many other NRI films) but because Indians are depicted as having the upper hand, whether in cricket, over neighbors, or at school. The opening frames of the segment of the film set in London begin with aerial views of such iconic landmarks as Big Ben, the Houses of Parliament, and Tower Bridge—but with an anthem of militant Hindu/Indian nationalism, "Vande Mataram," in the background.

5.1. Rohan arrives in London.

And while the subsequent frames depicting a newly arrived Rohan in London are campy in their portrayal of Indianness in London, their overriding tone is decidedly triumphant. Rohan is completely self-assured as he strides through the public spaces of London with the supreme self-confidence of a Global Indian who is at home anywhere in the world (figure 5.1).[26] The empire (or, at least, the postcolony) has struck back: Global India is not only alive but is thriving in London.[27] This is underscored by the ways in which Anjali keeps India alive in her home by insistently speaking to her British-born son in Hindi, singing patriotic Indian songs to him, and, most significantly, through her adherence to Hindu rituals.

Unsurprisingly given the dominance of hypergamy in patriarchal and heteronormative discourses of family, the difference in Anjali's and Rahul's class positions seems to get diluted after they marry and start living in London: Anjali has acquired upward mobility through her marriage with Rahul. Furthermore, as in several popular filmic and televisual narratives set in postliberalization India, in *K3G* the working classes have all but disappeared. To the extent that class conflict is depicted at all in *K3G*, it exists between the lower-middle and middle classes on the one hand, and the hyperaffluent on the other. Further, and perhaps more centrally, it is represented entirely in terms of the commodities that individuals can acquire and display, thus reinforcing how class difference is displaced onto the terrain of consumption in Global India. Yet, as I argue in chapter 4, the desire for commodities is never just that; it is often conjoined with the production and regulation of erotic desire and articulates a host of other desires, including the desire for upward mobility.

The lavish interiors of Rahul and Anjali's home in London point to NRI successes in diaspora; certainly, Rahul does not seem to lose his class position after Yash throws him out of his family.[28] If the family does provide the setting for the playing out of class difference, this is depicted in moral rather than structural terms as, for instance, in Yash's concerns that the lower-middle-class Anjali will be unable to follow Raichand family traditions or preserve its moral values. Significantly, he uses the Sanskrit word *samskara*, which explicitly equates moral values with religious values. In congruence with the disappearance of class conflict in this tale of a post-liberalization family in Global India is the disappearance of labor. In years past, several Bollywood films were set either in factories, in mills, among working-class neighborhoods, or, if they were set in villages, depicted changing class relationships in the countryside (and here I refer not only to films of the 1950s but also to films from the 1970s and 1980s such as *Kaala Pathar* [1979], *Namak Haram* [1973], and *Coolie* [1983]. In contrast, in *K3G* (as in many NRI films), we rarely see people at work; laboring bodies have been replaced by bodies of consumption. In *K3G*, we come across abundant evidence of the fact that Yash is a tycoon. He owns a private jet and helicopter; he appears on CNN as one of India's leading entrepreneurs; that he has business interests all over the world is foregrounded by the clocks in his office displaying the time in different global cities. We never, however, see him or any of his family members at work; all we see is the presence of global capital in the world they inhabit. We see flashes of Sayeeda, Rahul and Rohan's nanny, at work; her labor, however, is represented entirely in terms of her love for the Raichand sons. In this context, *K3G*'s representation of Muslims is telling. The film's most important (perhaps the only significant) Muslim character is Sayeeda, whose affection for the family is underscored by her subservience to them; at best, Muslims can only occupy a secondary position in Global India.

In *K3G*'s representation of Global India, ideal families are those that adopt and manifest select aspects of (capitalist) modernity through their consumption practices. At the same time, they must retain their samskaras, for it is these samskaras that define them as essentially Indian. In addition, class difference is represented not in terms of an antagonism between labor and capital or between different kinds of labor, but in terms of consumption, as in the clothes people wear, the cars they drive, and how they decorate their homes.[29] In the part of the film set in London, we constantly see the protagonists in front of high-end stores like Gucci and Armani; consumption provides the context for the imagination of a homogeneously affluent Indian diaspora, a diaspora that is, in fact, represented solely in terms of NRI capital.

Once again, I would like to caution against the hazards of reductively reading *K3G* as a Hindutva text, and foreground, again, my strategy of attending to the pleasures and complicities that constitute its resonances with Hindutva discourses. The discursive work performed by *K3G*'s spectacular

Raichand House
Diwali, 10 years ago

5.2. The Raichand mansion.

renditions of pujas (North Indian prayer ceremonies) and other Hindu rituals is especially significant here. Nandini's Diwali puja in the Raichand mansion introduces us to the politics of gender and generation in this household.
Anjali's pujas in London signal a different negotiation, in this case, the recuperation and maintenance of national identity in diaspora, an identity that
is coded in terms of Hindu ritual. Pooja's puja, also in London, is what marks
her complete transformation or rather the emergence of the Hindu Indian
Woman purportedly latent within her.[30] It is important to note that in these
specific narrative contexts the pujas signify not so much everyday religiosity or even faith per se, but instead serve as placeholders for Hindu Indian
identity in the face of globality.

Put another way, tradition does not indicate nostalgia for past modes
of living, but provides a blueprint for how to live in the future as moral
subjects of Global India. Thus conceived, tradition indexes futurity rather
than the past. Tradition, then, is invoked through distinct processes of
temporality. Other temporalizing processes play a significant role in K3G's
participation in the construction of moral subjects of the Global India of
the future. Spaces of domesticity form the mise-en-scène for these temporalizing processes. Not surprisingly, these spaces of intimate habitation
are profoundly mediated by class and gender. For instance, in India the
Raichand family lives in a mansion that literally combines East and West
and, in so doing, gestures toward the Global India of the future. An English
manor house from the outside (surrounded by lush green lawns that look
like they belong in England rather than in arid New Delhi; figure 5.2), the
mansion displays traditional Indian *haveli* architecture on the inside.

One scene in particular is striking in how it juxtaposes tradition and
modernity as represented by the wealth of the upper classes in the Global
India of the present as well as of the future. Nandini leads the family in a
Diwali puja. Spliced through scenes of the celebration of the puja are shots
depicting Rahul's return home in a helicopter (figures 5.3, 5.4). More im-

5.3. Rahul comes home for Diwali puja in a helicopter.

5.4. Nandini senses that Rahul has arrived.

portantly, as we will see below, the representation of this puja dramatizes the negotiated relationship between modernity (signified, in this case, in terms of global capital and consumption) and Indian tradition (coded, here, as religiosity). These intercutting frames depict the purportedly harmonious coming together of tradition and modernity in the ideal family of Global India.

Anjali is marked as lower middle class because of where she lives before her marriage. Chandni Chowk is located in one of the most congested areas of Old Delhi and is frequently associated with "backwardness" and traditionality. On the one hand, for all its apparent backwardness, Chandni Chowk is depicted in unmistakably nostalgic terms for a particular kind of past. It is a place of close and enduring social relations, where Muslims and Hindus live in harmony, and neighbors stand by one another; to this extent, it represents an older moral universe that belongs in the past. At the same time, however, it is full of billboards and advertisements that underscore its position at the cusp of India's encounter with globalized patterns of consumption; its temporal location, therefore, seems deliberately scrambled.

In contrast, the Raichand mansion is iconic of the spectacular wealth of a class of elites that has profited from its enthusiastic participation in the globalization of India's economy and, equally significantly, of a particular kind of cosmopolitan modernity, which is to say, a modernity that belongs in the future. At the same time, the film repeatedly portrays the Raichand home as the site of a (capitalist) modernity that retains select aspects of "tradition." Moreover, tradition becomes an unmistakable, unequivocal trope for morality, a morality that is represented in terms of both a pious and spectacular adherence to Hindu rituals and obedience and deferral to the wishes of the patriarch.

K3G thus participates in the constitution of notions of Global Indian-ness through several modalities. For one, the film exemplifies Bollywood cinema's articulation of the cultural politics of the purported homeland as it addresses spectators in multiple locations. Grewal (2005: 90) has pointed to how diaspora culture is marketed within India to create a new transnational imaginary and eventually a transnational nation. *K3G*'s significance lies neither in its mimetic function nor in its ability to rep-resent "the" diaspora but in how it forms an important node in the gen-eration and circulation for affective and temporalizing regimes pertaining to Global India. *K3G* is also pedagogical in that it purportedly teaches its implied spectators in India and across Indian diasporas how to be Global Indians who are equally at home in India and abroad. Crucially, Global In-dianness is defined through affective ties and moral obligations to family and particularly to one's parents, which must be preserved and reinforced for Global India to remain Indian; hence, the film's tagline, "It's all about loving your parents."

In the next section, I draw on my ethnographic research with Preeti Dhillon, a young working-class Sikh American who lived in the East Bay town of Fremont, to underscore that the moral and affective claims of Global India were neither monolithic nor totalizing: Preeti exemplifies how subjects located at the margins of the Indian and the U.S. nation-state draw on Bollywood cinema to formulate conceptions of Global India that diverge from those produced by Hindu nationalism. In presenting her appropriation and construction of Global India, I wish to foreground how minor narratives might unsettle the hegemony of dominant narratives of nation and community.

Gendered Longings: Intimacy and Morality in the Diaspora

Although I did not focus on youth per se in my ethnographic research in the San Francisco Bay Area, in the course of over a decade of fieldwork I interviewed, conducted participant observation with, and collated life narratives from over thirty young people.[31] When I first met Preeti Dhillon in the summer of 1998, she was a sophomore at San Jose State University. Her positionality was marginal on several registers. As a Sikh, she was marginalized by Hindu nationalist discourses of belonging and was racialized in complex ways in the United States. In addition, Preeti's family was working class. Her father worked in an automobile factory in Fremont, and her mother was employed as a sales clerk in a nearby Indian grocery store. Preeti's family history had been marked by multiple migrations: as argued in the introduction, such histories problematize normative assumptions of diaspora as unilinear or singular.[32] Her paternal grandfather had migrated from Punjab to Indonesia in the 1920s and both parents had been born and raised there. Her father's extended family lived in a village near the Indian-Pakistani border in Punjab and, despite the fact that her parents had never lived there, the entire family frequently spoke of Punjab, and India, as "back home." Preeti and her brother were born in Jakarta, and the family had immigrated to the United States when she was five. She had visited Punjab only once, for about two weeks, in the mid-1990s.[33]

Our meetings occurred in different settings over the year in which I got to know her. Our first meeting was at a Starbucks not far from the Dumbarton Bridge. This was followed by meetings at the mall by her home. One day I gave her a ride from her university to her friend's house and we chatted in the car for over an hour after we reached there. Shortly thereafter, she began to invite me to her home, where she introduced me to her grandmother and her parents, who were all somewhat surprised by my interest in her. Over time, however, their warm hospitality overrode any skepticism they might have harbored about me, and I began to meet with Preeti and her family on a biweekly basis. Our meetings drew to an end after about thirteen months, when Preeti, who was engaged to a distant relative in Connecticut, got married and left the Bay Area to live with her husband and his family. Despite our efforts to do so, Preeti and I were unable to stay in touch after her marriage: I got the sense that she was completely preoccupied with the responsibilities and duties of her new married life. For the most part, Preeti identified herself as Sikh American rather than as South Asian or Indian American. Yet, every now and then, she spoke of how she was an "Indian who is not from India." These claims about her Indianness seemed to emerge either when she spoke of feeling "out of place" in the United States or when we discussed Hindi films. As our friendship developed, I learned about the complexities of her positionality.

I had worked with young people of heterogeneous socioeconomic backgrounds over the course of my fieldwork, and my working-class informants constantly brought home to me the vast difference between their worlds and those inhabited by my students at Stanford University, where I was teaching at the time. Even in the case of my South Asian students who hailed from working-class or lower-middle-class families, being at Stanford itself yielded tremendous cultural and educational capital. In contrast to these students, most of whom assumed they had a fairly secure future to look forward to, Preeti was apprehensive about what the future held in store for her. Wryly describing herself as a "straight C" student, she did not fit the model minority stereotype in terms of her academic achievements.[34] Like other working-class youth that I got to know during my fieldwork, Preeti felt both elated and marginalized by the tech boom in Silicon Valley in the late 1990s. On the one hand, she frequently spoke of how proud she felt of Indian success in Silicon Valley. At the same time, as a working-class woman with neither the educational qualifications nor the cultural capital to participate in what she termed "the gold rush," she felt she had nothing to gain from the economic boom. She and her parents were waiting for her to get married; neither she nor they aspired to a job for her in the IT industry. Preeti's class position and gender thus foreclosed any possibility of her benefiting from the promise of technology that became hegemonic in Silicon Valley during the boom years of the 1990s (Shankar 2008).

Equally importantly, as a Sikh, Preeti felt acutely marginalized by the entrenched Hindu nationalism of many of the Indians surrounding her at school and in her neighborhood. Her relatives in India had experienced state violence against Sikhs and, even though she had not personally witnessed the Indian government's attack on the Golden Temple in Amritsar, she expressed grief and anger every time she spoke about it. Having witnessed the ascendance of Hindu nationalism among many of my informants in the San Francisco Bay Area, it did not surprise me to learn that Preeti felt acutely vulnerable among her Hindu classmates and neighbors. As she put it, the "mainstream Indian community" had no place for Sikhs like herself. Preeti's feeling of being out of place was further compounded by her sense of alienation from the *gurudwara* community in her neighborhood; most of the Sikhs she met there were from Punjab and she, and her family, felt foreign in their midst. However, Preeti lived in a part of Fremont that was racially heterogeneous. Most of her friends were either Afghan or Latina and she described to me, with great delight, how she had introduced them to the joys of Hindi films, which she and her friends would frequently go to the Naz 8 multiplex to watch.

Preeti's engagement with Bollywood films underscores how these films, as texts in motion, enable multiply marginalized subjects to negotiate complex, sometimes contradictory, constructions of Global India. Preeti's entire family watched Hindi films on a regular basis; indeed, favorite family pastimes consisted of either renting DVDs of Hindi films or going together to Naz 8. The "dynamic threshold between text, media, sensation, and bodies" that Rai (2009: 11) ascribes to engaging a Bollywood film in a theater applied equally well to watching a film with Preeti's family. Let me describe the first time I watched a Hindi film in their home.

It was a balmy October Sunday and the family had just returned from the neighborhood gurudwara when I rang their doorbell. Preeti's father welcomed me with a warm smile and sat me down on their couch as he regaled me with stories of his life in Jakarta, their last family trip to Punjab, and his impressions of New Delhi. He had found the international airport at New Delhi "smelly and disgusting, like a typical Third World airport," in contrast to the airport in Jakarta. As he chatted, his mother sat by smiling benevolently at me, while Preeti and her mother buzzed around the kitchen getting prelunch snacks ready. Preeti placed a plate of steaming hot *pakodas* on the coffee table in front of us and sat down next to me. After catching me up on a scandal concerning her classmate at San Jose State University, she asked me if we could watch a Hindi film that they had rented from a nearby grocery store. It was an old Raj Kapoor film from the 1970s, *Mera Naam Joker*, which I had watched multiple times. Preeti's father had seen it several times as well and for both of us this intensified, rather than undermined, our pleasure in the film. The volume was turned up very high as if to compete with the whistling of the pressure cooker in the kitchen, but this did not deter Preeti and her father from keeping up a running conversation with me, with each other, and with the character played by Raj Kapoor in the film. Their home was redolent with the fragrance of lamb *keema* and *cholas*. Watching *Mera Naam Joker* that day was a multisensorial experience par excellence, the aroma and tastes of the meal mingling with the auditory and visual pleasures of the film. As we sat balancing our plates on our laps, I thought to myself, if only fieldwork was always this much fun: amazing food, great company, and an old Raj Kapoor film. Although Preeti and her mother had prepared a particularly lavish meal in my honor, the family's experience of watching Bollywood films on Sundays was always deeply enmeshed with the sensuous pleasures of food. On subsequent visits, it became clear to me that watching films over lunch on Sundays was a ritual the entire family greatly enjoyed, to be surpassed only by visits to Naz 8.

As suggested in my discussion of K3G, for most of my informants, and for me, watching a Bollywood film was a deeply affective process. It not only entailed an engagement with the film's narrative but also constituted bodily, multisensorial, and intensely social experiences. Tapping one's feet to the music, whistling one's approval or titillation, hissing disgust at a turn of events, singing along, talking back to characters in the film, weeping or laughing in response to the filmic text and to each other, dipping in and out of the film to chat about seemingly unrelated subjects, imbibing the aroma of food and of surrounding bodies—none of these interrupted or supplemented our experiences of watching a film but, in fact, constituted it.

One day I took Preeti and her friend to the film *Mohabattein* (2000) at Naz 8. The story of *Mohabattein* is set in a fictional small town supposedly in the Himalayan foothills; it narrates the romantic relationships that develop between the young men and women attending two high schools (hence the name *Mohabattein*, which roughly translates to *Many Loves*). The boys' school references the ostensibly secular boarding schools that have been churning out cohorts of elites since Indian independence (Srivastava 1998), but is called Gurukul, a name that connotes an upper-caste Vedic education. The headmaster of Gurukul (played by Amitabh Bachchan) is a strict disciplinarian who has banned love from the school. His tenuous success in doing so is rendered even more precarious with the arrival of a music teacher, played by Shah Rukh Khan, who introduces his pupils to the sensuous joys of music and encourages them to pursue their love interests. As the film proceeds we learn that, many years before, the principal's daughter had fallen in love with the character played by Shah Rukh Khan and had committed suicide because her father disapproved of their love.

In several ways, *Mohabattein* is a conventional, somewhat banal, rendition of teenage romance and of a love thwarted and, ultimately, vindicated and redeemed. Yet, when I watched *Mohabattein* with Preeti and her friends at Naz 8, I sensed that she was deeply moved by the film. Unlike other times when she talked incessantly, she watched spellbound, getting irritated when her friend tried to talk to her. Although she was relatively quiet, her response to the film seemed intense, and contrasted with the somewhat lukewarm responses of most people surrounding us. As I described above, conversation and food—with audience members chatting loudly among themselves or walking in and out of the theater carrying popcorn or samosas—was always an integral part of being at Naz 8, but this time it seemed like audience members were not engaging the film with their characteristic enthusiasm and exuberance: they seemed bored and listless, and many walked out before the intermission. On other visits to Naz 8, audience members would typically repeat dialogue, hum songs, and clap with great gusto at different moments during the screening. Although this was not happening while we were watching *Mohabattein,* it did not undermine Preeti's deep engagement with the film.

Afterward, I asked Preeti if she liked the film, and she replied that she loved it. Her silence on our drive back to her house indicated to me that she continued to be profoundly affected by it. Once we returned to her house, she said to me that she felt the film was about a "lovely world." She elaborated that the film depicted not only scenes that were lovely, but a world in which everybody cared for each other. She appreciated the "moral of the film": that love conquers all. But more than anything else, she loved the friendships between the young people, the affection they felt for their music teacher, and how everybody "came together."

Preeti's engagement with the film was shaped by at least two factors: its depiction of love and romance, and its portrayal of India. Articulated in terms of heteronormatve erotic desire, Preeti's longing for romance and intimacy was shaped by her engagement with Bollywood film. She once confided that she hoped to, one day, meet "the right man." As she said, "A lot of people want to meet the right person. I do too. Girls want the first one to be the right one because it's a big risk for us. If he doesn't stay and you [have to] go with someone else, it's bad for your reputation. Girls even in high school want the right guy." Her dreams of meeting "the right guy" were fed by what she saw in romantic Hindi films: "[You] also see this in the movies. See what happens in *Mohabattein*! . . . You want to escape, but you also want that love, that romance, that acceptance."

As Shankar points out, when it comes to romance, "one place Desi teens look for support and inspiration is Bollywood films. Unlike depictions of American romance, which feature premarital sex and do not foreground family loyalty, romantic interaction portrayed in these films appeals to Desi teen sensibilities because it follows similar cultural codes as their upbringing" (2008: 172). Certainly, Bollywood films like *Mohabattein* seemed to give Preeti a language, so to speak, to articulate her anxieties and desires about romance. She insisted that "Films [are] not just about fantasy, but also about imagining yourself. So [they are] not just [about] escape." Preeti elaborated, "These films allow me to experience what I don't have. DDLJ did just that for me. It allowed me to enjoy something I may never have. . . . But, no matter where I live, I'm Indian at heart and always will be."

Although Preeti's conception of Global Indianness and, in particular, what it means to be an Indian abroad diverge sharply from the Hindu nationalist discourses analyzed earlier in this chapter, I was puzzled by her last sentence. I wanted to learn more about why she, a Sikh American woman born in Indonesia and raised in California, would claim to be

"Indian at heart." I pushed her to explain what she meant. She responded by listing what she deemed were the essential attributes of being Indian at heart: "That family comes first, respect [for] elders. Education is important; religion is important. Also, for girls, the question we're always asked is: can you cook and clean and run the house?" Here, Preeti's tone flattened to suggest an acute ambivalence, if not resentment, toward what she clearly felt were constraints on her behavior. Nevertheless, for her, being Indian consisted of moral attributes (respect for one's elders, loyalty to one's family, religious faith) and was often articulated in terms of hegemonic notions of appropriate womanhood. Regardless of where one lived, Global Indianness entailed performing, even if resentfully, one's duties as a daughter and as a potential wife and mother.

Thus, at the same time that it diverges sharply from Hindu nationalist conceptions of Resurgent India, Preeti's conception of Global India draws on similar discourses of morality having to do with the containment of erotic desire, deference to parental authority, and the reinscription of conventional gender roles. Certainly, being Indian at heart was contingent on policing one's erotic desires, thus underscoring the intimate relationship between erotics and morality at the heart of conceptions of Global India. Women and, in particular, daughters were deemed to play a central role in not just the biological reproduction of the community but, more importantly, in the cultural reproduction of its traditions. On another occasion, Preeti complained that she was forbidden from going to *bhangra* parties because alcohol was served there and because these parties were, as she put it, "full of boys." Her parents were afraid that attending these parties would harm her reputation and that of her family. Yet, for all the moralistic insistence on deference to parental authority, Preeti and her friends participated in practices that subverted it. Although she insisted that she understood her parents' point of view, Preeti frequently defied her parents by attending these parties on the sly.

As Shankar (2008: 168) points out, community surveillance and gossip are effective forms of the policing of erotic desire. Preeti was ambivalent about the prohibitions placed on attending bhangra parties. She argued that "parents have the wrong impression about bhangra parties," and that these parties offered an opportunity to socialize with Desi (South Asian) men. She also chafed against her parents' restrictions, insisting that she had to "experience certain things" in order to learn to protect herself: "That way you see someone on the street, you know this person I gotta stay away from." She added that an American (read: white) friend had pointed something out to her that she had been unaware of: "She said to me, 'If there's a group of Punjabi or Indian guys your head goes down automatically.' She said, 'You do that.' I said, 'I do? I didn't know I do that.'" Her body responded to the sight of unknown Punjabi or Indian men by assuming the affect of modesty; thus, Preeti literally embodied some of the discourses of morality so crucial to her identity as a woman who is Indian even if not "from India."

In this manner, twinned discourses of erotics and morality refract affectively charged conceptions of Global Indianness for subjects like Preeti. As several analysts have pointed out, socializing between the sexes and dating are matters of tremendous anxiety for South Asian American parents.[35] Community surveillance, the fragility of the reputations of young, unmarried women, and discourses of family honor make sexuality a prime site for anxieties about cultural identity and preservation, such that any deviation from norms surrounding heteronormative desire is condemned and "posed as synonymous with unprincipled and immoral behavior" (Dasgupta and Das Dasgupta 1998: 113). These anxieties, in turn, are frequently articulated in terms of discourses of morality around sexual and, therefore, cultural purity. Indeed, as Maira argues, "The discourse of chaste tradition and contaminated hybridity is socialized to some extent by immigrant parents in the context of *moral* codes that equate Indian with 'good' or 'pure' and American with 'culturally inferior' or 'polluted'" (2002: 178, emphasis added). If sexual "pollution" (indexed by Valentine's Day celebrations) provokes moral panics in India, it seems especially threatening in the diaspora, where the sexual mores of young women are supposedly even more vulnerable to cultural contamination. The stakes, in other words, are considerably higher in the diaspora, and discourses of morality are reconfigured to cope with the dangers of a new land.[36]

Furthermore, it was clear to me that Bollywood films did more than feed Preeti's desire for romance and fantasy. They also enabled her interpellation by moral discourses of intimacy and "home." Her yearnings for romance were, in turn, embedded in yearnings for social, as much as erotic, intimacy. She gave the example, once again, of *Mohabattein*, which, she said, was set in a small town "where everybody knows your name. That doesn't happen here where everybody is so busy." Bollywood films like *Mohabattein* enabled her to imagine a home that replaced her sense of disaffection with relationships of familiarity, even if these relationships were frequently sites of discomfort and ambivalence.

Preeti repeatedly spoke of how Bollywood films were an important link with "back home." Over time, it became clear to me that Bollywood films played a crucial role in her formulation of a complex, albeit decidedly ambivalent, production of an extraterritorial, Global India that contrasted sharply with that constructed by the Indian nation-state or Hindu nationalists. It is thus crucial that we note that Preeti's construction of a home/land based on her engagement with Bollywood film and her claims about being Indian at heart do not reveal a suturing of identity through a purportedly seamless process of identification with the Indian nation-state. Instead, it suggests a more complex affective engagement that is analogous to Gopinath's (2005) discussion of queer spectatorship. According to Gopinath, queer spectators "may very well not be completely at home in the ideological space of the cinema and may enact particular viewing strategies in order to remake such a space" (2005: 98). Preeti's engagement with Bollywood films like *Mohabattein* enables her to (even if temporarily) sidestep dominant discourses of Indian nationalism rampant among Indian communities in the San Francisco Bay Area. Indeed, Preeti frequently said to me that "Bollywood films allow me to remember how to be Indian." This was an Indianness that was not predicated on constructions of Hindu or, indeed, Indian nationalism.

In conjunction with producing Global India as a particular kind of place, these films also suggest ways of performing everyday constructions of Global Indianness. Preeti's memories of a place that she has never inhabited reminds us of the centrality of Bollywood to place making and to processes of emplacement for some of its spectators. These films construct landscapes that are rendered ever more affectively potent because of how they fuse moralistic prescriptions on how to be a gendered subject with longings for familiarity and social connectedness. Let us consider, for a moment, *Mohabattein*'s depiction of India as a particular kind of chronotope. It was clear to me that what appealed most to Preeti about *Mohabattein* was its depiction of India as the locus of a particular kind of sociality and, indeed, morality. Not only was its story set in a pristine (in Preeti's words, "lovely") small town in the hills (as opposed to a bustling, crime-ridden city), it is also the site of social cohesion and warmth where, according to Preeti, "everybody knows your name."

In the face of the ascendance of a violent, state-endorsed Hindu nationalism, deep polarizations between religious communities, and the state's brutal repression of insurgencies in several parts of India, *Mohabattein*'s depiction of "Indian" sociality in terms of cozy neighborliness and loyal friendships is profoundly disingenuous and, at the very least, clichéd. Class differences exist (as, for instance, between some of the boys at Gurukul), but are papered over by the elegant surroundings of the school. Sikhs, Christians, and Muslims live in harmony even as they are portrayed in stereotypical terms (the primary protagonists are all Hindu; secondary characters belong to other religious communities, with Sikhs providing comic relief). This is a Global India produced through the prism of homosocial bonding and intercommunal loyalties; it is a place of deep and abiding friendships in which friends make sacrifices for each other's happiness. At the same time, this Global India represents a moral world that is ruled by benevolent patriarchs and dominated by normative heterosexuality, embodied in the headmaster and the music teacher. Nevertheless, encapsulating but extending beyond the pristine surroundings and physical beauty of the hill town where *Mohabattein* is set, the film enables viewers like Preeti to inhabit particular landscapes of Global Indianness, where one can be Indian without being from India. Preeti's affective investment in the Global India represented by *Mohabattein* entailed a scrambling of temporalities; as she put it: "This is how life used to be. This is how it still is in many places in India."

Even though the film is purportedly set in a small town set in the Himalayan foothills, when I first saw this film I was convinced that the building that housed Gurukul and the grounds surrounding it were somewhere in Europe, most likely in England.[37] On the one hand, given the fact that some of *Mohabattein*'s songs were shot on location in Switzerland and, furthermore, that scenes of upper-class life in most Bollywood films (recall my discussion of *K3G* above) are set in Europe, this should not surprise us. However, rather than simply depicting landscapes in other countries, films like *Mohabattein* depict an India that is emplaced in the affluent West and, therefore, construct an India *that could be*. In so doing, they fuse the affective investments of a Global India based on fantasies of affluence and progress with temporalizing processes contingent on discourses of national futurity and potentiality. Put another way, the West functions as a place that Global India can become, an aspirational and affective location articulated in discourses of futurity. As Rai has argued in his discussion of *Mohabattein*, "Part of what is being marketed as traditional Indian culture in Hindi films is not simply a Sanskritized and chauvinistic brand of 'national' memory, but one with global ambitions as well" (2009: 34).

Bollywood films like *Mohabattein* represent a vision of Global India which, even as it functions as a node of moral discipline and social regulation, is constituted as an archive of affect and temporality. As a Sikh, Preeti belongs to a community that has been marginalized and targeted as an object of violence by the Indian state and by Hindu nationalists.[38] Further, her experiences of being out of place in the San Francisco Bay Area are compounded by her gender and class position and by her struggles to negotiate a complex, frequently hostile, racial landscape. Preeti's affective investment in her own version of Global India suggests how subjects situated at the margins of both the Indian and the U.S. nation-state construct a home/land even when they are not sutured to the nation. Contrasting with K3G's construction of the Indian nation in terms of its anteriority to diasporic subjectivity, Preeti's Global India refers neither to a geopolitical entity nor to a purported place of origin. Preeti's Global India, far from reifying or consolidating nationalist conceptions of India, unsettles them.

Conclusion

Insofar as it entailed the transnational circulation of specific, sometimes discrepant, discourses of morality, the construction of Global India was as much an affective and temporal project as a political-economic one. As we have seen, affectively charged processes of temporality were deeply imbricated in the Resurgent India campaign launched by the BJP-led state in 1998. In this campaign, representations of Resurgent India were contingent on the reclamation of a past glory deemed essential for the Hindu/Indian nation to march toward a glowing future. In other contexts, Global India was constituted through affectively charged discourses of tradition. Tradition emerged as an affective-temporal formation that entailed not so much the invocation of a past as the generation of a set of practices enabling subjects to imagine and embrace specific forms of futurity. In yet other instances, as in the case of Preeti, Global India represented a chronotope of social intimacy as well as social regulation, and represented ways of being Indian that eschewed any identification or affiliation with the Indian nation or state.

Differentiating time consciousness from objective, measurable time, Gingrich, Ochs, and Swedlund underscore that "time-keeping" is a "*moral matter*, implicating such notions as truth, virtue, authority, origins, memory, desire, progress, and anticipation" (2000: 83, emphasis added). We have seen how temporality and affect converge at the heart of the Resurgent India campaign through its promise to bring back a "glorious past when India had been 'surging'" (Chander 2001: 1066).[39] Discourses of Resurgent India draw sustenance from constructions of a mythic past of a pristine Hindu Golden Age that allegedly declined due to "Islamic invasion," British colonialism, and certain aspects of Western culture (through the specter of Westernization).[40] Discourses of contemporaneity are equally implicated, for it is in the present—a present marked by a selective adoption and rejection of Western and modern practices—where the blueprint of the future is to be formulated; for example, while the free market might be embraced, the "Westernization" of Indian women is abhorred. Since the invocation of the past connotes loss—the loss of glory and national supremacy—the present is haunted by a recurrent absence. But it is this sense of absence that forms the basis of conceptions of futurity in which India will, once again, become an important world power. The different forms of Hindu nationalist affect that adhere to conceptions of Global India pertain to how the contemporary nation must negotiate globality through economic liberalization and, equally importantly, through the production of particular kinds of moral subjects who participate in the production of a Global India of the future.

Thus, I have mapped the circulation of discontinuous trajectories of specific discourses of morality in order to trace how they articulate with conceptions of Global Indianness at specific nodes: the moral and affective claims of the Resurgent India campaign; the controversies surrounding romance in the celebration of Valentine's Day in India; the work of a Bollywood film in the production of patriarchal romance along axes of family, nation, and femininity; and the efforts of a young, working-class Sikh American woman to emplace herself vis-à-vis Global India. As I note above, my strategic juxtaposition of these apparently disparate nodes is intended to highlight their overlaps and their disjunctures.

My primary goal has been to demonstrate that, instead of consolidating or reifying India, these constructions of Global India in fact unsettle substantialist notions of India and Indian culture. For instance, in my analysis of the generation and policing of heteronormative erotics, I point out that, according to Hindutva ideology, ideal Hindutva women must channel their erotic energies into the task of producing a nation of Hindu/Indian patriots. Yet in the Global Indias constituted in *K3G* and in the celebration of Valentine's Day, erotic desire emerges as eruptive even as it is refracted by relations of power and inequality (see also chapters 2 and 4). In *K3G*, erotic desire tears the patriarchal family apart, even if temporarily, and overrides all reason and allegiances to family to constitute an agency all its own; for example, when Yash asks Rahul how he could possibly think that Anjali could fit into the Raichand family, Rahul responds, his eyes glazing with desire, "I didn't think, Papa, I just loved, just loved." The eruptive potential of erotic desire also suggests that Hindutva discourses of morality are not totalizing. For all their interpellation by globally circulating discourses of commodity capitalism, by celebrating Valentine's Day young men and women defy the moral policing of erotic desire in the face of considerable danger to their reputations and persons.

Constructions of Global India were profoundly affective in two senses of the term. On the one hand, they were saturated with distinct regimes of affect (ranging from an acute sense of loss or mourning about the purported or imminent loss of Indian culture to celebratory pride based on the belief that India has earned its rightful place on the global stage). At the same time, constructions of Global India were affective in that they were generative of agency, for instance, when they enabled, and sometimes incited, specific kinds of actions and practices on the part of individuals and communities, ranging from Hindu nationalist violence to the everyday negotiation of cultural identity on the part of heterogeneous subjects in the diaspora.

Moreover, my selection and staging of the foregoing ethnographic accounts serve to enact my larger argument, the objective of which is to examine how India is constructed as well as unsettled: I have foregrounded the overlaps and disjunctures characterizing how heterogeneous subjects construct India as an archive of affect and temporality. As Stewart succinctly puts it, affects "work not through 'meanings' per se, but rather in the way that they pick up density and texture as they move through bodies, dreams, dramas, and social worldings of all kinds" (2007: 3). As I have demonstrated throughout this book, conducting ethnographic analysis is itself a deeply affective process and entails an engagement with the entire being of the ethnographer (Ortner 1995). My affective engagements with some of my informants point to disjunctures that were political as much as affective: the accounts presented above highlight that, far from finding common ground with all my informants, there were occasions when I felt compelled to refuse identification or connection with them, thus challenging assumptions about ethnographic rapport and, extending beyond these ethnographic encounters, unsettling presumptions about a singular diasporic identity. These were moments of affective and temporal disconnect, when time stood still or felt out of joint with the humdrum placidity of our surroundings.

Yet my engagement with my informants—whether my visceral responses to those who expressed their hatred for Muslims or my corporeal participation in watching films with others—extended beyond the emotions or feelings that I might have shared (or not) with them. My concern was less with my informants' individual feelings or sentiments than with the ways in which they, and I, were emplaced and constituted through multiple affective regimes—whether generated by Hindutva, class mobility in the Bay Area, or Bollywood films. As Stewart argues, affects are "more directly compelling than ideologies, as well as more fractious, multiplicitous, and unpredictable than symbolic meanings" (2007: 3). The indeterminacy of affect is underscored in its centrality to the ways in which worlds are formed, sustained, and, also at times, unraveled.

Preeti's conception of Global Indianness draws, at least in part, on heteronormative constructions of erotics and, to this extent, may not be valorized as resistance or subversion. Nevertheless, in ways that are radically different from hegemonic representations of Global India, she constructs a vision of Global Indianness that challenges hypostasized and reified notions of Hindu/Indian culture that have been violent in their brutal exclusions of cultural and religious Others like herself. Her formulation of Global India also unsettles conceptions of Indianness that are predicated on discourses of origin (thus, according to her, one can be a Global Indian without being from India). Finally, by facilitating Preeti's navigation of a complex and hostile racial landscape in the United States, her constructions of Global India gesture toward the instability of processes of cultural assimilation and racialized minoritization that refract her formation as a Sikh American and a South Asian American woman.

In chapter 6, I examine other formations of (Global) India by focusing on the instability catalyzed by the uneven articulation of discourses of neoliberalism, particularly those pertaining to individual responsibility and entrepreneurship, in the lives of call center agents in Gurgaon and in a popular Hindi film, *Bunty aur Babli*. Pivoting around the trope of movement and mobility, these discourses of individual entrepreneurship are predicated on the intensification of the aspirations of lower-middle-class youth in contemporary India. These aspirations underscore how anticipation and hope are interwined with anxiety and uncertainty to produce a state of unsettlement.

CHAPTER 6

Aspirational India

Impersonation, Mobility, and Emplacement

In chapter 5, I analyzed how discrepant discourses of morality undergirded conceptions of Global India. Here, I focus on the impersonation practices of the protagonists of a Bollywood film, *Bunty aur Babli* (Bunty and Babli, 2005) and call center employees in Gurgaon to examine the place of aspiration in the formation of India as an archive of affect and temporality.[1] I use these two examples to trace how the metrics of progress, success, and class mobility have been recalibrated and, more crucially, aspired to by lower-middle-class youth in early twenty-first-century India.[2] I am interested in tracing the processes through which laboring subjects get emplaced in a world of apparently dizzying mobility and, hence, return to a theme I introduced in chapter 1: the intimate relationship between mobility and emplacement.[3] Finally, I examine the role of race in the emplacement of call center employees in India by drawing on analyses of the circulation of racialized labor in Asian American studies; in so doing, I interrogate the boundaries of South Asian studies and Asian American studies by pushing at the edges of nation-bound assumptions about identity and race.

That call center employees, or agents as they are called in the industry, assumed foreign identities by acquiring new names, modifying their accents (either through imitating foreign patterns of speech or, as happened recently, through supposedly neutralizing their regional accents), and, in many cases, adopting fictive personas and lives has attracted a great deal of media attention. For many call center agents, impersonation was a prerequisite of their jobs and, hence, a crucial strategy in their struggles for upward mobility. By focusing on impersonation as a cultural practice driven by aspiration, I wish to unsettle the binary between impersonation and personation, and fictive versus authentic identity: these forms of impersonation were not unique to call center employees but were, instead, part of larger discourses of upward mobility circulating in early twenty-first-century India.

Impersonation is neither unique nor unprecedented in scholarly and other discourses on identity and personhood. My conception of impersonation draws on the problematization of a stable and unitary identity implicit in the work of a wide range of scholars, including Erving Goffman (1959), whose work on the performance of everyday life has been foundational to much theorizing on the social bases of personhood. In a different vein, some of the canonical work in postcolonial studies foregrounds the destabilization of subjectivity in colonial contexts marked by radical asymmetries of power. For instance, Frantz Fanon (1967) has poignantly described how notions of authentic subjectivity are undermined, if not forestalled, through practices of mimicry, while Homi Bhabha asserts that "mimicry emerges as the representation of a difference that is itself a process of disavowal" (1994: 86). The place of mimicry in the construction of subjectivity has been reconceptualized by Parama Roy, who critiques its implicit teleology and locates it in the formation of gender, race, and sexual identities; in addition, in her discussion of Kipling's Kim, Roy (1998) argues that impersonation, unlike mimicry, is not always subversive and can, in fact, consolidate hierarchies of power and inequality.

Feminist and queer theory, most notably the work of Judith Butler (1993) and Marjorie Garber (1997) on performativity and masquerade respectively, also enable us to interrogate the relationship between impersonation and subject formation. In her canonical work on how imitation lies at the heart of the heterosexual project, Butler (1993: 125) posits that drag is not a secondary imitation that presupposes an a priori and original gender, but that hegemonic heterosexuality is itself a constant and repeated effort to imitate its own idealization. To put it differently, all impersonation is personation. Similarly, Garber (1997), in Vested Interests, argues that masquerade and cross-dressing reflect a blurring of gender roles and thus engages how impersonation occurs through the assumption of sartorial difference.

Conceptions of impersonation have a long and varied genealogy in South Asian public cultures. For instance, Hindu epics are rife with references to gods, goddesses, and lesser mortals who not only impersonate people but also assume the form of other beings including animals. The trope of the behroopiya (the being that changes its roop or form) is ubiquitous in many scriptural and vernacular traditions. In fact, impersonation has a rich history in the textual and performative traditions of Hindu South Asia, providing fascinating insights into the relationship between impersonation (variously conceived and defined), cultural production, and constructions of personhood. While engaging these traditions is beyond the scope of this chapter, a cursory review reveals multiple instances of impersonation. As analyzed by George Thompson (1997), folkloric and Sanskritic discourses of impersonation radically destabilize a notion of personhood as innate. Similarly, performative traditions such as the Ramlila of Ramnagar suggest an intimate relationship between impersonation and personation, as when actors imbibe the personas of divine beings. According to Anuradha Kapur (1990) actors playing mythic beings may acquire spiritual powers through their impersonation of them, thus blurring the boundary between impersonation and personation, and underscoring the mutual constitution of performance, performativity, and selfhood.

The modalities of impersonation that I am about to describe are different from those outlined above in that the impersonation practices followed by Bunty and Babli and by call center agents are fueled by their aspirations to mobility and growth. What do the specificities of these protocols of impersonation tell us about the relationship between aspiration and subject constitution in urban, postliberalization India? What are the social bases of these particular aspirations and, conversely, how are these aspirations productive of sociality? As Appadurai reminds us, aspirations are "never simply individual (as the language of wants and choices inclines us to think). They are always formed in interaction and in the thick of social life" (2004: 67). I am interested in how, at a particular historical moment in postcolonial India, the capacity to aspire was generated and the ways in which it shifted for some sections of urban youth, and in how these shifts in the capacity to aspire were, in turn, produced and acquired salience. I argue that aspirations are an affective-temporal formation: drawing sustenance from a disjuncture between how subjects navigate the present and imagine the future, they are generative of specific forms of action and agency; aspirations mediate how subjects form their worlds and inhabit and navigate them. Last but not least, the specific aspirations I focus on in this chapter are allegorical of the (re)constitution of the Indian nation as it seeks to position itself in the global economy. In focusing on the temporality and affectivity of aspiration, my primary objective is to explore how our assumptions about India and about cultural change are stirred up—unsettled—in contexts of neoliberalism and the circulation of transnational public cultures.

6.1. Babli sings of her dream of leaving her hometown.

Impersonation, Aspiration, and Gender

Bunty aur Babli is one of many Hindi films that, over the past decade, have narrated the recalibration of aspiration in postliberalization India. These films are too numerous to list and engaging a comparison between them is beyond the scope of this chapter. However, some notable examples include *Guru* (2007), a (purportedly) fictional representation of the rise of a textile tycoon; *Swades* (2004), which is exemplary in how it brings together discourses of rural development, national progress, diasporic longing, and neoliberal conceptions of self-sufficiency; and *Band Baaja Baraat* (2010), a romantic comedy that brilliantly marries neoliberal discourses of entrepreneurship with heteronormative formulations of erotic desire and romance (Mankekar 2013).

I focus here on *Bunty aur Babli* because it effectively conjoins tropes of movement and mobility with impersonation as metrics for aspirations to growth and entrepreneurial self-sufficiency. *Bunty aur Babli* is about the struggles of Rakesh and Vimmi, a young man and woman who seem to be riding the crest of the changes occurring in India in the early decades of the twenty-first century. Rakesh and Vimmi are ambitious, resourceful, and spunky—and desperately bored with their lives in their respective hometowns of Fursatganj and Pankinagar. They aspire to more, much more, than their small towns can promise. Rakesh wants to be a successful business tycoon, while Vimmi has her heart set on becoming a fashion model. Their respective hometowns are too small for them to realize their dreams of making it big. We are introduced to them through a song in which we see them dancing on a train that, they fantasize, will transport them to lives of glamour, success, and fame (figure 6.1). Their hunger for a life radically different from the one they are leading makes them destined to meet. The train serves as a trope for their aspirations to mobility; it also symbolizes the lure of elsewhere.[4] This song depicts Rakesh and Vimmi's boredom, as well as their aspirations for what their lives could be like were they to leave the "empty, bore [sic] afternoons" of their lives.

Rakesh and Vimmi's aspirations are contingent on their ability to be mobile. They meet by accident at a desolate railway station. They decide shortly afterward to set up a partnership and travel together to Bombay, the city of their dreams. Impersonation becomes a cornerstone of Rakesh and Vimmi's aspirations. They have to become other people in order to make it big—indeed, to acquire physical as well as social mobility. Their physical travel from Uttar Pradesh to Mumbai is enabled by their impersonation of a host of characters (ranging from gurus, business tycoons, and bureaucrats, to a minister and her secretary). Although their pursuit of freedom, adventure, and glamour is laden with hardship and risk, like the call center agents introduced later in this chapter, their aspirations for making it big have material effects on the choices they make and the lives they lead. Mobility is the key to their success, indeed, to their very ability to leave the claustrophobia of their hometowns.

Rakesh and Vimmi's mobility is thus predicated on the adoption of new identities, and on their journey to Bombay they adopt new names: Bunty and Babli. Impersonation blends into personation as Rakesh morphs into Bunty and Vimmi into Babli. They proceed to assume several new personas and identities that will enable them to embark on a string of con jobs: Babli Bose, a health inspector out to investigate complaints against a restaurant, and her assistant; a gangster and his moll who wish to buy a fancy foreign car; tourist guides; a guru and his assistant; a business tycoon and his wife out to purchase a hotel; and so on (figures 6.2 and 6.3). Their different personas are marked by the disguises they don: as they change clothes, we realize they have become different people.

Their undoing occurs when they try to con the Indian state by stealing gold that the government is attempting to transport from one city to another. At that point, Dashrath Singh, a Criminal Investigation Department (CID) inspector played by the leading Bollywood star Amitabh Bachchan, who has been pursuing them in vain for years, catches up with the couple and arrests them. Ironically, their arrest occurs at the very moment when they decide to mend their ways: Babli has just delivered their first child and has made Bunty promise that they will return to Fursatganj and lead law-abiding lives. Bunty and Babli plead with Dashrath Singh that they have indeed turned a new leaf. Miraculously, Singh believes them and lets them go, and they return to Fursatganj as Rakesh and Vimmi. Three years later they are surprised by a visit from Dashrath Singh, who invites

6.2 and 6.3. Bunty and Babli's impersonations.

them to join the government as secret agents. Their ability to impersonate others, Dashrath claims, is exactly what the Indian government needs in order to track down criminals. The film ends on a triumphant note that celebrates the ways in which impersonation can now be put to the service of the state itself.

At a critical moment in the film, Bunty proclaims that he wants to be a business tycoon like Tata, Birla, or Ambani (three leading Indian industrialists) and that, in order to do so, he has to leave his hometown of Fursatganj and go to Mumbai: "If Tata-Birla-Ambani had stayed on in their hometowns, do you think they would have reached anywhere?" Mobility is valorized as the key to their success, indeed to their very ability to flee the claustrophobia of their hometowns. The film portrays them perpetually on the move in trains, in buses and cars, on top of trucks, running away from irate mobs. They so enjoy being on the move that they derive immense pleasure from being fugitives. In fact, in one instance when we see the two of them fleeing an enraged mob that has (presumably) caught on to them, Bunty comments that he enjoys being chased by the mob because he finally feels that he too is someone (*hum bhi kuch hain*).

Bunty and Babli's subjectivities are also shaped by their practices of consumption. Their flashy new clothes, and the pleasure they derive from eating at high-end restaurants and staying at fancy hotels, are all markers of how far they have traveled in their journey toward a successful and glamorous life. In one scene where they decide that they can never make enough money, we see that they have reached the acme of consumption: she is preening in her new dress and eating a large chocolate cake; he has donned a loud shirt and a flashy new watch.[5] In fact, throughout the film, we see that their joy in buying new clothes, new cars, and living the high life is second only to the sheer pleasure they derive from getting away with impersonating others.

Significantly, even as *Bunty aur Babli* is purportedly about the aspirations of lower-middle-class youth in small towns and rural and semirural India, it represents the obstacles they face almost entirely in terms of the alleged lack of opportunities of small towns and semirural parts of India.[6] The film never touches on the hurdles to upward mobility faced by lower-middle-class (or indeed working-class) youth in terms of their structural positions, and it leaves untouched, for instance, the role of class and caste. They strive to embody their newfangled class positions through other markers of distinction (Bourdieu 1984). Bunty and Babli embody the symbolic capital they acquire through their new clothes, the new ways in which they inhabit their bodies, and their ability to move through space.

Bunty and Babli's aspirations to mobility, glamour, and success are fed by transnational media. This is particularly true of Vimmi. The film's scriptwriter, Jaideep Sahni, describes her as a young woman who lives in a small town but derives her knowledge of the world from cable TV (*The Making of Bunty aur Babli* 2005). Very early in the film, we see her mother lamenting that, ever since she started watching "cable TV," she has "lost her mind." Her bedroom in Pankinagar is plastered with photographs of international models and Bollywood and Hollywood film stars. She aspires to be a star and, singing in a heady mix of Hindi and English, she dreams about how it is not easy to live among stars (*taaron mein jeena-weena* easy *nahin*). We see her talking to a photograph of Sushmita Sen, one of the first Indian women of her generation to win an international beauty pageant; Sen is clearly one of Vimmi's role models. In another scene, we see her take a photograph torn from a glossy fashion magazine to her tailor in Pankinagar so that he can copy the outfit worn by the model.

Impersonation blends into personation through the ways in which gender and sexuality refract Vimmi's ability to become other people. When we first see her in the film, her parents are trying to arrange her marriage to a head clerk in a bank. When she protests, her mother advises her to forget about her aspirations to become a model because, as she points out, once she is married she will have to live her life according to the customs and wishes of her in-laws. Vimmi is horrified; her fiancé might be a fantastic catch for another lower-middle-class woman in a small town, but she is well aware that getting married will prevent her from pursuing her aspirations to become a supermodel. She decides to run away from home to Lucknow, where she plans to compete in the Miss India pageant.

But because she is a woman traveling by herself, Vimmi has to depend on some degree of protection by Rakesh as her travel companion; for instance, when they first meet she asks Rakesh to escort her to the women's restroom in a desultory corner of the railway station. Nevertheless, she more than holds her own against him. When, at one point in the film, Bunty suggests to her that they should part ways so he can continue his life of impersonation and she can pursue her dream of becoming a model, Babli demands to know if he could ever have attained anything without her. Shortly after the birth of their child, she tells Bunty that the time has come for them to change their ways. Delivering the baby while fleeing the police has terrified her, and she is afraid that their child will end up being raised in a prison. Although it is difficult, she is able to persuade Bunty to switch to a life of respectability and honesty.

Like other Bollywood heroines, Babli is eroticized throughout the film; unlike many other heroines, however, she is portrayed as having relative control of her own sexuality (see chapter 4 for an extended analysis of Hindi television's representation of women as agentive subjects of erotic desire). Very early in the film, when the clerk at an office of the Miss India beauty pageant makes a pass at her, she beats him up in a decidedly unfeminine way. Further, in the course of becoming Babli, she never hesitates to deploy her sexuality to get what she wants, as is evident in her seductive behavior with Qureshi, the bureaucrat who cheats Rakesh, and in her flirtation with the manager of a large appliance store from which they steal a huge amount of merchandise. The film's depiction of Bunty and Babli's wedding night transgresses conventional Bollywood representations of the wedding night or *suhaag raat*, in which coy brides are seduced by their grooms. After getting drunk and falling asleep on her wedding night, it is Babli who takes the initiative the next day to consummate their relationship. The two sing an erotic song that underscores her unequivocal pleasure in her sexuality.

When they first arrive in Bombay, Bunty tells Babli that he wishes to continue his life of impersonation. He realizes that he had never been Rakesh but, in fact, had been Bunty all along. He adds that he is happy being Bunty; this is the path he wants to follow for the rest of his life.

When they return to Fursatganj, Rakesh's hometown, with their child, we see that Bunty appears to have reverted to being Rakesh and works in an office (much like his father), while Babli has been transformed into—or rather impersonates—Vimmi, a dutiful wife, daughter, and daughter-in-law who spends her time cooking and taking care of her family. But it remains ambiguous whether they have returned to who they truly are, or if they are impersonating Rakesh and Vimmi.

When Dashrath Singh visits them in Fursatganj, he sees that they are leading law-abiding lives but are desperately bored. He invites them to return to their life of impersonation but, this time, they are to form a special investigative team and, rather than return to their earlier life of fraud and petty crime, they will serve the Indian state by deploying their uncanny ability to impersonate others to hunt down criminals. Rakesh falls at Dashrath Singh's feet and begs him to rescue him from his life of respectability, and Babli pleads, "If I have to bottle another jar of mango pickle, I will die!" Returning to the life of impersonation will allow her to escape, once again, the tedium and claustrophobia of the stereotypical life of a small-town woman who measures her accomplishments by the amount of mango pickles she can make. For all the freedom that they enjoy after running away from home, Bunty and Babli eventually return to Bunty/Rakesh's hometown of Fursatganj where they live with his parents, thus reinforcing patriarchal notions of belonging and emplacement. Even when, at the end of the film, they leave Fursatganj for the second time, they do not (and cannot) do so as autonomous subjects: their uncanny ability to impersonate others is harnessed by the Indian state itself.

This hilarious but remarkably insightful film is a masterful depiction of a brave new world of aspirations, daring and, most pertinent to my argument here, impersonation. I want to suggest that the impersonation practices of Bunty and Babli, and the aspirations that fuel them, were not unique to them but were, in fact, ubiquitous in discourses of upward mobility circulating in India during the first decade of the twenty-first century (compare Mankekar 2013). One commentator has described call center agents as "liberalization's children . . . [who have] a hunger in the belly for achievement and all the good things that money can buy" (Rama Bijapurkar in Shome 2006: 120). The things that money can buy were important indexes of making it big in a brave new world. This way of living (and moving up) in the world—this ethic—is profoundly shaped by a commitment to individual initiative and a spirit of entrepreneurship, and is sometimes predicated on a profound ambivalence toward an older world of conventional roles and duties. *Bunty aur Babli* effectively materializes a particular zeitgeist: as two lower-middle-class youths from small towns, Rakesh and Vimmi are motivated by the same "hunger in the belly" to pursue their aspirations (to make money, to earn fame, to acquire a glamorous lifestyle) as many call center agents.

Impersonation and Personation in Call Centers

On a muggy July night in 2003, Akhil Gupta and I, accompanied by an old school friend of mine, first ventured into the world of call centers. As we entered a nondescript building in Gurgaon, a two-story, whitewashed building that looked for all intents and purposes like a house, we were confronted by a high metal gate watched over by a security guard. We gave him our names, and he called in to see if we had permission to enter. Much to the astonishment of the guard, who probably did not expect the sahib himself to come out to identify us, we were greeted by the owner. But the sahib, Harjeet, aka Harry, Sethi, was a former student of my friend's and evidently felt obliged to greet us personally. At the time, Harry was in his early twenties; he was casually, but expensively, dressed and looked too young to be the owner of a business of any sort.

Harry took us up two flights of stairs into his office, a spartan room, furnished with a few chairs and a desk on which, of course, sat a PC. But there were no windows, no carpets, no bookshelves, and nothing adorning the walls. The room had a strangely transient air. Akhil Gupta and I began by describing our interest in the cultural dimensions of the call center industry and in learning more about the organizational culture of companies like his, and were particularly concerned with investigating how the work of call center employees intersected with their personal lives. Harry, a smart and articulate young man, became visibly excited as we spoke and was so full of suggestions for us that he barely allowed us to complete our sentences.

Harry insisted on giving us a personal tour. He first took us to the cafeteria, a large room that was clearly inspired by representations of high school cafeterias in Hollywood films. It had a shiny linoleum floor and brightly colored plastic tables and chairs. Glossy prints of pizza, hamburgers, and spaghetti jostled with posters of Hollywood stars on vividly colored walls. American pop music was playing softly in the background. We peered over at the steam tables—no "American" food was sold here. Instead, we saw *daal*, *rajmah* (kidney beans), spicy okra, *raita*, and a stack of rapidly-cooling chapatis. It was past midnight (and, apparently, too early for most employees to be eating their midnight meal), there were very few people in the cafeteria. We next took the elevator to the basement and entered a room that Harry described as the gym. A large, cavernous room with bare walls, it contained brand new weight machines, a few treadmills and stationary bikes, and a large ping-pong table. The room did not look like it was used very much; there wasn't a soul in sight.

We decided to walk up two flights of stairs to the main office, the shop floor where the call center employees, or agents, did their work. We took a stairway outside the building, and it was full of young men and women on cigarette breaks. They shuffled their feet restlessly when they saw their boss walking toward them. Harry, who is a Sikh, shook his head in disgust and explained to us that, since they could not smoke inside the building, the agents used the stairs to smoke and socialize. Most of them were in their early or mid-twenties, either the same age or a little older than the young man who owned their company. All, without exception, were trendily dressed and impeccably groomed. Some of them sported a fashionably bored look; others seemed nervous to be in the presence of their boss and looked away uneasily.

Harry led us into the main working area, a large room filled with cubicles. There was a perceptible buzz in the room, a sense of excitement and industry. Most of the cubicles were filled with young men and women sitting in front of flickering computer monitors, wearing headsets, and speaking in low voices. The cubicles were bare, unadorned with any personal items. I wondered if this was because the agents moved from one cubicle to another or because they simply didn't bother to mark their space in any way. A few looked up and smiled, somewhat uncertainly, at us. Harry introduced us to the floor supervisor. We hung around in the room somewhat awkwardly, until the supervisor asked if we wanted to listen in on a call.

TEMPORALITY AND AFFECTIVE LABOR IN CALL CENTERS

Call centers are a part of the business process outsourcing (BPO) industry, which took off in India in the late 1990s. The BPO industry has been shaped by a phenomenon whereby Indian companies, many of which are "homegrown" and locally based, are contracted by companies in the United States, the United Kingdom, and Australia to perform a range of functions, including telemarketing and customer services; business process management; back-office clerical work; medical transcription processing; account services; building and maintaining legal databases; and data entry, digitization, and management. By the time we started our fieldwork in Gurgaon, a range of multinational companies had established their back offices in India, the most prominent of which were Citibank, GE, AOL, AT&T, and Goldman Sachs. The shift to digitization meant that large quantities of data were rapidly transmitted across vast geographical distances, resulting in new regimes of labor (Aneesh 2006; Freeman 2000; Shome 2006; Vora 2010). Hundreds of thousands of Indian men and women were recruited, trained, and then put to work on the shop floor in the BPO industry as agents, where they earned entry-level salaries that were relatively substantial for most middle- and lower-middle-class Indian youth.[7]

Central to offshore production since the 1970s, labor arbitrage has acquired new forms in recent years and has been fundamental to the offshore outsourcing of services. This is particularly true of the information technology (IT) industry, where jobs ranging from software programming to back-office work have been outsourced from the Global North to other countries. Labor arbitrage refers to the "ability to pay one labor pool less than another labor pool for accomplishing the same work, typically by substituting labor in one geography for labor in a different locale" (Ong 2006: 161). Labor arbitrage enables cost cutting, a crucial survival strategy for many IT companies after the dot-com bust. Labor arbitrage replaces one form of outsourcing, the hiring of imported labor in the form of H-1B visa holders (chapter 3), with the offshore outsourcing of labor to other countries. For over a decade, Asian countries like India, China, and the Philippines have become the primary sites for offshore outsourcing. Labor arbitrage is also facilitated by IT because of its ability to synchronize the performance of online labor in different parts of the world.

Sharma and Gupta point out, "As a symbol of economic globalization, call centers have come to occupy a central place in debates on the 'outsourcing' of jobs from the North" (2006: 2). Typically, Indian firms lease dedicated telecommunication networks to connect with online databases and with overseas companies and clients. Thus, for instance, call center agents sitting in Gurgaon could look up a customer's purchasing habits to prep for a sales call, and debt collectors could tap into their customers' credit histories. According to one call center owner that we interviewed, customer services were no longer as lucrative as they used to be in the 1990s and some Indian firms were switching to debt collection and medical transcription services.

In theory, call centers may recruit from a fairly diverse employee pool, including homemakers, retired military officers, and so on. Yet all the trainers and owners of call centers we worked with were unanimous in insisting that they preferred to hire young people, either those still in college or, preferably, recent graduates. One call center owner was very explicit in his reasons for preferring young people: "Older people don't have the stamina to do this kind of work," he said. "If you're over thirty, you're basically too old. Plus, most people have families of their own by that age. And [in those cases] families get in the way of the work." Working hours were such as to preclude having a normal family life.

We interviewed one call center agent who was in his late twenties and did, in fact, have a family. He had previously worked as a wholesale agent for laundry detergent and had had to travel constantly to sell his wares. Since his income was tied to his sales, he had been under tremendous pressure to perform. He told us that, even though it meant that he had to do night work, he preferred working in call centers. Despite the fact that here, too, he was under great pressure to meet targets, he claimed that he got less tired than when he had to go from shop to shop selling detergent. He liked the "young crowd" because they were fun to be around and made him feel young; the salary was much better and, most of all, he enjoyed interacting with "foreigners." When Akhil Gupta and I asked him whether this was a job he would stick with long term and if he thought he could advance in his new career, he admitted that he did not know. Slightly older than his coworkers, he seemed fairly realistic about the precarious prospects for advancement in his current workplace. However, he claimed, this job was enabling him to grow in other ways by providing him with a range of "soft skills" and, equally important, the confidence that would enable him to find another—hopefully better—job.

Many call center agents inhabited multiple temporalities: the time difference between India and most overseas clients meant that Indian agents had to work at night to be able to interact with them in real time. When Akhil Gupta and I first visited a call center in Gurgaon, we experienced firsthand some of the temporal dissonances faced by agents. We left after 9 p.m., just as our family was retiring for the night, and drove for an hour through the gray darkness of the outskirts of New Delhi into Gurgaon. It was considerably darker by the time we arrived. Street-corner stores and shacks selling tea and samosas were shuttered, and the buzz of the streets was winding down for the night.

The inky blue of residential neighborhoods was punctuated by brightly lit buildings. Every now and then the drowsy streets would be jolted awake by the squealing of the tires of vans and SUVs transporting employees of the BPO industry, which zoomed around jumping over potholes and narrowly avoiding sleeping street dogs. By the time we arrived at the call center it was close to midnight, and we were drowsy and tired from the activities of our day. But within a few moments of walking in we were swept up into its high-energy atmosphere. As Gupta and Sharma (2006: 1) have remarked elsewhere, the shop floor represented all the speed up and electricity of a news room just before a deadline, and threw into sharp relief the slumber of the city around us. Call center agents sat in cubicles in a large room that was humming with the sound of their voices as they spoke in low tones to their clients. Several agents had a can of Coke or a paper cup of coffee by their side and seemed wide awake (agents are said to depend on the "3Cs"—coffee, Coke, and cigarettes—to keep awake and stay energized). The rest of the city felt very distant and, by the time we left and reentered New Delhi, our sense of dislocation felt complete.

The temporal disconnect entailed in working in call centers required a great deal of stamina and resilience and had consequences for the health and social relationships of agents. Agents in the call centers we visited would typically return to their homes in the early hours of the morning and eat, shower, and try to rest. Several agents described the difficulty of "switching off" when they left the call center; they said they found it impossible to fall asleep when they got home, no matter how tired they were. One agent spoke of how she never quite got used to this routine; always aware of the city buzzing around her, she was unable to sleep soundly during the day. Agents described how they would awaken in the late afternoon, go shopping, hang out, visit friends, and then leave for work just as their friends and families were ending their day. All the agents and supervisors we interviewed described their work as physically exhausting and spoke of how working the night shift on a continuous basis disrupted their sleep cycles and circadian rhythms.

The temporalities call center agents inhabited were disjunctive also because, in the words of one agent, they always felt out of sync with family members, neighbors, and friends. Many agents experienced a contraction of their social worlds. While they strove to keep up with the daily lives of relatives and friends who did not have to work night shifts, this was a struggle that many of the agents found overwhelming. As a result, most agents socialized primarily with each other, forming friendships and intimate relationships that frequently spring up in communities cut off from a larger social world. But these relations of sociality and intimacy were often fraught because agents were also encouraged to compete with each other to meet the quotas set by their supervisors.

Through our fieldwork in call centers in Gurgaon, Akhil Gupta and I learned that affective regimes constitute a central, if not foundational, aspect of the labor of call center agents. In the United States, a perceptible shift from manufacturing to the service economy began during the 1970s and gained momentum in the last two decades of the twentieth century. The service economy includes education, the so-called knowledge industries, transportation, health care, and food services, many sectors of which depend on working-class and immigrant labor and demand highly mobile and flexible skills. The service economy has had widespread ramifications for the world economy. Like some other countries in the Global South (for instance, the Philippines), India has emerged as a hub for the global service economy. The call center industry is an important component of the service sector of the Indian economy.

On a global scale, the convergence of the service industry with IT, or what Michael Hardt (1999: 90) calls the postindustrial informational economy, is characterized by labor regimes predicated on transactions involving knowledge, information, communication, and affect. Hardt uses the term "affective labor" to foreground the corporeal and intellectual aspects of the new forms of labor performed by the "new cognitariat" (2007: xi).[8] Arguing that affective labor is one dimension of what he terms "immaterial labor," Hardt posits, "Since the production of services results in no material and durable good, we might define the labor involved in this production as immaterial labor—that is, labor that produces an immaterial good, such as a service, knowledge, or communication" (1999: 94). Hardt points to how these sectors of the economy are "focused on the creation and manipulation of affects" (1999: 96) and insists that, while affective labor was never outside the capitalist economy, it now represents "the very pinnacle of the hierarchy of labor forms" (1999: 90).

Although the teleology implicit in this formulation is problematic, it is evident that affective labor has always been part of capitalist economies. I would, in fact, argue that high-tech capitalism is dependent on forms of affective labor, particularly in political-economic contexts shaped by the convergence of IT and the service economy, as in the case of the call centers. The call centers that Akhil Gupta and I observed were part of a multinational service economy based on the continual and transnational exchange of information and knowledges.[9]

Furthermore, while many forms of affective labor entail physical contact between service provider and client/customer, affective labor also exists in contexts of virtual contact, as in the case of call centers.[10] Although Hardt's conception of affective labor (and those who perform it) might, at first glance, appear monolithic, it is an apt description of the labor performed by the call center workers Akhil Gupta and I worked with whose self-constitution and self-regulation as laboring subjects revealed the convergence of cognitive labor, embodiment, and affect.[11] Agents were trained to talk to their overseas clients about the most recent sports event (for instance, in baseball or American football) with the appropriate degree of enthusiasm so as to be able to make a sale, clinch a deal, or extract necessary information from them. Sometimes it helped to chat about their families. Hence, agents had to acquire not only American names but, frequently, American families as well. Agents were trained to adopt the appropriate affect in their dealings with clients; familiar yet respectful of boundaries, they had to learn to be polite and friendly yet persistent. Their training was oriented to their incorporation into affective regimes foundational to the service and informational sectors of the global economy. These affective regimes reconstituted not only the work habits, daily routines, and speech patterns of call center agents but, equally, habits of the mind and the body.

Several scholars have posited that the modulation of affect is a crucial component of the training of workers in the service economy (for instance, Ducey 2010; Hochschild 2003b).[12] In our fieldwork in call centers in Gurgaon, Gupta and I learned that the affective regimes enjoined by training programs aimed at agents entailed distinct processes of embodiment. Bridging, and blurring, the line between cognition and emotion, mind and body, the training of call center agents relies on the adoption of particular kinds of affective repertoires and underscores how certain modes of affect—of courtesy, familiarity, friendliness, helpfulness, and, above all, caring—became central to their self-constitution and self-regulation as laboring subjects.

For instance, as a trainer of agents in a multinational BPO pointed out to us, "becoming American" involved not just talking like an "American" but, equally importantly, learning to inhabit an "American" body and learning anew how to navigate different spaces and temporalities.[13] She explained to us that she taught agents how to groom themselves, use deodorant, enter and leave elevators ("while entering an elevator they should first wait for those inside to come out and then enter—they shouldn't rush in as if they are boarding a Delhi bus"), stand in the hallways ("they should not stand with one foot against the wall"), and, last but not least, how to use Western-style toilets. It is important to note that affective labor had other corporeal and material consequences for call center agents, such as repetitive strain injury and carpal tunnel syndrome, the disruption of circadian rhythms, eyestrain, radiation hazards, and depression, to name a few (see also Dyer-Witherford 2001: 71). As Hardt argues, "Affective labor, in this sense, is ontological—it reveals living labor constituting a form of life and thus demonstrates again the potential of biopolitical production" (1999: 99).

Through their processes of im/personation, call center agents crafted themselves into particular kinds of subjects because of their incorporation into particular affective regimes.[14] These affective regimes shaped agents' capacities to navigate and inhabit the world around them. As several scholars have pointed out, affective labor is productive of sociality (Hardt 1999; Lazzarato 1996; Ducey 2010). The modulation and, I would add, the production and circulation of regimes of affect were central to the generation of call center agents as laboring subjects. Furthermore, affective modulation was central to the production of the aspirations of call center agents. These aspirations were affective because they were generative of their action, agency, and subjectivity, and their capacity to act and be acted upon. These aspirations were affective also because they blurred the boundaries between corporeality and sociality: despite their struggles to acquire class mobility, neither call center agents nor Bunty and Babli ever became part of the bourgeoisie in a conventional Marxian sense because they never got to own the means of production (compare Freeman 2000: 49); if anything, their means of production were their very bodies, which they refashioned through their practices of impersonation.

LEARNING TO BE SOMEONE ELSE

> We live in a make believe world. . . . Right now, when you come to our campus, you are leaving India behind
> —Narayan Murthy, founder and former CEO of Infosys, a leading IT company based in India, quoted in Shome, "Thinking through the Diaspora."

As Sharma and Gupta point out, "Outsourcing is seen as both a sign of state 'openness,' modernity, good macroeconomic liberalization by the defenders of transnational capitalism, and as a charged symbol of decreasing state sovereignty and control by economic nationalists" (2006: 4). As noted above, since the call center and BPO industry first took off in India (and other Asian nations), media accounts in India and abroad have centered on two issues: one, debates about outsourcing and, two, the fact that call center employees are trained to impersonate people living in their clients' countries. In many of these accounts, impersonation is represented as a marker of the duplicity of companies that outsource jobs to foreign workers. For instance, in the widely circulated Australian documentary *Di-*

verted to Delhi (2002), one commentator (a white Australian) expresses his anger at the fact that agents pretend to be Australian: "Do they think we're stupid?" he asks, enraged. What clearly upsets him is the very practice of impersonation: the fact that young men and women in India pretend to be someone else. In more sympathetic accounts, impersonation is deemed indexical of the economic exploitation and cultural oppression of agents who are forced to disavow their own identities as part of a larger process of being disciplined as "techno-coolies."[15]

Undoubtedly, call center companies invested a great deal of effort in teaching agents to be someone else. Shakuntala was a trainer with a major multinational BPO company based in the United States whom we interviewed in December 2005. A short, smartly dressed, middle-aged woman with close-cropped hair, she greeted us warmly when we visited her early one evening in her elegant, two-story bungalow in Gurgaon. When we entered her living room we saw a young man fast asleep on the couch. It was her son; he seemed to be in his late twenties and was wearing a formal shirt and trousers and still had his socks on. As we gingerly lowered ourselves into chairs adjacent to his couch, Gupta asked Shakuntala in a low voice if our conversation would disturb him. No, she replied, dismissing our worries with a wave of her hand; he had returned from his shift in a BPO earlier that day and was sleeping too soundly to be awakened by us.

As she served us tea and biscuits, Shakuntala informed us that training sessions for call center agents in her company usually lasted six to eight weeks. The computer screens in front of agents provided the script that they were supposed to follow and flashed information regarding the weather in the city where the customer was located. They were required to know about weather conditions in the place where the client lived; after all, what better way to pass as local and inhabiting the same time-space as their clients than talking about the weather? But Shakuntala's job was to teach the agents in her charge not only the protocols of what to say to clients but how to interact with them. It was crucial that agents be clued in to the responses and personalities of their clients: this entailed not only cultural training but also affective training. Shakuntala taught them how to make small talk with their clients and befriend them. The agents had to have an intimate knowledge of the contexts in which their clients lived and, more importantly, had to learn to affectively engage with them appropriately. Their work with clients and, indeed, their ability to meet the quotas set by their supervisors was predicated on their ability to assume the culturally appropriate affect in their interactions with clients (see also Vora 2010).

In the call centers Gupta and I visited, transnational media played a significant role in their training in practices of im/personation (compare Shome 2006: 112). For one, these media were centrally implicated in the formal training of agents, who were required to watch Hollywood films and multiple episodes of U.S. television shows such as *Friends*, and used them as resources for acquiring American accents, adopting American colloquialisms, and learning about American lifeways and relationship patterns—in short, for "becoming American." These media also worked more subtly in enabling them to imagine American spaces and landscapes that they could inhabit. For instance, as my description of a call center cafeteria suggests, some of the physical spaces of call centers were explicitly modeled after their imagination of American spaces as depicted in Hollywood films.

Of course, the work of transnational media began well before agents commenced their formal training and, certainly, their reach and influence extended far beyond call centers: as with Bunty and Babli, their aspirations to mobility, glamour, and success were fed by transnational media.[16] Transnational media such as satellite television and Hollywood cinema had become ubiquitous in the lives of many young men and women in urban and semi-urban parts of India for several decades and had been centrally implicated in the fueling of multiple desires, ranging from the craving for the commodities flooding Indian markets since the 1980s to shaping erotic longings (see, for instance, chapters 4 and 5; compare Mankekar 2013). For many agents, "America" and "the West" were synonymous with aspirations to high-tech (post)modernity, success, and a high standard of living. Mobina Hashimi (2006: 246) has argued that "desire for American style" was what drove many young men and women to become call center agents. The agents' imagining of the West was fed primarily by their consumption of transnational media. These media, which included Hollywood films, American magazines such as *Glamour* and *Elle*, and television shows imported from the United States, the United Kingdom, and Australia, converged with portrayals of cosmopolitan lifestyles in Bollywood films, print media like *India Today* and Indian editions of magazines like *Cosmopolitan*, and depictions of the West in transnational television networks like Zee TV and Asia TV (see chapter 4). Although most agents probably watched (or formerly watched) imported television shows and Hollywood films in their leisure, they now mined these media as pedagogical texts for learning how to become American, further blurring the line between impersonation and personation.

I believe that these modes of im/personation are a crucial analytic for understanding the kinds of subjectivities being constituted not just in the

BPO industry but in the larger sociohistorical conjuncture in postliberalization India.[17] Hence, we might well conceive of these forms of impersonation as modes of personation. The modes of impersonation practiced by call center agents were therefore not diametrically opposed to an authentic self, nor were they facades that covered up a deeper truth. Instead, these modes of impersonation were central to their subject formation. For instance, like Bunty and Babli, for whom growth is measured in terms of the things that money can buy, impersonation blended into personation in the consumption practices of call center agents in Gurgaon—and this happened with men as much as women, albeit in terms of specifically gendered modalities. The construction of malls in close proximity to call centers in Gurgaon was surely not a coincidence, and several observers (including trainers and owners of call centers) remarked to us that these malls provided spaces where agents could socialize and, more importantly, offered the high-end commodities they so desired.[18] As noted earlier, most of the call center agents we met were exceptionally well groomed and fashionably dressed; the sartorial signifiers of globality were evident. Shopping was a major form of consumption and a favorite leisure activity for them, as was going to restaurants and pubs. Call center agents perceived new forms of consumption as markers of a cosmopolitan lifestyle, and of being part of a modern generation that was participating in globalization and the glamour they associated with it.

Despite the misperception that agents of consumption were primarily women, men as much as women were seduced by the lure of commodities (see also chapter 4). In fact, men's enthusiastic participation in the cultures of consumption became so ubiquitous in urban (particularly metropolitan) India in the past two decades as to result in the emergence of a new phenomenon, that of the metrosexual male. Further, it is crucial to note that, while not all call center agents might have the money or time to engage in these consumption activities, it was the aspiration to do so that drove many of them to seek jobs in call centers in the first place. Ironically, while both men and women engaged in consumption practices, women who participated in transnational fashion were singled out as "ultra-Westernized" or, worse, sexually promiscuous and, therefore, asking for trouble.

Growth, Mobility, and Emplacement

Drawing on Massumi's (2002) notion of movement as integral to social process, I wish to foreground the emergent nature of subjectivity entailed in the protocols of impersonation followed by call center agents.

Im/personation exemplifies how subjectivity is always in motion, in tandem with the physical and imaginative travel of subjects through space and time. Extending Massumi, I conceptualize these emergent subjectivities as formed not just through movement but as forged in contexts of struggles for social mobility and as always already co-implicated with processes of emplacement.

I have noted above that, as in the case of Bunty and Babli, call center agents' impersonation practices were driven by their aspirations to mobility. Bunty and Babli's mobility might be measured along different registers, ranging from the spatial and physical mobility that enables them to escape the claustrophobia of small towns for the bright lights of the big city, to social mobility, as symbolized by their acquisition of wealth and the trappings of an upper-class and glamorous lifestyle. As countless agents, trainers, and call center owners in Gurgaon attested, the desire for mobility was the primary motivation for hundreds of thousands of young men and women to work in call centers. An overwhelming majority of the call center agents we worked with sought these jobs not just because they promised employment in the face of rampant under- and unemployment, but because they offered opportunities for different kinds of mobility from, for instance, the tedium of small towns to the busy, border-crossing world of call centers, and from the humdrum anonymity of lower-middle-class lives to the flamboyantly glitzy world of malls and the erotic mysteries of pubs and bars. While in the early years of BPO industry agents were drawn from metropolitan centers and nearby universities and colleges, by 2005 they were being recruited from small towns and cities far and wide. (Indeed, some small towns had also become new venues for call centers.) For instance, agents in the call centers we observed came not only from small towns in nearby Uttar Pradesh and Rajasthan, but also from Meghalaya, Mizoram, and Assam in northeastern India. Additionally, agents' mobility up the professional ladder was indexed by their ability to move from call centers run by less-known Indian companies in small towns or lower-middle-class neighborhoods in Delhi to plush, high-status multinational BPOs in Gurgaon or Bangalore. Their consumption of transnational media and their interaction with overseas clients also facilitated the imaginative travel that enabled them to engage with faraway places and people.[19]

Last but not least, call center agents were able to engage in virtual migration through their labor. In his trailblazing work on the electronics industry, A. Aneesh describes virtual migration thus: "The new space of transnational labor has reversed its relationship with the worker's body. Rather than move the body across enormous distances, new mechanisms allow it to stay put while moving vast quantities of data at the speed of light" (2006: 2). He explains, "The speed of electronic flows brings different time zones together and connects . . . [agents] in real time. Work is integrated across geographies, aided by the logic of programming schemes, including information protocols that facilitate electronic flows through adaptive routing" (2006: 84). At the same time, as my analysis of the impersonation practices of call center agents has suggested, corporeality and embodiment were salient to their constitution as laboring subjects.

Virtual migration was necessitated and conditioned by the economic imperative of profit as many multinational companies sought to maintain twenty-four-hour offices, taking a "follow-the-sun approach" (Aneesh 2006: 84). This was done in different ways. For example, airlines or computer companies offering technical support employed agents to engage in night work so that they could interact with customers in the United States or the United Kingdom in real time, which is to say, during normal business hours in these countries. In other instances, doctors in a hospital in the United States could send a lab report to India at the end of their workday. As that time coincided with the beginning of the workday in India, medical technicians in India could interpret lab results and electronically transmit them back to the United States so that by the time the doctors returned to work the following day, the lab reports were ready.

Struggles for mobility, through social, national, and transnational space, thus constituted the driving force behind agents' practices of impersonation and became crucibles for the forging of their identities and subjectivities. Impersonation and mobility converged when these young men and women began their work as agents. As described earlier, when agents engaged in night work they inhabited different time zones simultaneously—what Raka Shome describes as the "collision of multiple times" (2006: 108)—and hence engaged in transnational border crossing. Other kinds of crossing also occurred when agents adopted fictive names, personas, identities, and, in some cases, lives. Thus, for instance, the film *Diverted to Delhi* depicts a naming ceremony that call center agents undergo when they take on new names. This ceremony functions as a ritual in which agents are reborn, as it were, with new identities. Agents we worked with were frequently under great pressure to perform their new identities seamlessly (they were often not allowed to use their real names within the call center and coworkers and supervisors called them by their new names) such that impersonation often blurred into personation.

Fundamentally, in all these contexts, impersonation was predicated on aspiration—in particular, aspirations to upward mobility, globality, and to making it big. Call center jobs were tremendously attractive to educated youth in India because of the aspirations they engendered. They promised relatively high salaries (in most cases, agents earned more than their parents ever had or would) that ostensibly enabled high-end lifestyles, the sense of freedom and adventure associated with doing night work, the glamour attached to call centers, and, last but not least, the notion that working in call centers would enable them to grow.

In all our interviews about why people wanted to work in call centers, managers, agents, and trainers named "growth" as a primary motivation. But what exactly did they mean by growth? Aspirations to upward mobility, indexed by the ability to acquire the trappings of a middle- or upper-class lifestyle, were obviously deemed essential components of growth, as was the possibility of rising within a company from being an agent on the shop floor to becoming a team leader, supervisor, manager, and so on. It was clear to us that, at the beginning of their careers, many agents believed that the sky was the limit when it came to their professional growth: all they had to do was work hard to meet quotas and, whenever possible, impress their supervisors and managers by exceeding them. Growth was measured largely in terms of mobility, which, as we have seen above, could be experienced and measured along several different registers ranging from spatial and social mobility to imaginative travel and virtual migration.

Indeed, there seemed to be a particularly close relationship between the aspirations of the agents we interviewed and the ubiquity of the trope of growth in their discourses. We quickly learned that, for many of our informants, growth also referred to the acquisition of significant cultural and symbolic capital: chiefly, becoming fluent in English and acquiring the soft skills required for succeeding in the border-crossing world of globalized capital. Aspirations to growth and mobility were hence inextricably entangled. For several agents, this mobility brought with it an exhilarating sense of being part of India's rise as an economic power on the global stage. As some agents informed us, growth entailed moving from being passive onlookers to feeling that they were participants in a drama much larger than themselves, the drama of India's growth as an economic power. For these agents, then, growth encapsulated both their personal aspirations to being part of a transnational and globalized world and their interpellation by nationalist aspirations to growth and to ascendance to economic power.

Certainly, for most of them, being employed in the BPO industry was itself a mode of participating in the (post)modernity engendered by high-tech capitalism, symbolized by the physical environments in which they worked, such as their air-conditioned and Westernized workspaces (which contrasted sharply with the dusty and grimy spaces in which most of their parents had labored); the fact that they worked with computers, the ultimate icons of the new age of informatics; and the imaginative travel enabled by their constant interactions with clients in the West.[20]

We also found that lateral mobility within the BPO industry was valorized as essential for one's growth, that is, for advancing in one's career. Managers, trainers, owners of call centers, and agents themselves spoke constantly of how agents frequently changed jobs to get raises and better perks. Rapid turnover was thus a serious problem for owners and managers, who found that, after investing the time and resources in hiring and training agents (many of whom were fresh recruits), they moved on to the next employer who offered them a few additional thousand rupees or a better package of perks. In fact, as much as income per se, it was the perks that enabled companies to lure agents into working with them, including higher bonuses, cell phones, expense accounts, and, in some cases, free junkets to nearby countries like Singapore and Malaysia.

Indeed, changing jobs was the most effective strategy for growth in an industry where, many of them believed, it was easy to get stuck in a rut. Thus, at the same time that managers and human resources personnel were frustrated by the frequent turnover in their companies, they also seemed to believe that, in contrast to agents who were perceived as slackers because they stayed in one company, those who moved around from company to company were deemed hot because they were ambitious, productive, and displayed aspirations to advance. Immobility, therefore, was deemed detrimental to their careers, thus underscoring the inextricability of discourses of growth and mobility.

As in the case of Bunty and Babli, it should be evident that the impersonation practices of call center agents were neither inherently empowering nor subversive. The mobility of call center agents was obviously shaped by specific relations of power, such as relations of inequality between agents and supervisors, or call center owners and their client companies, which could cancel their contract if the quota was not met or if "accent interference" angered customers. Thus, despite the ways in which it was romanticized in their own aspirations to growth and success, the mobility of agents was highly precarious. As we learned from our interviews, many agents quickly discovered that their dreams of upward mobility were fragile and could easily be dashed to the ground by the ongoing surveillance to which they were subjected in the name of quality control; the quotas and targets that they had to meet on an hourly basis; the constant threat of layoffs; the vulnerability of their jobs, and indeed of their companies, to the vicissitudes of global markets; and, equally debilitating, the physical and psychic burnout that many of them experienced because of the relentless rhythms of their labor and the imperative to inhabit disjunctive temporalities. Like other workers in the informatics industry, the call center agents we met were under constant pressure to update or, to use their favorite buzzword, "revamp" their skills in order to remain employable.

Further, call center agents' physical mobility in their workplaces was highly circumscribed at a more fundamental level for, even as IT enabled specific forms of mobility, it also emplaced agents through technologies of regulation and surveillance. Agents were generally given a time limit to complete a call and, even though they had to engage in some degree of small talk to soften up their clients, were discouraged from talking too long because they had to meet a specific quota of calls every day. Their breaks were closely regulated, and they were subjected to unceasing surveillance while at work, as indicated by the ubiquitous presence of close-circuit cameras; the daily monitoring and evaluation of calls by the floor supervisor; the monotonous repetition of formulaic scripts several hundred times a day and a prohibition on deviating from that script; and the constant monitoring of their work by team leaders who, in turn, had to report to supervisors.

Caren Kaplan's eloquent description of the relationship between informatics and processes of emplacement seems particularly pertinent to the call center agents Gupta and I worked with: "The promise of new technologies is couched in terms of ever-increasing powers of transformation and transport—of information, business, and self—and the benefits of surveillance and tracking. . . . What or who counts as a person becomes transformed. The self is believed to have expanded capacities as soon as it is released from the fixed location of the body, built environment or nation. But the self is always somewhere, always located in some sense in some place, and cannot be totally unhoused" (2003: 210). The virtual migration of call center agents coexisted with forms of emplacement and immobility (and, in some cases, virtual incarceration). For, even as they engaged in imaginative travel and virtual migration, agents were also fixed in place. As Kaplan insists, much of the mobility and displacement enabled by information technologies "fixes and locates through the appearance of movement and flux" (2003: 216).

Mobility is crucially refracted through gender (see, for instance, Kaplan 2003; Massey 1993; Rose 1993) and, I would add, by race—all of which served to emplace call center agents in fundamental ways. Freeman

(2000) suggests that gender is a crucial modality in the disciplining of the new kind of laborer embodied in call center agents in Barbados. Media accounts of Indian call centers portray women agents, many of whom come from small towns and/or from middle-class and lower-middle-class families, as simultaneously sexually emancipated, transgressive, and vulnerable. This is particularly true of portrayals of women who work night shifts. Certainly in Delhi and New Delhi, whose public spaces have long been notorious for the sexual harassment of women, going out at night to work is fraught with risk and danger. The call centers Gupta and I worked with provided transportation for all employees. Most of these companies hired or owned Toyota Qualis SUVs, and company drivers would pick up agents at the beginning of their shifts and drop them off at home when they finished work. It was clear that managers and owners were particularly worried about the safety of their women employees.

Although, in general, call center managers seemed to adopt a "don't ask, don't tell" policy toward the gendered and sexual dynamics among their men and women employees, they took great pains to portray their work spaces as safe (read: respectable) spaces to mollify the fears of the parents and families of their employees. One manager we interviewed talked of how she frequently organized picnics and Family Days to which agents could invite their families. The idea was that, on family days, agents could bring family members to their places of work so that they could see for themselves the "healthy atmosphere" in which they worked.

Physical and spatial mobility also brought with it increased social surveillance, which had crucial consequences for how these laboring subjects were gendered. Freeman describes the gendered surveillance of women working in the informatics industry in terms of the Foucauldian trope of the panopticon: "the gaze of computer, the gaze of supervisor, the manager, the fellow production worker, and finally the internal gaze of the self" (2000: 28). The gender and sexual politics faced by women call center agents as they negotiated the physical and social spaces around them were multiple and complex, and ranged from the pressure to be part of the "in crowd" and sexual harassment at work to the surveillance of family and neighbors.

Anxieties surrounding women who work outside the confines of the home are far from new in urban India.[21] But these anxieties assumed an added dimension when women engaged in night work, as highlighted by the moral panics surrounding women call center workers.[22] For, despite the best efforts of call center owners, it was obvious that the specter of women doing night work alongside men continued to be a huge source of anxiety for parents and families. While this also applied to some extent to male agents, it was particularly true in the case of female agents whose families felt tremendous pressure to explain their daughters' unconventional hours and work habits to other members of the community. Thus, despite the fact that many of them seemed to be the financial backbone of their families (most tended to earn more than their fathers or other relatives), they were subjected to increased surveillance from members of their families and communities.

Women's mobility was refracted by the fact that they were subjected to pressure from all sides. At work, they had to deal with the stresses and anxieties of not only meeting performance targets but, in many cases, of working alongside men for the first time in their lives. As noted above, because the demand for agents far exceeded supply, agents were recruited from all over India. In these instances, women agents faced particularly daunting challenges. These women not only had to leave their homes and hometowns but also had to find a place to live in distant New Delhi and negotiate its hostile public spaces on their own. They were subjected to particularly harsh scrutiny by landlords and neighbors because they had migrated from a different part of India and were living on their own, ostensibly beyond the control of their families.[23]

Regimes of affective labor also shaped ideologies of masculinity. After all, call centers also employed men to perform the affective labor entailed in what was essentially clerical and/or service work—work that is conventionally performed by women—and entailed developing the affect of domesticity and caregiving.[24] Further, these young men had to learn to work alongside women and, when the team leader, supervisor, or owner was a woman, in subordinate positions to them. While male agents were unlikely to be subjected to the same degree of parental and community surveillance as women, they nevertheless had to learn to negotiate the apparently paradoxical experience of increased mobility and the promise of sexual freedom associated with night work, along with increased social surveillance and their subsequent emplacement as gendered and sexual subjects (see also Vora 2010).

Last but not least, as much as the agents were interpellated by Indian nationalist discourses about their role in the upward mobility of India's economy and in consolidating the nation's presence on the global stage, their constitution as laboring subjects was also inflected by transnational discourses of race. Insights from Asian American studies on the relationship between racialized labor and high-tech capitalism have been particularly helpful to my understanding of how transnational discourses of race have shaped (and, for the most part, curtailed) the mobility of call center agents in India by emplacing them in particular ways. As several scholars have argued, the globalization of the world economy is predicated on striations of race as much as it is on class and gender. The mapping of race onto place in the political economy of digitized capitalism is underscored by Rachel Lee and Cynthia Sau-ling Wong, who argue, "As these scenes of production and labor make clear, Internet technologies are not mere free-standing tools either for enhancing sociality or reducing human life to a monitored existence, but historically specific inventions dependent upon uneven political relations between the 'first' and 'third' worlds, and between Northern and Southern hemispheres" (2003: xiii).

The everyday lives of call center agents in Gurgaon were shaped by discourses of race and national origin in the United States in multiple ways.[25] Agents described the unpredictability of their overseas customers: they could be friendly and cooperative, or they could be cranky, suspicious, or disorganized about the information solicited from them. But, for the most part, customers tended to become enraged when they learned that they were speaking to someone in India. Their rage was often articulated in terms of dissatisfaction or frustration with the services provided by the agents (as in complaints about "lack of quality control" or "incompetence") or in terms of communication problems with them; for instance, Dell Computers closed down its customer service operations in India following complaints from its customers about the alleged communication problems they faced while dealing with agents in India. Many customers became overtly racist when they learned that the agent was located in India; consequently, at the time most of the agents we worked with were explicitly forbidden from revealing where they were to their clients. They were frequently subjected to racial epithets and abuse by clients who found out where they were located, thus suggesting how race and location were mapped onto each other.

Lee and Wong argue that Asians and Asian Americans have a "vexed relation" to IT (2003: xv). Racist responses to the offshore outsourcing of IT jobs are not unprecedented and are only the most recent instantiation of the close association between digitalized capitalism and racializing discourses. As argued in chapter 3, nativist and racist rage against the alleged loss of jobs to Asians rose rapidly in the late 1990s at the height of the body-shopping boom when software engineers were brought as contract labor on H-1B visas from countries like India to the United States.[26] "Outsourcing" surfaced as a dirty word in the 2004, 2008, and, most recently, the 2012 U.S. presidential campaigns, which facilitated virulent attacks on the offshore outsourcing of IT jobs. Undoubtedly, race has always played a role in the discourses about Asians in the IT industry, whether in perceptions of "nimble-fingered" Asian women performing assembly-line labor in the production of computer hardware or in stereotypical discourses of "Asian geeks" writing code. Notwithstanding a deep history of imperial policies in Asia and their marginalization and exploitation in the United States, Asians and Asian Americans are deemed particularly threatening to the self-representation of the U.S. nation as a technological leader.[27]

Let us not forget that the impersonation practices of call center agents were necessitated by racist and xenophobic anger against offshore outsourcing to countries in Asia (we rarely see the same virulence in discussions about outsourcing to Israel or Ireland, which also emerged as hubs for the global IT industry in the 1990s). Thus, for instance, media reports in the United States were about how American jobs are going to India. As Hashimi argues, "The globalization of IT labour is threatening partly because it suggests that the U.S. may not be able to control the nature and direction of global flows of people, capital and commodities" (2006: 246). The racialization of call center agents in India hence went beyond instances of racist abuse or discriminatory business practices.

These expressions of outrage are reminiscent of earlier debates about the alleged stealing of "American" jobs by Asians and Asian immigrants—but with a crucial twist.[28] The BPO phenomenon points to a new configuration of the relationship between labor, migration, and nationhood. At issue was not the physical presence of Asians in America who had allegedly snatched jobs that ought to have gone to "native-born" Americans, but the labor of workers located in Asia. Recall also the use of the term "techno-coolie" to describe call center agents by critics of the BPO industry. The word "coolie," as we know, is tied to the profoundly racialized process of labor extraction under colonialism (as in the indenture of laborers from South Asia to the West Indies) and to the use of Asian (Chinese) labor in the United States.

As Lee and Wong point out in another context, the racialization of call center agents emerges as "a material and gendered relation in the flexible, offshore, capitalist production processes of the wired world" (2003: xx). After all, the mapping of race onto geographic location shaped much of the training of agents. At the time that Gupta and I worked in a call center in Gurgaon in December 2005, we learned that, despite the switch in the industry from training agents to speak in American English to a "global English," agents calling a customer in, say, a Midwestern state in the United States were still expected to assume a Midwestern accent, take on a local name, and learn about local customs and lifeways (sometimes to the extent of creating a local family). These claims about switching from American English to global English were predicated on an assumption that one could become accentless by erasing Indianness from one's speech.

Accent "neutralization" involved voice modulation and stressing syllables in particular ways and perfecting specific inflections and tones, all of which were necessary in order to assume the appropriate affect while speaking with overseas clients. Trainees were required to perform facial exercises to get the right inflection and had to learn to breathe in particular ways to be able to aspirate their *p*'s and *t*'s, thus underscoring the corporeal aspects of learning to speak like an American. One trainer we interviewed described global English as a strategy to deal with "communication problems caused by the language interference factor." As a result, "de–Indianization" was deemed an important part of the impersonation strategies in which agents were trained. These claims about global English were themselves founded on discourses that mapped race onto place. While the term accent neutralization implies that agents were being decultured or deracialized, the fact is that they were being reracialized in new ways. Accent thus emerged as a code for race and national location. For example, we learned that in the process of learning global English, agents were taught to say "skedule" instead of "shedule," "zee" instead of "zed," and so on. While learning global English was about acquiring modes of speech that are (supposedly) culturally neutral, speaking in an American accent was a measure of fluency in global English, in contrast to speaking in an Indian accent, which was derided as regional.

My analysis of the relationship between language training and racialization converges with that of Shome, who insists that the training call center agents undergo reracializes them in new ways: "The training is not just about teaching English. It is about the control and regulation of 'voice,' tone, phonology, (American) 'speech codes' (word choices, inflections, emotions, affects, stresses, etc.) and thus behavior itself that provides an example of what Ferguson and Gupta, following Foucault, have termed 'transnational governmentality'" (2006: 110). Hence, although the explicit goal was to train agents to become cosmopolitan subjects who were ostensibly unlocatable because they spoke global English with accents that had been de-Indianized, these notions of Americanness were deemed indexical of globality itself and became the unstated, yet normative, ideal to which they were all to strive.

Shome also posits that, unlike canonical studies of racial formation where racial identity is tied to visuality, "in the culture of call centers and outsourcing of telematics, we see a crisis of this logic of race. We see a shift from a regime of visuality to aurality where the racism occurs through a control of language, voice, and accent all carried out under the label of 'cultural neutralization'" (2006: 108). This leads her to assert that we need to reframe the politics of race in terms of aurality and disembodiment rather than visuality and embodiment. Yet, as we observed in our ethnographic research, accent neutralization and the de–Indianization of one's speech patterns formed only one modality of the reconfiguration of the identities of Indian call center agents and their formation as racialized laboring subjects. After all, processes of impersonation extended beyond linguistic shifts and included processes of affective embodiment. Impersonation and personation came together in the ways in which call center agents were taught to inhabit particular kinds of bodies and spaces, and these bodies and spaces were often cast in terms of an imagined (white) Americanness. On the one hand, cultural and racial differences were sought to be made invisible through the act of speaking global English that supposedly rendered one unlocatable. At the same time, processes of embodiment inherent in other aspects of an agent's training underscored the agent's marginalized location in the dominant racial regime of digitalized capitalism.

Thus, while the virtual migration of call center agents demonstrates an unhooking of conceptions of migration from territoriality, gender, race, and geographic location emplace call center agents in concrete ways. Ahmed et al. critique the "romanticization of mobility as travel, transcendence and transformation" (2003: 1). Likewise, we have to be extremely wary of the valorization of mobility in the discourses of call center agents. As noted above, the mobility of call center agents is precarious: at the same time that mobility is enabled and, in the case of some agents, speeded up by IT, it is also accompanied by processes of regulation and surveillance, the fixing of the body in particular spaces, and confinement.

Neoliberalism and the Production of Aspiration

Drawing on Amartya Sen's insistence on engaging with social values in economic analyses, Appadurai (2004) asks us to think of aspiration as a cultural capacity. Although Appadurai focuses on the development of aspiration as essential to the (self-)mobilization and empowerment of the poor, his assertion that aspirations must be located in larger social and cultural fields is particularly pertinent to my engagement with the aspirations of lower-middle-class urban youth who worked in call centers in Gurgaon. But how was their capacity to aspire produced, and what were its temporal and affective dimensions? In what ways was the capacity to aspire itself generative of action and agency, of affecting others and being affected, of building a world and of inhabiting and navigating it?

Clough (2007) posits that there has been a shift from disciplinary technologies of normalization to societies of control in late twentieth-century capitalism. Drawing on the work of Parisi and Terranova, she insists that with the expansion and disorganization catalyzed by globalization, structural adjustment, and flexibilization, there is a "transformation in biopolitics such that control becomes the effect and the condition of possibility of an investment in the reorganization of material forces, of bodily matter" (Clough 2007: 17). To what extent is this description of control societies pertinent to the world of call centers and their employees in late twentieth-century India? Clough asserts that the "target" of control is not "the production of subjects whose behaviors express internalized social norms"; instead, control aims at "a never-ending modulation of moods, capacities, affects, and potentialities" (2007: 19). What might this conception of control offer to an analysis of the impersonation practices of call center agents, of Bunty and Babli, and, in particular, of the affective production of their aspirations?

The impersonation practices of call center agents and Bunty and Babli, and the aspirations that fueled them, were shaped by a larger political-economic and historical context refracted by neoliberal discourses of progress, growth, and mobility. Put another way, their aspirations, and the affectivity of these aspirations, did not emerge in a vacuum but were constitutive of the sociohistorical conjuncture of which they were a part. One scene from *Bunty aur Babli* is particularly revealing in how it foregrounds the affective potency of aspiration. As they draw close to Bombay, Babli tells Bunty that now that they have made enough money, they can put an end to their lives of impersonation and fraud. But Bunty has different ideas. "There are two kinds of people in this world," he claims. "Those who feel they've collected enough money, and others who never feel they've collected enough. Birla-Tata-Ambani never feel they've collected enough money and that is why they are where they are." While an insatiable desire for making money is an indispensable prerequisite of the success of these celebrated tycoons, for Bunty and Babli aspiration or, rather, the capacity to aspire is an end in itself. Bunty easily persuades Babli that they should continue their lives of impersonation. It is evident that what drives them is not simply the desire to make money. Instead, they seem to derive sustenance from their ability to aspire and, in so doing, defy the rest of the world, become famous, and enjoy the trappings of glamour and success.

Their aspirations are in and of themselves foundational to the formation of their subjectivities which are always emergent, constantly in motion: it is no surprise, then, that they never "settle down."

Indeed, as suggested above, their aspirations are affective precisely because they are generative of their capacities to act and be acted upon, in short, of their agency, their subjectivity, and of the ways in which they inhabit and navigate the world; their aspirations are affective not only because they spur their individual actions but because they suffuse (and, to some extent, generate) their social world. Bunty and Babli and the call center agents we worked with in Gurgaon foreground the self-production and self-regulation of subjects in contexts marked by new configurations of technology, bodies, and aspirations under neoliberalism. Certainly, the impersonation practices of call center agents as well as Bunty and Babli shared much with some of the cultural and discursive traits associated with neoliberalism, such as a valorization of entrepreneurial energy, risk taking, an individualist ethos, an emphasis that individuals must own and take responsibility for their ambitions, and so on (see also Mankekar 2013 and Rose 1993).

Thus, although it would be misguided and reductionist to assume that neoliberalism was the singular or even dominant political-economic formation in place in early twenty-first-century India, the impersonation practices analyzed above suggest how some of the normative imperatives of neoliberalism functioned to produce the laboring subject as an entrepreneurial subject.[29] Early in *Bunty aur Babli*, Rakesh and his mother discuss the different financial schemes he has designed to make money. In one such scheme, he invests in a shower in his backyard. When his mother complains that he has wasted money on the shower and that he should stand in line at the communal bathroom down the street, he responds, "There are two kinds of people in this world: those who stand in line in front of taps, and those who construct taps so that they never have to stand in line." We are left with no doubt that he belongs to the latter group; his entrepreneurial energy, embrace of risk, and can-do spirit is foregrounded throughout the film. Similarly, Vimmi defies her parents and leaves home to follow her dream of becoming a supermodel. Like Rakesh, she is willing to risk venturing out on her own and to assume responsibility for fulfilling her ambitions.

Gupta and Sharma describe neoliberal governmentality in terms of the "direction of conduct towards specific ends, which has as its objects both individuals and populations, and which combines techniques of domination and discipline with technologies of self-government" (2006: 1).[30]

I wish, therefore, to reject the binary constructed in some analyses of post-liberalization India of the economic effects of policies versus the discourses and affective regimes that emerged in conjunction with economic liberalization (which, of course, have material consequences for individual lives, fortunes, and subjectivities). For while the discursive aspects of neoliberalism pertain not to economic policy per se but to distinctive techniques by which subjects and citizens are constituted and governed (Brown 2003), there was clearly a complex and intimate relationship between the liberalization of the Indian economy and the salience, in the BPO industry, of neoliberalism as an ethic of self-governance and self-production.

The BPO industry, and call centers in particular, demonstrate the intersection of capital flows and IT in contexts of neoliberalism. While the strategy of labor arbitrage provided the economic rationale for the offshore outsourcing of services to sites like India, as evident in the im/personation practices of call center agents, the informatics industry was particularly dependent on the manipulability and fungibility of labor prescribed by neoliberalism. Hence, beyond the imperative to save costs through labor arbitrage, as impersonation blends into personation we see that it is not just labor practices but subjects themselves who become fungible: as suggested by the title of a popular documentary about call centers, agents have to be *Nancy by Night, Nandini by Day* (2005).

As we have seen, in the discourses of many agents, mobility was romanticized and valorized because it connoted growth and freedom. Yet, as noted above, their mobility was highly fragile, their opportunities for growth precarious, and their sense of freedom illusory. The BPO industry, like many others that were inextricably entangled with global capital, was extremely vulnerable to changes in the international economy. The capriciousness of the global market, the fact that most call centers survived solely on the basis of their contracts with multinational companies, and fluctuations in the stock market meant that agents could be laid off at a moment's notice, regardless of their performance on the job. The free agent of neoliberalism was thus not a sovereign or autonomous subject; on the contrary, freedom became the very means by which the self was disciplined to "take care" of himself or herself (Foucault 1988, Harvey 2005).

Even so, it would be a mistake to assume that neoliberalism had flattened out the agency of call center employees. For one, neoliberalism is neither a singular nor a monolithic discursive formation. Instead, as defined by Ong, it consists of "mobile calculative techniques of governing that can be decontextualized from their original sources and recontextualized in constellations of mutually exclusive and contingent relationships"

(2006: 13). Moreover, neoliberalism is discontinuous and unpredictable in its effects: it is neither homogenizing nor totalizing, nor can it be viewed in teleological terms. As Wendy Brown argues, "Neo-liberalism can become dominant as governmentality without being dominant as ideology—the former refers to governing practices and the latter to a popular order of belief that may or may not be fully in line with the former, indeed may even be a site of resistance to it" (2005: 49). In *Bunty aur Babli*, as well as in the lives of many call center agents, the neoliberal ethic of entrepreneurship as self-care sat uneasily alongside other moral imperatives prescribed by discourses of gender, sexuality, family, and nation—and, equally importantly, was held in check by them and unsettled by them.[31]

Brown points to a reading of neoliberalism in terms of an extension of Weber's conception of rationalization and disenchantment: "The extension of market rationality to every sphere, and especially the reduction of moral and political judgment to a cost/benefit calculus, would represent precisely the evisceration of substantive values by instrumental rationality that Weber predicted as the future of a disenchanted world" (2005: 45).[32] I would like to insist that this did not seem to be happening in the world of call center agents or indeed in *Bunty aur Babli*. Theirs was not a disenchanted world but was, in fact, a world that had its own sources of enchantment—the enchantments provided by transnational media that enabled young, lower-middle-class men and women who lived in small towns to acquire the capacity to imagine life in other places. This was a world shaped by the enchantments of aspiration and impersonation.[33] However tenuous and short-lived they might ultimately have been, like the impersonation practices they engendered, these aspirations were affective in that they fundamentally refracted the subjectivities of call center agents (and Bunty and Babli) and their capacities to act and be acted upon.

Aspiration and the Time(s) of the Nation

Bunty aur Babli begins with a commentary that situates its narrative within two coexisting Indias, an Aspirational India and an Other India. In a voice-over, Amitabh Bachchan describes Aspirational India: "This is India. Sparkling, dazzling, whispering that if you have a dream, come, fulfill it. [Yeh hai India. Chamchamata, jagmagata, phusphusata hai, ki agar tera sapna hai to aaja, karle poora]." As the titles roll, we see a cityscape of skyscrapers sparkling along a seashore—presumably, that of Mumbai. The dazzling skyline beckons all those who dare to dream. Bachchan adds, his voice turning seductive: "If there is a hunger within you, come, satisfy it. Respect, glamour, money, power—all will become your friends, and your life will become a never-ending golden dream. Yes, this is India. The India that Bunty and Babli dreamed of. [Agar tera sapna hai to aaja, karle poora. Aur agar tere me koi bhookh hai, to aaja aur karle poori. Izzat, shohrat, paisa, taakat, sab tere dost ban jayenge aur teri zindagi kabhi na khatam hone vala sapan ho jayega. Haanh, yeh India hai, voh India jo Bunty aur Babli ka sapna tha.]"

Then, quickly, abruptly, there is a perceptible shift in Bachchan's tone, and the landscape is completely transformed. Instead of the enticing skyline of Mumbai, we now get glimpses of small-town and rural India. Bachchan continues, his voice flat with irony: "And this is India as well. The India that was their reality. Which said, dream only of those things within your reach. Allow yourself only that hunger that you can satisfy. Move ahead, but only when those around you want to move ahead as well. Move up, but never by stepping on the shoulders of anybody else. Respect, honesty, community. These are your legacy. Yes, this is India. The India where Bunty and Babli grew up. The India where they felt suffocated." These landscapes contrast with the cityscapes portrayed earlier: even as they invoke respect, honesty, and community, they are suffused with a sense of claustrophobia; they evoke stasis; they are suffocating because they represent a snuffing out of the capacity to aspire to, much less acquire, a different way of inhabiting the world. In Aspirational India, individuals are, ostensibly, driven by their hunger for wealth, glamour, and power. In the Other India one can dream only of those things that are already within one's reach. Aspirational India is marked by individual progress, by constant mobility produced by an insatiable hunger. The Other India is ruled by familial obligations and duty, but is also characterized by the corruption, protocols of patronage, and stagnancy so derided in discourses sympathetic to the liberalization of the Indian economy.

It is crucial to note that the film never portrays these two Indias in terms of a linear temporality in which the modern and/or neoliberal order succeeds an older one. Instead, it portrays them in terms of its characters' inhabitation of coexisting, yet distinct, temporalities. The moral and affective framing of both these two temporalities is markedly ambivalent: the India of obligation and duty is also corrupt, as characterized by the bureaucrat who steals Rakesh's business plan and the beauty pageant official who tries to get Vimmi to sleep with him in exchange for bending the rules to let her compete in the pageant; yet it is also marked by the presence of Dashrath Singh, who is incorruptible and is completely dedicated to his job of ridding India of crime. The contrast between the two Indias, then, is portrayed largely in terms of their contrasting temporalities. Aspirational India is constantly unfolding and moving toward the future; the Other India appears mired in stasis. Primarily, Aspirational India is represented as always emergent, marked by potentiality—and as chronically unsettled.

What does the valorization of the constant mobility of Bunty and Babli indicate about the temporality of aspiration, specifically of aspirations to growth, upward mobility, and success circulating in urban India in the early years of the twenty-first century? Let us recall that temporalizing processes are central to the impersonation practices adopted by Bunty and Babli and by call center agents. Bunty and Babli's peripatetic journeys back and forth between two coexisting, apparently contradictory, Indias enact the temporality of contemporaneity. And, as we saw above, call center agents traveled back and forth across different temporalities. Furthermore, temporalizing processes powerfully refracted their efforts to fulfill their aspirations: undergirding their protocols of impersonation, their aspirations to growth and mobility were driven by their perception of being out of step with a fast-moving world because of their fears of being mired in a different temporality, specifically, a temporality of lag. To most (if not all) of the call center agents we worked with in Gurgaon, call centers held out the possibility of their getting *in step* with the world of post/modern capitalism.

But what happens when the remade self inhabits multiple chronotopes? The virtual migration of call center agents resulted in complex forms of displacement compounded by their emplacement in disjunctive temporalities. As we have seen, these forms of mobility did not necessarily entail physical movement but were, in fact, contingent on the affective transformation of bodies. Thus, even when these bodies had to stay in place, as it were, they were transformed through their incorporation into transnational regimes of affective labor. By working night shifts, agents inhabited multiple time zones simultaneously which, in turn, meant that they had to navigate and inhabit parallel, often discrepant, social worlds.

Predicated upon a transformation of affect and the body, of the experience of space and temporality, and of the imagination and sociality, the impersonation practices of call center agents and Bunty and Babli materialize the generative aspects of aspiration. Appadurai (2004) has insisted on the importance of understanding the normative contexts in which aspirations are produced. He reminds us that the capacity to aspire is not evenly distributed across social formations but, instead, is a "resource that is unequally tilted in favor of the wealthier people in any society" (2004:

68–69).[34] Working in call centers enabled lower-middle-class and working-class youth, who had until that point tended to aspire only to those things that were within their reach, to expand their conceptions of what they could yearn for.

The agents we worked with in Gurgaon reminded me that aspiration is fueled by the desire to *change* something about the present—whether by transforming their place in the world or by securing it—even if the fulfillment of this desire is perpetually deferred to the future. Thus, rather than disavowing the weight of the past or the urgency of the present, foregrounding the futurity of aspiration, its potentiality enables us to parse out the temporal weight of the past, present, and future. My engagement with how my informants experienced these multiple temporalities serves as a point of departure for tracing the ways in which, even as it is generative of sociality, the temporality of aspiration unsettles received ways of thinking and being in the world. The future-oriented temporality of aspiration generally arises out of a perceived chasm between life as it is experienced in the present moment (and/or was lived in the past), and the imagination of what that life can be like in the future. For many of the call center agents with whom we worked in Gurgaon, the very horizon of possibilities had been transformed; even for those among our informants for whom this horizon seemed to be ever-receding, it had become considerably more expansive than it had been for many of their parents' generation. The temporality of aspiration was thus underscored by how aspirations might change across generations (as in the dramatic contrasts between the aspirations of call center agents and those of many of their parents and other family members) as well as over the course of agents' lifetimes. Yet while aspirations to growth and mobility drove the practices of impersonation so necessary to their work in call centers, not all of their aspirations were centered on moving forward exclusively in their individual lives: many, if not most, aspired to improving the well-being of their families and, often, of their extended families and clans. Nor must we forget that for a considerable proportion of the call center agents with whom we worked, personal aspirations to growth and success were sutured to their aspirations for India's rise in the world economy. Thus we need to be extremely wary of leaping to the conclusion that these practices of impersonation were driven solely by an obsession with individual (or individualistic) desires or yearnings.

Furthermore, and most importantly, we need to recall the high burnout rates of call center agents. Gupta and I came across several instances in which, in the poignant words of one of our informants, "the body simply gives up." The physical and emotional strain of working long hours, doing night shifts, being cut off from family and friends, being constantly under surveillance at work and, in the case of many of our informants, at home and in neighborhoods, the repetitive stress injuries of agents who worked in data entry, and the psychic wounds of those who faced racial abuse and/or sexual harassment from clients—all underscored the ways in which, for many call center agents, these aspirations came perilously close to meeting with failure.

As with Bunty and Babli, the emergent subjectivities of call center agents reveal how aspiration may blur the boundaries between impersonation and personation, and problematize the distinction between fictive and authentic identities. In particular, the impersonation practices of call center agents in Gurgaon has compelled me to rethink the relationship between aspiration, cultural continuity, and social change in contexts of neoliberalism. Rofel proposes that, rather than assume that neoliberalism is "a set of universal principles from which derives, in a deterministic fashion, a singular type of neoliberal subject," we examine "the historical specificity and heterogeneity of global practices fostered in the name of neoliberal capitalism" (2007: 2; see especially Ong 2006, for analyses of neoliberalism that exemplify such a nuanced approach). In dialogue with Rofel, I have sought to examine how aspirations, chiefly those pertaining to mobility and growth, are situated in a larger historical context marked by the liberalization of the Indian economy and the proliferation of transnational media: I have been interested in how these aspirations acquire affective and temporal significance by engendering particular kinds of action and agency. Rofel describes the cultural transformations wrought by neoliberalism in China as a "sea-change" predicated on a model of human nature that "has the desiring subject at its core: the individual who operates through sexual, material, and affective self-interest" (2007: 3). In contrast, I hold that, as exemplified by Bunty and Babli and the call center agents I worked with in Gurgaon, neoliberal aspirations to growth and mobility and the practices of impersonation they engender do not replace other constructions of agency (such as those shaped by duty and collective well-being) but, instead, exist alongside them—even as they unsettle them and are unsettled by them.

Appadurai suggests that we foreground aspiration in order to "place futurity, rather than pastness, at the heart of our thinking about culture" (2004: 84). He asserts that most conceptions of culture, while not ignoring the future, "smuggle it in indirectly, when they speak of norms, beliefs, and values as being central to cultures, conceived as specific and multiple designs for social life. But by not elaborating the implications of norms for futurity as a cultural capacity, these definitions tend to allow the sense of culture as pastness to dominate" (2004: 60–61). Drawing on these provocative insights, I wish to ask after the implications of the future-oriented temporality of aspirations for how India and Indian culture are (re)constituted. Far from ignoring or disavowing patterns and sedimented traditions, by deploying unsettlement as an analytic I have attempted to foreground the practices that undergird them. By tracking and unpacking and by critiquing and thus denaturalizing how these patterns and sedimented traditions get variously reconstituted and, equally frequently, reified or fetishized, I underscore that unsettlement is intrinsic to culture and, hence, to the temporalities of cultural change.

Bunty aur Babli's representation of two apparently oppositional and coexisting Indias—the India of self-driven and self-created opportunities for success and the India of collective welfare—is critically significant in how it materializes tensions between contrasting conceptions of national and individual progress and success. Conceived in temporal and affective terms, the aspirations of Bunty and Babli and the call center agents we worked with in Gurgaon may be allegorical of the complex ways in which India or, rather, multiple Indias are constituted as archives of affect and temporality in contexts shaped by transnational public cultures and neoliberalism. Aspirational India engages a temporality of self-advancement and futurity; it is about overcoming a sense of inferiority based on a sense of a temporal lag vis-à-vis the so-called developed world. Yet the Other India, although positioned at the margins of Aspirational India, is also necessary to its very existence—not only because it serves as a foil to it, but also because of how it shapes it and reins it in. Thus conceived, aspiration emerges as an affective-temporal ontology for the nation itself.

When Akhil Gupta and I first started working in call centers in Gurgaon, we were struck by the nervous energy that suffused them. Some of this nervous energy resulted from the pressure felt by all employees to meet deadlines and quotas. But we sensed that there was more to it than that. A nervousness tinged with euphoria appeared to saturate the lives of the call center agents with whom we worked. For most of our informants, this was a time of excitement but also of uncertainty. And for many of them, this was a time marked by an exhilarating sense of participating in India's ostensible rise as an economic power as well as a painfully acute awareness of the risks of being left out of (and by) India's hasty race to the future. For all of them, these were unsettled times indeed.

My primary focus throughout this book has been to examine how, at specific nodes in the transnational circulation of images, texts, and commodities, India was constituted as an archive of affect and temporality for my informants in New Delhi and the San Francisco Bay Area. In tracing the modalities through which India is simultaneously reified and reconfigured, my objective has been to unsettle India. In the brief coda that follows, I outline the experiences of my informants in the San Francisco Bay Area immediately after September 11, 2001, to deploy unsettlement as both an ethnographic lens and an analytic to critique the repressive and totalizing claims of the U.S. nation-state. In so doing, I wish to extend the framework developed in this book to sketch the contours of a theoretical and political project that will enable me to unsettle the U.S. nation-state.

Unsettling Nations

My family and I were living in the San Francisco Bay Area when we learned about the attacks on the World Trade Center and the Pentagon. Desperate to shake off our sense of foreboding, we decided to go to nearby Mountain View to get some lunch. At the time, restaurant row in Mountain View was full of immigrant businesses. It had been just a few hours since the attacks on the World Trade Center and the Pentagon, but the U.S. national flag was flying outside almost all the businesses we drove past.[1] We entered an Indian restaurant that also functioned as a grocery store. Unlike other occasions when a Bollywood film song would be playing loudly in the background, this time the store was pervaded by an eerie silence. Compared with all other times when the space had been bustling with customers, largely South Asians shopping, eating, or socializing, now there were very few people. Those that were present spoke in hushed tones. Many seemed to avoid eye contact with each other: it was almost as if they were afraid of the fear they would see mirrored in each other's eyes. Our sense of uneasiness grew; we rushed out and returned home. The public spaces that we had long experienced as familiar had now turned strange.

I do not assume that my experiences, refracted as they were by my class position, national origin, and gender, represent those of all South Asians; in presenting the foregoing vignette I wish to evoke the acute sense of uneasiness and fear that I, and many of my informants, felt immediately after September 11, 2001. Certainly, the South Asians I met in the days and months following September 11 did not respond in identical ways to what had happened: men and women, adults and children, upper-class elites and working folk, queer and straight communities, and Sikhs, Muslims,

Christians, and Hindus were implicated differently. Yet it became clear to me that I was not alone in experiencing these complex emotions. Over phone lines, on the Internet, and in our hushed conversations with each other, grief, fear, and, in some cases, rage spread like a contagion through the communities of which I was a part. Judith Butler offers the following caution with regard to first-person framings of September 11, 2001: "We start the story by invoking a first-person narrative point of view, and tell what happened on September 11. And it is that date, and the unexpected and fully terrible experience of violence, that propels the narrative" (2002: 179).[2] The individualist I of the first-person narrative is particularly problematic when it is complicit with nationalist narcissism. My intention, then, is to decenter the I of such a narrative framing by asking what September 11, 2001, might have meant for some racialized subjects positioned at the margins of the U.S. nation-state.[3] My intention is to invoke forms of temporality that neither originate nor culminate in a nationalist telos exemplified by the "attack on America" and, thereby, to point to ways in which we may unsettle the U.S. nation at the very moment when it was consolidated and reified through practices of exclusion.[4]

Throughout this book I have deployed unsettlement as an analytic and as an ethnographic strategy to foreground how transnational public cultures produce India as an archive of affect and temporality. I ended the preceding chapter by arguing that the aspirations of call center agents and the protagonists of a Hindi film, *Bunty aur Babli*, emblematize a particular zeitgeist in early twenty-first-century India in which boundaries between impersonation and authentic identity were blurred. Aspirations (whether articulated in terms of excitement, hopefulness, anxiety, or a combination of all of the above) entail a temporality of waiting and of uncertainty, in short, a temporality of unsettlement.[5] Here I draw on the sense of unsettlement experienced by some of my informants in the San Francisco Bay Area, their sense of nothing being the same anymore after September 11, 2001. I briefly trace how the U.S. state and dominant media represented the attacks on September 11, 2001, and, in so doing, participated and, to a large degree, endorsed the generation of regimes of fear and hate in its attempts to consolidate a national community predicated on the exclusion and excision of cultural and racial Others. In the introduction to this book I inquired after the affective regimes that enable the formation of national communities (Anderson 1991). Now I am concerned with how regimes of affect and temporality enabled the creation of a national community in the United States that was predicated on the marginalization and demonization of racial and cultural Others.

Jasbir Puar describes the complex historicity of September 11 eloquently: "The event-ness of September 11 refuses the binary of watershed moment and turning point of radical change, versus intensification of more of the same, tethered between its status as a 'history-making moment' and a 'history-vanishing moment'" (2007: xviii). On the one hand, for many of my informants September 11, 2001, was an event of some singularity. To this day, many people (including me) can vividly remember what we were doing when we heard about what happened, and can recount in considerable detail our initial reactions. In dominant discourses of U.S. nationalism, September 11, 2001, is narrated as an emergency and I have no doubt that it was experienced as such by those who were directly affected by its violence. Yet, as Craig Calhoun (2004) points out, constructions of emergencies are embedded in particular kinds of social imaginaries. I would add that they also invoke particular renditions of temporality. For one, in the modern world, emergencies call for specific responses and interventions (humanitarian, managerial, and so on); the implication is that there is something abnormal and unpredictable about them. The concept of emergencies often obscures their mediation by prior histories and by technologies of power and control that exist in the realm of the everyday and the "normal." As such, emergencies invoke the temporality of interruption, specifically, the interruption of the normal and the everyday, the safe and the orderly, eliding the obvious question of how (and at whose expense) conceptions of normalcy, the everyday, safety, and order are constructed in the first place.

Even as it deepened their sense of vulnerability, several of the South Asians I was to work with in the aftermath September 11, 2001, did not experience the hate violence that followed as a rupture or a watershed in their lives in the United States. This was particularly true of many of my working-class informants, for whom it represented a violent exacerbation of the racial tensions they and their communities had experienced for many years rather than a rupture. Several scholars have pointed to the political and discursive continuities of September 11, 2001, with preceding conjunctures.[6] Grewal makes an important and persuasive argument that, far from representing a break, September 11 constitutes "a fulfillment of some of the directions taken by neoliberal American nationalism, in particular the articulation of a consumer nationalism, the link between geopolitics and biopolitics, and the changing and uneven gendered, racial, and multicultural subjects produced within transnational connectivities" (2005: 197).

In the San Francisco Bay Area, arguably one of the most ethnically diverse parts of the nation, the days immediately following September 11 were marred by acts of hate violence: rocks were thrown into a mosque in the East Bay; the body of a sixty-year-old Sikh man was found floating in a canal near his house; an Indian man and his Australian friend were stabbed in the yuppie SOMA district of San Francisco; a flyer posted in San Francisco's Islamic Center read, "Allah is dead; Rambo killed him" (ACLU 2002). On September 15, a Sikh man, Balbir Singh Sodhi, was shot dead in Mesa, Arizona. His assailant claimed that he had killed him "because he was dark-skinned, bearded, and wore a turban" (2002). By the end of the month, there were forty-eight reported hate crimes in San Francisco itself, and in Santa Clara County reported hate crimes rose 2,500 percent in 2001 over 2000. Of course these statistics reveal nothing of the everyday experiences of violence, humiliation, and suffering experienced by many Sikhs and Muslims solely because of their religion, ethnic affiliation, and/or national origin; furthermore, it is critical that we note that these numbers are not entirely reliable because hate violence is typically underreported.[7]

Next I draw on a sliver of the ethnographic research I conducted from October 2001 through September 2005 to trace how my Sikh and Muslim informants living in the San Francisco Bay Area were positioned in this national community.[8] Hate violence against people of South Asian and Middle Eastern origin, in particular those "deemed to be Muslim," was engendered through the creation of an affectively charged national community. This national community was galvanized by the production of affective regimes of fear and hate, as evident in the speeches and enunciations of national leaders, and the policies and actions of governmental agencies such as the FBI, the Immigration and Naturalization Service, and the Department of Homeland Security.

What sorts of affective and temporal economies undergirded the formation of the U.S. nation after September 11? Building on Ahmed's (2004: 10) claims about the circulation of affect between bodies and its nonresidence in individuals, I am interested in how the U.S. nation was affectively constituted through the contagion of fear and hate. The articulation of religion and race that occurred after September 11, 2001, was not unprecedented: these forms of racialization were at once old and new; they invoked older signs of racial difference and engendered new ones. These old-new signs of racialization displayed multiple temporalities through an accumulation of affective value (Ahmed 2004: 11). In the hours following the terrorist attacks, patriotism shaded into xenophobic nationalism and, here, national leaders led the way. This xenophobic nationalism was buttressed by the production of the affects of fear; in turn, the circulation of fear was accelerated and intensified by the policies and enunciations of state officials.

Grewal (2005: 201) has pointed out that concepts of danger and security were allied after September 11, 2001. Strategies of surveillance, incarceration, and deportation deployed by the state closely allied danger with cultural and religious Others who were racialized in specific ways. The U.S. state swung into action by putting in place domestic (and, of course, foreign) policies of surveillance predicated on the assertion of a state of emergency. For instance, on the evening of September 11, 2001, Attorney General John Ashcroft declared that justice would be done and that individuals could report any information they knew about these crimes to a website set up by the FBI.[9] The ensuing "war on terror" allowed for no dissent—either nationally or internationally—and exacerbated the circulation of fear. In his address to the nation, President Bush reassured "Americans" that "we" would not be intimidated by terror, that America would prevail, and, last but not least, that the rest of the world now had a decision to make: "Either you are with us or you are with the terrorists" (Bush 2002). Ironically, but not surprisingly, the state's counterterrorism measures accelerated the circulation of fear and hate which, in turn, encouraged a space for violence against these racial Others.[10]

The months following September 11 reveal innumerable instances of the U.S. state's role in generating affective economies of fear and hate. Ashcroft unveiled a plan to prevent terrorist acts "by rounding up suspects early on, before they get a chance to act." This was a strategy the U.S. Justice Department had rejected in the late 1970s because of its ineffectiveness and because it had led to abuses of civil rights (Volpp 2002).[11] Human rights and civil rights advocates were especially outraged that noncitizen immigrants would be arrested on suspicion of terrorism and detained indefinitely without judicial review.[12] The affects of fear produced by terrorist acts on September 11, 2001, were exacerbated a thousandfold by some political leaders who, even as they called for calm and resolve, also made inflammatory statements about racial and cultural Others in "our" midst. National(ist) leaders warned against "enemies within" and terrorist "cells" operating not just abroad but also in "quiet suburbs" within America, and insisted that all Americans now had to be in a state of high alert.[13]

Ahmed argues that, rather than being a tool or a symptom, "the language of fear involves the intensification of 'threats,' which works to create a distinction between those who are 'under threat' and those who threaten. . . . Through the generation of 'the threat,' fear works to align bodies with and against others" (2004: 72). Articulating with previously existing racial hierarchies, a new racial formation was created in contradistinction to the nationalist Self that was hailed into being.[14] The creation of an affectively charged national community was fundamentally enabled by the coercive power of the state. The triangulation of the affective economies of hate and fear, the circulation of media representations of racial Otherness as signs of danger, and the formation of the national community converged in the production of a space for violence.

The media played a central role in the production of this space for violence by highlighting the dangers posed to the U.S. nation by religious and racial Others, whose very presence were now represented as indexical of danger. Newspapers, television coverage, and Internet chat rooms were replete with discourses of how "America" was under attack by religious and racial Others. Religious differences were coded as an immutable "civilizational difference" and collapsed under the sign of a monolithic Islam. Religious differences were explicitly racialized so that people were targeted for looking Muslim and having Muslim names. On television screens, on the Internet, and in newspapers, the relentless reiteration of images of the carnage of September 11, together with representations of those allegedly responsible for what had happened, intensified the circulation of fear and rage and, in the process, enabled the production of a space for violence in which institutional, physical, and psychic assaults on those deemed of South Asian and Middle Eastern "origin" were engendered, condoned, and, in many instances, rendered invisible.

State violence assumed the form of the systematic targeting of particular communities because of their religious affiliation; how this difference got read became central to the processes by which these communities became reracialized. As Ahmed points out, "Hate is economic; it circulates between signifiers in relationships of difference and displacement" (2004: 44). Signs of religious difference such as the hijab, turban, beard, or "foreign-sounding" names, visible—and public—markers of Sikh and Muslim affiliation, became charged with affective potency: the affect of fear began to congeal around these signs of Otherness, reconfigured as signs of danger. Affective regimes of fear and hate against these religious and racial Others became so potent that acts of hate violence emerged not as extraordinary eruptions of disorder into the everyday, but as quotidian, even normal, and constitutive of a newly configured racial order (compare Goldberg 1995).

I would add that these figures acquired political potency precisely because of their affective freight. In his analysis of representations of hate violence, Muneer Ahmad (2002) describes the murders of Balbir Singh Sodhi and others as crimes of passion, as inappropriate, perhaps extreme, expressions of an appropriate, "normal" passion—the passion for one's nation. Patriotism was now expressed as nationalist affect. The words of

Sodhi's killer are especially telling in this regard. He is reported to have said, "I'm a patriot. I'm a damn American all the way." Similarly, a man who tried to run over a Pakistani woman with his car claimed that he was doing so because she was "destroying [his] country" (Ahmad 2002: 108). Implicit in these examples is the production of masculinist regimes of affect: hate violence against racial Others was condoned as an archetypal crime of passion because it exemplified specifically masculinist expressions of grief and mourning.

If the reconfiguration of space in the aftermath of September 11 bore marks of the accumulation of affective value, it also bore the marks of multiple and displaced temporalities so that past, present, and future intermixed. This came home to me most powerfully when Baldeep Singh, an employee at a 7-Eleven in Sunnyvale, spoke of how, when he went home one night, his teenage son came to him weeping and asked, "Dad, what is a raghead?" Apparently, one of his son's classmates had called him a raghead because he wore a turban. Baldeep Singh sat at a counter in his store, his eyes glazed with bewildered misery, his palm squeezing a paper coffee cup. I was at first dumbstruck by what he said, but I also understood what his son's classmate was talking about. Baldeep Singh, a recent immigrant who had come to the United States about twelve years earlier, had no idea what "raghead" referred to, but had no doubt that it was a term of repugnance. I let Baldeep Singh know that "raghead" was a racial epithet used against Sikhs who had migrated to rural California in the early part of the twentieth century, referring to the fact that they wore turbans. Baldeep was stunned. Why would a young white boy who had played with his son since the two of them were four years old use such a word? How would he, living as he did nearly a hundred years afterward in Sunnyvale, a place that symbolized the cosmopolitan globality of Silicon Valley, even know this word? What explained this outpouring of hate on the part of a young boy who had known his Sikh friend for most of his life? Could it be that he did not know what the word meant? If so, how did he come to use it, and why did he use it now?

Ahmed cautions that, although "affects cannot be determined in advance" (2004: 59), some signs of hate are repeated. She asks why this happens: "Is it because they keep open a history which is already open insofar as it is affective?" (59). The use of the term "raghead" suggests a collapse of the past into the present and underscores how a younger generation of immigrants is haunted by the experiences of its ancestors. Sikh children who had borne racial slurs about their appearance and accents and complaints about their "smelly lunches" were now facing a different order of race-based hate, one that was at once old because it bore the traces of the experiences of an earlier generation and another era, and new in that it drew on contemporary representations of racial and cultural Others. The dominant explanation in the media for the hate violence that proliferated after September 11, 2001, was that it was perpetrated by strangers who ostensibly had misidentified or misrecognized Sikhs and others from the Middle East and South Asia as followers of Osama bin Laden and as real or potential terrorists.[15] Yet, according to most of my working-class informants in the San Francisco Bay Area, the perpetrators were frequently people who knew who they were: these were neighbors, playmates, teachers, and coworkers.

The temporality of racial identity was foregrounded by several informants who said that, while they had faced racial discrimination in the past, it had acquired an especially virulent edge after September 11, 2001. Particularly after the murders of Balbir Singh Sodhi in Arizona in September 2001 and his brother Sukhpal Singh Sodhi, who was killed while driving his taxi in San Francisco in August 2002, they were forced to reposition themselves in the ever-shifting racial landscape of the United States.[16] This, in turn, compelled them to rethink their future as working-class Sikhs in the United States. As one of them said to Veena Dubal and me, the murder of the Sodhi brothers reinforced to them that "things can change suddenly," thus reinforcing how, during moments of danger, temporalizing processes become reconfigured by a sense of radical contingency.

The temporality of racial identity necessarily entails recalling the racial violence faced by other communities of color at specific historical moments in the United States. As several scholars have pointed out (see, for instance, Ahmad 2002; Puar and Rai 2002), the racial profiling techniques faced by South Asians after September 11, 2001, had been perfected on the bodies of African American and Latina/o communities.[17] The temporality of racial identity also underscores shifting relations between communities of color. I began to observe how, after September 11, 2001, antiracist and progressive South Asian activists and some community leaders engaged in much soul-searching with regard to their own and their communities' responses to racial violence against other communities of color, in particular against African Americans. Many had to painfully confront their own racism. Several of these activists participated in antiracism workshops with members of other communities, including other Asian American communities who reached out to them after September 11, 2001, and Arab American communities with whom they found that they had something in common in terms of the histories of their racialization in the United States.[18]

The case of South Asians and those perceived as "coming from" the Middle East was further complicated by being framed in terms of disjunctive temporalities. For instance, we see hegemonic representations of a battle between "civilizations" (Huntington 1996) in which modernity, democracy, and civilization are identified with a particular model of a Christian state versus a radicalized and militant Islam that is, in turn, indexical of a temporal lag, a backward slide into an era of barbarism. The process of marking these men and women as objects of fear was based as much on conceptions of temporality as it was on spatial mappings. These men and women embodied a place as well as a time of barbarism and irrational violence, a disjuncture and an anachronism in the supposedly rational space of modernity; their very presence effected a temporal, and threatening, disjuncture.[19]

As Maira argues, "A crucial point is that the 'post-9/11' moment is not a radical historical or political rupture, but rather a moment of renewed contestation over the state's imperial power and ongoing issues of war and repression, citizenship and nationalism, civil rights and immigrant rights" (2009: 23). Indeed, the hate violence against South Asians after September 11, 2001, needs to be located in a longer history of racist policies against Asians in the United States, most notably Asian exclusion laws and, more recently, the internment of Japanese Americans during World War II. It also needs to be situated vis-à-vis representations of Asian Americans as perpetual foreigners and unassimilable Others. As Chuh puts it, "'Asian American' in this regard connotes the violence, exclusion, dislocation, and disenfranchisement that has attended the codification of certain bodies as, variously, Oriental, yellow, sometimes brown, inscrutable, devious, always alien. . . . 'Asian American' provides entry into these histories of resistance and racism" (2003: 27). What Lowe describes as "the unfixed liminality of the Asian immigrant" (1996: 19) seems to have been particularly salient with South Asians in the United States—both before and after September 11, 2001.

At the same time, as Chuh (2003) and several other scholars have pointed out, "Asian American" is itself a conjunctural and epistemological formation. Aligning South Asian histories of racial violence vis-à-vis Asian American histories is thus both a political and epistemological imperative. Signaling the urgent necessity of learning from each other's experiences at the level of activism and everyday practices, it also underscores the importance of the production of knowledges that enable struggles for social justice across communities of color.[20] The very term "Asian American" foregrounds the political imperative to claim cultural and legal citizenship vis-à-vis a white supremacist state and is often necessitated by racist conceptions of Asian Americans as chronically unassimilable. Yet this emphasis on nation-bound political struggles has, in the past, resulted in a distancing of Asian American scholarship from Asia (Chuh 2003: 87–88). As I have argued in my analysis of the transnational racial logics positioning call center agents in India, the demands of flexible citizenship on the part of global capital and the changing demographics of Asian communities in the United States have rendered nation-bound assumptions about migration, belonging, and racialization inadequate.[21] For close to two decades now, Asian American studies scholars have realigned their perspectives accordingly (see, for instance, Hune 2001; Kim and Lowe 1997). This shift in perspective is not just a matter of providing a more empirically accurate or complete portrayal of Asians in the United States. At stake are an alertness to the politics of knowledge production and a vigilance against how our epistemological strategies may inadvertently reinscribe a white supremacist and imperialist nation-state.

Indeed, the project of unsettling nations is rendered particularly urgent because of the persistence of the violence, exclusions, and hegemonic claims of nation-states. The disjuncture between formal citizenship and the sense of unsettlement experienced by some of my informants in the San Francisco Bay Area left them feeling acutely anxious about their location vis-à-vis the dominant (national) community. Although many of them did not experience hate violence after September 11, 2001, as a rupture, the exacerbation of the racism and racial violence many of them had suffered their entire life resulted in a profound sense of uncertainty; as one of them said to me, "It felt like the ground shifted under our feet." As immigrants of color, many of them had long felt disoriented. After September 11, 2001, they felt that they were losing their footing in a terrain that was unstable to begin with. In mining these informants' profound sense of unsettlement, and deploying it as an analytic, I have wished to sketch the contours of a conceptual and political framework that may enable us to unsettle the exclusionary and violent claims of the U.S. nation.

Some Concluding Thoughts

This book has been about how, at specific nodes in the circulation of transnational public cultures, the lush sensoria of grocery stores, the eruptive potentialities of erotics, the (often) irresistible draw of commodity affect, and the enchantments and uncertainties of aspiration participate in the discontinuous and heterogeneous production of India as an archive of affect and temporality. Richard and Rudnyckj underscore that affect is both a noun and a transitive verb; they emphasize that the analytical value of this conceptualization stems from its dynamic and reflexive quality and its coimbrication with action and agency; they add, "Affect is a means of sub-jectification that simultaneously produces those who enact it and those upon whom it acts" (2009: 59, 61–62). The affective regimes examined in this book are generative because of the thoughts, feelings, and actions they engendered for my informants: these affects index their capacities for world making, in short, their abilities to inhabit and navigate the social world.

My project of unsettling static conceptions of India and Indian culture is necessitated by a cultural and political context in which notions of the authenticity of Indianness and Indian identity have been staged as the basis for the marginalization of, if not violence against, subjects minori-tized along axes of religion, caste, class, gender, and sexuality.[22]

My analysis of the simultaneous reification and unsettlement of India as it gets produced and circulated across diverse nodes in a transnational circuit of capital, goods, and media underscores how the temporality of processes of simultaneity undergirds the unsettlement of India.[23] My point, moreover, has been to trace how unsettlement might be *intrinsic* to the production of India such that Indian culture emerges as endemi-cally and chronically in flux. At the same time, and critically, eschewing the temptation to engage in epochal thinking (as exemplified in discourses of the New India), my effort has been to ethnographically engage the speci-ficities of particular historical moments without exceptionalizing them.[24] By unsettling India I also problematize the modernist hubris of assuming the plasticity of time according to which we can shape time into what we will, in favor of a recognition that it is time that does its work on us, leaves its mark on us, makes us into who we were, are, and will become (compare Das 1996 and, especially, 2006). Recall also my discussion in chapter 1 of Fehmida Khan's articulation of the unpredictability of what time can do for and to us; as she said, "There is no saying what time will bring" (kuch keh nahin sakte ki waqt apne saath kya layega).

In this book I have gestured toward the different forms taken by uncer-tainty in the lives of my informants in New Delhi and the San Francisco Bay Area: Harbhajan's claustrophobic sense of being stuck in a rut and, hence, being left out by the onward march of a nation indifferent to her pain (chapter 1); the eruptive potential of erotics (chapters 2 and 4); the sense of flux articulated by informants like Omvati, Fehmida, and Vishnu (chapter 4); the backward slide feared by Beena, who worries that Muslims will make India regress (chapter 5); the myriad ways in which commodity affects promise, then defer and, in many cases, deny the gratification of desire for lower-caste and lower-middle-class and working-class men and women in New Delhi (chapter 5); the hopeful yet nervous anticipation of the future entailed in aspirations of lower-middle-class youth who wish to suture their upward social mobility to the purported rise of the Indian nation (chapter 6); and the contagion of fear and how it shook up the tempo of everyday life for my informants in the San Francisco Bay Area after September 11, 2001. Yet my primary focus has been less on my informants' individual experiences of the passage of time, nor on time consciousness as a collective experience (as postulated by Durkheim), than on what temporality does, its affectivity.[25] Diverging from conceptions of time as homogeneous or empty, I have been concerned with the fullness of time as a durée that encapsulates but, more importantly, exceeds individual consciousness (Bergson 1910), and of temporality as multiple and productive of sociality.

Contemporary battles over Indian identity and, indeed, over India in political and popular culture seem to be undergirded either by assumptions of cultural stasis (as in conceptions of tradition that have existed since "time immemorial"), fears about cultural contamination, or of cultural transformations of such magnitude as to be unrecognizable. Thus, for instance, we hear of how globalization (which has become a gloss for, among other things, urbanization, transnational media, the liberalization of the Indian economy, or neoliberalism) has resulted in a fundamental transformation of Indian culture; or, in contrast, we are told that (static) tradition exists alongside rapid cultural transformation. As argued in preceding chapters, each of these representations of culture and cultural change implies very specific notions of temporality, all of which are affectively charged. Deploying unsettlement as an analytic and ethnographic strategy has enabled me to rethink conceptions of cultural change. Ethnographically, this has involved remaining attuned to the "apparent momentum of the present" (Pandian 2012: 548) in order to construct an archive based on everyday affects and selectively compiling them into something that is unsettling yet productive of subjects, communities, and nations.[26] Conceptually, this has entailed allowing for the coincidence of past, present, and future, or a sense of acute disjunctures between different temporalities. Finally, this project has entailed remaining open to how the generative power of the everyday can unsettle any possible taken-for-grantedness of identity and understanding and, hence, throw into sharp relief how contingent are our ways of knowing and becoming.

The sense of uncertainty of so many of my informants—what they shared with me as well as that which remained unspoken between us—suffuses everything that I have learned about the affectivity of temporality and the marks that it leaves on subjects, communities, and nations. By training an ethnographic eye on the "weighted and reeling present" (Stewart 2007: 1), I have sought to avoid hypostasizing my informants' sense of flux, uncertainty, and unsettlement in terms of crisis, emergency, or watershed moments. Instead, I have examined how the circulation of transnational media and public cultures compels us to rethink conceptions of cultural change and, thereby, conceive of culture as inherently unsettled. Insofar as the political and affective claims of nation-states are predicated on assumptions about the stability and fixity of national culture and identity, my insistence on the fundamental unsettledness of India has consequences that are political as much as epistemological. As implicit throughout this book, the task of politically responsible feminist critique is precisely to hold still the reeling present in order to unsettle the reifications and violences unleashed by the repressive projects of nations and states.

Chapter 1. Unsettlement

1. I join forces here with several other feminist scholars who have sought to complicate the notion of patriarchy as relations of inequality produced by sexual difference (in this regard, the work of women of color in the United States and postcolonial feminists working in South Asia has been particularly helpful; for instance, Alexander 2005; Anzaldua and Keating 2002; Combahee River Collective 1984; Grewal and Kaplan 1994; Mani 1989; Mohanty 1988, 2003; Moraga and Anzaldua 1984, Sangari and Vaid 1990; Sunder Rajan 1993, 2003). My conception of patriarchy hence refers to the gendered relations of inequality that exist not just between men and women but also among women, and as shaped by multiple relations of power. Thus, for instance, my stories about Omvati, Ashutosh Sen, and Harbhajan Kaur (whom we will meet shortly) reveal how their lives and subjectivities have been formed through gendered relations of inequality that have left their imprint on their discourses of family, kinship, and sexuality. Equally, gendered relations of inequality are also refracted by and, in turn, shape the articulation of caste, class, religious minoritization, and politics of family. Thus conceptualized, the theme of patriarchal relations of power and inequality is threaded through subsequent chapters as well, for instance, in my discussion of the slippage between the sexual purity of women and the cultural purity of nations in both the homeland and the diaspora (chapters 2 and 5); of how gender and sexuality intersect with race and class to constitute Indian grocery stores as social spaces that are generative of particular kinds of sensuous knowledges (chapter 3); of the gendered inflections of the conjunction of erotic affects and commodity affects and fears about the "contamination" of Indian culture (chapter 4); of how gender and sexuality inflect neoliberal conceptions of entrepreneurship and growth in contexts of changing aspirations of young people (chapter 6); and finally, in terms of the profound salience of gender and sexuality to the construction of regimes of fear and rage in the "post–September 11" conjuncture in the United States (coda). I am grateful to one of the anonymous readers of this book for pushing me to clarify this point.

2. Compare with Allison (2012). In this remarkable essay, Allison (2012: 345) describes social precarity in contemporary Japan in terms of economic decline combined with an "evisceration of social ties" and a loss of hope in the future. My formulation of uncertainty (and unsettlement) is in dialogue with Allison's conceptualization of precarity but also contrasts with it. As I demonstrate in this book, the uncertainty of

my informants encapsulated a range of affects including anxiety fueled by a rapidly changing social milieu and, also, the hopeful, yet nervous, anticipation of the future.

3. Having done so once, I will no longer use quotation marks to foreground the constructed and contested nature of India: it should be clear that the primary objective of this project is precisely to unpack what is meant by India.

4. As I elaborate later in this book, in focusing on nodes in a global circuit of discourses, images, and texts, I draw on a rich methodological archive of feminist analyses of transnationalism (for instance, Alexander 2005; Grewal 2005; Shih 2007). See, in particular, the pioneering scholarship of Kondo (1997) and Manalansan (2003) on transnational cultural formations, which brings together feminist and queer anthropology, Asian studies, and Asian American studies.

5. Lynn Spigel (2004) has asserted that, even with a single medium like television, modes of engagement have been transformed as audiences in the United States (variegated, of course, by class, income, race, and age) now draw on a number of media outlets ranging from television to print media and the Internet. I believe that this description is apt for public cultures in contemporary Indian cities.

6. It goes without saying that at no point do I make universalistic claims about Indian public cultures in their dizzying totality—such a claim would be methodologically unviable and politically untenable.

7. In an insightful discussion of the relationship between affect, discourse, and narration, Massumi argues that while "affect is indeed unformed and unstructured, . . . it is nevertheless highly organized and effectively analyzable. . . . It is not entirely containable in knowledge but is analyzable in effect, as affect" (2002: 260, see also 45, 62).

8. For the most part in this book, I trace the constitution of notions of India rather than South Asia. I refer to transnational public cultures, in particular media produced in India and circulated across diverse Indian diasporas, as South Asian when they self-consciously and deliberately address (and, in so doing, *create*) a South Asian audience. There are yet other instances, as when I draw on my ethnographic research with activists and others who identify as South Asian rather than as Indian, when I use the term South Asian to flag the construction of a politics of solidarity by these individuals and collectivities.

In invoking the categories of India and South Asia, my intention is to foreground their discursive construction as discontinuous knowledge formations that are irreducible to each other: in so doing, I aim to draw attention to the overlaps as well as tensions between India and South Asia as produced by the Indian state, by transnational media, and in the everyday lives of my informants.

9. This is a rich and voluminous body of scholarship (for some early examples, see Chuh 2003; Chuh and Shimakawa 2001; Espiritu 2003; Hing 1993; Hune 1991; Kim 1982; Kim and Lowe 1997; Ong et al. 1994; Palumbo-Liu 1999; Shimakawa 2002). In particular, I draw on the work of scholars who bring an ethnographic sensibility to their transnational analyses of Asian American community and identity formation (notably Kondo 1997; Siu 2007; Maira 2002, 2009; Manalansan 2003; Shankar 2008).

10. I elaborate on these themes in Mankekar (n.d.).

11. See Leonard (1993), Takaki (1989). Compare Visweswaran (1997) for critiques of an overemphasis on West Coast histories of Asian communities in the United States. On dwelling and travel, see Clifford (1997). For feminist critiques of the politics of travel, see Grewal (1996), Kaplan (1996), and Pratt (2007).

12. It goes without saying that Asian and Asian American are nonequivalent and discontinuous identity categories. Yet, as Kandice Chuh has argued, it is important to recognize that "'Asians in America' and 'Asians in Asia' can only be held as separate and distinct within a symbolic economy that, more than refusing recognition of the 'Asian' as 'American,' does not accord standing as equal person to those racialized as 'Asian'" (2003: 88).

13. For an excellent ethnography of youth in the San Francisco Bay Area, see Shankar (2008).

14. A comparison of the 2000 and 2010 data reveals an 81 percent increase in the population of South Asians in the United States.

15. See also George (1997), Shah (2001, 2012), Shankar (2008), and Visweswaran (1997) on the complex racialization of South Asians in California.

16. To clarify: affect may have biological manifestations but cannot be explained in terms of biological processes.

17. In an important critique of "affect theory," Emily Martin argues against locating affect and, in particular, potentiality in the brain (2013). A more detailed engagement with Martin's thoughtful and provocative critique is beyond the scope of this chapter. For now suffice to say that, while her concerns about the "move away from the social" (2013: S154) in some affect theory are valid, my conceptualization of affects foregrounds their complex entanglement with the social; hence my insistence on conceptualizing affective *regimes* that congeal around social institutions like the state, the nation, and media. Martin also critiques affect theory for doing away with the subject and subjectivity (2013). As noted above and throughout this ethnography, I demonstrate how affective regimes are, in fact, productive of subjects.

18. See Ahmed (2004: 119) for a similar discussion.

19. Compare Appadurai (1996) on the imagination as a particular modality of modernity at large.

20. Compare Martin 2013.

21. My understanding of the relationship between time, temporality, and everyday life owes much to the work of Veena Das (for example, 1990, 2006, 2007); indeed, the subheading above is taken from the title of one of her important essays on time and violence (Das 2000).

22. Compare Munn (1992: 116) who foregrounds the symbolic dimensions of time.

23. Bergson makes an important distinction between durée as qualitative time and spatialized time that may be objectively measured through clocks and calendars. He conceives of durée as process and movement, an unfolding, as opposed to static units of time reckoning (see also Munn 1992: 95, 96).

24. My argument here converges with Rai's (2009) assertion that media assemblages in postliberalization India have established new rituals of life. However, rather than posit that media assemblages gesture toward the subsumption of life itself

(Clough 2007; Rai 2009), my interest lies in the articulations and disarticulations between temporality of everyday life and those of media consumption.

25. Compare Althusser (2001), Hall (1986), Sahlins (1987); on feminist conjuncturalism, see Mani and Frankenberg (1993); on conjunctural analyses of media, see Mankekar (1999a).

26. Compare Gupta (1992) on representations of time in "East" and "West."

27. In contrast to Peter van der Veer, I see no necessary contradiction between the territoriality of nationalism and the "transgressive fact of migration" (1995: 2); as I indicate above and elaborate in subsequent chapters, migration and immigration might sometimes renew affective investments in territoriality even as they reterritorialize identity.

28. This young man's description of the erotic love of soldiers who had died for the nation was neither idiosyncratic nor exceptional—he was, in fact, drawing on discourses of nationalism that conjoined erotic love (*mohabbat*) with martyrdom (*shahadat*) ubiquitous in contemporary Indian popular culture. As I have argued in a previous study of the affective bases of nationalism, nationalist affect in militaristic discourses of nationhood frequently slides between an asexual love for the motherland and erotic longing (Mankekar 1999a).

29. Compare Schein (2013) and Manalansan (2013) for excellent analyses of the articulation of erotic desire with a desire for return to the homeland.

30. See also Gopinath's (2005) powerful critique of assumptions about the backward-looking glance of diasporas.

31. I provide a brief history of the politico-legal category of the NRI in chapter 2.

32. See Axel (2004) for a somewhat different perspective on the "context" of diaspora.

33. See Boellstorff (2005), Gopinath (2005), and Manalansan (2003, 2012) for important critiques of universalistic assumptions of coming out as a critical modality for gay and lesbian identity.

34. See Weston (1997) for a pathbreaking ethnography of kin networks constructed by gay and lesbian communities in California; for a brilliant queer reading of Bollywood cinema, see Gopinath (2005).

35. My conception of home and homelessness builds on a rich and voluminous body of scholarship produced by feminist theorists, in particular feminist theorists of color in the United States (for instance, hooks 1999, 2000; see also Ahmed et al. 2003; Martin and Mohanty 1997; Pratt, Smith, and Bulkin 1988).

36. As Steedman argues, the archive's "condition deflects outrage: in its quiet folders and bundles is the neatest demonstration of how state power has operated, through ledgers and lists and indictments, and through what is missing from them" (2002: 68).

37. Although my focus in this book is on the period following the liberalization of the Indian economy and the expansion of transnational media, as will be evident shortly I do not by any means exceptionalize the current historical moment by implying that these cultural transformations are unprecedented, or that they have been "caused" by transnational media or globalized capital.

38. Obviously, transnational media are themselves part of my ethnographic archive. See Gupta (1992) for a trenchant critique of the tendency to assume that media texts are somehow less authentic than historical archives.

Chapter 2. Moving Images

1. I first published an analysis of DDLJ in 1999 but, as I note later in this chapter, had to fundamentally rethink my earlier discussion of this film after conducting ethnographic fieldwork in New Delhi and the San Francisco Bay Area. This chapter represents a substantial revision of my original analysis.

Since the publication of my article in 1999, there has been a large body of scholarship on this film. I would like to note, with particular pleasure, the resonances between my argument in this chapter and those in Uberoi (1998) and Sharpe (2005).

2. In this regard, my repeat viewing practices were similar to those of many of my informants who watched the film multiple times. They, and I, could sing most of its songs and recite much of the dialogue from memory.

3. This information is corroborated in Chopra (2002: 14). According to Chopra, Jiwani claims that he earned $200,000 from his screenings of DDLJ at Naz 8 Cinemas. Chopra also posits that the film earned 2.5 million pounds in its first year in the United Kingdom.

4. Of course, DDLJ was by no means the first popular Hindi film to circulate transnationally. The most cursory glimpse of the history of Indian cinema reveals that Hindi films have been transnational from the outset. From the earliest productions of Dadasaheb Phalke (*Raja Harishchandra* and *Lanka Dahan* in 1913 and 1917 respectively), who was inspired by the work of the Lumière brothers and films like the *Birth of Christ*, to films like Raj Kapoor's *Awaara* (1951), which made the two lead actors household names in many parts of Southeast Asia, East Africa, the People's Republic of China, and the former Soviet Union, popular Hindi films have been transnational in both their intertextual inspiration and in their circulation across the globe. A multitude of South Asian fiction, including that of Salman Rushdie (for instance, *Midnight's Children*, 1980) and Meera Syal (*Anita and Me*, 1996), suggests how the very language of Hindi cinema is deeply implicated in the formation of diasporic subjectivities in heterogeneous South Asian communities in different parts of the world.

5. Chopra (2002: 23) estimates that DDLJ earned over $5 million worldwide.

6. See Favero (2003, 2005) on the place of "the global" in the construction of young men's identities in New Delhi in the 1990s.

7. My most intensive ethnographic fieldwork on informants' engagement with DDLJ was conducted in the San Francisco Bay Area; my analysis of the film, therefore, draws largely on insights obtained there.

8. Compare Ochs and Schieffelin (1989) on how linguistic expressions of affect include both verbal and nonverbal cues.

9. The sociological and cultural changes resulting from the liberalization of the Indian economy are only just being comprehended (see, for example, Fernandes 2006; Gupta and Sivaramakrishnan 2012; Jeffrey, Jeffery, and Jeffery 2010; Sharma 2008;

Sharma and Gupta 2006). Let me be clear that I am, by no means, suggesting that these developments in the Indian economy determined shifts in nationalist affect; nor am I arguing for simplistically mapping affective economies onto political economy.

10. I place "middle classes" in quotes to foreground the highly contested nature of this social formation in the context of postliberalization India (see, for instance, Fernandes 2006; Mankekar 1999a; Mazzarella 2005).

11. For extended analyses of the state in postliberalization India, see Gupta and Sivaramkrishnan (2012).

12. In chapter 6 I attend to some of the cultural implications of these policies of economic liberalization in terms of the proliferation of discourses of neoliberalism and their implications for the production of normative discourses of entrepreneurship and individual self-sufficiency.

13. For a detailed analysis of the reforms introduced in 1991, see Nayak (1991).

14. For a more sanguine view of the reforms see Sharma (1996). The consequences of liberalization for organized and unorganized labor are worthy of a separate investigation. See, for example, Lakdawala (1991).

15. Compare Visweswaran (1997) on the implied masculinity of global capital; see also George (1997).

16. Based on the exchange prevalent at that time, these figures translate into $1.763 billion, $41 billion, and $7.5 billion respectively.

17. For excellent analyses of the Indian state's policies with regards to NRIs and PIOs (Persons of Indian Origin), see Shukla (2003) and Raj (2003).

18. My argument about the accrual of affect resonates with Sara Ahmed's (2004) formulation of affect as cumulative.

19. Recall Raymond Williams's (1977) formulation of how, even as they are "in solution" and "on the cusp of semantic availability," structures of feeling may be materialized in the literary or aesthetic form. However, what I am foregrounding here is not feelings but affects. For an explication of the difference (and overlaps) between feelings and affects, see the introduction to this book.

20. As several film theorists have argued, several senses come into play when we "watch" a film: the auditory, the tactile and haptic, kinesthetic, and other senses are engaged simultaneously so as to be corporeal and extracognitive: put another way, at work is not simply a cognitive decoding of symbols but practices of bodily engagement (Deleuze 1986; Marks 2000; Sobchak 2004; Linda Williams 2008). These scholars remind us that we make sense of films through our senses. Similarly, our engagement with films is nonlinear and, in the case of popular Hindi films like DDLJ, music and songs neither interrupt the narrative nor disrupt it (compare Gopalan 2008; Rai 2009).

21. For a detailed comparison between DDLJ and *Purab Aur Paschim*, see Mankekar (1999b).

22. My use of the term "deterritorialization" draws on Gupta and Ferguson's (1997b) critique of the assumed mapping of cultures onto specific places.

23. Compare Ochs (1992: 341) on how linguistic indexical signs are constitutive of particular affects.

24. There is a rich and voluminous scholarship theorizing travel. Some notable examples include Behdad (1994), Clifford (1997), Grewal (1996), Kaplan (1996), and Pratt (2007).

25. Simran's sexual purity is indexical because it has both an existential and a causal relationship with the preservation of Indian tradition in diaspora. See Ochs on how some indexical linguistic signs may be represented through "two-headed arrows" in that they "help to constitute other domains of social reality" (1992: 343).

26. Here Simran contrasts with Preeti of *Purab Aur Paschim*, who smokes, drinks, does not respect her father, and wears a blonde wig.

27. It goes without saying that DDLJ also elides the existence of heterogeneous South Asian diasporas in other parts of the world.

28. Significantly, Gopinath is not interested in simply bringing same-sex desire into visibility; instead, she attempts to trace the workings of same-sex desire that weave through "mainstream" texts like those of Bollywood cinema. She describes queer spectatorship as "strategies by which queer counterpublics actively read, resist, and reappropriate dominant cinematic representations" (Gopinath 2005: 93). For Gopinath, then, queer spectatorship "names a mode of reading, of rendering intelligible that which is unintelligible and indeed impossible within dominant diasporic and nationalist logic" (187).

29. See also Sharpe (2005: 67) for a similar analysis of Simran's innocent sensuality.

30. The spectacularization of Hindu rituals seems to have become a central part of films that purport to represent Indian culture, particularly to diasporic audiences. See chapter 5 for my analysis of Hindu rituals in another such film, *Kabhi Khushi Kabhie Gham*.

Chapter 3. Affective Objects

1. See Shankar (2008) for a brilliant ethnography of South Asians, in particular South Asian youth, living in the San Francisco Bay Area.

2. In sociocultural anthropology, there has been a long-standing interest in the analysis of objects as spheres of exchange and in terms of gift giving (see, for instance, Bohannon 1955; Gregory 1982). On the semiotics of material culture, see Sahlins (1976) and Shanks and Tilley (1986). Important examples of the symbolic analysis of goods may be found in Douglas and Isherwood (1978), Appadurai (1986), and Miller (1995a). See also "Objects on the Loose: Ethnographic Encounters with Unruly Artifacts," a special issue of *Ethnos* (1999). Recent decades have seen a proliferation of interdisciplinary scholarship on consumption and on the affectivity of objects. While it is impossible to cite all the works that represent this body of work, some notable examples are Bennett (2010), Burke (1996), and Miller (1995 a and b, 1998, 2009).

3. In this chapter I focus on the sensuous and embodied aspects of affect and veer, therefore, toward a post-phenomenological orientation to affect (see Gregg and Seigworth 2010). In so doing, I draw largely on theorizations of sensuous knowledges in Marks (2000).

4. Compare Grewal (2005: 6–7) and Kondo (1997: 6) for similar formulations of gender and racial identities that are refracted by nationalist discourses but not over-written by them.

5. For eloquent arguments for the sociocultural bases of sensuous knowledges, see Marks (2000) and Manalansan (2007).

6. Compare Ameeriar (2012) for an examination of the place of smell in the pro-duction of the radical alterity of Pakistani women in multicultural Toronto; see also Manalansan (2006, 2007) for powerful analyses of smell, racial alterity, and immigrant subjectivity.

7. See Manalansan (2007) for a sensitive discussion of the relationship between cuisine and the racialization of Asian Americans. See also "Asian Americans on Meat vs. Rice," a special issue of *Amerasia Journal* (2006), for excellent analyses of the re-lationship between cuisine and the semiotics and politics of Asian American subject formation.

8. Compare Allison (1991) on bento boxes and the (re)production of mothering in Japan.

9. Compare Appadurai (1988) on the formation of Indian "national" cuisine.

10. I borrow the term "diasporic affect" from Brian Axel (2002). However, I hasten to add that, far from reducing it to nostalgia, Axel provides us with a complex and nu-anced understanding of diasporic affect.

11. See also Mazumdar (1989: 25) for a discussion of the acute "color consciousness" of South Asians in the United States.

12. To clarify: while skin color is only one aspect of the racialization of South Asians in the United States, events following September 11, 2001, have only highlighted that chromatics are far from irrelevant to the racial mapping of these extremely heteroge-neous communities. As I argue in this chapter, class position and discourses of culture and cultural difference continued to hold a great deal of salience for how my infor-mants emplaced themselves in the racial landscape of the San Francisco Bay Area.

13. Compare Grewal (2005: 118). See especially Maira (2002) for powerful critiques of Indian cool in contexts of consumption.

14. Compare Maira (2002, 2009) and Shankar (2008).

15. See also Kondo (1997) for a powerful critique of U.S. multiculturalism.

16. For a discussion of the reification of notions of culture and cultural difference within South Asian communities, see also Prashad (2000: 113–15) and Shankar (2008). For an insightful discussion of racialization and multiculturalist aesthetics in contexts of neoliberalism, see Manalansan (2005).

17. On the complex relationships between racial minorities in the United States, and on antagonisms between Asian Americans and African Americans in particular, see the important work of Kyeyoung Park (1996, 1999) and Biju Mathew (2008).

18. Vijay Prashad (2000: 4) has argued that an explanation for poverty that es-chews structural analysis and focuses, instead, on a "conceptualization of a people as having discrete qualities" is inherently racist. Prashad also claims that the expansion of Asian immigration after the 1965 Immigration and Nationality Act and the resulting proliferation of the model minority stereotype resulted in increased state-endorsed

violence against African Americans. These discourses hinged upon an alleged contrast between the model South Asian family and the dysfunctional African American family (see, for instance, the Moynihan Report 1965).

19. Before the 1923 Supreme Court decision (United States v. Bhagat Singh Thind) that made Indians ineligible for citizenship on racial grounds, some Indians had claimed that because of their allegedly Aryan heritage, they were entitled to naturalization (see George 1997; Leonard 1993; Mazumdar 1989; Takaki 1989). According to Mazumdar (1989: 50–51), the South Asian community in the United States continues to seek access to "whiteness" using Aryan racial myths (see also George 1997: 41–42).

20. See Visweswaran (1997: 7, 11) for a discussion of the relationship between class privileges of Indian Americans and colonialism.

21. As George points out, "When pressed, the commonly offered affiliation approaching a racial category that is seen as acceptable is 'Aryan'" (1997: 41–42).

22. Proposition 187 (also known as the Save Our State initiative) was a referendum passed by voters in California in 1994 that aimed to exclude undocumented immigrants from access to social services and other entitlements. Although it ostensibly targeted undocumented immigrants, it was part of a larger backlash against immigrants of color, particularly Latina/os and Asians. Proposition 209, while targeting all communities of color, reinforced nativist hostility toward Latina/o and Asian immigrants. Also known as the California Civil Rights initiative, this proposition was passed by the California electorate in 1996 and aimed at prohibiting government institutions from considering race, ethnicity, or gender in public education and government jobs.

23. See Shankar's (2008) analysis of ideologies of success among South Asian American youth in the Bay Area.

24. See Dhaliwal (1995) and Wadhwani (1998) for excellent analyses of labor politics within Indian family-run stores in the San Francisco Bay Area.

25. Several scholars have analyzed the cultural and political shifts that occurred within South Asian communities as a result of changes in U.S. immigration policy, for instance, Prashad (2000: 76–81).

26. For studies of body shopping and Indian workers, see Aneesh (2006) and Xiang (2007). See especially Grewal (2005) on the networks of class, nationality, and race that undergirded body shopping in the late 1990s.

27. See Grewal (2005) for an important discussion of the symbolics of the U.S. flag for South Asians, and Sikh Americans in particular, after September 11, 2001.

Chapter 4. Transnational Hindi Television

1. Compare Clough (2007), Grossberg (2010), Massumi (2002).

2. As Page and Crawley state, "Before the international satellite invasion hit India, over 90 per cent of the country was covered by satellite-fed terrestrial signals" (2001: 75).

3. It is important to reiterate that television did not work in isolation in accelerating the proliferation of commodity culture. I am grateful to one of the anonymous reviewers for pushing me to clarify this.

4. The most important networks to emerge in South India in the 1990s were the Tamil Sun TV group, owned by Kalanidhi Maran, who has close family links with the DMK, one of the most important political parties in Tamil Nadu; Eenadu TV and Gemini TV in Telugu; Udaya TV in Kannada; and Asianet in Malayalam.

5. For statistical and marketing data on the correlation between proliferation of transnational television, the acceleration of advertising, and the increase in consumer spending, see Mankekar (2004).

6. Haug also cautions us that commodity aesthetics form just one "functional complex, one aspect among others in our social reality" (1986: 138).

7. I elaborate on processes of embodiment evoked by the synesthetic pleasures of television elsewhere (Mankekar 2014).

8. In foregrounding the centrality of television to the construction of commodity affect, I am by no means claiming that other media like film or print advertisements became irrelevant or even less powerful. Cinema, for instance, continued to play a critical role in popularizing consumerist lifestyles, fashions, and so on; as noted above, I return to this theme in chapter 5. I am, however, concerned here with how the ubiquity of television in the everyday lives and spaces of my informants in New Delhi made all the more potent the commodity affects that proliferated at that historical moment. In Mankekar (2012) I argue that the temporalizing regimes generated by television, particularly as they shape the everyday lives of viewers, has consolidated its significance to the formation of subjectivities in late twentieth- and early twenty-first-century India.

9. To clarify, although many of my informants could afford some of the less-expensive commodities that had come into the market (e.g., cosmetics; some varieties of packaged foods; small appliances such as mixers, gas stoves, and electric fans), they were unable to purchase most of the high-end consumer goods advertised, such as automobiles, air conditioners, and expensive clothing.

10. The existing literature on commodities and consumption in sociocultural anthropology, history, and cultural studies is voluminous. For a groundbreaking and theoretically rigorous analysis of shopping in a non-Western context, see Chua Beng Huat's (2003) *Life Is Not Complete without Shopping: Consumption Culture in Singapore*. On the positionality of the feminist researcher in studies of shopping, see Meaghan Morris (1993). As this chapter (and the previous one) demonstrates, I concur with Morris's argument that rather than adopt either a vantage point of voyeurism or condescension or, at the other extreme, a perspective that valorizes consumption, cultural studies scholars need to adopt a critically informed perspective of "ambivalence" (1993: 300). She suggests that, much like "effective shopping," we deploy a "sharpened focus, [a] narrowed gaze" in our analyses of consumption (300).

11. There is an important story to be told about the precarious class mobility of my working-class informants like Raju—certainly the irony of a working-class man policing the entry and movements of other working-class men and women in stores previously frequented by rich people should not be lost (see Fernandes [2000, 2006] on the precarious class positions of working-class communities in postliberalization India). For now, my primary concern in this chapter lies with how some of the affective

regimes and temporalizing processes generated and circulated by transnational television participated in the reconfiguration of notions of India and Indianness.

12. Lenore Manderson and Margaret Jolly's (1997) excellent critique of the binary of universalistic versus indigenous sexualities applies equally to erotics. As Manderson and Jolly posit with respect to cross-cultural studies of sexuality, erotic desire is most fruitfully analyzed in terms of cultural encounters and confluences. By situating contemporary expressions of erotic desire in India in the larger context of globalization and transnational media, I argue both against exoticizing an essentially Indian form of erotics and assuming that expressions of erotics in India are the same as in other parts of the world. See also Boellstorff's (2012) important intervention against unproductive binaries such as those of similitude and difference in transnational and cross-cultural frameworks on sexuality.

A related project, but one that lies outside the scope of this chapter, is the place India occupies in transnational discourses of erotics. See, for instance, Manderson and Jolly for a discussion of "Western-imagined Oriental sexuality" (1997: 8).

13. The scholarship on erotics in Indian literature, myth, and popular culture is voluminous; see, for instance, Bannerjee (1989), Bhattacharya (1975), Doniger (1996), Kakar (1989), Nandy (1980), and Rege (1996). On the politics of sexuality in colonial and nationalist contexts, see Arondekar (2009), Das (1996), C. Gupta (2012), Orsini (2002), Sinha (1997), Srinivasan (1985), Thapan (1997), and Uberoi (1996).

14. Although the authorship of the Kamasutra has been attributed to Vatsayana, it is more likely a composite text. See Roy (1998) for an excellent discussion of the politics underlying the translations and appropriations of the Kamasutra in the modern era.

15. For more information on erotics within Sanskritic *rasa* theory, see Dimock et al. (1974) and Siegel (1978).

16. The relationship between same-sex erotics and the formation of gay and lesbian identities in modern India has been a site of controversy among analysts of popular culture, queer theorists, and gay and lesbian activists in India. Scholars such as Rachel Dwyer have argued, "In India, some people enjoy same-sex sexual activity without wishing to claim a gay or lesbian or even bisexual identity; it is simply that they have sex with someone of the same sex but they expect to marry and live in a heterosexual relationship" (2000: 51–52), thus drawing a distinction between same-sex desire and the formation of gay and lesbian identities in urban India. Giti Thadani (1996) offers another perspective in pointing to the ways in which heteropatriarchal discourses have rendered gay and lesbian desire so invisible that they have foreclosed the articulation (until very recently) of gay and lesbian identities. In this regard, the heteronormativity of the representations that I analyze in this chapter may serve to reinforce the hegemonic invisibility and illegibility of gay and lesbian identities. There is, nevertheless, a burgeoning gay and lesbian movement in India. The cultural productions and interventions of Indian gay and lesbian activists and scholars are an important topic for further research but, regrettably, are beyond the scope of this chapter. See the pioneering work of Arondekar (2009) on homoerotic desire in a historical frame, and also Abraham (2004), Balachandran (2004), Bandyopadhyay (2007), Bose and Bhattacharya (2007), Biswas (2007), Cohen (1995), Gandhi (2007), Ghosh (2007), Merchant

(2007), Mutneja (2007), Pandey (2004), Patel (1998, 2007), Reddy (2005, 2007), Shahani (2008), Srivastava (2004), and Thadani (1996) on same-sex and gay and lesbian erotics in contemporary India.

17. For instance, a STAR Plus serial titled *Maryada: Aakhir Kab Tak* featured love between two men in an important subplot. This serial ran from October 2010 to April 2012.

18. Engagements with global/local axes of sexuality and erotics include Allison (2012), Boellstorff (2005, 2012); Manalansan (2003, 2012); and Mankekar and Schein (2012).

19. V. Geetha (1998) notes the entanglement of sexuality, erotics, and violence in her research on sexual violence among lower-middle-class and working-class women in Chennai. Although my focus is not on sexual violence but on erotic affects circulated by transnational media, the mutual imbrication of erotics and power in the lives of my informants is inescapable.

20. Compare Geetha's (1998) discussion of the covert and indirect expression of women's erotic desires (and frustrations). In one instance, Geetha observes that a woman expressed her erotic estrangement from her husband by saying, "The child sleeps between us these days" (1998: 307).

21. For a poignant and powerful discussion of the relationship between cosmetics and desire in another sociocultural context, see Peiss (2011).

22. Omvati's discomfort with the relationship between her son and daughter-in-law is far from unusual in the context of the gendered politics of patrilineal (and patriarchal) extended families in northern India (see, for instance, Raheja and Gold's [1994] discussion of the tensions surrounding conjugality in rural northern India). It also articulates with the new visibility of conjugality in the public sphere; I return to this theme later in the chapter.

23. Let us not forget that the yearning for commodities implicated women in more ways than one. In some cases, the febrile consumerism of the middle and lower-middle classes led to a rise in demands for increasingly ostentatious dowries. Consequently, young brides were particularly vulnerable to being harassed for dowries. Almost all the lower-middle-class men and women I interviewed, in particular those with daughters of marriageable age, expressed intense anxieties about the kinds of dowries that they would be expected to provide, and many young women were terrified about the kind of treatment that they would receive if their in-laws were dissatisfied with their dowries. As V. Geetha notes, "It is not accidental that dowry demands are never simply that: they inscribe themselves literally and metaphorically on the wifely body. They constitute this body as a thing, which may be discarded if it cannot yield its essential 'use' value" (1998: 314). For many of the women with whom I did fieldwork, on the other side of the pleasures of yearning for commodities lay a sinister nexus of consumerist desire, avarice, and the gendered (female) body.

24. On the co-implication of intimacy and capitalism, see Berlant (2000), Giddens (1992), Mankekar (2013), and Wilson (2004).

25. For years popular films have provided ample opportunities for the construction of erotic affects. But how was the production of erotic affects on transnational Hindi

television different from those dominant in popular cinema? Since the Indian film industry is so large and heterogeneous, I focus on popular Hindi films. As Rachel Dwyer (2000) points out, in Hindi films, erotic longing is frequently portrayed in terms of romance and expressed through the use of song, fetishization, and metaphor (see also Uberoi 1997).

Representations of erotics in Hindi films have shifted over time. As one of my informants pointed out to me, in older Hindi films, sexual desire tended to be portrayed rather elliptically (which, she claimed, accentuated rather than diffused or deflected their erotic power). But starting in the 1990s, with songs such as "Jumma Chumma de de" (Give me, give me a kiss, in *Hum* [Us, 1991]) or "Choli ke Peeche kya hai" (What lies beneath my blouse? in *Khalnayak* [1993]), Hindi films started to represent erotic desire more explicitly. Representations of erotics in these films drew on diverse aesthetic practices ranging from "folk" performative conventions to MTV-influenced song-and-dance sequences—including several that focused not only on the sexualized female body but also on the sexualized male body.

Recent representations of the latter are not unprecedented. Male stars have frequently been eroticized—for instance, Shammi Kapoor, a 1960s star who apparently drew inspiration from the gyrating Elvis Presley (Rai 1994). By the late 1990s, Bollywood films featured actors like Salman Khan, whose buffed body was explicitly staged as an object of erotic desire.

26. But see Sangita Gopal's (2012) provocative analysis of these films as renegotiating the relationship between conjugality, romance, and patterns of authority in the family.

27. For a discussion of how erotic desire was foregrounded in some cinematic representations of conjugality in the 1990s, see John (1998) and Niranjana (1995).

28. Conflicts between conjugal desire and duties toward the extended family are the subject of innumerable folk tales, songs, and novels; see, for instance, Raheja and Gold (1994). However, as I argue, representations of this conflict in transnational Hindi television serials became particularly disconcerting to my informants when they foregrounded women's erotic agency.

29. These anxieties were also mirrored in and perhaps fueled by television serials that focused on tensions between the conjugal unit and the extended family. Serials such as *Kuch Jhuki Palkein* (2002–2003) and *Gharana* (2003) focused centrally on conflicts between the two, even as others (e.g., *Justajoo* 2005) depicted the trials but also the clandestine pleasures of extramarital sexual relationships. *Justajoo*, in fact, was about an incestuous extramarital relationship and problematized dominant discourses of family and kinship by making explicit the politics of desire among members of a family.

30. Some Hindi films of the time, such as *Drishti* (1990) or *Paroma* (1984), narrate the erotic awakening of married women. Note that these are not conventional Bollywood films, but are deemed crossover films made by directors who have established their reputations in alternative or "middle cinema."

31. Page and Crawley corroborate this by reporting that the middle-class students they surveyed in Ahmedabad did not find Savi bold. When asked whether *Hasratein* was bold, one student replied, "It is bold, but Savitri does not act bold. She is like a

traditional wife"; another responded, "She respects everyone and teaches me to respect everyone" (Page and Crawley 2001: 166).

32. Compare Giddens's reminder that sexuality might also be "worrying, disturbing, fraught with tensions" (1992: 177).

33. Most notable among them was *Kyunki Saas Bhi Kahbhi Bahu Thi* (Because a mother-in-law was once a daughter-in-law too, 2000–2008), which was the longest-running serial on television to date with 1,830 episodes, and received some of the highest ratings in India and, indeed, in Asia (it received a TRP or Television Rating Point of 5.6). Another notable serial was *Kahaani Ghar Ghar Kii* (The story of every home), which ran in the early 2000s and, with 1,700 episodes, was the second-longest-running serial on Indian television. This serial was immensely popular both within India and abroad and was estimated to have an audience of over 90 million viewers. It received a TRP rating of 4.9. Both these serials set the trend for many that followed in their wake, so much so that many scholars of Indian television have tended to overlook the efflorescence of programs that foregrounded the erotic during the 1990s.

34. My ethnographic observations are corroborated by quantitative data collected by a Pathfinders India Study, according to which 41.8 percent of a total sample size of 10,955 individuals believed that "Western influence on TV programmes is harmful to Indian culture" (1998: 25, table 2.8.7).

35. As many feminist historians and cultural analysts have reminded us, contests over tradition are profoundly gendered and are frequently predicated on the containment of women (see, for instance, Mani 1989; Sunder Rajan 1993).

36. Recall, also, controversies surrounding the Miss World pageant in Bangalore in December 1996 and the portrayal of a lesbian relationship between the heroines of Deepa Mehta's film *Fire* that same year. In the case of the Miss World pageant, a large coalition of protesters criticized the decision to hold the pageant in India as symptomatic of the contamination of Indian culture by Western discourses of gender, sexuality, and the erotic (see John 1998; Oza 2001). Similarly, protesters against *Fire* represented the lesbian relationship between the heroines as foreign and therefore antinational. In these protests, Indian culture was reified, and its difference from so-called Western culture was essentialized and fetishized (Bandyopadhyay 2007 and Patel 1998).

37. My argument about the temporalizing discourses undergirding the idea that India had been lagging behind and had to catch up draws on Akhil Gupta's (1998) theorization of (under)development as an identity in postcolonial India.

Chapter 5. Global India and Moral Subjects

1. My focus on nodal points in the production, circulation, and unsettlement of India is at once a methodological and epistemological strategy, and draws on similar strategies deployed by some feminist scholars of transnationalism, most notably Shih (2007) and Grewal (2005); it also draws on the delineation of feminist conjuncturalism in Frankenberg and Mani (1993).

2. It goes without saying that I am by no means attempting to generalize that all viewing communities (in India or overseas) engage Hindi cinema in ways similar to

those of my informants: the heterogeneous affective regimes generated by Hindi cinema for members of Indian diasporas can only be postulated through a rigorous attention to the complex interplay between texts, audiences, and contexts in specific sociohistorical locations. My focus in this chapter is on the role of Hindi cinema in the construction of Global India for a group of men and women located in a particular place (the San Francisco Bay Area) and time (the early 2000s). I would therefore like to caution against assumptions about its appeal to viewers in diverse sociohistorical contexts. See Kaur and Sinha (2005), Kavoori and Punathambekar (2006), and Larkin (2008) for examples of important analyses of the multiple modalities of the pleasures provided by Hindi cinema to viewers across the world.

Furthermore, and more importantly, my analysis in this chapter (see also chapters 1, 2, and 3) is intended precisely to foreground how gender and sexuality, class and racial identity, and migration history and geography problematize assumptions about the Indian diaspora as a transhistorical and/or transcultural identity.

3. The concept of resurgence is neither unique to nor unprecedented in Hindu nationalism. But what lent moral and affective potency to Hindu nationalist conceptions of resurgence was the insistence on vengeful recovery enabled only by the excision of Muslims from the nation.

4. See Gopinath (2005), Lal (1999), Prashad (1998), and Rajagopal (2001) for detailed analyses of the diasporic bases of Hindu nationalism.

5. Valentine's Day continues to enrage Hindu nationalists who have persisted in their moral policing against it. In February 2009, Hindu nationalist goons, allegedly instigated by Pramod Muthalik, the leader of the Hindu nationalist organization Sri Ram Sene, physically assaulted a group of women in a pub in the southern Indian city of Mangalore. The Sri Ram Sene had long been an important part of the moral police lashing out at young men and women celebrating Valentine's Day. In response to the attack on women in the pub, a group of activists launched a Facebook campaign against Muthalik and the Sri Ram Sene. Named the Pink Chaddi (Underwear) Campaign, the campaign called on volunteers to mail pink panties to Muthalik and his followers as a counterprotest to their moral policing.

6. Gopinath (2005) has pointed to significant lacunae in some feminist critiques regarding the heteronormativity of Indian nationalism. See also Paola Bachetta (1999) on the conjunction of discourses of moral purity and homophobia in Hindu nationalism.

7. Interestingly, but not surprisingly, many orthodox Muslim organizations and leaders also expressed their displeasure at Valentine's Day celebrations. As one report pointed out, it was "the only point upon which organisations like Shiv Sena, Hindu Jagran Manch, Jamait-e-Islami, the All India Muslim Forum, Hussaini Tigers, and Dukhtaran-e-Jainib holding diverse views, share a common front" (Rastogi 2007: 1). A crucial difference between orthodox Muslim and Hindu nationalist mobilization against Valentine's Day celebrations is that the latter had the endorsement of the state and, indeed, functioned with its complicity if not its active collusion.

8. The blackening of faces symbolizes public humiliation and harkens back to days when ash was smeared on the faces of those who transgressed social norms to index their ritual pollution.

9. Several commentators pointed to an apparent contradiction between Bal Thackeray's warm welcome to Michael Jackson when he came to Bombay in 2001 to give a concert, and his call to action against the celebration of Valentine's Day as something against "Hindu/Indian culture." There was some speculation in the press that Thackeray's welcome to Jackson might have to do with Jackson's alleged donation to a family enterprise (see, for example, "Tussle for Turf in the Love Bazaar" 2001).

10. While there is a supreme irony in the Sangh Parivar's appropriation of Gandhi's call to swadeshi (launched against British imports during the anticolonial struggles) to Hindutva ends, it is not unprecedented. Hindu nationalist groups have frequently used the rhetoric of swadeshi in other antiglobalization statements against multinational companies.

11. See also Paola Bachetta (1999) on the queering of Muslim sexuality in Hindutva discourses.

12. In these representations of arranged marriages, transnational discourses of morality are sometimes couched in the rhetoric of human rights or women's rights. While it is beyond the scope of this chapter to analyze them, controversies in Britain and other parts of northern Europe on the issue of "forced marriages" among South Asian and other "Third World" immigrants over the past several decades exemplify how the sovereign individual is posited as the normative subject of romance in purportedly universal discourses of the moral. For now, suffice to say that attempts by these European states to deploy discourses of morality to regulate the erotic desires of racial Others are part of longer colonial and neocolonial legacies.

13. See Gopal (2011) for a provocative analysis of this film and its significance to director Karan Johar's oeuvre.

14. Gopal (2011: 65, 67) accurately points out that the opening up of the diasporic market to Hindi cinema coincided with the production of several films that thematized the family.

15. In her nuanced and innovative analysis of the history of conjugality in Hindi cinema, Gopal describes *K3G* as a moment of transition between films in which the law of the family overrides "the couple's right to be" and those that she describes as the New Bollywood, which depict the lives of couples who are already married such that their story begins with their marriage rather than depicting marriage as a happy ending. As she puts it, *K3G* represents "a very important temporal and aesthetic bridge between Hindi cinema's courting duo and New Bollywood's postnuptial dyad" (2011: 65).

16. Gopal points out that, like many other films by Johar, *K3G* "fully harnesses the technological potential of cinema to immerse spectators in a consumerist utopia" (2011: 79).

17. See Srinivas (2002: 170) for a comparison between her experience of watching a film in a "half empty" theater in Los Angeles, and her observations of audiences in Bangalore.

18. See Srinivas (2002) on cinema going as a collective experience.

19. For a delightful description of the scene at Naz 8, see Shankar (2008). See also Sharma (2003) and Rai's (2009) rich and insightful analysis of the emergence of the "malltiplex" in India.

20. Srinivas (2002) underscores the sociality of moviegoing for her informants in Bangalore. See, especially, her discussion of how members of audiences talk back to characters on screen, move around (she describes this as an "ambulatory viewing style"), and engage in social interactions with each other (165). Srinivas also emphasizes that "repeat viewing" and the participatory modes in which audience members engage the filmic text makes for "differentiated experiences" (166).

21. I owe this insight to Faye Ginsburg (personal communication, February 1, 2008).

22. Jaya Bachchan is reported to have suspended her hugely successful Bollywood career for several decades after she married superstar Amitabh Bachchan.

23. In this, *K3G* contrasts with *DDLJ*, which suggests a much more extraterritorial and portable notion of home and homeland (see Mankekar 1999a; chapter 2).

24. As Gopinath has argued, *Hum Aapke Hain Kaun* is exemplary in its "seamless reconciliation of the tensions between India's economic liberalization of the early 1990s and 'traditional' Indian/Hindu values by reconstituting conventional patriarchal gender relations in the context of a newly globalized Indian middle class" (2005: 117). *Hum Saath Saath Hain*, on the other hand, might well be described as a contemporary rendering of the Ramayana in a context marked by neoliberal capitalism (for more on the place of neoliberal capitalism in contemporary, urban India, see chapter 6). *K3G* also evokes Karan Johar's previous film, *Kuch Kuch Hota Hai*, in several ways, not least of which is the casting of one of its star pairs, Shah Rukh Khan and Kaajol. Most of all, it references films like *Dilwale Dulhaniya Le Jayenge* in its evocation of NRI nostalgia.

25. Here it is important to note that, for most of my informants among the Indian diaspora in the San Francisco Bay Area, nostalgia for India did not automatically or inevitably imply a desire to return to India (see chapter 3 for a detailed problematization of nostalgia as the affective basis of diasporic subjectivity).

26. *K3G* is not unique in its depiction of Global Indians who are at home everywhere in the world. Several films, including a few that do not concern themselves with NRIs, such as *Dil Chahta Hai* (2001), depict the self-confidence of upper-class (predominantly, but not exclusively, male) Indians who travel the world as transnational and, most often, corporate elites and are at home wherever they go.

27. In *K3G*, some public spaces in London display the Indian flag. Another significant display of *K3G*'s version of NRI patriotism is its allusion to India's victory over England in a cricket match. Interestingly, but not surprisingly, the match is against England and not Pakistan; as one viewer suggested to me, this was probably in deference to the film's Pakistani audiences.

28. As Gopal suggests, it is clear that "the family wields merely emotional power over its members. The allegiance that Rahul owes his father is underwritten not by necessity but by affect" (2011: 81).

29. The valorization of consumption in *K3G* contrasts with its gaudy representation in films like Sooraj Barjatya's *Hum Aapke Hain Kaun* (1994), where the interiors of homes index the ostentatious display of wealth by the nouveau riche in postliberalization India. *K3G*'s sophisticated opulence is naturalized to emblematize a cosmopolitan domesticity enabled by a liberalized economy. On cinema's centrality to consumption, see Gopal (2011: 15).

30. The film also contains a long and spectacular representation of another Hindu religious ceremony, the cremation of Yash's mother, grandmother to Rahul and Rohan.

31. For a particularly insightful ethnography of South Asian youth in Silicon Valley, see Shankar (2008).

32. See Parminder Bhachu (1986) for an excellent analysis of multiple migration.

33. While it is beyond the scope of this chapter to examine how members of diasporic communities in different parts of the world engage Hindi cinema, I narrate Preeti's story in order to foreground the multiple trajectories of members of communities that we might term "diasporic": hence, I problematize assumptions about diaspora that flatten out the complexities of subject formation. My objective here is to trace how the jagged trajectories of imaginative and physical travel articulate with regimes of affect and temporality in contexts of transnationality.

34. Scholars in Asian American studies have produced powerful critiques of model minority discourses. For instance, see Zhou and Lee (2004) for an important sociological analysis of the implications of model minority discourses for Asian American communities, and Shankar (2008) for critiques of the relationship between model minority discourses, the racialization of South Asians, and the marginalization of working-class Desi youth. As Prashad (1998) argues, model minority discourses are predicated on valorizing Asian Americans' achievements at the expense of African Americans who, by implication, are represented as underachievers, with dysfunctional families, dependent on welfare and state social services, and so on. For South Asian Americans, and for Sikh and Muslim South Asians in particular, model minority discourses became particularly fraught after September 11, 2001 (see also Maira 2009).

35. See, for instance, Dasgupta and Das Dasgupta (2002), Maira (2002), and Shankar (2008).

36. See especially Espiritu (2003) for an analysis of similar discourses of gender and sexuality in Filipino American communities.

37. My suspicions were confirmed when, years later, I read Amit Rai's (2009: 343) identification of *Mohabattein*'s Gurukul as a manor house near Wiltshire, England.

38. As Puar (2007: 282n59) points out, Hindu nationalism in India and the diaspora renders Sikhs and Muslims doubly vulnerable.

39. See Lal (1999) for a detailed discussion of Hindutva versions of Indian history.

40. See Bachetta's (1999) examination of the role of Hindu notions of time, chiefly notions of *satyug* and *kalyug*, in how the past and the future are constructed in Hindutva.

Chapter 6. Aspirational India

1. In addition to drawing on my ethnographic field research over the past decade on the cultural politics surrounding transnational public cultures, I base my analysis of impersonation on ethnographic research conducted by Akhil Gupta and myself in call centers in Gurgaon, India, in 2003 and 2005, and a close textual reading of the film *Bunty aur Babli*.

2. It is critical that we note that these aspirations coexist with a loss of hope for many youths in India; see especially Chua (2011, 2014) on the prevalence of suicide

among youth in Kerala, Jeffrey (2011) on unemployment and its production of a temporality of waiting, and Jeffrey, Jeffery, and Jeffery (2010) on unemployment and gender identity among youth in rural North India. In addition, there exists a rich and voluminous scholarly literature on how the so-called rise of India as an economic power may be belied by the persistence of high rates of malnutrition and poverty among many segments of the Indian population (see, for instance, Gupta 2012). For a nonacademic and powerful indictment of how economic progress might have bypassed the urban poor, see Boo (2012).

My point is not to suggest that the aspirations I analyze in this chapter are examples of false consciousness but, indeed, to underscore how aspirations and precarity may be intertwined: as I emphasize later in this chapter, the proximity of precarity is precisely what generates the co-implication of aspiration and uncertainty. On precarity outside the context of South Asia, see Allison (2012b).

3. Compare with Julie Chu's study of mobility and emplacement in Fuzhou, China, where, she argues, mobility emerges a "key trope in projects of capitalist development and modernity" (2010: 4).

4. In much of Indian popular culture, the train has long been represented as a harbinger of change. In particular, the train is a trope for both the enchantments of modernity and its destructive and traumatic dimensions. In postcolonial India, the train has also become evocative of communal violence, as evident in its association with the bloodshed of Partition and the 1984 violence against Sikhs. In February 2002, images of the burning train in Godhra spurred pogroms against Muslims across the state of Gujarat.

5. Fernandes (2000) has argued that some studies of middle classes in South Asia focus exclusively on consumption. Extending her important critique, the research Akhil Gupta and I conducted in call centers demonstrates the inextricability of labor and consumption: call center agents labor in order to consume and, conversely, their consumption practices fuel their need to work in call centers.

6. Here *Bunty aur Babli* contrasts sharply with films like *Satya* (1988), *Yuva* (2004), and *Laaga Chunari Mein Daag* (2007), which belong to a genre of Bollywood films that focuses on the traps and dangers faced by migrants to the city and thus provide accounts that are far from celebratory. More recent films like *Oye Lucky! Lucky Oye!* (2008) and *Shanghai* (2012) similarly foreground the dark underbelly of aspiration.

7. See Sharma and Gupta (2006) for an analysis of the relationship between IT, outsourcing, and the postliberalization state in India.

8. Several theorists have commented on the relationship between affect and labor, most notably feminist scholars who underscore the affective bases of what is frequently deemed women's work. Formulations of affective labor by scholars of "late" capitalism such as Hardt (1999, 2007), Hardt and Negri (2000, esp. 289–94), and Lazzarato (1996) have launched intense debates regarding the viability of this concept, its applicability to different segments of global and local economies, and so on. It is beyond the scope of this chapter to parse out this debate, but for a powerful feminist engagement with Hardt's conception of affective labor, see Kathi Weeks (2007).

9. Call center agents problematize the binary sometimes constructed between the intellectual labor of men in the North versus the material labor of women in the South (compare Dyer-Witheford 2001: 71).

10. See Hardt (1999: 96) for a similar argument about virtual presence in affective labor.

11. By no means am I extrapolating from the experiences of the call center workers I interviewed to suggest that affective labor is the only or even a dominant mode of labor in India today. India has a mixed economy with the coexistence of industrial and manufacturing sectors, agriculture, and informational and service sectors. More importantly, physical labor continues to be the dominant mode of work for the overwhelming majority of the population. Furthermore, the offshore outsourcing of informatics and business processing is just one facet of the mobile and flexible labor entailed by high-tech capitalism in India. For a trenchant critique of the violence inherent in the political economy of contemporary India, see Gupta (2012).

12. In her pioneering book, Arlie Hochschild (2003b) analyzes how training programs teach flight attendants how to manage emotions and channel them to profit for the company. Working with theories of affect and affective labor, Ariel Ducey points to the complex relationship between consciousness, the noncognitive, and the realm of the potential implicit in the training of health care workers; as she puts it, "The level of noncognitive intensity is autonomous from what emerges in consciousness, but it is nonetheless the realm of potential from which any cognitive realizations will be drawn" (2010: 23).

13. In the next section I elaborate on some of the training undergone by our informants in Gurgaon's call centers.

14. I allude, of course, to Dorinne Kondo's (1990) groundbreaking analysis of how Japanese factory workers craft themselves as laboring subjects. My focus here is on distinct processes of embodiment enjoined by working in sectors of the economy driven primarily by affective labor.

15. Morrison (2004) is an example of a media report that expresses outrage at the impersonation practices of call center agents; for a more sympathetic account, see Prathap (2005). Interestingly, both accounts describe the agents as techno-coolies. Later in this chapter, I comment on the connotations of racialized labor enfolded in the term "coolie."

16. It must be noted that media are centrally implicated in all forms of impersonation. Chakravarty (1993: 202–3), for instance, has analyzed how disguise, masquerade, and impersonation are the visual means that constitute spectatorship. Furthermore, impersonation is an important modality for imagining and, more significantly, inhabiting alternative worlds created through media. See chapter 5 for how media, and Bollywood cinema in particular, enables the (in)habitation of spaces of globality.

17. See, for instance, Fernandes's (2006) rigorous examination of "style training" in MBA institutes in contemporary India.

18. For a brilliant study of modes of consumption associated with the informatics industry in Barbados, see Freeman (2000: 23). On the centrality of consumer culture to processes that are both "subject-producing" and "subjectifying," see Grewal (2005: 31).

19. As Chu argues in her analyses of spatial-temporal extension among Fuzhounese peasants, "One did not need to physically leave China to feel emplaced within a larger global and transnational social field" (2010: 39).

20. See Freeman (2000: 22) for similar markers of modernity among pink-collar workers in Barbados.

21. Compare Satyajit Ray's film *Mahanagar* (1962). In an earlier work I analyze some of the anxieties surrounding middle-class women working outside the home (Mankekar 1999a).

22. Some of these anxieties are not unfounded in light of the dangers of physical assault faced by women who work at night. For instance, in the early hours of December 13, 2006, Pratibha Murthy, who was working for HP's GlobalSoft in Bangalore, was murdered by the driver who was transporting her back to her home. In July of the same year, Tanya Bannerjee, employed as an agent in the BPO Aviva-24/7, was murdered by her coworker. Justifiably, tragedies such as these have raised questions about the safety of women employed by BPOs. Unfortunately, however, these tragedies have also been portrayed by the media as scandals, stirring considerable *moral* panics surrounding the specter of middle-class women doing night work.

23. I comment on anxieties surrounding women who travel and, thereby, step out of the control of their families in chapter 2.

24. Compare with Ducey (2010).

25. The place of race and racial identity in contemporary India has been inadequately theorized—in sharp contrast to the rich scholarship on class, caste, communal identity, and gender. For an important discussion of the implications of this silence for our understanding of culture, nation, and identity, see the debate between Ghosh and Chakrabarty (2002, esp. 150–60). As Ghosh argues in this debate, "Racism is comparable to casteism and communalism only in that it has the same murderous effects: its internal logic is quite different" (159). Compare Ashis Nandy (1980) for a pioneering study of the role of colonial discourses of race in the formation of postcolonial identity; see also Bhabha 1994.

In our ongoing research on outsourcing in the IT sector in contemporary India, Akhil Gupta and I seek to foreground the coimplication of race with regimes of labor.

26. Yet labor displacements are not new in the history of the U.S. economy, making it evident that it is the loss of white-collar and middle-class jobs that is deemed so threatening to American national(ist) identity. Ong (2006: 160, see also 157–59) foregrounds the convergence of gender and xenophobia by pointing out that nativist rage against offshore outsourcing was frequently articulated in terms of a blow to American middle-class masculinity, which took the rewards of technical education for granted. Evidently, being an upper-class male American citizen no longer guarantees entitlements to the purported (and illusory) fruits of global capitalism.

27. As Ong points out, "With the offshore outsourcing of high-tech jobs to Asian professionals, it appears that another Asian-American nexus has opened up, not in the factory jobs but in the realm of knowledge-based work, the kind of expertise that has symbolized twentieth-century American identity and character" (2006: 158).

28. The murder of Vincent Chin on June 19, 1982, became a flashpoint for the Asian American movement and civil rights struggle and foregrounded the positionalities of Asian Americans as "perpetual foreigners" at the margins of a white supremacist U.S. nation-state. Chin, a young draftsman living in Detroit, was bludgeoned to death with a baseball bat by two white men. As they attacked him, one of them is alleged to have said, "It's because of you little motherfuckers that we're out of work," thus expressing their belief that they (and countless others) had been laid off from their jobs as auto workers because of the global success of the Japanese automobile industry. Chin's murder underscores how changes in the global economy might affect the place of Asian Americans in tragic ways.

Of course, Chin was Chinese American and not, as his murderers assumed, Japanese or Japanese American. His murder was a horrific case of mistaken identity: as I argue in the coda to this book, these instances of "mistaken identity" do not occur in a historical or discursive vacuum but are embedded in complex discourses about dangerous Oriental/Asiatic Others.

29. In her important work on neoliberalism in China, Rofel points out that new technologies of governance reconstrue "individual citizens as subjects of entrepreneurial choices" (2007: 16).

30. Compare Foucault (2004) on the relationship between biopolitics and governmentality.

31. See also Freeman (2007) for an insightful and succinct analysis of how neoliberal discourses of entrepreneurship and reputation articulate with prevalent conceptions of respectability in Barbados.

32. It is important to clarify that Brown critiques this reading of neoliberalism. She believes that Weber's theory of rationalization does not "bring into view the historical-institutional rupture it signifies, the form of governmentality it replaces and the form it inaugurates, and hence the modalities of resistance it renders outmoded and those that must be developed if it must be effectively challenged" (2005: 45).

33. Compare with Chu (2010: 5). Chu argues that among her Fuzhounese informants, the enchantments of modernity are "integral to the production of modern imaginaries themselves" (6).

34. Appadurai (2004: 69) asserts that aspiration must be nurtured among the poor because poverty can diminish the capacity to aspire. He presents us with a case study of what happens when one group of poor people begins to "mobilize its capacity to aspire in a specific political and cultural regime" as an example of new social movements that can strengthen the capacity to aspire (70).

Coda. Unsettling Nations

1. For an excellent discussion of the complex semiotics surrounding the display of the U.S. flag by minoritized subjects after September 11, 2001, see Grewal (2005: 211–12, 217–19).

2. Butler elaborates: "I do not mean that the story that begins with September 11 should not be told. These stories have to be told, and they are being told, despite the

enormous trauma that undermines narrative capacity in these instances. . . . We need to emerge from the narrative perspective of U.S. unilateralism and, as it were, its defensive structures, to consider the ways in which our lives are profoundly implicated in the lives of others" (2002: 180).

3. With my research assistants Veena Dubal and Amina Chaudhry, I interviewed antiracist and antihate activists, members of Sikh and Muslim community organizations, and men and women who were on the front lines of the attacks, such as taxi drivers and those working in convenience stores and gas stations. We conducted participant observation at workshops aiming to educate Sikh and Muslim communities on their legal rights, worked with mosque communities, attended meetings with law enforcement officials and members of other communities of color, participated in interfaith vigils, and observed a children's camp at a local *gurudwara* (Sikh temple) in which children were encouraged to share their experiences of hate violence and develop strategies for coping with them. For an ethnography of the experiences of my informants and the construction of national publics and counterpublics after September 11, 2001, see Mankekar (n.d.).

4. Such a project must necessarily engage frameworks emerging from critical ethnic studies and critiques of settler colonialism in Native American studies that interrogate and foreground the foundational violence and modes of exclusion on which the U.S. nation is predicated. While I am unable to do justice to this important task in this brief coda, as in the other chapters I draw on insights provided by scholars in Asian American studies to point to a framework that might enable us to unsettle the hegemonic claims of the U.S. nation.

5. Compare Biehl and Locke (2010).

6. See, for instance, Maira (2009), Dudziak (2003), and Žižek (2002) who make this argument from radically different perspectives.

7. I am particularly grateful to Veena Dubal for reminding me of the underreporting of hate violence (e-mail communication, May 17, 2013).

8. See, especially, Leti Volpp (2002) for an important discussion of the racialization of religious difference after September 11, 2001.

9. As Veena Dubal points out, this practice of reporting "suspicious persons and activities" has been institutionalized by "Suspicious Activities Reporting," which essentially encourages neighbors to spy on each other. She adds that this "results in thousands of open investigations on innocent people" (e-mail communication, May 17, 2013).

10. Compare with Pradeep Jeganathan (2001).

11. Over twelve thousand immigrants of South Asian and Middle Eastern descent were arrested and detained on suspicion of terrorism and, to date, no conclusive data have been made available on how many of these detainees have been convicted of terrorism.

12. In March 2002, Ashcroft announced the results of the Interview Project, which, he claimed, had been a resounding success: there were seventeen arrests for visa violations, three arrests for criminal activities unrelated to September 11, and no arrests for crimes related to terrorism (ACLU 2002).

13. Dubal posits that, "in recent years, the term 'home grown' terrorist has made its way into the government's lexicon" (e-mail communication, May 17, 2013).

14. See Grewal (2005: 208) for a similar argument.

15. See Mankekar (n.d.) for an elaboration of this discussion. For a critique of the mistaken identity thesis that resonates with the one presented here, see Puar (2007).

16. As Dubal points out, ironically, in contrast to the murder of his brother, Sukhpal Singh Sodhi's killing was never considered a hate crime because, allegedly, the perpetrator was not heard making racial slurs while killing him. As Dubal argues, "The law did not permit the recognition of what was so obvious: a working-class man with a turban was shot in a public space because of the hate-filled energy suffusing the city" (e-mail communication, May 17, 2013).

17. Thus, it is essential to note that, although these histories are not equivalent, racial profiling has hardly been the preserve of South Asians and, in fact, has long been inflicted on other communities of color in the United States. Any analysis of racial profiling, therefore, must be part of a larger project of comparative racialization.

18. See Maira and Shihade (2006) for an important discussion on the importance of rethinking the boundaries of (South) Asian American studies and Arab American studies.

19. Lowe points out that the U.S. orientalism of the twentieth century "may be rhetorically continuous but is materially discontinuous with an earlier European orientalism. . . . It has been transformed by a quite different state apparatus and a different global and national context of material conditions, purposes, and possibilities" (1996: 178n7; compare Grewal 2005: 209, for a similar argument). See also Maira (2009: 200) and Volpp (2002: 572).

20. Several scholars have commented on the complicated relationship between South Asian American and Asian American political and intellectual formations (see, for instance, Das Gupta 2006; Dayal 1998; Maira 2002, 2009; Prashad 2000; Shankar and Srikanth 1998; Visweswaran 1997; Visweswaran and Mir 1999).

21. Compare Chuh (2003).

22. My political intervention here converges with that of Shih in her formulation of a Sinophone formation that exceeds hegemonic and exclusionary notions of "Chineseness" (2007: 183).

23. Compare Alexander (2005) on nodes of instability in the transnational circulation of discourses.

24. For important insights on the anthropology of the contemporary, see Pandian (2012); Rabinow (2007); and Rabinow, Marcus, Faubion, and Rees (2008).

25. In contrast to Munn (1992: 116), who sketches a notion of temporalization as a symbolic process, I have been interested in its extrasymbolic and extraphenomenological aspects.

26. Compare Cvetkovich (2003) and Stewart (2007).

Print and Online Sources

Abraham, Leena. 2004. "Redrawing the Lakshman Rekha: Gender Differences and Cultural Constructions of Youth Sexuality in Urban India." In *Sexual Sites, Seminal Attitudes: Sexualities, Masculinities, and Culture in South Asia,* edited by Sanjay Srivastava, 209–41. New Delhi: Sage.

Agamben, Giorgio. 1993. *Stanzas: Word and Phantasm in Western Culture.* Minneapolis: University of Minnesota Press.

Agarwal, Purshottam. 1995. "Surat, Savarkar and Draupadi: Legitimising Rape as a Political Weapon." In *Women and the Hindu Right,* edited by Tanika Sarkar and Urvashi Butalia, 29–57. New Delhi: Kali for Women.

Ahmad, Muneer. 2002. "Homeland Insecurities: Racial Violence the Day after September 11." *Social Text* 20 (3): 101–15.

Ahmed, Sara. 2004. *The Cultural Politics of Emotion.* New York: Routledge.

Ahmed, Sara, Claudia Castaneda, Anne-Marie Fortier, and Mimi Sheller. 2003. "Introduction: Uprootings/Regroundings: Questions of Home and Migration." In *Uprootings/Regroundings: Questions of Home and Migration,* edited by Sara Ahmed et al., 1–15. Oxford: Berg.

Alexander, M. Jacqui. 1991. "Redrafting Morality: The Postcolonial State and the Sexual Offences Bill of Trinidad and Tobago." In *Third World Women and the Politics of Feminism,* edited by Chandra Mohanty, Ann Russo Talpade, and Lourdes Torres. Bloomington: Indiana University Press.

Alexander, M. Jacqui. 2005. *Pedagogies of Crossing: Meditations on Feminism, Sexual Politics, Memory, and the Sacred.* Durham, NC: Duke University Press.

Allison, Anne. 1991. "Japanese Mothers and Obentos: The Lunch-Box as Ideological State Apparatus." *Anthropological Quarterly* 64 (4): 195–208.

Allison, Anne. 2012a. "American Geishas and Oriental/ist Fantasies." In *Media, Erotics, and Transnational Asia,* edited by Purnima Mankekar and Louisa Schein, 297–321. Durham, NC: Duke University Press.

Allison, Anne. 2012b. "Ordinary Refugees: Social Precarity and Soul in Twenty-First Century Japan." *Anthropological Quarterly* 85 (2): 345–70.

Althusser, Louis. 2001. *Lenin and Philosophy and Other Essays.* London: Monthly Review Press.

Ameeriar, Lalaie. 2012. "The Sanitized Sensorium." *American Anthropologist* 114 (3): 509–20.

American Civil Liberties Union. 2002. "Caught in the Backlash: Stories from Northern California." https://www.aclunc.org/sites/default/files/asset_upload_file532 _4380_0.pdf.

Anderson, Benedict. 1991. *Imagined Communities: Reflections on the Origin and Spread of Nationalism*. London: Verso.

Aneesh, A. 2006. *Virtual Migration: The Programming of Globalization*. Durham, NC: Duke University Press.

Anzaldua, Gloria, and AnaLouise Keating. 2002. *This Bridge We Call Home*. New York: Routledge.

Appadurai, Arjun. 1986. "Introduction: Commodities and the Politics of Value." In *The Social Life of Things: Commodities in Cultural Perspective*, edited by Arjun Appadurai, 3–63. Cambridge: Cambridge University Press.

Appadurai, Arjun. 1988. "How to Make a National Cuisine: Cookbooks in Contemporary India." *Comparative Studies in Society and History* 30 (1): 3–24.

Appadurai, Arjun. 1996. *Modernity at Large: Cultural Dimensions of Globalization*. Minneapolis: University of Minnesota Press.

Appadurai, Arjun. 2004. "The Capacity to Aspire: Culture and the Terms of Recognition." In *Culture and Public Action*, edited by Vijayendra Rao and Michael Walton. Stanford, CA: Stanford University Press.

Appadurai, Arjun. 2006. *Fear of Small Numbers: An Essay on the Geography of Anger*. Durham: Duke University Press.

Arijit, Sen. 2012. "From Curry Mahals to Chaat Café's: Spatialities of the South Asian Culinary Landscape." In *Curried Cultures: Globalization, Food, and South Asia*, edited by Krishnendu Ray and Tulasi Srinivas, 196. London, England: University of California Press.

Arondekar, Anjali. 2007. "The Voyage Out: Transacting Sex under Globalization." *Feminist Studies* 33 (2): 337–49.

Arondekar, Anjali. 2009. *For the Record: On Sexuality and the Colonial Archive in India*. Durham, NC: Duke University Press.

Axel, Brian Keith. 2002. "The Diasporic Imaginary." *Public Culture* 14 (2): 411–28.

Axel, Brian Keith. 2004. "The Context of Diaspora." *Cultural Anthropology* 19 (1): 26–60.

Axel, Brian Keith. 2005. "Diasporic Sublime: Sikh Martyrs, Internet Mediations, and the Question of the Unimaginable." *Sikh Formations* 1 (1): 127–54.

Bachetta, Paola. 1999. "When the (Hindu) Nation Exiles Its Queers." *Social Text* 17 (4): 141–66.

Bahri, Deepika, and Mary Vasudeva. 1996. *Between the Lines: South Asians and Postcoloniality*. Philadelphia: Temple University Press.

Balachandran, Chandra S. 2004. "A Preliminary Report on Emerging Gay Geographies in Bangalore, India." In *Sexual Sites, Seminal Attitudes: Sexualities, Masculinities, and Culture in South Asia*, edited by Sanjay Srivastava, 165–87. New Delhi: Sage.

Bandyopadhyay, Sibaji. 2007. "The Pre-text: The Fire Controversy." In *The Phobic and the Erotic: The Politics of Sexualities in Contemporary India*, edited by Brinda Bose and Subhabrata Bhattacharya, 17–90. Calcutta: Seagull Books.

Banerjee, Sikata. 1995. "Hindu Nationalism and the Construction of Woman: The Shiv Sena Organises Women in Bombay." *Women and Right Wing Movements: Indian Experiences*, edited by Tanika Sarkar and Urvashi Butalia, 216–32. London: Zed.

Bannerjee, Sumanta. 1989. "Marginalisation of Women's Popular Culture." In *Recasting Women: Essays in Colonial History*, edited by Kumkum Sangari and Sudesh Vaid. New Delhi: Kali.

Bartwal, Hemendra Singh. 2002. "V-Day Troubles." *Hindustan Times Online*, February 12. http://www.hindustantimes.com/.

Basu, Amrita. 1995. "Feminism Inverted: The Gendered Imagery and Real Women of Hindu Nationalism." In *Women and Right Wing Movements: Indian Experiences*, edited by Tanika Sarkar and Urvashi Butalia, 158–80. London: Zed.

Baudrillard, Jean. 1994. *Simulacra and Simulation*. Ann Arbor: University of Michigan Press.

Beary, Habib. 2000. "Bangalore's Valentine Boom." BBC *News Online*, February 4. http://news.bbc.co.uk/2/hi/south_asia/630951.stm.

Behdad, Ali. 1994. *Belated Travelers: Orientalism in the Age of Colonial Dissolution*. Durham, NC: Duke University Press.

Benjamin, Walter. 1973. *Illuminations*. London: Fontana/Collins.

Bennett, Jane. 2010. *Vibrant Matter: A Political Ecology of Things*. Durham, NC: Duke University Press.

Berdahl, Daphne. 1999. "'(N)Ostalgie' for the Present: Memory, Longing, and East German Things." *Ethnos* 64 (2): 192–211.

Bergson, Henri. 1910. *Time and Free Will*. London: Allen and Unwin.

Bergson, Henri. (1911) 1988. *Matter and Memory*. Translated by Nancy Margaret Paul and W. Scott Palmer. New York: Zone.

Berlant, Lauren. 2000. *Intimacy*. Chicago: University of Chicago Press.

Berlant, Lauren. 2008. *The Female Complaint: The Unfinished Business of Sentimentality in American Culture*. Durham, NC: Duke University Press.

Bhabha, Homi. 1994. "Of Mimicry and Men: The Ambivalence of Colonial Discourse." In *The Location of Culture*. London: Routledge.

Bhachu, Parminder. 1986. *Twice Migrants: East African Sikh Settlers in Britain*. London: Tavistock.

Bhattacharya, Narendra Nath. 1975. *History of Erotic Indian Literature*. Delhi: Munshiram Manohar.

Bhonsle, Sudesh, and Kavita Krishnamurthy. 1991. "Jumma Jumma De De" (Give me, give me a kiss). Lyrics by Anand Bakshi. In *Hum (Us)*. Dir. Makul S. Anand. Music dir. Laxmikant-Pyarelal. Dharma Productions.

Biehl, Joao and Peter Locke. 2010. "Deleuze and the Anthropology of Becoming." *Current Anthropology* 51 (3): 317–51.

Bijapukar, Rama. 2007. *Winning the Indian Market: Understanding the Transformation of Consumer India*. New York: Wiley.

Biswas, Ranjita. 2007. "The Lesbian Standpoint." In *The Phobic and the Erotic: The Politics of Sexualities in Contemporary India,* edited by Brinda Bose and Subhabrata Bhattacharya, 263–90. Calcutta: Seagull Books.

Boellstorff, Tom. 2005. *The Gay Archipelago: Sexuality and Nation in Indonesia.* Princeton, NJ: Princeton University Press.

Boellstorff, Tom. 2012. "The Politics of Similitude: Global Sexuality Activism, Ethnography, and the Western Subject." *Transcriptions* 2: 22–39.

Bohannan, Paul. 1955. "Some Principles of Exchange and Investment among the Tiv." *American Anthropologist* 57: 60–70.

Bonus, Enrique. 1994. "Marking and Marketing 'Difference': Filipino Oriental Stores in Southern California." *Positions* 5 (2): 643–69.

Boo, Katherine. 2012. *Behind the Beautiful Forevers: Life, Death, and Hope in a Mumbai Undercity.* New York: Random House.

Bose, Brinda, and Subhabrata Bhattacharya, eds. 2007. *The Phobic and the Erotic: The Politics of Sexualities in Contemporary India.* Calcutta: Seagull Books.

Bose, Sugata. 2009. *A Hundred Horizons: The Indian Ocean in the Age of Global Empire.* Cambridge, MA: Harvard University Press.

Bourdieu, Pierre. 1984. *Distinction: A Social Critique of the Judgement of Taste.* Abingdon: Routledge.

Breckenridge, Carol Appadurai. 1995. *Consuming Modernity: Public Culture in a South Asian World.* Minneapolis: University of Minnesota Press.

Brennan, Teresa. 2004. *The Transmission of Affect.* Ithaca, NY: Cornell University Press.

Brown, Wendy. 2003. "Neo-liberalism and the End of Liberal Democracy." In *Theory and Event* 7 (1).

Brown, Wendy. 2005. *Edgework: Critical Essays on Knowledge and Politics.* Princeton, NJ: Princeton University Press.

Burke, Peter. 1996. *Popular Culture in Early Modern Europe.* Aldershot, England: Scolar Press.

Bush, George W. 2001. "You Are Either With Us, Or With the Terrorists." *VOA,* September 21. http://www.voanews.com/content/a-13-a-2001-09-21-14-bush-66411197/549664.html.

Butler, Judith. 1993. *Bodies That Matter: On the Discursive Limits of Sex.* New York: Routledge.

Butler, Judith. 1999. *Gender Trouble: Feminism and the Subversion of Identity.* London: Routledge.

Butler, Judith. 2002. "Explanation and Exoneration, or What We Can Hear." *Social Text* 20(3): 177–88.

Caldwell, John. 2013. "Para-Industry: Researching Hollywood's Backwaters." *Cinema Journal* 52 (3): 157–65.

Calhoun, Craig. 2004. "A World of Emergencies: Fear, Intervention, and the Limits of Cosmopolitan Order." *CRSA/RCSA* 41 (4): 373–95.

Chakravarty, Sumita S. 1993. *National Identity in Indian Popular Cinema, 1947–1987.* Austin: University of Texas Press.

"The Challenge of Modernism." 1989. *India Today*, January 15.

Chander, Anupam. 2001. "Diaspora Bonds." *New York University Law Review* 76: 1060–94.

Chandra, Anupama. 1995. "Opening New Channels of Conversation." *India Today*, March 15.

Chatterjee, Partha. 1993. *The Nation and Its Fragments: Colonial and Postcolonial Histories*. Princeton, NJ: Princeton University Press.

Chaudhuri, K. N. 1985. *Trade and Civilisation in the Indian Ocean: An Economic History from the Rise of Islam to 1750*. Cambridge: Cambridge University Press.

Chopra, Anupama. 2002. *Dilwale Dulhania Le Jayenge (The Bravehearted Will Take the Bride)*. London: British Film Institute.

Chu, Julie. 2010. *Cosmologies of Credit: Transnational Mobility and the Politics of Destination in China*. Durham, NC: Duke University Press.

Chua, Jocelyn Lim. 2011. "Making Time For The Children: Self-Temporalization and Cultivation of the Antisuicidal Subject in South India." *Cultural Anthropology*, 26 (1): 112–37.

Chua, Jocelyn Lim. 2014. *In Pursuit of the Good Life: Aspiration and Suicide in Globalizing South India*. Berkeley: University of California Press.

Chuh, Kandice. 2003. *Imagine Otherwise: On Asian Americanist Critique*. Durham, NC: Duke University Press.

Chuh, Kandice, and Karen Shimakawa. 2001. *Orientations: Mapping Studies in the Asian Diaspora*. Durham, NC: Duke University Press.

Clifford, James. 1997. *Routes: Travel and Translation in the Late Twentieth Century*. Cambridge, MA: Harvard University Press.

Clough, Patricia Ticineto. 2007. "Introduction." In *The Affective Turn: Theorizing the Social*, edited by Patricia Ticineto Clough with Jean Halley, 11–33. Durham, NC: Duke University Press.

Cohen, Lawrence. 1995. "The Pleasures of Castration: The Postoperative Status of Hijras, Jankhas, and Academics." In *Sexual Nature, Sexual Culture*, edited by Paul R. Abramson and Steven D. Pinkerton. Chicago: University of Chicago Press.

Combahee River Collective. 1984. "A Black Feminist Statement." In *This Bridge Called My Back*, edited by Cherrie Moraga and Gloria Anzaldua, 210–18. New York: Kitchen Table/Women of Color Press.

Cvetkovich, Ann. 2003. *An Archive of Feelings: Trauma, Sexuality, and Lesbian Public Cultures*. Durham, NC: Duke University Press.

Daniel, Valentine E. 1996. *Charred Lullabies: Chapters in an Anthropography of Violence*. Princeton, NJ: Princeton University Press.

Das, Veena. 1990. *Mirrors of Violence: Communities, Riots, and Survivors in South Asia*. Delhi: Oxford University Press.

Das, Veena. 1996. *Critical Events: An Anthropological Perspective on Contemporary India*. New York: Oxford University Press.

Das, Veena. 2000. "Violence and the Work of Time." In *Signifying Identities: Anthropological Perspectives on Boundaries and Contested Values*, edited by Anthony P. Cohen, 59–74. London: Routledge.

Das, Veena. 2006. *Life and Words: Violence and the Descent into the Ordinary*. Berkeley: University of California Press.

Das Gupta, Monisha. 2004. "A View of Post-9/11 Justice from Below." *Peace Review* 16 (2): 141–48.

Das Gupta, Monisha. 2005. "Of Hardship and Hostility: The Impact of 9/11 on New York City Taxi Drivers." In *Wounded City: The Social Impact of 9/11*, edited by Nancy Foner. New York: Russell Sage.

Das Gupta, Monisha. 2006. *Unruly Immigrants: Rights, Activism, and Transnational South Asian Politics in the United States*. Durham: Duke University Press.

Dasgupta, Sayantani, and Shamita Das Dasgupta. 2002. "Sex, Lies, and Women's Lives: An International Dialogue." In *A Patchwork Shawl: Chronicles of South Asian Women in America*, edited by Shamita Das Dasgupta, 111–28. New Brunswick, NJ: Rutgers University Press.

Dayal, Samir. 1998. "Min(d)ing the Gap: South Asian Americans and Diaspora." In *A Part, Yet Apart: South Asians in Asian America*, 235–65. Philadelphia: Temple University Press.

Deleuze, Gilles. 1986. *Cinema 1: The Movement Image*. Minneapolis: University of Minnesota Press.

Deleuze, Gilles. 1989. *Cinema 2: The Time Image*. London: Athlone.

Deleuze, Gilles. 1997. *Essays Critical and Clinical*. Minneapolis: University of Minnesota Press.

Derrida, Jacques. 1996. *Archive Fever: A Freudian Impression*. Translated by Eric Prenowitz. Chicago: University of Chicago Press.

Dhaliwal, Amarpal K. 1995. "Gender at Work: The Renegotiation of Middle-Class Womanhood in a South Asian-Owned Business." In *Reviewing Asian America: Locating Diversity*, edited by Wendy L. Ng, Soo-Young Chin, James S. Moy, and Gary Y. Okihiro, 57–85. Pullman: Washington State University Press.

Dimock, Edward C., Jr., Edwin Gerow, C. M. Naim, A. K. Ramunjan, Gordon Roadarmel, and J. A. B. Van Buitenen. 1974. *The Literatures of India: An Introduction*. Chicago: University of Chicago Press.

Doniger, Wendy. 1996. "Sexual Masquerade in Hindu Myths: Aspects of the Transmission of Knowledge in Ancient India." In *The Transmission of Knowledge in South Asia: Religion, History, Politics*, edited by Nigel Crook. Delhi: Oxford University Press.

Douglas, Mary, and Baron Isherwood. 1978. *The World of Goods*. London: Allen Lane.

Ducey, Ariel. 2010. "Technologies of Caring Labor: From Objects to Affect." In *Intimate Labors: Cultures, Technologies, and the Politics of Care*, edited by Eileen Boris and Rhacel Salazar Parrenas, 18–32. Stanford, CA: Stanford University Press.

Dudziak, Mary L., ed. 2003. *September 11 in History: A Watershed Moment?* Durham, NC: Duke University Press.

Dwyer, Rachel. 2000. *All You Want Is Money, All You Need Is Love: Sex and Romance in Modern India*. London: Cassell.

Dyer-Witheford, Nick. 2001. "Empire, Immaterial Labor, the New Combinations, and the Global Worker." *Rethinking Marxism* 13 (3): 70.

"Economic Liberalisation: Cut Short by Politics." 1996. *India Today*, March 15, 66.

Espiritu, Yen Le. 2003. *Home Bound: Filipino American Lives across Cultures, Communities, and Countries*. Berkeley: University of California Press.

Evans-Pritchard, E. E. 1969. *The Nuer: A Description of the Modes of Life and Political Institutions of a Nilotic People*. Oxford: Oxford University Press.

"Exchange Reserves: Neglected Factor." 1992. *Economic and Political Weekly* 27 (1–2): 4.

"Express News Service." 2002. *India Express Online*, February 14. http://www.indian-express.com/.

Fabian, Johannes. 1983. *Time and the Other: How Anthropology Makes Its Object*. New York: Columbia University Press.

Fanon, Frantz. 1967. *Black Skin, White Masks*. New York: Grove Press.

Favero, Paolo. 2003. "Phantasms in a Starry Place: Space and Identification in a Central New Delhi Market." *Cultural Anthropology* 18 (4): 551–84.

Favero, Paolo. 2005. *India Dreams: Cultural Identity among Young Middle Class Men in New Delhi*. Stockholm: Dept. of Social Anthropology, Stockholm University.

Ferguson, James, and Akhil Gupta. 2002. "Spatializing States: Toward an Ethnography of Neoliberal Geography." *American Ethnologist* 29 (4): 981–1002.

Fernandes, Leela. 2000. "Restructuring the New Middle Class in Liberalizing India." *Comparative Studies of South Asia, Africa, and the Middle East* 20 (1–2): 88–104.

Fernandes, Leela. 2006. *India's New Middle Class: Democratic Politics in an Era of Economic Reform*. Minneapolis: University of Minnesota Press.

"Foreign Banks: A Profitable Presence." 1988. *India Today*, December 31, 54–56.

"Foreign Investment: Discovering India." 1988. *India Today*, December 31, 75.

Foucault, Michel. 1980. *The History of Sexuality, Volume 1: An Introduction*. New York: Vintage.

Foucault, Michel. 1988. *The History of Sexuality, Volume 3: The Care of the Self*. New York: Vintage.

Foucault, Michel. 2004. *The Birth of Biopolitics: Lectures at the College de France, 1978–1979*. New York: Palgrave Macmillan.

Frankenberg, Ruth and Lata Mani. 1993. "Crosscurrents, Crosstalk: Race, "Postcoloniality," and the Politics of Location." *Cultural Studies* 7 (2): 292–310.

Freeman, Carla. 2000. *High Tech and High Heels in the Global Economy*. Durham, NC: Duke University Press.

Freeman, Carla. 2007. "Middle-Class Conundrums—the 'Reputation' of Neoliberalism." *American Ethnologist* 34 (2): 252.

Gandhi, Leela. 2007. "A Case of Radical Kinship: Edward Carpenter and the Politics of Anti–colonial Sexual Dissidence." In *The Phobic and the Erotic: The Politics of Sexualities in Contemporary India*, edited by Brinda Bose and Subhabrata Bhattacharya, 91–116. Calcutta: Seagull Books.

Garber, Marjorie B. 1997. *Vested Interests: Cross Dressing and Cultural Anxiety*. New York: Routledge.

Geertz, Clifford. 1966. *Person, Time, and Conduct in Bali: An Essay in Cultural Analysis*. New Haven, CT: Yale University Press.

Geetha, V. 1998. "On Bodily Love and Hurt." In *A Question of Silence? The Sexual Economies of Modern India*, edited by Mary E. John and Janaki Nair. New Delhi: Kali.

George, Kenneth M. (editor) "Objects on the Loose: Ethnographic Encounters with Unruly Artifacts." 1999. Special issue, *Ethnos* 64 (2).

George, Rosemary Marangoly. 1997. "'From Expatriate Aristocrat to Immigrant Nobody': South Asian Racial Strategies in the Southern California Context." *Diaspora* 6 (1): 31–60.

Ghosh, Amitav. 1992. *In an Antique Land*. London: Granta.

Ghosh, Amitav, and Dipesh Chakrabarty. 2002. "A Correspondence on Provincializing Europe." *Radical History Review* 83: 146–72.

Ghosh, Shohini. 2007. "False Appearances and Mistaken Identities: The Phobic and the Erotic in Bombay Cinema's Queer Vision." In *The Phobic and the Erotic: The Politics of Sexualities in Contemporary India,* edited by Brinda Bose and Subhabrata Bhattacharya, 417–36. Calcutta: Seagull Books.

Giddens, Anthony. 1990. *The Consequences of Modernity*. Stanford, CA: Stanford University Press.

Giddens, Anthony. 1992. *The Transformation of Intimacy: Sexuality, Love, and Eroticism in Modern Societies*. Stanford, CA: Stanford University Press.

Gillespie, Marie. 1995. *Television, Ethnicity, and Cultural Change*. London: Routledge.

Gingrich, Andre, Elinor Ochs, and Alan Swedlund. 2002. "Repertoires of Timekeeping in Anthropology." *Current Anthropology* 43: S3–S4.

Goffman, Erving. 1959. *The Presentation of Self in Everyday Life*. New York: Anchor.

Goldberg, David Theo. 1995. "Afterword: Hate, or Power?" In *Hate Speech*, edited by Rita Kirk Whillock and David Slayden. Thousand Oaks, CA: Sage.

Gopal, Sangita. 2011. *Conjugations: Marriage and Form in New Bollywood Cinema*. London: The University of Chicago Press.

Gopalan, Lalitha. 2008. *Cinema of Interruptions: Action Genres in Contemporary Indian Cinema*. London: British Film Institute.

Gopinath, Gayatri. 2005. *Impossible Desires: Queer Diasporas and South Asian Public Cultures*. Durham, NC: Duke University Press.

Gray, Ann. 1992. *Video Playtime: The Gendering of a Leisure Technology*. London: Routledge.

Gregg, Melissa, and Gregory J. Seigworth, eds. 2010. *The Affect Theory Reader*. Durham, NC: Duke University Press.

Gregory, Christopher. 1982. *Gifts and Commodities*. London: Academic Press.

Grewal, Inderpal. 1996. *Home and Harem: Nation, Gender, Empire, and the Cultures of Travel*. Durham, NC: Duke University Press.

Grewal, Inderpal. 2005. *Transnational America: Feminisms, Diasporas, Neoliberalisms*. Durham, NC: Duke University Press.

Grewal, Inderpal, and Caren Kaplan. 1994. *Scattered Hegemonies: Postmodernity and Transnational Feminist Practices*. Minneapolis: University of Minnesota Press.

Grossberg, Lawrence. 2010. *Cultural Studies in the Future Tense*. Durham, NC: Duke University Press.

Guha, Ranajit. 1999. *Elementary Aspects of Peasant Insurgency in Colonial India*. Durham, NC: Duke University Press.

Gupta, Akhil. 1992. "The Reincarnation of Souls and the Rebirth of Commodities: Representations of Time in 'East' and 'West.'" *Cultural Critique* 22: 187–211.

Gupta, Akhil. 1995. "Blurred Boundaries: The Discourse of Corruption, the Culture of Politics, and the Imagined State." *American Ethnologist* 22: 375–402. doi: 10.1525 /ae.1995.22.2.02a00090.

Gupta, Akhil. 1998. *Postcolonial Developments: Agriculture in the Making of Modern India*. Durham, NC: Duke University Press.

Gupta, Akhil. 2012. *Red Tape: Bureaucracy, Structural Violence, and Poverty in India*. Durham: Duke University Press.

Gupta, Akhil, and James Ferguson. 1997a. *Anthropological Locations: Boundaries and Grounds of a Field Science*. Berkeley: University of California Press.

Gupta, Akhil, and James Ferguson. 1997b. *Culture, Power, Place: Explorations in Critical Anthropology*. Durham, NC: Duke University Press.

Gupta, Akhil, and Aradhana Sharma. 2006. "Globalization and Postcolonial States." *Current Anthropology* 47 (2): 277–307.

Gupta, Akhil, and K. Sivaramakrishnan. 2012. *The State in India after Liberalization: Interdisciplinary Perspectives*. London: Routledge.

Gupta, Charu. 2012. *Gendering Colonial India: Reforms, Print, Caste and Communalism*. New Delhi: Orient Blackswan.

Hall, Stuart. 1981. "Notes on Deconstructing 'The Popular.'" In *People's History and Socialist Theory*, edited by R. Samuel, 227–40. London: Routledge and Kegan Paul.

Hall, Stuart. 1986. "Gramsci's Relevance for the Study of Race and Ethnicity." *Journal of Communication Inquiry* 10 (2): 5–27.

Hall, Stuart. 1990. "Cultural Identity and Diaspora." In *Identity: Community, Culture, Difference*, edited by Jonathan Rutherford. London: Lawrence and Wishart.

Hannerz, Ulf. 1996. *Transnational Connections: Culture, People, Places*. London: Routledge.

Hardt, Michael. 1999. "Affective Labor." *Boundary 2* 26 (2): 89–100.

Hardt, Michael. 2007. "Foreword: What Affects Are Good For." In *The Affective Turn: Theorizing the Social*, edited by Patricia Ticineto Clough with Jean Halley, ix–xiii. Durham, NC: Duke University Press.

Hardt, Michael, and Antonio Negri. 2000. *Empire*. Cambridge, MA: Harvard University Press.

Harvey, David. 2005. *A Brief History of Neoliberalism*. Oxford: Oxford University Press.

Hashimi, Mobina. 2006. "Outsourcing the American Dream? Representing the Stakes of IT Globalisation." *Economic and Political Weekly* 41 (3): 242–49.

Haug, Wolfgang Fritz. 1986. *Critique of Commodity Aesthetics: Appearance, Sexuality, and Advertising in Capitalist Society*. Translated by Robert Bock. New York: Polity.

Helmreich, Stefan. 1992. "Kinship, Nation, and Paul Gilroy's Concept of Diaspora." *Diaspora* 2 (2): 243–49.

Hing, Bill Ong. 1993. *Making and Remaking Asian America through Immigration Policy, 1850–1990*. Stanford, CA: Stanford University Press.

Hochschild, Arlie Russell. 2003a. *The Commercialization of Intimate Life: Notes from Home and Work*. Berkeley: University of California Press.

Hochschild, Arlie Russell. 2003b. *The Managed Heart: Commercialization of Human Feeling*, 20th anniversary ed. Berkeley: University of California Press.

Honig, Bonnie. 1998. *Immigrant America? How Foreignness "Solves" Democracy's Problems*. Chicago: American Bar Foundation.

Huat, Chua Beng. 2003. *Life Is Not Complete without Shopping: Consumption Culture in Singapore*. Singapore: National University of Singapore Press.

Hune, Shirley. 1991. *Asian Americans: Comparative and Global Perspectives*. Pullman: Washington State University Press.

Huntington, Samuel. 1996. *The Clash of Civilizations and the Remaking of World Order*. New York: Simon and Schuster.

Irigaray, Luce. 1985. *This Sex Which Is Not One*. Ithaca, NY: Cornell University Press.

Ivy, Marilyn. 1995. *Discourses of the Vanishing: Modernity, Phantasm, Japan*. Chicago: University of Chicago Press.

Jain, Madhu and Nandita Chowdhury. 1997. "Coming Home." *India Today*, August 4: 88–90.

Jeffrey, Craig. 2011. *Timepass: Youth, Class, and the Politics of Waiting in India*. Stanford, CA: Stanford University Press.

Jeffrey, Craig, Patricia Jeffery, and Roger Jeffery. 2010. *Education, Unemployment, and Masculinities in India*. New Delhi: Social Science.

Jeganathan, Pradeep. "A Space for Violence: Anthropology, Politics, and the Location of a Sinhala Practice of Masculinity." In *Subaltern Studies XI: Community, Gender, and Violence*, edited by Partha Chatterjee and Pradeep Jeganathan, 37–65. New York: Columbia University Press.

John, Mary E. 1998. "Globalisation, Sexuality, and the Visual Field: Issues and Nonissues for Cultural Critique." In *A Question of Silence? The Sexual Economies of Modern India*, edited by Mary E. John and Janaki Nair. New Delhi: Kali.

Joseph, Sherry. 1996. "Gay and Lesbian Movement in India." *Economic and Political Weekly* 31 (33): 2228–33.

Kabhi Khushi Kabhie Gham . . . 2001. Web database entry. Internet Movie Database. http://www.imdb.com/title/tt0248126/.

Kakar, Sudhir. 1989. *Intimate Relations: Exploring Indian Sexuality*. New Delhi: Penguin.

Kaplan, Caren. 1996. *Questions of Travel: Postmodern Discourses of Displacement*. Durham, NC: Duke University Press.

Kaplan, Caren. 2003. "Transporting the Subject: Technologies of Mobility and Location in an Era of Globalization." In *Uprootings/Regroundings: Questions of Home and Migration*, edited by Sara Ahmed, Claudia Castaneda, Anne-Marie Fortier, and Mimi Sheller, 207–224. London: Berg.

Kapur, Anuradha. 1990. *Actors, Pilgrims, Kings and Gods: The Ramlila at Ramnagar*. Calcutta: Seagull Books.

Kapur, Ratna, and Brenda Cossman. 1995. "Communalizing Gender and Engendering Community: Women, Legal Discourse and the Saffron Agenda." In *Women and the Hindu Right*, edited by Tanika Sarkar and Urvashi Butalia. New Delhi: Kali for Women.

Kaur, Ravinder and Ajay Sinha. 2005. *Bollyworld: Popular Indian Cinema through a Transnational Lens*, New Delhi: Sage.

Kavoori, Anandam P. and Aswin Punathambekar. 2008. *Global Bollywood*. New York: New York University Press.

Khandelwal, Madhulika S. 1995. "Indian Immigrants in Queens, New York City: Patterns of Spatial Concentration and Distribution, 1965–1990." In *Nation and Migration: The Politics of Space in South Asian Diaspora*, edited by Peter van der Veer. Philadelphia: University of Pennsylvania Press.

Kim, Elaine. 1992. *Asian American Literature: An Introduction to the Writings and Their Social Contexts*. Philadelphia: Temple University Press.

Kim, Elaine H., and Lisa Lowe. 1997. *New Formations, New Questions: Asian American Studies*. Durham, NC: Duke University Press.

Kondo, Dorinne K. 1990. *Crafting Selves: Power, Gender, and Discourses of Identity in a Japanese Workplace*. Chicago: University of Chicago Press.

Kondo, Dorinne K. 1997. *About Face: Performing Race in Fashion and Theater*. New York: Routledge.

"K3G Opens to Record Breaking Collections." 2001. *ApunKa Choice*, December 15. http://www.apunkachoice.com/scoop/bollywood/20011215–1.html.

Lakdawala, D. T. 1991. "New Policy Measures." *Economic and Political Weekly* 26 (34).

Lal, Vinay. 1999. "The Politics of History on the Internet: Cyber-diasporic Hinduism and the North American Hindu Diaspora." *Diaspora* 8 (2): 137–72.

Larkin, Brian. 2008. *Signal and Noise: Media, Infrastructure, and Urban Culture in Nigeria*. Duham: Duke University Press.

Lazzarato, M. 1996. "Immaterial Labour." In *Radical Thought in Italy: A Potential Politics*, edited by M. Hardt and P. Virno, 133–47. Minneapolis: University of Minnesota Press.

Lee, Rachel C., and Sau-ling Cynthia Wong. 2003. *Asian America.Net: Ethnicity, Nationalism, and Cyberspace*. New York: Routledge.

Lele, Jayant, ed. 1981. *Tradition and Modernity in Bhakti Movements*. Leiden: E. J. Brill.

Leonard, Karen Isaksen. 1992. *Making Ethnic Choices: California's Punjabi Mexican Americans*. Philadelphia: Temple University Press.

Leonard, Karen Isaksen. 1993. "Historical Constructions of Ethnicity: Research on Punjabi Immigrants in California." *Journal of American Ethnic History* 12 (4): 3.

Lowe, Lisa. 1996. *Immigrant Acts: On Asian American Cultural Studies*. Durham, NC: Duke University Press.

Lutz, Catherine, and Lila Abu-Lughod. 1990. *Language and the Politics of Emotion*. Cambridge: Cambridge University Press.

M., B. 1991. "Towards Neo-colonial Dependency." *Economic and Political Weekly* 26 (31–32): 1837–39.

Maira, Sunaina. 2002. *Desis in the House: Indian American Youth Culture in New York City*. Philadelphia: Temple University Press.

Maira, Sunaina. 2009. *Missing: Youth, Citizenship, and Empire after 9/11*. Durham, NC: Duke University Press.

Maira, Sunaina, and Magid Shihade. 2006. "Meeting Asian/Arab American Studies: Thinking Race, Empire and Zionism in the U.S." *Journal of Asian American Studies* 9 (2): 117–40.

Malkki, Liisa. 1997. "National Geographic: The Rooting of Peoples and the Territorialization of Identity among Scholars and Refugees." In *Culture, Power, Place: Explorations in Critical Anthropology.* Edited by Akhil Gupta and James Ferguson, 52–74. Durham, NC: Duke University Press.

Manalansan IV, Martin F. 2003. *Global Divas: Filipino Gay Men in the Diaspora.* Durham, NC: Duke University Press.

Manalansan IV, Martin F. 2005. "Race, Violence, and Neoliberal Spatial Politics in the Global City." *Social Text* 23 (3–4): 84–85.

Manalansan IV, Martin F. 2006. "Immigrant Domesticity and the Politics of Olfaction in the Global City." In *The Smell Reader*, edited by Jim Drobnick, 41–52. New York: Berg.

Manalansan IV, Martin F. 2007. "Cooking up the Senses: A Critical Embodied Approach to the Study of Food and Asian American Television Audiences." In *Alien Encounters: Asian Americans in Popular Culture*, edited by Thuy Linh Nguyen Tu and Mimi Nguyen, 179–93. Durham, NC: Duke University Press.

Manalansan IV, Martin F. 2012. "Wayward Erotics: Mediating Queer Diasporic Return." In *Media, Erotics, and Transnational Asia*, edited by Purnima Mankekar and Louisa Schein, 33–52. Durham, NC: Duke University Press.

Manderson, Lenore, and Margaret T. Jolly. 1997. "Sites of Desire/Economies of Pleasure in Asia and the Pacific." In *Sites of Desire/Economies of Pleasure: Sexualities in Asia and the Pacific.* Chicago: University of Chicago Press.

Mani, Lata. 1989. "Contentious Traditions: The Debate on Sati in Colonial India." In *Recasting Women: Essays in Colonial History*, edited by Kumkum Sangari and Sudesh Vaid. New Delhi: Kali.

Mankekar, Purnima. 1993. "Television Tales and a Woman's Rage: A Nationalist Recasting of Draupadi's 'Disrobing.'" *Public Culture* 5 (3): 469–92.

Mankekar, Purnima. 1999a. *Screening Culture, Viewing Politics: An Ethnography of Television, Womanhood, and Nation in Postcolonial India.* Durham, NC: Duke University Press.

Mankekar, Purnima. 1999b. "Brides Who Travel: Gender, Transnationalism, and Nationalism in Hindi Film." *Positions* 7 (3): 731–62.

Mankekar, Purnima. 2004. "Dangerous Desires: Television and Erotics in Late-Twentieth Century India." *Journal of Asian Studies* 63 (2): 403–31.

Mankekar, Purnima. 2007. "Media and Mobility in a Transnational World." In *The Media and Social Theory*, edited by David Hesmondhalgh and Jason Toynbee, 145–58. London: Routledge.

Mankekar, Purnima. 2011. "Becoming Entrepreneurial Subjects: Neoliberalism and Media." in *The State in India after Liberalization: Interdisciplinary Perspectives*, edited by Akhil Gupta and K. Sivaramakrishnan, 213–22. New York: Routledge.

Mankekar, Purnima, and Louisa Schein, eds. 2012. *Media, Erotics, and Transnational Asia.* Durham, NC: Duke University Press.

Mankekar, Purnima. 2012a. "Dangerous Desires: Erotics, Public Culture, and Identity in Late Twentieth-Century India." In *Media, Erotics, and Transnational Asia*, edited by Purnima Mankekar and Louisa Schein, 173–202. Durham, NC: Duke University Press.

Mankekar, Purnima. 2012b. "Television and Embodiment: A Speculative Essay." *Journal of South Asian History and Culture* 3 (4): 603–14.

Mankekar, Purnima. 2013. "'We Are Like This Only': Aspiration, *Jugaad*, and Love in Enterprise Culture." In *Enterprise Culture in Neoliberal India: Studies in Youth, Class, Work and Media*, edited by Nandini Gooptu, 27–42. London: Routledge.

Mankekar, Purnima. 2014. "Televisual Temporalities and the Affective Organization of Everyday Life." In *Channeling Cultures: Television Studies from India*, edited by Biswarup Sen and Abhijit Roy, 41–55. New Delhi: Oxford University Press.

Mankekar, Purnima n.d. "Spaces of Danger: Affective Publics and National Belonging after September 11, 2001."

Mannur, Anita and Valerie Matsumoto, eds. 2006. "Asian Americans on Meat versus Rice." *Amerasia Journal* 32 (2).

Manuel, Peter. 1993. *Cassette Culture: Popular Music and Technology in North India*. Chicago: University of Chicago Press.

Markovits, Claude François, Jacques Pouchepadass, and Sanjay Subrahmanyam. 2003. *Society and Circulation*. Delhi: Permanent Black.

Marks, Laura U. 2000. *The Skin of the Film: Intercultural Cinema, Embodiment, and the Senses*. Durham, NC: Duke University Press.

Martin, Biddy, and Chandra Talpade Mohanty. 1986. "Feminist Politics: What's Home Got to Do with It?" In *Feminist Studies, Critical Studies*, edited by Teresa de Lauretis, 191–212. Bloomington: Indiana University Press.

Martin, Emily. 2013. "The Potentiality of Ethnography and the Limits of Affect Theory." *Current Anthropology* 54, Supplement 7: S149–158.

Massey, Doreen. 1991. "A Global Sense of Place." *Marxism Today*, June 1991: 24–29.

Massey, Doreen. 1993. "Power-Geometry and a Progressive Sense of Place." In *Mapping the Futures: Local Cultures, Global Change*, edited by J. Bird, B. Curtis, T. Putnam, G. Robertson, and L. Tickner, 59–69. London: Routledge.

Massey, Doreen. 1994. *Space, Place, and Gender*. Cambridge: Polity.

Massumi, Brian. 1997. *Deleuze, Guattari, and the Philosophy of Expression*. Toronto: University of Toronto Press.

Massumi, Brian. 2002. *Parables for the Virtual: Movement, Affect, Sensation*. Durham, NC: Duke University Press.

Mathew, Biju. 2008. *Taxi!: Cabs and Capitalism in New York City*. New York: Cornell University Press.

Mazumdar, Sucheta. 1989. "Racist Responses to Racism: The Aryan Myth and South Asians in the United States." *South Asia Bulletin* 9 (1): 47–55.

Mazzarella, William T. S. 2003a. *Shoveling Smoke: Advertising and Globalization in Contemporary India*. Durham, NC: Duke University Press.

Mazzarella, William T. S. 2003b. "'Very Bombay': Contending with the Global in an Indian Advertising Agency." *Cultural Anthropology* 18 (1): 33–71.

Mazzarella, William. 2005. "Indian Middle Class." Published as part of Rachel Dwyer, ed., *South Asia Keywords*, an online encyclopedia maintained by SOAS. http://d3qioqp55mx5f5.cloudfront.net/anthrolpology/docs/mazz_middleclass.pdf.

Mazzarella, William T. S. 2009. "Affect: What Is It Good For." In *Enchantments of Modernity: Empire, Nation, Globalization*, edited by Saurabh Dube. New Delhi: Routledge.

McRobbie, Angela. 1994. *Postmodernism and Popular Culture*. London: Routledge.

McRobbie, Angela. 2000. *Feminism and Youth Culture*. London: Routledge.

Merchant, Hoshang. 2007. "Agha Shahid Ali's Kashmir and the Gay Nation." In *The Phobic and the Erotic: The Politics of Sexualities in Contemporary India*, edited by Brinda Bose and Subhabrata Bhattacharya, 465–70. Calcutta: Seagull Books.

Miller, Daniel, ed. 1995a. *Acknowledging Consumption*. London: Routledge.

Miller, Daniel, ed. 1995b. "Consumption as the Vanguard of History." In *Acknowledging Consumption*, edited by Daniel Miller, 1–57. London: Routledge.

Miller, Daniel, ed. 2009. *The Comfort of Things*. Cambridge, UK: Polity.

Mohanty, Chandra. 1988. Under Western Eyes. *Feminist Review* 30 (Autumn): 61–88.

Mohanty, Chandra. 2003. *Feminism without Borders: Decolonizing Theory, Practicing Solidarity*. Durham, NC: Duke University Press.

Moraga, Cherrie and Gloria Anzaldua. 1984. *This Bridge Called My Back: Writings by Radical Women of Color*. Boston, MA: Kitchen Table/Women of Color Press.

Morley, David. 1992. *Television, Audiences, and Cultural Studies*. London: Routledge.

Morley, David. 2000. *Home Territories: Media, Mobility and Identity*. London: Routledge.

Morris, Meaghan. 1993. "Things to Do with Shopping Centres." In *The Cultural Studies Reader*, edited by Simon During, 295–319. New York: Routledge.

Morrison, Patt. 2004. "A Labor Problem Made in the U.S.A." *Los Angeles Times Online*, February 24. http://articles.latimes.com/2004/feb/24/local/me-patt24.

Moss, Pamela. 2002. *Feminist Geography in Practice: Research and Methods*. Oxford: Blackwell.

Moss, Pamela, and Karen Falconer Al-Hindi. 2007. *Feminisms in Geography: Rethinking Space, Place, and Knowledges*. Lanham, MD: Rowman and Littlefield.

Moynihan, Daniel Patrick. 1965. *The Negro Family: The Case for National Action*. Office of Policy Planning and Research. United States Department of Labor. http://www.stanford.edu/~mrosenfe/Moynihan<#213>s%20The%20Negro%20Family.pdf.

Mukherjee, Bharati. 1989. *Jasmine*. New York: Grove.

Munn, Nancy D. 1992. "The Cultural Anthropology of Time: A Critical Essay." *Annual Review of Anthropology* 21: 93–123.

Mutneja, Shivani. 2007. "East-West Myth/Making in Suniti Namjoshi's Feminist-Lesbian Fables." In *The Phobic and the Erotic: The Politics of Sexualities in Contemporary India*, edited by Brinda Bose and Subhabrata Bhattacharya, 471–76. Calcutta: Seagull Books.

Naficy, Hamid. 1993. *The Making of Exile Cultures: Iranian Television in Los Angeles*. Minneapolis: University of Minnesota Press.

Nandy, Ashis. 1980. "Woman versus Womanliness: An Essay in Social and Political Psychology." In *At the Edge of Psychology: Essays in Politics and Culture*. Delhi: Oxford University Press.

Nayak, Pulin B. 1991. "On the Crisis and the Remedies." *Economic and Political Weekly* 26 (34): 1993–97.

Ngai, Sianne. 2004. *Ugly Feelings*. Cambridge, MA: Harvard University Press.

Niranjana Tejaswini. 1995. "Banning 'Bombayi': Nationalism, Communalism, and Gender." *Economic and Political Weekly* 30 (22): 1291–92.

"Non-Resident Indians Asking for More." 1990. *India Today*, December 31: 53.

"NRIs: A Relationship Worth Nurturing." 1991. *India Today*, October 15: 54.

"NRI Remittances—Why This Neglect?" 1991. *Economic and Political Weekly* 26 (33): 1885.

Ochs, Elinor. 1992. "Indexing Gender." In *Rethinking Context: Language as an Interactive Phenomenon*, edited by Alessandro Duranti and Charles Goodwin, 335–58. Cambridge: Cambridge University Press.

Ochs, Elinor and Bambi Schieffelin. 1989. "Language Has a Heart." *Text* 9 (1): 7–25.

Omi, Michael and Howard Winant. 1994. *Racial Formation in the United States: From the 1960s to the 1990s (Critical Social Thought)*. New York: Routledge.

Ong, Aiwha. 2006. *Neoliberalism as Exception: Mutations in Citizenship and Sovereignty.* Durham, NC: Duke University Press.

Ong, Paul, Edna Bonacich, and Lucie Cheng. 1994. *The New Asian Immigration in Los Angeles and Global Restructuring*. Philadelphia: Temple University Press.

Orsini, Francesca. 2002. *The Hindi Public Sphere 1920–1940: Language and Literature in the Age of Nationalism*. New Delhi: Oxford University Press.

Ortner, Sherry B. 1995. "Resistance and the Problem of Ethnographic Refusal." *Comparative Studies in Society and History*. 37 (1): 173–93.

Oza, Rupal. 2001. "Showcasing India: Gender, Geography, and Globalization." *Signs* 26 (4): 1067–96.

Page, David, and William Crawley. 2001. *Satellites over South Asia: Broadcasting, Culture, and the Public Interest*. New Delhi: Sage.

Palumbo-Liu, David. 1999. *Asian/American Historical Crossings of a Racial Frontier*. Stanford, CA: Stanford University Press.

Pandey, Vikash N. 2004. "Emancipated Bodies/Embodying Liberation: Debating through Fire." In *Sexual Sites, Seminal Attitudes: Sexualities, Masculinities, and Culture in South Asia,* edited by Sanjay Srivastava, 188–208. New Delhi: Sage.

Pandian, Anand. 2012. "The Time of Anthropology: Notes from a Field of Contemporary Experience." *Cultural Anthropology* 27 (4): 547–71.

Parisi, L., and Tiziana Terranova. 2000. "Heat-Death: Emergence and Control in Genetic Engineering and Artificial Life." *CTheory*, May 10. http://www.ctheory.net/articles.aspx?id=127.

Park, Kyeyoung. 1996. "Use and Abuse of Race and Culture: Black-Korean Tension in America." *American Anthropologist* 98 (3): 492–99.

Park, Kyeyoung. 1999. "'I Am Floating in the Air': Creation of a Korean Transnational Space among Korean-Latino American Remigrants." *positions* 7 (3): 667–95.

Patel, Geeta. 1998. "Home, Homo, Hybrid: Translating Gender." *College Literature* 25 (2): 133–50.

Patel, Geeta. 2007. "Risky Lives." In *The Phobic and the Erotic: The Politics of Sexualities in Contemporary India,* edited by Brinda Bose and Subhabrata Bhattacharya, 201–34. Calcutta: Seagull Books.

Pathfinders India Study. 1998. "Survey of Women." N.p.

Peirce, Charles Sanders. 1958. *Collected Papers*, vols. 1–6. A. Bucks, ed. Cambridge: Harvard University Press.

Peiss, Kathy. 2011. *Hope in a Jar: The Making of America's Beauty Culture*. Philadelphia: University of Pennsylvania Press.

Prashad, Vijay. 1998. "Crafting Solidarities." In *A Part, Yet Apart: South Asians in Asian America*, edited by Rajini Srikanth and Lavina Dhingra Shankar. Philadelphia: Temple University Press.

Prashad, Vijay. 2000. *The Karma of Brown Folk*. Minneapolis: University of Minnesota Press.

Prathap, Gangan. 2005. Editorial. *Current Science* 89: 1063–64.

Pratt, Mary Louise. 2007. *Imperial Eyes: Travel Writing and Transculturation*. New York: Routledge.

Pratt, Minnie Bruce, Barbara Smith, and Elly Bulkin. 1988. *Yours in Struggle: 3 Feminist Perspectives on Anti-Semitism and Racism*. Ithaca, NY: Firebrand.

"President Bush 9/11/2001." 2002. September 11 News.com. http://www.september11news.com/PresidentBush.htm.

Puar, Jasbir K. 2007. *Terrorist Assemblages: Homonationalism in Queer Times*. Durham, NC: Duke University Press.

Puar, Jasbir K., and Amit S. Rai. 2002. "Monster, Terrorist, Fag: The War on Terrorism and the Production of Docile Patriots." *Social Text* 20 (3): 117–48.

Rabinow, Paul. 2007. *Marking Time: On the Anthropology of the Contemporary*. Princeton, NJ: Princeton University Press.

Rabinow, Paul, George E. Marcus, James D. Faubion, and Tobias Rees. 2008. *Designs for an Anthropology of the Contemporary*. Durham, NC: Duke University Press.

Raheja, Gloria Goodwin, and Ann Grodzins Gold. 1994. *Listen to the Heron's Words: Reimagining Gender and Kinship in North India*. Berkeley: University of California Press.

Rai, Amit. 1994. "An American Raj in Filmistan: Images of Elvis in Indian Films." *Screen* 35 (1): 51–77.

Rai, Amit. 2009. *Untimely Bollywood: Globalization and India's New Media Assemblage*. Durham, NC: Duke University Press.

Raj, Dhooleka Sarhadi. 2003. *Where Are You From? Middle-Class Migrants in the Modern World*. Berkeley: University of California.

Rajagopal, Arvind. 1999a. "Thinking about the New Indian Middle Class: Gender, Advertising, and Politics in an Age of Globalisation." In *Signposts: Gender Issues in Post-Independence India*, edited by Rajeshwari Sunder Rajan. New Delhi: Kali.

Rajagopal, Arvind. 1999b. "Thinking through Emerging Markets: Brand Logics and the Cultural Forms of Political Society in India." *Social Text* 60 (Fall): 131–49.

Rajagopal, Arvind. 2001. *Politics after Television: Religious Nationalism and the Reshaping of the Indian Public*. Cambridge: Cambridge University Press.

Ramanujan, A. K. 1973. *Speaking of Siva*. Harmondsworth, U.K.: Penguin.

Rastogi, Alka. 2007. "V-Day Is Behuda Divas for These Groups." February 13. http://www.hindustantimes.com/StoryPage/Print/205585.aspx.

Reddy, Gayatri. 2005. *With Respect to Sex: Negotiating Hijra Identity in South India*. Chicago: University of Chicago Press.

Reddy, Gayatri. 2007. "Sexual Differences and Their Discontents: Shifting Contexts of 'Thirdness' in Hyderabad." In *The Phobic and the Erotic: The Politics of Sexualities in Contemporary India*, edited by Brinda Bose and Subhabrata Bhattacharya, 301–23. Calcutta: Seagull Books.

Rege, Sharmila. 1996. "The Hegemonic Appropriation of Sexuality: The Case of the Lavani Performer of Maharashtra." In *Social Reform, Sexuality, and the State*, edited by Patricia Uberoi. New Delhi: Sage.

Richard, Analiese and Daromir Rudnyckyj. 2009. "Economies of Affect." *Journal of the Royal Anthropological Institute*. 15: 57–77.

Rofel, Lisa. 2007. *Desiring China: Experiments in Neoliberalism, Sexuality, and Public Culture*. Durham, NC: Duke University Press.

Rosaldo, Michelle Z. 1984. "Toward an Anthropology of Self and Feeling." In *Culture Theory: Essays on Mind, Self, and Emotion*, edited by R. A. Shweder and R. A. LeVine, 137–57. Cambridge: Cambridge University Press.

Rose, Gillian. 1993. *Feminism and Geography: The Limits of Geographical Knowledge*. Cambridge: Polity Press.

Rouse, Roger. 1995. "Thinking through Transnationalism: Notes on the Cultural Politics of Class Relations in the Contemporary United States." *Public Culture* 7 (2): 353–402.

Roy, Kumkum. 1998. "Unravelling the Kamasutra." In *A Question of Silence? The Sexual Economies of Modern India*, edited by Mary E. John and Janaki Nair. New Delhi: Kali.

Roy, Parama. 1998. *Indian Traffic: Identities in Question in Colonial and Postcolonial India*. Berkeley: University of California Press.

Roy, Parama. 2002. "Reading Communities and Culinary Communities: The Gastropoetics of the South Asian Diaspora." *Positions* 10 (2): 471–502.

Sahlins, Marshall. 1976. *Culture and Practical Reason*. Chicago: University of Chicago Press.

Sahlins, Marshall. 1987. Islands of History. London and New York: Tavistock.

Sangari, Kumkum and Sudesh Vaid. 1989. *Recasting Women: Essays in Colonial History*. New Delhi: Kali for Women.

Sarkar, Tanika. 1995. "Heroic Women, Mother Goddesses: Family and Organisation in Hindutva Politics." In *Women and the Hindu Right*, edited by Tanika Sarkar and Urvashi Butalia, 181–215. New Delhi: Kali for Women.

Schein, Louisa. 1999. "Of Cargo and Satellites: Imagined Cosmopolitanism." *Postcolonial Studies* 2 (3): 345–75.

Schein, Louisa. 2013. "Homeland Beauty: Transnational Longing and Hmong American Video." In *Media, Erotics, and Transnational Asia*, edited by Purnima Mankekar and Louisa Schein, 203–32. Durham, NC: Duke University Press.

Schimmel, Annemarie. 1975. *Mystical Dimensions of Islam*. Chapel Hill: University of North Carolina Press.

Schultz, Vicki. 2006. "Sex and Work." *Yale Journal of Law and Feminism*. 18: 223–34.

Sengupta, Somini. 1998. "India Taps into Its Diaspora: Investing for Love of Country, and 7.75% Interest." *New York Times*, August 19, B1.

Setalvad, Teesta. 1995. "The Woman Shiv Sainik and Her Sister Swayamsevika." In *Women and Right Wing Movements: Indian Experiences*, edited by Tanika Sarkar and Urvashi Butalia, 233–44. London: Zed.

Shah, Nayan. 2001. *Contagious Divides: Epidemics and Race in San Francisco's Chinatown*. Berkeley: University of California Press.

Shah, Nayan. 2012. *Stranger Intimacy: Contesting Race, Sexuality and the Law in the North American West*. Berkeley: University of California Press.

Shah, Svati. 2014. *Street Corner Secrets: Sex, Work, and Migration in the City of Mumbai*. Durham, NC: Duke University Press.

Shahani, Parmesh. 2008. *Gay Bombay: Globalization, Love and (Be)Longing in Contemporary India*. New Delhi: Sage Publications.

Shankar, Lavina Dhingra, and Rajini Srikanth. 1998. *A Part, Yet Apart: South Asians in Asian America*. Philadelphia: Temple University Press.

Shankar, Shalini. 2008. *Desi Land: Teen Culture, Class, and Success in Silicon Valley*. Durham, NC: Duke University Press.

Shanks, Michael, and Christopher Tilley. 1986. *Re-constructing Archaeology*. London: Routledge.

Sharma, Amit. 2001. "Valentine's Day Victim of Sangh Wrath in UP." *Indian Express Online*. February 12. http://www.indian-express.com/.

Sharma, Amit and Harish Deshmukh. 2002. "Loving to Hate." *Indian Express Online*. February 14. http://www.indian-express.com/.

Sharma, Aparna. 2003. "India's Experience with the Multiplex." *Seminar*525. www.india-seminar.com.

Sharma, Aradhana. 2008. *Logics of Empowerment: Development, Gender, and Governance in Neoliberal India*. Minneapolis: University of Minnesota Press.

Sharma, Aradhana, and Akhil Gupta, eds. 2006. *The Anthropology of the State: A Reader*. Malden, MA: Blackwell.

Sharma, Shailendra. 1996. "India's Economic Liberalization: The Elephant Comes of Age." *Current History* 95: 414–18.

Sharpe, Jenny. 2005. "Gender, Nation, and Globalization in Monsoon Wedding and Dilwale Dulhania Le Jayenge." *Meridians: Feminism, Race, Transnationalism* 6 (1): 58–81.

Shih, Shu-mei. 2007. *Visuality and Identity: Sinophone Articulations across the Pacific*. Berkeley: University of California Press.

Shimakawa, Karen. 2002. *National Abjection: The Asian American Body Onstage*. Durham, NC: Duke University Press.

Shome, Raka. 2006. "Thinking through the Diaspora: Call Centers, India, and New Technologies of Hybridity." *International Journal of Cultural Studies* 9 (1): 105–24.

Shukla, Sandhya Rajendra. 2003. *India Abroad: Diasporic Cultures of Postwar America and England*. Princeton, NJ: Princeton University Press.

Siegel, Lee. 1978. *Sacred and Profane Dimensions of Love in Indian Traditions as Exemplified in the Gitagovinda of Jayadeva*. Delhi: Oxford University Press.

Sinha, Mrinalini. 1997. *Colonial Masculinity: The "Manly Englishman" and the "Effeminate Bengali" in the Late Nineteenth Century*. New Delhi: Kali.

Siu, Lok. 2007. "The Queen of the Chinese Colony: Contesting Nationalism, Engendering Diaspora." In *Asian Diasporas: New Formations, New Conceptions*, edited by Rhacel S. Parreñas and Lok C. D. Siu, 105–40. Stanford, CA: Stanford University Press.

Sobchack, Vivian Carol. 2004. *Carnal Thoughts: Embodiment and Moving Image Culture*. Berkeley: University of California Press.

Spigel, Lynn, and Jan Olsson. 2004. *Television after TV: Essays on a Medium in Transition*. Durham, NC: Duke University Press.

Spinoza, Benedictus de. 1985. *The Collected Works of Spinoza*. Edited and translated by E. M. Curley. Princeton, NJ: Princeton University Press.

Springer, Richard. 2012. "Analysis of the Indian American Community from Census 2010 Data." *India West*, March 29. http://www.indiawest.com/news/article_03307c37-88d7-5665-88d1-cda4af353a3d.html.

Srinivas, Lakshmi. 2002. "The Active Audience: Spectatorship, Social Relations and the Experience of Cinema in India." *Media Culture Society* 24 (2): 155–73.

Srinivasan, Amrit. 1985. "Reform and Revival: The Devadasi and Her Dance." *Economic and Political Weekly* 20 (44): 1869–76.

Srivastava, Sanjay. 1998. *Constructing Post-colonial India: National Character and the Doon School*. London: Routledge.

Srivastava, Sanjeev. 2000. "India Takes Valentine's Day to Heart." *BBC News*, February 14. http://news.bbc.co.uk/2/hi/south_asia/642644.stm.

Steedman, Carolyn. 2002. *Dust: The Archive and Cultural History*. New Brunswick, NJ: Rutgers University Press.

Stewart, Kathleen. 2007. *Ordinary Affects*. Durham, NC: Duke University Press.

Stewart, Susan. 1984. *On Longing: Narratives of the Miniature, the Gigantic, the Souvenir, the Collection*. Baltimore, MD: Johns Hopkins University Press.

Stoler, Ann Laura. 2009. *Along the Archival Grain: Epistemic Anxieties and Colonial Common Sense*. Princeton, NJ: Princeton University Press.

Subrahmanyam, Sanjay. 1998. *The Career and Legend of Vasco da Gama*. Cambridge: Cambridge University Press.

Subrahmanyam, Sanjay. 2013. *Is Indian Civilization a Myth? Fictions and Histories*. New Delhi: Permanent Black.

Sunder Rajan, Rajeshwari. 1993. *Real and Imagined Women: Gender, Culture, and Postcolonialism*. London: Routledge.

Sunder Rajan, Rajeshwari. 1999. "Introduction." In *Signposts: Gender Issues in Post-Independence India*. New Delhi: Kali.

Sunder Rajan, Rajeshwari. 2003. *The Scandal of the State: Women, Law, and Citizenship in Postcolonial India*. Durham, NC: Duke University Press.

Takaki, Ronald T. 1989. *Strangers from a Different Shore: A History of Asian Americans*. Boston: Little, Brown.

Tan, Amy. 1989. *The Joy Luck Club*. New York: Putnam.

Thadani, Giti. 1996. *Sakhiyani: Lesbian Desire in Ancient and Modern India*. London: Cassell.

Thapan, Meenakshi, ed. 1997. *Embodiment: Essays on Gender and Identity*. Delhi: Oxford University Press.

Tharu, Susie. 1989. "Tracing Savitri's Pedigree: Victorian Racism and the Image of Women in Indo-Anglian Literature." In *Recasting Women: Essays in Colonial History*, edited by Kumkum Sangari and Sudesh Vaid. New Delhi: Kali.

Thompson, George. 1997. "Ahamkara and Atmastuti: Self-Assertion and Impersonation in the Rgveda." *History of Religions* 37 (2): 141–71.

Thrift, Nigel. 2007. *Non-Representational Theory: Space, Politics, Affect.* New York: Routledge.

Thrift, Nigel. 2010. "Understanding the Material Practices of Glamour." In *The Affect Theory Reader*, edited by Melissa Gregg and Gregory J. Seigworth, 289–308. Durham, NC: Duke University Press.

Tölölyan, Khachig. 1991. "The Nation-State and Its Others: In Lieu of a Preface." *Diaspora* 1 (1): 3–7.

"Tough Love for Indian Valentines." 2001. *BBC News*, February 14. http://news.bbc.co.uk/2/hi/south_asia/1169077.stm.

Tsing, Anna. 2004. *Friction: An Ethnography of Global Connection.* Princeton, NJ: Princeton University Press.

"Tussle for Turf in the Love Bazaar." 2001. *Hindustan Times.com*, February 14. http://www.hindustantimes.com/.

Uberoi, Patricia, ed. 1996. *Social Reform, Sexuality, and the State.* New Delhi: Sage.

Uberoi, Patricia. 1997. "Dharma and Desire, Freedom and Destiny: Rescripting the Man-Woman Relationship in Popular Hindi Cinema." In *Embodiment: Essays on Gender and Identity*, edited by Meenakshi Thapan. Delhi: Oxford University Press.

Uberoi, Patricia. 1998. "The Diaspora Comes Home: Disciplining Desire in *DDLJ*." *Contributions to Indian Sociology* 32 (2): 305–36.

Uberoi, Patricia. 2001. "Imagining the Family: An Ethnography of Viewing Hum Aapke Hain Kaun . . . !" In *Pleasure and the Nation*, edited by Rachel Dwyer and Christopher Pinney, 309–51. New Delhi: Oxford University Press.

van der Veer, Peter. 1994. *Religious Nationalism: Hindus and Muslims in India.* Berkeley: University of California Press.

van der Veer, Peter. 1995. *Nation and Migration: The Politics of Space in the South Asian Diaspora.* Philadelphia: University of Pennsylvania Press.

"V-Day Couples Humiliated in Kanpur." 2000. *Hindustan Times*, February 15. http://www.hindustantimes.com/.

Visweswaran, Kamala. 1997. "Diaspora by Design: Flexible Citizenship and South Asians in U.S. Racial Formations." *Diaspora* 6 (1): 5–29.

Visweswaran, Kamala, and Ali Mir. 1999. "On the Politics of Community in South Asian-American Studies." *Amerasia Journal* 25 (3): 97–110.

Volpp, Leti. 2002. "The Citizen and the Terrorist." *Berkeley Law Scholarship Repository*. 23: 561–86.

Vora, Kalindi. 2010. "The Transmission of Care: Affective Economies and Indian Call Centers." In *Intimate Labors: Cultures, Technologies, and the Politics of Care*, edited by Eileen Boris and Rhacel Salazar Parreñas, 33–48. Stanford, CA: Stanford University Press.

Wadhwani, Anita. 1998. "Working Overtime." *India Currents*, December. https://www .indiacurrents.com/articles/1998/12/22/working-overtime.

Weeks, Kathi. 2007. "Life Within and Against Work: Affective Labor, Feminist Critique, and Post-Fordist Politics." *Ephemera: Theory and Politics in Organization* 7 (1): 233–49. www.ephemeraweb.org/.

Weston, Kath. 1997. *Families We Choose: Lesbians, Gays, Kinship*. New York: Columbia University Press.

Williams, Linda. 2008. *Screening Sex*. Durham, NC: Duke University Press.

Williams, Raymond. 1954. *Drama in Performance*. London: F. Muller.

Williams, Raymond. 1977. *Marxism and Literature*. Oxford: Oxford University Press.

Wilson, Ara. 2004. *The Intimate Economies of Bangkok: Tomboys, Tycoons, and Avon Ladies in the Global City*. Berkeley: University of California Press.

Wissinger, Elizabeth. 2007. "Always on Display: Affective Production in the Modeling Industry." In *The Affective Turn: Theorizing the Social*, edited by Patricia Ticineto Clough with Jean Halley. Durham, NC: Duke University Press.

Xiang, Biao. 2007. *Global "Body Shopping": An Indian Labor System in the Information Technology Industry*. Princeton, NJ: Princeton University Press.

Yanagisako, Sylvia Junko. 2002. *Producing Culture and Capital: Family Firms in Italy*. Princeton, NJ: Princeton University Press.

Zavella, Patricia. 1997. "'Playing with Fire': The Gendered Construction of Chicana/ Mexicana Sexuality." In *The Gender/Sexuality Reader: Culture, History, Political Economy*, edited by Roger Lancaster and Micaela di Leonardo. New York: Routledge.

Zeman, J. Jay. 1977. "Peirce's Theory of Signs." In *A Perfusion of Signs*, edited by Thomas A. Sebeok and Diana Agrest. Bloomington: Indiana University Press.

Zhou, Min, and Jennifer Lee. 2004. "The Making of Culture, Identity, and Ethnicity among Asian American Youth." In *Sociology: Exploring the Architecture of Everyday Life Readings*, 8th ed., edited by David M. Newman and Jodi O'Brien, 98–105. Thousand Oaks, CA: Pine Forge Press.

Žižek, Slavoj. 1989. *The Sublime Object of Ideology*. London: Verso.

Žižek, Slavoj. 2002. *Welcome to the Desert of the Real*. New York: Verso.

Films and Television Programs

Aa Ab Laut Chalein. 1999. Dir. Rishi Kapoor. R. K. Films, Chembur, India.

Band Baaja Baraat. 2010. Dir. Maneesh Sharma. Yash Raj Films, Mumbai, India.

Baywatch. 1989–2001. NBC. GTC Entertainment, Los Angeles, CA.

Bhaji on the Beach. 1993. Dir. Gurinder Chadha. Film Four International, London, UK.

Bunty aur Babli. 2005. Dir. Shaad Ali. Yash Raj Films, Mumbai, India.

Coolie. 1983. Dir. Manmohan Desai. Aasia Films Pvt. Ltd.; M.K.D. Films Combine.

Dil Chahta Hai. 2001. Dir. Farhan Akhtar. Excel Entertainment, Mumbai, India.

Dilwale Dulhaniya Le Jayenge. 1995. Dir. Aditya Chopra. Yash Raj Films, Mumbai, India.

Diverted to Delhi. 2002. Dir. Greg Stitt. Australia Broadcasting Company, Sydney, Australia.

Drishti. 1990. Dir. Govind Nihalani. Udbhav Productions, Mumbai, India.

Gharana. 2003. Zee TV, Mumbai, India.

Guru. 2007. Dir. Mani Ratnam. Madras Talkies Film, Madras, India.

Hasratein. 1995. Dir. Ajai Sinha. Ananda Films. Zee TV, Mumbai, India.

Hum Aapke Hain Kaun. 1994. Dir. Sooraj Barjatya. Rajshri Productions, Mumbai, India.

Hum Saath Saath Hain. 1999. Dir. Sooraj Barjatya. Rajshri Productions, Mumbai, India.

India Calling. November 14, 2005–October 5, 2006. Rose Audiovisuals. STAR One, Mumbai, India.

Justajoo. 2005. Dir. Ajai Sinha. Zee TV, Mumbai, India.

Kaala Pathar. 1979. Dir. Yash Chopra. Yash Raj Films, Mumbai, India.

Kabhi Alvida Na Kehna. 2006. Dir. Karan Johar. Dharma Productions; Yash Raj Films, Mumbai, India.

Kabhi Khushi Kabhie Gham. 2001. Dir. Karan Johar. Yash Raj Films, Mumbai, India.

Kahaani Ghar Ghar Kii. October 16, 2000–October 9, 2008. Balaji Telefilms. STAR Plus, Mumbai, India.

Kal Ho Na Ho. 2003. Dir. Karan Johar. Yash Raj Films, Mumbai, India.

Kuch Jhuki Palkein. April 29, 2002–January 8, 2003. Dir. Rahul Kapoor and Shyam Maheshwari. Sony Entertainment, Los Angeles, CA.

Kuch Kuch Hota Hai. 1999. Dir. Karan Johar. Yash Raj Films, Mumbai, India.

Kyunki Saas Bhi Kahbhi Bahu Thi. July 3, 2000–November 6, 2008. Balaji Telefilms. STAR Plus, Mumbai, India.

Laaga Chunari Mein Daag. 2007. Dir. Pradeep Sarkar. Yash Raj Films, Mumbai, India.

Mahanagar. 1962. Dir. Satyajit Ray. Dist. Edward Harrison. R. D. Banshal & Co., India.

Making of Bunty aur Babli, The. 2005. Dir. Shaad Ali. Yash Raj Films, Mumbai, India.

Making of Kabhi Khushi Kabhie Gham, The. 2001. Dir. Karan Johar. Yash Raj Films, Mumbai, India.

Maryada: Aakhir Kab Tak. October 18, 2010–April 13, 2012. Dir. Waseem Sabir, Imtiaz Punjabi, and Iqbal Rizvi. STAR Plus, Mumbai, India.

Mississippi Masala. 1991. Dir. Mira Nair. MGM, Beverly Hills, CA.

Mohabattein. 2000. Dir. Aditya Chopra. Yash Raj Films, Mumbai, India.

Namak Haram. 1973. Dir. Hrishikesh Mukherjee. R.S.J. Productions, Media City, UK.

Nancy by Night, Nandini by Day. 2005. Dir. Sonali Gulati. Women Make Movies, New York, NY.

New York. 2009. Dir. Kabir Khan. Yash Raj Films, Mumbai, India.

Oprah Winfrey Show. 1986–2011. Harpo Productions. Dist. King World Productions; CBS Television Distribution, Santa Monica, CA.

Oye Lucky! Lucky Oye! 2008. Dir. Dibakar Banerjee. UTV Motion Pictures, Mumbai, India.

Pardes. 1997. Dir. Subhash Ghai. Mukta Arts, Mumbai, India.

Paroma. 1984. Dir. Aparna Sen. Usha Enterprises, New Delhi, India.

The Priya Tendulkar Show. 1994. El TV, Mumbai, India.

Purab Aur Paschim. 1970. Dir. Manoj Kumar. Vishal International Productions, Mumbai, India.

Purush Kshetra. 1994. El TV, Mumbai, India.

Raavan. 2006–2008. Zee TV, Mumbai, India.

Rajani. 1984. Doordarshan, New Delhi, India.

Ramayan. 1987–1988. Dir. Ramanand Sagar. Doordarshan, New Delhi, India.

Salaam Namaste. 2005. Dir. Siddharth Anand. Yash Raj Films, Mumbai, India.

Sa Re Ga Ma Pa. 1995–2013. Dir. Gajendra Singh. Zee TV, Mumbai, India.

Satya. 1988. Dir. Suresh Krishna. Pyramid Saimira Films, Chennai, India.

Shanghai. 2012. Dir. Dibakar Banerjee. PVR Productions, Mumbai, India.

Shanti—Ek Aurat Ki Kahani. 1994. Dir. Adi Pocha. DD National, New Delhi, India.

Swabhimaan. 1995–1997. Dir. Mahesh Bhatt. DD National, New Delhi, India.

Swades. 2004. Dir. Ashutosh Gowariker. Ashutosh Gowariker Productions Pvt. Ltd., Dillywood, UTV Motion Pictures, Mumbai, India.

Tara. February 1993–1997. Dir. Raman Kumar. Zee TV, Mumbai, India.

Yuva. 2004. Dir. Mani Ratnam. Madras Talkies Film Co., Madras, India.

Note: page numbers followed by "n" indicate endnotes.

Doordarshan (state-controlled television), 46, 110, 111–12, 133
dowries, 254n23
dress codes, 157
Drishti (film), 255n30
Dubal, Veena, 236, 265n3, 265n9, 266n13, 266n16
Ducey, Ariel, 262n12
durée, 19–20, 240, 245n23
Dwyer, Rachel, 134, 253n16, 255n25

economic liberalization policies in India, 46–49, 68, 111, 221
emergency narratives, 231
emplacement: call center agents and, 215–18, 224; *DDLJ* and, 36; Global India in Bollywood films and, 183; Indian grocery stores and, 72, 90–92; informatics and, 212. *See also* migration and immigration
English, "global," 216–17
erotics and erotic affect: in *Bunty aur Babli*, 195; caste and class position and, 122–26; commodity affect and erotic affect, 120–22, 139–43; ethnographic practice and, 119; in film, 117–18, 255n25, 255n30; gender and, 126–27; genealogies of the erotic in South Asia, 116–19; global capitalism and, 161; heteronormative desire, policing of, 179, 180–81, 185; India eroticized in *DDLJ*, 56; indirect expression of, 120, 254n20; *K3G*, patriarchal romance, and, 162–63, 166–67, 185; and landscape in *DDLJ*, 54; nationalism, martyrdom, and, 246n28; same-sex desire and relationships, 61, 118, 249n28, 253n16, 254n17, 256n36; television and erotic affect, 119–27, 138–39; television representation of eroticized intimacy, 127–38; territoriality and, 23–24; Valentine's Day panics and, 160–61
ethnic identity and cultural difference, 93–96. *See also* race

families: extended family in *K3G*, 168–69; television representations and, 134–35, 138–39

Fanon, Frantz, 189
fantasy, 124–25, 166
Favero, Paolo, 10, 12, 73
Ferguson, James, 217
Fernandes, Remo, 113, 261n5
film: commodity aesthetic and, 115; commodity affect and, 252n8; erotics and, 117–18, 255n25, 255n30; Hollywood films used for call center training, 206; media assemblages, affective experience, and, 164–65; sensory engagement and, 248n20. *See also* Bollywood cinema and Hindi film; Bollywood/Hindi films
Fire (film), 256n36
food as cultural signifier, 83–87
Foreign Exchange Regulation Act (FERA), 48
foreign investments in India, 46–49
Fortier, Anne-Marie, 15
Foucault, Michel, 129, 213, 217
Freeman, Carla, 212–13
Freud, Sigmund, 44–45

Gandhi, Mahatma, 147, 258n10
Gandhi, Rajiv, 47
Garber, Marjorie, 189
gay and lesbian movement in India, 253n16. *See also* same-sex desire and relationships
Geetha, V., 254nn19–20, 254n23
gender: call centers, mobility, and, 212–14; consumer subjectivity and, 125–27; diaspora and, 28–29, 61–62; gustatory memory and gender politics, 84–87; Hindutva ideologies and, 159; inequality, gendered relations of, 243n1; *K3G*, Hindu rituals, and, 167; modernity mediated through gendered NRI bodies, 61; soundscapes of surveillance and, 82–83; Valentine's Day panics and, 158–60; women's subjectivity in *DDLJ*, 62. *See also* masculine subjectivity; sexuality; womanhood
George, Rosemary, 92, 96, 251n20
Gharana (TV), 255n29
Ghosh, Shohini, 96, 263n25
Giddens, Anthony, 106
Gingrich, Andre, 184

landscapes: affective iconicity of, in *DDLJ*, 51–56; commodity affect and, 115; of Global Indianness, 182–83; physical, social, and cultural landscapes of Indian grocery stores, 75

language in call centers, 216–18

Lee, Rachel, 215

loss: in *DDLJ*, 52–53, 55; diaspora and trope of loss, 27

Lowe, Lisa, 94, 97, 103, 237, 266n19

Lutz, Catherine, 13

Maira, Sunaina, 181, 237

Manalansan, Martin, 42, 83, 244n9

Mandal Commission Bill (1990), 122

Manderson, Lenore, 253n12

Maran, Kalanidhi, 252n4

Marks, Laura, 73–74, 78–79, 80, 83, 84, 88

marriage, in *DDLJ*, 59–60, 61–62

Martin, Emily, 245n17

Marx, Karl, 44–45

maryada (appropriate rules of conduct), 129, 134

Maryada: Aakhir Kab Tak (serial), 254n17

masculine subjectivity: affective labor and, 214; 9/11 hate violence and, 235; NRIS and, 49, 60–61. *See also* gender

Massey, Doreen, 10, 12

Massumi, Brian, 13, 26, 45, 207–8, 244n7

matri shakti ("strength of motherhood"), 159

Mazumdar, Sucheta, 251n19

Mazzarella, William T., 17, 140

media: affect and, 14–15, 17–18, 45–46; affective economies and, 45; aspirations and, 194, 206; circulation of, 7; commodity affects and, 115, 118; consolidation of, 7; impersonation and, 206; media assemblages, 164; nationhood, gender, subject formation, and, 33; NRIS and, 49, 146; proliferation of, 7; reconfiguration of Indianness and, 41, 67, 111, 127, 138, 163; Sept. 11 and, 230, 234; spatiotemporal rupture and, 24–25; temporalization and, 19–20; travel aspirations and, 16, 208

mediation: affect and, 15, 45; archive and, 33–35

Mehra, Nidhi, 158

Mehta, Deepa, 256n36

memory: food as cultural signifier and, 83–87; nostalgia and, 88–90; sensuous knowledges and sense memory, 78–79

Mera Naam Joker (film), 177

migration and immigration: Asian American perspective on, 11, 250n18; fraught relationship between, 103; H-1B visas, 102–3, 199, 215; Indian grocery stores and patterns in, 101–3; multiple, trajectory of, 25–26; return to India, 25–26; South Asians and, 11; territoriality and, 246n27; U.S. policy, 11, 101–3, 250n18; virtual migration, 208–9, 212; xenophilia, xenophobia, and myth of immigrant success, 98–99

Miller, Daniel, 88

minority rights discourse, 148–49, 153, 154

Mississippi Masala (film), 67

Miss World pageant (Bangalore, 1996), 256n36

mobility and movement: affective transformation bodies and, 224; *Bunty aur Babli* and, 191–95; call centers agents and, 207–18, 221; neoliberalism and, 221; and NRI bodies in *DDLJ*, 58; NRI men in *DDLJ* and, 60–61; train trope, 191–92; of women, 214. *See also* migration and immigration

model minority discourses, 176, 260n34

modernity: commodity affect and, 123, 143; gendered NRI bodies in *DDLJ* and, 61; national identity and, 143; phantasm and, 106; "westernism" vs. modernism, 156

Mohabattein (film), 178–79, 181, 182–83

Monteiro, Anjali, 129

morality, discourses of. *See* Global India and transnational discourses of morality

moral panics over Valentine's Day. *See* Valentine's Day moral panics moral panics over women and night work, 263n22

Morris, Meaghan, 252n10

movement. *See* migration and immigration; mobility and movement

multiculturalism, U.S., 94

Munn, Nancy D., 20, 266n25

Murthy, Pratibha, 263n22

music in Indian grocery stores, 81–82

music videos, Indipop, 131–32

Muslims: Gujarat pogroms against, 150; Hindutva sentiments against, 150–52; Sept. 11 and racial positionality of, 232–37; Valentine's Day and, 257n7

Muthalik, Pramod, 257n5

Nair, Mira, 67

narration and affect, 13

nationalism and nationalist affect: affective economies and, 44–45; Bollywood cinema and reconfiguration of, 67–68; call center agents and, 214; commodity affect, erotic affect, and, 142–43; *DDLJ* and, 55–57, 61, 66–69; erotics, martyrdom, and, 246n28; family-nation metonymy in *K3G*, 169; purity discourses and, 142; Sept. 11 and U.S. nationalism, 231, 232–38; temporalization and, 22; territoriality of, 246n27; U.S. patriotism, 104; women's bodies and, 61; xenophilia, xenophobia, and, 99. *See also* Hindutva

Natyashastra (Bharata), 117

neoliberalism, 218–22, 226, 264n32

New Delhi, 10, 31, 41. See also *Dilwale Dulhaniya Le Jayenge*; television, Hindi transnational

New York (film), 50

9/11. *See* September 11, 2001, and aftermath

nonresident Indians (NRIs): as foreign investors, 48–49, 68, 145–46, 148; Hindi films' preoccupation with, 50; as indexical of shifting Indianness, 58; *K3G* and NRI nostalgia, 259n24; masculine subjectivity and, 49, 60–61; national-

foreign, Self-Other binaries and, in *DDLJ*, 68–69; Resurgent India campaign and, 145–54; returning (RNRIs), 26–27; supreme self-confidence of the Global Indian, 170, 259n26; and territoriality in *DDLJ*, 57, 65–67

nostalgia, 87–90, 172, 259n24

nuclear testing, 145, 146

objects: Indian grocery stores and objects in motion, 78; on the move in *DDLJ*, 58–59; recollection-objects, 88. *See also* commodities and commodity affect

Ochs, Elinor, 57, 184

Ong, Aiwha, 221–22, 263nn26–27

orientalism, 83, 117, 140, 266n19

outsourcing, 199, 204, 215–16, 263nn26–27. *See also* call centers

Overseas Friends of BJP, 148

Page, David, 113, 251n2, 255n31

panopticon, 213

Pardes (film), 50

Park, Kyeyoung, 95–97

Paroma (film), 255n30

Pathfinders India Study, 256n34

Patodia, Hemant, 158

patriarchy: conception of, 243n1; eroticized bodies in *DDLJ* and, 63; *K3G* and, 162–63, 166–67, 168

patriotism: *K3G* and NRI patriotism, 259n27; Sept. 11 and, 104, 234–35. *See also* nationalism and nationalist affect

Peirce, Charles Sanders, 13, 18, 45, 50–51

Phalke, Dadasaheb, 247n4

phantasm: concept of, 72–73; India as, 73, 75, 106, 107

Pink Chaddi Campaign, 257n5

Plato, 73

poverty: aspiration and, 264n34; racism and explanations for, 250n18; "rise of India" and, 261n2

Prasad, Rajendra, 157

Prashad, Vijay, 250n18, 260n34

Proposition 187 (CA), 96, 251n20

Proposition 209 (CA), 96, 251n20

Puar, Jasbir, 231

Punjab and nation in *DDLJ*, 55–56

Purab Aur Paschim (film), 57, 65, 249n26

purity: cultural purity and contamination, 128, 143–44, 151; policing of heteronormative desire and, 181; sexual and cultural, in *DDLJ*, 59–60; Valentine's Day panics and, 154, 157, 159

Purush Kshetra (talk show), 130–31

queer spectatorship, 182, 249n28

race: call centers and racialized labor, 214–18; denial of, 96; minority communities, racial tensions between, 95–97; Omi and Winant on, 90–91; Sept. 11 and, 103–4, 232–37; skin color, beauty regimes, and cosmetics, 91–92; visuality vs. aurality of racism, 217–18

Rai, Amit, 7, 164, 177, 183, 245n24

Rajagopal, Arvind, 147

Rajan, Rajeshwari Sunder, 120

Rajani (TV), 133

Ramayana, 168–69, 259n24

recognition and landscape in *DDLJ*, 55

recollection-objects, 88

religious differences and 9/11, 234

religious minorities and moral cleansing discourse, 151–52. *See also* Muslims; Sikh positionality

remittances, 48

Resurgent India campaign, 145–54, 184–85

returning nonresident Indias (RNRIs), 26–27

Richard, Analiese, 239

Rofel, Lisa, 226, 264n29

Rosaldo, Michelle, 13

Roy, Parama, 84, 189

Rudnyckyj, Daromir, 239

saas bahu ("mother-in-law–daughter-in-law" serials), 138–39, 256n33

Sahni, Jaideep, 194

Salaam Namaste (film), 50

same-sex desire and relationships: activism and controversy in India over,

253n16; Gopinath on, 61, 249n28; in Mehta's *Fire*, 256n36; television and, 118, 254n17

samskaras, 171

Samsung advertisement, 120–22

San Francisco Bay Area as nodal space, 11–12. *See also* grocery stores, Indian

Sangh Parivar, 147, 154, 155–57, 160

Sa Re Ga Ma Pa (TV), 14–15

satellite television technology, 111–12

Seigworth, Gregory J., 44

semeiotic theory, 45, 50–52, 58–61, 63–64

Sen, Amartya, 218

senses and sensoria: film and sensory engagement, 248n20; grocery store as sensorium, 79–83; sensuous knowledges and sense memory, 78–79, 86; smells, 80–81; taste and sense memory, 84–87; television and, 114–16

September 11, 2001, and aftermath: affective value and, 20; affects of fear and hate, 229–30, 233–37; emergency narratives and event-ness of, 231; first-person narrative and, 229–30; hate violence, 231–32, 234–35; media representations and, 234; racial tensions, Indian grocery stores, and, 103–4; temporalities and, 235–38; unsettlement and, 230, 238; U.S. nationalism and racial positioning of Sikhs and Muslims, 232–38

serials and soap operas, 132–36, 138–39, 255n29, 255n31, 256n33

service economy, 202

sexuality: in *Bunty aur Babli*, 195; call center agents and anxieties around, 213–14; community surveillance of, 180–81; control over, in *DDLJ*, 59–60; diaspora and, 28–29; Hindutva ideologies and, 159; Valentine's Day panics and sexual purity, 157. *See also* erotics and erotic affect; purity

Shankar, Shalini, 179, 180

Sharma, Aradhana, 199, 201, 220

Sheller, Mimi, 15

Shih, Shi-mei, 29, 144, 266n22

Shiv Sena, 156

Shome, Raka, 209, 217–18
Sikh positionality, 175, 176, 232–37
Singhal, Ashok, 147
Sinha, Mridula, 160
SITE (Satellite Instructional Television Education) project, 111
skin color and cosmetics, 91–92
smells in Indian grocery stores, 80–81
soap operas and serials, 132–36, 138–39, 255n29, 255n31, 256n33
Sodhi, Balbir Singh, 232, 234–35, 236
Sodhi, Sukhpal Singh, 236, 266n16
soundscapes in Indian grocery stores, 82–83
"South Asian" as term, 244n8
South Asian immigration, 11
Srinivas, Lakshmi, 259n20
Sri Ram Sene, 257n5
Steedman, Carolyn, 32, 33–34, 246n36
Stewart, Kathleen, 13, 51, 186–87
structures of feeling (Williams), 12–13, 248n19
subject formation: affect and, 13, 14, 15, 17, 18, 20, 22; impersonation and, 189, 207; Indian grocery stores and, 72, 106; mobility of bodies and, 15–16; return to India and, 25–26; temporality and, 21–22; unsettlement and, 18
surveillance: call centers and, 213; community surveillance, 180–81; Sept. 11 and, 233; soundscapes in Indian grocery stores and, 82–83
Suspicious Activities Reporting, 265n9
Swabhimaan (TV), 133
Swades (film), 191
swadeshi (self-rule) discourse, 147, 258n10
Swedlund, Alan, 184
symbolic capital, 194, 210
symbolic vs. extrasymbolic temporalization, 266n25
symbols in semeiotic theory, 51

talk shows, 130–31
Tara (TV), 133
"techno-coolies," 205, 216, 262n15

television: commodity consumption, relationship with, 112–14; regional networks, 113, 252n4; sensoria and, 114–16; state-controlled (Doordarshan), 46, 110, 111–12, 133; U.S. shows used for call center training, 206
television, Hindi transnational: commodity affect and, 111–16; erotic affects and, 119–27, 137–38; expansion of, 111–12; Hindi cinema contrasted with, 133–34; "Indianized" programming and, 113, 128; and Indianness, renegotiation of, 138–43; Indipop music videos, 131–32; satellite technology and, 111–12; soap operas and serials, 132–36, 138–39, 255n29, 255n31, 256n33; state-controlled television vs., 109–10, 111–12; talk shows, 130–31; unsettlement and representations of eroticized intimacy in, 127–38
temporality and temporalizing discourses: affect and, 16–19, 184–85; of aspiration, 223–27; call centers and, 200–201, 209; of commodity affect, 139–41, 143; contemporaneity, 20–21, 22, 143, 154, 184–85, 224; cultural change conceptions, reconsideration of, 240; *durée*, 19–20, 240; Global India and, 183–85; Hindutva ideology and, 152–54; of identity, 29; indexicality and, 58; India as archive of, 32–33; *K3G* and, 163; nostalgia and, 88–90; Sept. 11 and, 235–38; as symbolic vs. extrasymbolic, 266n25; time consciousness, 184; tradition vs. modernity in *K3G*, 172–74; the work of time, 19–22. *See also* modernity
territoriality: erotic longing and, 23–24; and Indianness in *DDLJ*, 56–57, 65–67; subject formation and, 23. *See also* homeland
Thackeray, Bal, 155, 156, 258n9
Thadani, Giti, 253n16
Thompson, George, 190
Titanic (film), 161
Tölölyan, Khachig, 68
tradition vs. modernity in *K3G*, 172–74
train as trope, 191–92, 261n4

transnational public cultures: affective regimes and, 14–15; constitution of India as archive and, 4, 7, 18, 19, 23, 32–33, 230; economic liberalization and, 111; heterogeneity of media and multiplicity of, 6; media consolidation and, 7; mobility and, 16; proliferation of, 10; San Francisco Bay Area and, 11; South Asian vs. Indian, 244n8; temporalities and, 20–21; unsettlement and, 4, 20

transnational regimes of morality. *See* Global India and transnational discourses of morality

travel: commodity affect and imaginative travel, 115; in *DDLJ*, 58, 62–63; imaginative, 16; media and aspirations to, 16; train as trope, 191–92, 261n4. *See also* migration and immigration; mobility and movement

unsettlement: archive and, 34; cultural change conceptions, reconsideration of, 240; diaspora, displacement, and, 29–32; as ethnographic lens and analytic, 5, 18, 38, 145, 228, 230, 238; Global India and, 185; and India, production of, 9, 34, 36, 37, 72, 109, 110, 137–39, 142; Indian grocery stores and, 72; intimacy and, 127; narratives of, 29; Sept. 11 and, 230, 238; temporality and, 20, 32; temporality of aspiration and, 227; temporality of cultural change and, 227; on two registers, 18

Vaidya, M. G., 156

Valentine's Day moral panics, 154–62, 257n5, 257n7

value and affective value: Ahmed's affective economies and, 19, 44–45; beauty products and, 91–92; commodity exchange and regimes of value, 78, 87; mediated images and, 20

van der Veer, Peter, 246n27

Vishwa Hindu Parishad (World Hindu Organization), 147, 157

"war on terror," 233

Weber, Max, 222, 264n32

the West: aspiration and, 206; modernism vs. "westernism," 156; purity discourses and "Western"/"Indian" boundaries, 142

Williams, Raymond, 12–13, 248n19

womanhood: consumerism discourses and the "new" woman, 125; food preparation and, 85–86; "Hindu Woman" or "new Hindu woman," 158–60; *matri shakti* ("strength of motherhood"), 159; in soap operas, 134–35; Valentine's Day panics and, 154

Wong, Cynthia Sau-ling, 215

xenophilia and xenophobia, 98–99

Yanagisako, Sylvia, 13

youth: hope, loss of, 260n2; Indian grocery stores and, 93; marginal positionality, Global India, and, 174–84; rural, 194; Valentine's Day panics and erotic agency of, 160–61

Zee TV, 14–15, 113

Zeman, J. Jay, 51

Žižek, Slavoj, 124–25

Made in the USA
Lexington, KY
01 May 2017